Totalitarian Dictatorship and Autocracy

Totalitarian Dictatorship
and Autocracy

CARL J. FRIEDRICH
AND
ZBIGNIEW K. BRZEZINSKI

SECOND EDITION, REVISED BY
CARL J. FRIEDRICH

HARVARD UNIVERSITY PRESS

Cambridge, Massachusetts

1965

To Lenore and Muška

FOREWORD TO THE REVISED EDITION

The numerous developments in the practice of totalitarian dictatorship, the greatly increased documentation of past activities, and the vigorous discussion concerning the nature of this form of government have made it seem imperative that a new edition be prepared. Unfortunately, Zbigniew Brzezinski could not participate in this task, owing to other pressing commitments. It seemed to us, in any event, that the collaboration which at one time enabled us to produce an integrated whole could not be resurrected ten years later without undue loss of time and effort.

As far as the general theory is concerned, my discussion has been in part a critique of the position advanced by us nearly ten years ago. I have tried to take into account all the major points that have been raised in the interim. Writers like Tucker, Buchheim, Wittfogel, and Lifton have made highly significant contributions, deepening and broadening our understanding of totalitarian regimes. They have not altered my basic conviction that totalitarian dictatorship is a novel form of government exhibiting features that distinguish it from other types of autocracy. To clarify this general issue, I have added a new introductory chapter on autocracy; it has gained added perspective by Eisenstadt's remarkable study. Here and there I have given references to the broad general theory of politics that I published in 1963, as well as a number of references to works in the general area of Soviet totalitarianism which Brzezinski has published since this book appeared and which impressively implement the general analysis, especially his *The Soviet Bloc* and *Political Power: USA/USSR* (with Samuel P. Huntington). In thus developing further a morphological and operational theory of totalitarian regimes, I should like to make it clear that I still believe that we are as yet unable to offer a genetic one. Some interesting further arguments have been advanced in the intervening years, and elements of such a theory are scattered throughout this book, as they are through other writings on totalitarianism, but no one in my opinion has fully answered the question: why? Unforeseen and still unfolding, totalitarianism has shaped or, if one prefers, distorted the political and governmental scene of the twentieth century. It promises to continue to do so to the end of the century.

On the whole I feel that both the theory and the practice of totalitarian dictatorship have tended to confirm the analysis we offered. But with the spread and elaboration of totalitarianism, especially into non-European lands, new facets were bound to appear and older ones to change in some significant respects. Especially the evolution of Communist China, which is much more fully known (though still quite inadequately documented), has added highly suggestive points; I have attempted to take greater account of them than was possible a decade ago. But the style of rule that Khrushchev introduced, while in some respects bringing the political dynamics of the Soviet Union closer to some Fascist regimes, has in other respects raised the serious question of whether the course of the Soviet Union is not in fact one that will end in the abandonment of totalitarianism. The theory offered here will make it a bit easier to deal with that vexed question. At present the Soviet Union still exhibits all the criteria of totalitarian dictatorship, even though the extent of terror may in some respects have dropped to the level prevalent in national Fascist regimes, which could always count on a considerable amount of political consensus. The psychic terror exercised by holistic groups can be more terrifying than the threat of death and torture.

To take account of these changes, the chapters on terror have been recast. A new chapter on the constitution, law, and justice has been added to provide an adequate setting for the changed perspective. The writings of a number of highly competent legal scholars, including Berman and Meissner, have made this possible, especially since they can now be extensively based on the work of Soviet jurists. While the general order of the chapters remains as before, there have been some adjustments. The most important is the gathering together of three chapters on totalitarian expansionism in the final section, even though I have not been able to persuade myself that expansionism should be added to the essential features of totalitarian regimes, as was suggested by some learned critics. Altogether, about a quarter to a third of the text and bibliography is new.

In preparing this revision, I have had the help of Mrs. Gail Lapidus, who has also contributed Chapter 25. Her special competence in the field of Soviet studies compensated me somewhat for the loss of Brzezinski's contribution to the earlier volume. I want to thank her most heartily for her patience and industry. My long-time editorial assistant, Miss Roberta Hill, proofread the manuscript and prepared the new Index to Authors Cited. She too deserves my sincere thanks, which are gladly offered.

C. J. F.

January 1965

PREFACE TO THE FIRST EDITION

The present study of totalitarian dictatorship seeks to give a general, descriptive theory of a novel form of government. It does not seek to explain why this dictatorship came into being, for the authors are convinced that such an explanation is not feasible at the present time, though some of the essential conditions can be described. Some brilliant efforts have been made in this field, but they have remained speculative and controversial. The authors' is a humbler task: to delineate, on the basis of fairly generally known and acknowledged factual data, the general model of totalitarian dictatorship and of the society which it has created. In attempting such a general assessment, they hope to provide a basis not only for more effective teaching but also for a more informed discussion of particular issues and further developments. It might be objected that their study is not addressed to any definite group, that it is too elementary for the scholar, too difficult for the general reader, and too learned for the beginner. But is not any study of this kind partly esoteric, partly exoteric? There is no doubt that a book which seeks to delineate in fairly clear and comprehensive form the general nature of totalitarian dictatorship, on the basis of what are reasonably well-established matters of fact, will traverse much ground that is familiar to the specialist. At the same time, its argument will involve recondite matter which may well go beyond the range of interest of the intelligent lay reader and the student. The authors hope, nonetheless, to have succeeded in producing a volume that has something to offer each of these groups, and which may contribute something of an answer to the question — what is a totalitarian dictatorship, and how does it fit into the general framework of our knowledge of government and politics?

This volume is the product of very close collaboration between the authors not only in the course of writing but also in teaching and research. To be sure, the studies of C. J. Friedrich in this field go much further back; the main framework was developed by him in the late thirties in a nearly completed book-length manuscript, but the knowledge and understanding of both the Nazi and Soviet dictatorships was then very limited and it was decided not to publish it when the war broke out. In the years following, Merle Fainsod became associated with him in the course he was then teaching on totalitarian dictatorship — a most fruitful cooperation which grew out of their joint direction of the Civil Affairs Training School at Harvard. This training effort in turn led to Friedrich's work in military government and the seminar in this field, taught for several years in conjunction with the continuing work on totalitarian dictatorship. For the constitutional dictatorship of Western military government provided an interesting contrast to the totalitarian pattern. Z. K. Brzezinski became associated with this seminar in 1951, and out of their joint work this study eventually emerged.

The main reason for relating this background is to emphasize the method of joint authorship of which this book is the fruit. Unlike many books by two or more authors, this one was written by both authors chapter by chapter, now one, now the other providing the first draft. The general conception, as outlined in chapter one, is Friedrich's and was first offered in *Totalitarianism,* a volume of proceedings edited by him for the American Academy of Arts and Sciences in 1953. But even this, dating back to prewar days, was considerably refined in constant discussions between the authors and with others, notably members of the Russian Research Center and the many acute students who have participated in the seminar these past years. Beyond this general beginning, the authors worked out the book together and consider it their joint product. As far as concrete material is concerned, the authors' divergent linguistic background and source knowledge combined to provide the necessary breadth. Brzezinski wishes to acknowledge with sincere gratitude the generous support given to him in this connection, as in the past, by the Russian Research Center at Harvard University of which he is a staff member; similarly, Friedrich wishes to thank the director and staff of the Institut für Zeitgeschichte at Munich for their critical reading and helpful criticisms, though neither of these learned bodies thereby assumes any responsibility for this interpretation. Many helpful suggestions and criticism were made by colleagues, particularly Professor Merle Fainsod, who read the entire manuscript. Similarly Dr. Dante Germino read the manuscript, especially the sections dealing with Fascist Italy, and kindly gave counsel on the basis of his able study of the Fascist Party. Between March 1955 and April 1956, Friedrich directed a research project for the Human Relations Area Files, Yale University, on the Soviet Zone of Germany, which has since appeared as one of their studies and contains the names of the numerous collaborators. The authors' debt to many others will, it is hoped, be largely apparent from the notes, though certain "consultants" of the seminar, notably Hannah Arendt, Sigmund Neumann, Franz Neumann, Adam Ulam, and Alex Inkeles call for special mention. Finally, the authors would like to express their profound appreciation for the help of Miss Roberta G. Hill, the seminar's secretary, who devoted untold hours to editorial and related chores.

The manuscript was completed in December 1955. In view of the events in the Soviet Union surrounding the Twentieth Party Congress, held in February 1956, a few minor revisions and additions to the text were made. But the hard core of the analysis has not been changed; developments up to now do not appear to call for any such revision; as yet no fundamental change seems to have occurred in the Soviet system. The party continues to play its crucially important and predominant role and, indeed, the significance of the party as the mainspring of the system has increased. The leadership is now attempting to shift somewhat from its reliance on terroristic measures to more subtle incentives as the basis for continued drives in "the socialist construction." This search for a new basis of authority, in which the post-Stalinist regime is now engaged, has resulted in some relaxation of police controls over the population, but the use of arbitrary violence against the opponents of the regime has not been abandoned. No effective restraints against the employment of terror have yet been developed. The potential of terror still is present, and the party would not hesitate to use violence to defend its monopoly of power. Nonetheless, it is heartening to see that even Stalin's closest collaborators feel compelled to renounce his activities.

Z. K. B.
C. J. F.

April 1956

CONTENTS

I

Introduction

1

AUTOCRACY AND THE PROBLEM
OF THE STATE

"We have created a new type of state!" Lenin repeatedly claimed. He made it clear at the same time that he considered this new state to be radically different from a constitutional democracy with its civil liberties. With the creation of this new type of state, "a turn in world history had occurred . . . the epoch of bourgeois-democratic parliamentarism is ended; a new chapter of world history began: the epoch of the proletarian dictatorship." (207a) By these statements, which are still orthodox doctrine in accordance with the reemphasis on Lenin's views, the great revolutionary fanatic made it amply explicit that the Soviet state was different. He considered it a new kind of democracy, in which the masses of workers and peasants are activated for participation through the party. Democracy in this context means a nonautocratic system of the tsarist type, and certainly the Soviet Union from its very beginning has constituted a radical departure from that traditional and hereditary autocracy which was the tsars'. And yet a more comprehensive analysis shows it to be a new species of autocracy. In order to justify this statement, we first need such an analysis.

Totalitarian dictatorships have been labeled with every one of the expressions used to signify older autocracies. They have been called tyrannies, despotisms, and absolutisms. Yet all these terms are highly misleading. In any historically valid sense, the resemblance between twentieth-century totalitarian dictatorships and such older autocracies as oriental despotism and Greek tyranny is very partial. The autocratic regimes of the past were not nearly as thorough as the totalitarian dictatorships of today. (389a) They did not seek to get hold of the entire man, the human being in his totality, but were satisfied with excluding him from certain spheres and exploiting him more or less mercilessly in others. Yet one also maligns totalitarian dictatorship by these analogical descriptions. For whereas tyranny was conducted for the benefit of the tyrant, as Aristotle pointed out, it is not very realistic to make that kind of egoism the basis of an interpretation of totalitarian dictatorship. Whatever Lenin's new type of state was, it was not conducted in the personal interest of Lenin.

There have, then, been many types of autocracy in the history of government. Certain forms of primitive kingship, the several forms of despotism often associated with the deification of the ruler characteristic of the Orient, as well as the later Roman empire, the tyranny in the Greek city-states and in Renaissance Italy, and the absolutist monarchies of modern Europe, including tsarist Russia, are the more familiar types of autocracy. Any typology of broad empirical scope must include these models, as well as military dictatorship and related forms of emergency rule. It has been shown elsewhere (110i) that the thirteen identifiable types of rule fall into a rough developmental pattern, but this pattern is devoid of any inherent value constituting "progress" from the first to the last. Rather it should be recognized that the value of any particular political order corresponding to one of these types is, from a pragmatic viewpoint, the consequence of the degree of its "working." From an ideological viewpoint, its value may result from the purposes to which the particular regime is addressing itself, from the national or class group that predominates, from the religion prevalent therein, from the degree of general consensus it enjoys, and from various other considerations. Autocracy is therefore not "in itself" bad; it has worked over long periods of time, and the question of its value now is its workability, as well as the ideological considerations just enumerated. Totalitarian dictatorship may, in a preliminary characterization, be called an autocracy based upon modern technology and mass legitimation.

In all autocratic regimes, the distinguishing feature is that the ruler is not accountable to anyone else for what he does. He is the *autos* who himself wields power; that is to say, makes the decisions and reaps the results. The logical opposite of autocracy, therefore, would be any rule in which another, as the *heteros,* shared the power of ruling through the fact that the ruler is accountable to him or them. In the modern West, it has become customary to speak of such systems as responsible or constitutional government.* Among such constitutional systems, constitutional democracy has become the predominant type, though there have existed other types, such as constitutional monarchies, aristocracies, and theocracies. (431)

Since any system of accountability must be expressed in rules of some kind which together constitute the "constitution" and, as rules, are properly speaking a kind of legal norm, it has been customary since Plato and Aristotle to stress the role of law and to distinguish political systems according to whether or not they are characterized by the subordination of the political rulers to law. From this viewpoint, an autocracy is any political system in which the rulers are insufficiently, or not at all, subject to antecedent and enforceable rules of law — enforceable, that is, by other authorities who share in the government and who have sufficient power to compel the lawbreaking rulers to submit to the law.

This problem of the control of the rulers by the law must be distinguished from the problem of the role of law in a given society. All human societies, communities, and groups of any sort have some kind of law, and the totalitarian dictatorships of our time are characterized by a vast amount of "legislation," necessitated by the requirements of a technically industrialized economy and of the masses of dependent operators involved in such a society. (19; 102a) Similarly the Roman empire saw an increase, not a decline, in the detailed complexity of its legal system during the very period when it was becoming more and more autocratic. This autocracy eventually reached the point of deifying the emperor, while the detailed development of the legal system continued. Long before this time, all enforceable control of the ruler had vanished and the responsibility of which the republic had been so proud had completely disappeared. The will of the emperor was the ultimate source of all law. (81a) This conception was expressed in a number

---

* The term *heterocracy* has never been suggested, though it is the genuine logical alternative to autocracy. Some such general term would be highly useful, since "constitutional government" is a much more restricted type, limited to the modern West. (104)

of celebrated phrases, which eventually became the basis of the doctrine of sovereignty that provided the rationalization of absolute monarchs in the seventeenth century. (105a)

It is at this point that the analysis is faced with the problem of the "state." The notion of the state arose in the sixteenth century and has since become generalized to mean any political order or government. But in view of the problem of law as a restraint upon government, it may be instructive to go back to the origins of the concept. The state as an institutional manifold developed in response to the challenge presented by the Christian church's secular ambitions. It embodies a political order institutionally divorced from the ecclesiastical establishment. Even where a "state church" has survived, as in England, this church is separated from the political order in terms of authority, legitimacy, and representation. This sharp separation of the state from religion and church distinguishes it from the political order of Greece and Rome as much as from the Asiatic and African monarchies. The state in this distinct historical sense is almost entirely "Western," and some of the perplexities of contemporary state-building are connected with this fact. (110j) The "new type of state" that Lenin spoke of so proudly is, in this perspective, an effort to transcend this modern state; for the official ideology encompasses a pseudo-religion that is intended to replace the separated religions of the past. It marks in that sense a return to the sort of political order that characterized the Greek and Roman world, as well as older autocracies.

The state, as already mentioned, was recognized as a new order in the sixteenth century. Jean Bodin more especially formalized its understanding by linking the state with sovereignty. The claim that the ruler of a state must be sovereign, if the state is to epitomize a good order, amounted to claiming that the ruler must be free of all restraints. Jean Bodin did not, in fact, dare to go that far, though some of his more radical formulations do. But Hobbes did and thus completed the doctrine of the modern state. Among the restraints that particularly concerned Bodin, Hobbes, and their contemporaries in the sixteenth and seventeenth centuries was that of fixed and established law. The ruler must be free to change all laws to enable him to rule effectively. Yet even Hobbes could not bring himself to go quite that far. The arbitrary discretion of the ruler found its limit in the right of self-preservation of each of his subjects. But the trend was clear: power must be concentrated so as to produce order and peace. It was this doctrine that remained at the core of absolutism in its characteristic monarchical form. Tsarist autocracy rested upon it as clearly as Western monarchies, with one highly significant difference: the separation from the church that had been the heart of the matter in the West never occurred.

This is not the place to sketch the evolution of these absolutist regimes or the doctrines; nor can we even sketch the constitutional alternative which, inherited from the Middle Ages, was fashioned to supersede them in conjunction with those revolutions, English, American, and French, that Lenin contemptuously brushed aside as bourgeois. Let us merely state again that the state was by the sixteenth century a large-scale governmental organization effectively centralized by means of a strictly secular bureaucracy, often implemented by some kind of representative body. Suffice it merely to point out that the contradictory implications, in theory and practice, of this monarchical absolutism, this autocracy, prevented its maintenance. It broke down because as the economy became more complex — stimulated by these very autocracies — the centralized bureaucracy was unable to handle the ever larger number of decisions that had to be taken.* In order to salvage the state concept, political philosophers and jurists attributed sovereignty either to the people or to the state. Both of these collectives were sufficiently intangible to negate the real meaning of the doctrines of Bodin and Hobbes. For, as has been pointed out, the essence of the doctrine of sovereignty was that a determinate person or group of persons wield an unlimited power of deciding what is in the public interest. The truth of the matter is that, as once was said rather picturesquely by the great Sir Edward Coke, "sovereignty and the common law make strange bedfellows," by which he meant that the common-law tradition of the supremacy of the law could not be reconciled with the new theory of the state as unlimited in fact.†
The genuine state concept calls for an absolute ruler, an autocrat.

---

* There is a striking analogy here to the present difficulties in the Soviet Union, which are highlighted in the controversy over decentralization and its implementation.

† The present debate among lawyers in the Soviet bloc, and more especially the USSR, over legal restraints to prevent a return to the Stalinist terror therefore raises this central issue, and it is understandable that the lawyers (as always) are clashing with the party and its politicians on this score. (449b)

Doctrines such as that of "democratic centralism" or the "mass line of leadership," just as much as Hitler's *Führerprinzip,* constitute a return to this autocratic conception of the state. The retention of the "people," the "masses," or the "Volk" as ultimate reference points does not alter the fact that decision making is concentrated and unlimited at the apex of the official hierarchy. And this is the quintessence of autocracy: that the autocrat is able to determine by and for himself to what extent he will use his power. Any self-imposed limits — and there always are such — do not alter this key criterion, as long as the autocrat retains the power to discard them, whenever he deems it desirable in the interest of the regime. Such autocracy may be collective; it still is autocratic, as long as the collective or a part of it possesses the "highest and perpetual power over citizens and subjects, unrestricted by laws" (Bodin), and therefore does not have to account for its use "except to immortal God" (or some other intangible entity such as "the people"). Such ultimate decisional power of the sovereign has been given a shorthand description, that of "the last word."

No complete concentration of power being possible, then, the matter is ultimately one of degree, and a state in the classical sense is found to be that form of political order in which power is in fact fairly concentrated, and potentially may be deployed to handle any situation, including the autocrat's own tenure. When seen in this perspective, the totalitarian regimes of the twentieth century are the outcome of movements directed against the denigration of the state in the liberal age. This reassertion of the state is not limited to totalitarian systems. It is found, in more restricted form, in those military dictatorships which have replaced ineffectual constitutional orders, as in Pakistan, Portugal, or Brazil. Such dictatorships are often instituted in order to ward off the threat of a possible takeover by a totalitarian movement; yet to confuse them with totalitarian regimes may have serious practical consequences as well as being theoretically unsound.

It is interesting at this point to consider briefly the personal regimes of Franco in Spain and of De Gaulle in France. Both represent a reassertion of the need for a strong state with an autocrat at the head, intended to ensure the functioning of the body politic. The Gaullist republic is still a constitutional order of sorts, though the General has taken it upon himself to set the constitution aside when it interfered with his plans for the succession, thereby demonstrating the trend toward autocracy. The Caudillo, on the other hand, has been moving in the opposite direction. In the heyday of the Falangist party, Spain had many of the hallmarks of a totalitarian regime in the making. But the regime has been gradually transformed into a personal military dictatorship of essentially reactionary propensities, lacking both a total ideology and a party to support and embody it. It has many parallels in Latin America, past and present. As such, it rests upon military support and ecclesiastical sanction and a kind of negative legitimation of popular apathy, reinforced by some pseudo-democratic rituals, such as rigged elections and plebiscites. Its essence is nevertheless autocratic in the general sense here developed and is epitomized by the absence of any genuine opposition, a free press, and the like.

Such military dictatorships are distinguished from the older autocracies of monarchy and tyranny not only by their curious legitimation, but also by their essentially technical outlook on politics. This is true whether their propensity is conservative-reactionary, as in Spain or Brazil, or progressive, as in Pakistan and *ceteris paribus* the Turkey of Kemal. Such pragmatic "functions" suggest the term "functional dictatorship." The absolute monarchies of seventeenth- and eighteenth-century Europe had a much more deep-rooted cultural concern, even though their mercantilist policies fostered technical progress. The oriental despotic regimes (when they were despotic) were typically expansionist. In both the legitimacy rests upon a divinely sanctioned blood descent and some sort of identification of the ruler with the deity as master of the universe. This outlook provided an underpinning for expansionist policies. Finally the tyrannies of Greece and Italy, both products of periods of profound anomie and a disruption of traditional order, sought to substitute personal valor and violence for any satisfactory and satisfying claim to legitimacy — hence their extreme instability. Such instability is by no means the hallmark of other autocracies. On the contrary, some have exhibited to a remarkable degree a capacity to endure over long periods.

In this connection, it should be remembered that autocratic regimes are not necessarily possessed of a greater degree of authority than nonautocratic ones; in fact they often arise when authority is difficult to maintain. The role of authority in government is a ubiquitous one, and for that reason it is rather misleading to speak of autocratic regimes as "authoritarian" (264); a constitutional democracy or a traditional monarchy, neither of them autocratic, may be highly authoritarian in fact. Every government of whatever type will seek to achieve as much authority as possible, because authority contributes to stability and longevity. (110m) This problem of longevity calls for further comment.

The totalitarian dictatorship in the Soviet Union is by now over a generation old. No one can be sure at the present time what the lasting qualities of this system of government will turn out to be. At first it was rather generally believed that such dictatorships would, like the tyrannies of ancient Greece, prove short-lived. Aristotle, reasoning in terms of the Greek passion for the citizen's free participation in the affairs of his polis, believed high mortality to be a built-in feature of tyranny. But the historical record of autocracy suggests that these Greek tyrannies were the exception proving the rule that autocracies tend to last. They have shown an extraordinary capacity for survival. Not only the Roman empire, but also the despotic monarchies of the Near and Far East lasted for centuries, the Chinese empire for millennia. (52 p. 198ff) To be sure, the dynasties changed and there were recurrent internal times of trouble, as well as foreign invasions, but the systems endured in Egypt, in Mesopotamia, in Persia, in India, China, and Japan, to mention only the most important. When they did fall, it was usually because of conquest by a rival empire, Babylon, Assur, Egypt, and India being cases in point. It is similarly quite conceivable, as Orwell hints in *1984,* that by the end of this century rival totalitarian empires will from time to time engage in mortal combat; for there is certainly no reason to assume that the world-wide triumph of totalitarianism would necessarily usher in a period of universal peace. The mounting conflicts between the USSR and China are a hint of what might be in store for mankind along this line (see Chapter 27).

The autocratic regimes of the past, while lasting over long periods, witnessed considerable ups and downs in the degree or intensity of violence employed for their maintenance. Periods of relative order and domestic peace, such as that of the Antonines, alternated with periods of fierce oppression and tyrannical abuse of power. The first century of the Roman *principatus* saw the benevolent rule of Augustus turn into the fierce absolutism of Tiberius and the criminal license of Nero; comparable contrasts are part of the historical record of every such autocracy. Medieval political thought elaborated these alternatives into the dichotomy of monarch and tyrant, the latter being a monarch who by abuse of his power raised serious doubts about his title to rule. The historical record suggests that some sort of cycle is involved in this alternation between intensification and relaxation of autocratic power, though the adventitious change in rulers who brought a different personality to the task of ruling disrupted the cycle from time to time. Extraneous events, whether natural or man-made, such as plagues, disasters, and foreign threats, may also cause deviations from the natural cycle of gradual intensification of violence that increase until a certain extreme is reached, to be followed by a more or less violent reversal, a return to the original state, and the recommencement of the cycle. Thus the long rule of Stalin saw a gradual increase in totalitarian violence that came to an end with his death, which some believe to have been a murder committed by persons in his entourage who were in danger of becoming victims of his suspicion. This cycle seems to have recommenced after a period of transition. The process resembles a familiar and repetitive pattern, which characterized Russian tsardom. Time and again, the new hope raised by a young emperor, that autocracy would end, died as the reign matured and methods became violent once more.

The oscillation between tight and loose control in an autocratic regime is probably linked to its origin. Born in violence, it remains confronted by the problem of how far it can go in abandoning violence. The autocratic regimes of modern times, at least, have all had such a violent beginning. Absolute monarchy and military and totalitarian dictatorships share this trait, even though the violence is in one case an extension of traditional discretion by usurpation, in another counterrevolutionary reaction, and only in the third the revolutionary seizure of power. By analogical reasoning, one might presume that the origin of older autocracies is similarly conditioned. This is certainly true for the rise of the Roman emperors, even though it was accomplished by gradual steps and disguised behind a curtain of traditional republican claptrap. It is also historically confirmed for the Macedonian rulers and for the tyrants of Italy and Greece. In the case of oriental despotism and its primi-

tive antecedents, we are left to surmises. The origins are shrouded
in the mists of legend and myth, telling of divine descent, as in
Egypt and China. Recent scholarship has advanced the argument
that at the dawn of history nomadic herdsmen, and more especially
conquerors on horseback, subjected large peasant populations to
their exploitative rule and thereby laid the foundations for the
growth of civilization. (306a) This process of superimposition
(*Überlagerung*) was certainly also extremely violent, and if further
research should confirm the theory it would place the expansionist
totalitarians in line with the earliest forebears in the practice of
autocracy.

That even these early autocracies faced the problem of how to
tame the extremes of senseless violence, is clear. It has been shown
that the growth of elaborate bureaucracies in response to complex
technical tasks of administration produced the bureaucratic empires.
Of these it has been said that they arose within the various types of
autocratic rule, when torn by strife and dissension. Usually, we are
told, it was "the objective of the ruler to reestablish peace and
order." (81b) As the scope of the activities of these bureaucracies
grew and their performance depended increasingly on experience
and know-how, the rulers found that they had to grant them a
certain autonomy, which in turn was embodied in rules, traditions,
and supervisory controls. These measures did not go nearly as far as
in modern autocracies, but they constituted a means of ordering
and institutionalizing autocratic procedures under law. The most
important conditions for the institutionalization of such bureaucratic empires were (1) the tendency of rulers toward implementing
autonomous political goals, and (2) the development of certain relatively limited levels of differentiation in all the major institutional
spheres. It should therefore not occasion any surprise that the autocracies of our time are confronted by similar problems.

Two other general hypotheses concerning the empirical evidence
on autocracies deserve to be mentioned. One is the existence of
widespread consensus. Such consensus on the broad goals of peace
and order, as well as on the more particular and parochial goals of
specific deities and the cultures associated with them, is to be found
throughout the history of autocracy. Only in the initial phase of the
establishment or re-establishment of an autocracy is that consensus
lacking. The formation of such consensus will in part occur in

response to efforts by the ruler as he seeks to provide his rule with a basis of legitimacy (110k); it will also "grow" as a result of the subject population's becoming accustomed to the rule, as its more active members are given or discover opportunities for personal advancement and gain. Indeed, in a certain sense, it can be said that general consensus is a specific characteristic of autocratic regimes that last more than one generation, in contrast to nonautocratic ones wherein a measure of sharp dissent is unavoidable and may even be cultivated.

The other hypothesis concerns consultation of the subject population, as implied in Lenin's democratic centralism, Mao's mass line, and Hitler's *Volksbefragung* through plebiscites. Autocratic regimes have often in the past engaged in such consultative practices, from Harun al-Rashid's legendary wanderings through the taverns of Baghdad to Frederick the Great's extended solicitation of popular responses to his proposed code of laws, to be repeated by Napoleon Bonaparte. In Frederick's case, we know the extent to which opinions were in fact expressed and later sifted by the drafters for possibly valid criticism, much as the Soviet Union has often through the party engaged in stimulating widespread popular discussion of impending changes. Such consultation is, therefore, not "democratic" in the Western sense of representative government, because the ruler retains full and complete power to decide what to accept and what to reject, because he alone is in charge. He has, as we mentioned, "the last word." He is sovereign in the full sense of the word.

In summary and conclusion, it might be said that autocracy appears to have been the prevailing form of government over long stretches of mankind's history. It should therefore not occasion any great surprise that it has reappeared in recent times, wherever public order seemed threatened by revolutionary movements or wherever such movements sought to institutionalize their power. The latter process has given rise to totalitarian dictatorships. It is the main purpose of this study to discover what is the actual nature of such a system, what its structure and the conduct of its affairs, and in the course of that inquiry to throw some light on the possible answer to the question of why such systems have arisen in the twentieth century. There has been much general speculation on this score, but the results have been rather unsatisfactory from a scientific viewpoint, even when impressive in their brilliance as literary exercises. In any case, scientific method seems to us to require that a phenomenon first be identified in its full complexity, before an attempt can be made to "explain" its existence.

2

THE GENERAL CHARACTERISTICS
OF TOTALITARIAN DICTATORSHIP

Totalitarian regimes are autocracies. When they are said to be tyrannies, despotisms, or absolutisms, the basic general nature of such regimes is being denounced, for all these words have a strongly pejorative flavor. When they call themselves "democracies," qualifying it by the adjective "popular," they are not contradicting these indictments, except in trying to suggest that they are good or at least praiseworthy. An inspection of the meaning the totalitarians attach to the term "popular democracy" reveals that they mean by it a species of autocracy. The leaders of the people, identified with the leaders of the ruling party, have the last word. Once they have decided and been acclaimed by a party gathering, their decision is final. Whether it be a rule, a judgment, or a measure or any other act of government, they are the *autokrator,* the ruler accountable only to himself. Totalitarian dictatorship, in a sense, is the adaptation of autocracy to twentieth-century industrial society. (19)

Thus, as far as this characteristic absence of accountability is concerned, totalitarian dictatorship resembles earlier forms of autocracy. But it is our contention in this volume that totalitarian dictatorship is historically an innovation (cf. 133; 389; 52) and *sui generis.* It is also our conclusion from all the facts available to us that fascist and communist totalitarian dictatorships are basically alike, or at any rate more nearly like each other than like any other system of government, including earlier forms of autocracy. These two theses are closely linked and must be examined together. They are also linked to a third, that totalitarian dictatorship as it actually developed was not intended by those who created it — Mussolini talked of it, though he meant something different — but resulted from the political situations in which the anticonstitutionalist and antidemocratic revolutionary movements and their leaders found themselves. Before we explore these propositions, one very widespread theory of totalitarianism needs consideration.

It is a theory that centers on the regime's efforts to remold and transform the human beings under its control in the image of its ideology. As such, it might be called an ideological or anthropological theory of totalitarianism. The theory holds that the "essence" of totalitarianism is to be seen in such a regime's total control of the everyday life of its citizens, of its control, more particularly, of their thoughts and attitudes as well as their activities. "The particular criterion of totalitarian rule is the creeping rape [*sic*] of man by the perversion of his thoughts and his social life," a leading exponent of this view has written. "Totalitarian rule," he added, "is the claim transformed into political action that the world and social life are changeable without limit." (44a) As compared with this "essence," it is asserted that organization and method are criteria of secondary importance. There are a number of serious objections to this theory. The first is purely pragmatic. For while it may be the intent of the totalitarians to achieve total control, it is certainly doomed to disappointment; no such control is actually achieved, even within the ranks of their party membership or cadres, let alone over the population at large. The specific procedures generated by this desire for total control, this "passion for unanimity" as we call it later in our analysis, are highly significant, have evolved over time, and have varied greatly at different stages. They have perhaps been carried farthest by the Chinese Communists in their methods of thought control, but they were also different under Stalin and under Lenin, under Hitler and under Mussolini. Apart from this pragmatic objection, however, there also arises a comparative historical one. For such ideologically motivated concern for the whole man, such intent upon total control, has been characteristic of other regimes in the past, notably theocratic ones such as the Puritans' or the Moslems'. It has also found expression in some of the most elevated philosophical systems, especially that of Plato who certainly in *The Republic, The Statesman,* and *The Laws* advocates total control in the interest of good order in the political community. This in turn has led to the profound and unfortunate misunderstanding of Plato as a totalitarian (284; 111a; 353); he was an authoritarian, favoring the autocracy of the wise. The misunderstanding has further occasioned the misinterpretation of certain forms of tyrannical rule in classical antiquity as "totalitarian," on the ground that in Sparta, for instance, "the life and activity of the entire population are continuously subject to a close regimentation by the state." (114) Finally, it would be necessary to describe the order of the medieval monastery as totalitarian; for it was certainly characterized by such a scheme of total control. Indeed, much "primitive" government also appears then to be totalitarian (223) because of its close control of all participants. What is really the specific difference, the innovation of the totalitarian regimes, is the organization and methods developed and employed with the aid of modern technical devices in an effort to resuscitate such total control in the service of an ideologically motivated movement, dedicated to the total destruction and reconstruction of a mass society. It seems therefore highly desirable to use the term "totalism" to distinguish the much more general phenomenon just sketched, as has recently been proposed by a careful analyst of the methods of Chinese thought control. (217; 314)

Totalitarian dictatorship then emerges as a system of rule for realizing totalist intentions under modern political and technical conditions, as a novel type of autocracy. (301) The declared intention of creating a "new man," according to numerous reports, has had significant results where the regime has lasted long enough, as in Russia. In the view of one leading authority, "the most appealing traits of the Russians — their naturalness and candor — have suffered most." He considers this a "profound and apparently permanent transformation," and an "astonishing" one. (238a) In short, the effort at total control, while not achieving such control, has highly significant human effects.

The fascist and communist systems evolved in response to a series of grave crises — they are forms of crisis government. Even so, there is no reason to conclude that the existing totalitarian systems will disappear as a result of internal evolution, though there can be no doubt that they are undergoing continuous changes. The two totalitarian governments that have perished thus far have done so as the result of wars with outside powers, but this does not mean that the Soviet Union, Communist China, or any of the others necessarily will become involved in war. We do not presuppose that totalitarian societies are fixed and static entities but, on the contrary, that they have undergone and continue to undergo a steady evolution, presumably involving both growth and deterioration. (209f)

But what about the origins? If it is evident that the regimes came into being because a totalitarian movement achieved dominance over a society and its government, where did the movement come from? The answer to this question remains highly controversial. A great many explanations have been attempted in terms of the various ingredients of these ideologies. Not only Marx and Engels, where the case seems obvious, but Hegel, Luther, and a great many others have come in for their share of blame. Yet none of these thinkers was, of course, a totalitarian at all, and each would have rejected these regimes, if any presumption like that were to be tested in terms of his thought. They were humanists and religious men of intense spirituality of the kind the totalitarians explicitly reject. In short, all such "explanations," while interesting in illuminating particular elements of the totalitarian ideologies, are based on serious invalidating distortions of historical facts. (182; 126; 145.1; 280) If we leave aside such ideological explanations (and they are linked of course to the "ideological" theory of totalitarian dictatorship as criticized above), we find several other unsatisfactory genetic theories.

The debate about the causes or origins of totalitarianism has run all the way from a primitive bad-man theory (46a) to the "moral crisis of our time" kind of argument. A detailed inspection of the available evidence suggests that virtually every one of the factors which has been offered by itself as an explanation of the origin of totalitarian dictatorship has played its role. For example, in the case of Germany, Hitler's moral and personal defects, weaknesses in the German constitutional tradition, certain traits involved in the German "national character," the Versailles Treaty and its aftermath, the economic crisis and the "contradictions" of an aging capitalism, the "threat" of communism, the decline of Christianity and of such other spiritual moorings as the belief in the reason and the reasonableness of man — all have played a role in the total configuration of factors contributing to the over-all result. As in the case of other broad developments in history, only a multiple-factor analysis will yield an adequate account. But at the present time, we cannot fully explain the rise of totalitarian dictatorship. All we can do is to explain it partially by identifying some of the antecedent and concomitant conditions. To repeat: totalitarian dictatorship is a new phenomenon; there has never been anything quite like it before.

The discarding of ideological explanations — highly objectionable to all totalitarians, to be sure — opens up an understanding of and insight into the basic similarity of totalitarian regimes, whether communist or fascist. They are, in terms of organization and procedures — that is to say, in terms of structure, institutions, and processes of rule — *basically alike*. What does this mean? In the first place, it means that they are *not wholly alike*. Popular and journalistic interpretation has oscillated between two extremes; some have said that the communist and fascist dictatorships are wholly alike, others that they are not at all alike. The latter view was the prevailing one during the popular-front days in Europe as well as in liberal circles in the United States. It was even more popular during the Second World War, especially among Allied propagandists. Besides, it was and is the official communist and fascist party line. It is only natural that these regimes, conceiving of themselves as bitter enemies, dedicated to the task of liquidating each other, should take the view that they have nothing in common. This has happened before in history. When the Protestants and Catholics were fighting during the religious wars of the sixteenth and seventeenth centuries, they very commonly denied to one another the name of "Christians," and each argued about the other that it was not a "true church." Actually, and in the perspective of time, both were indeed Christian churches.

The other view, that communist and fascist dictatorships are wholly alike, was during the cold war demonstrably favored in the United States and in Western Europe to an increasing extent. Yet they are demonstrably not wholly alike. For example, they differ in their acknowledged purposes and intentions. Everyone knows that the communists say they seek the world revolution of the proletariat, while the fascists proclaimed their determination to establish the imperial predominance of a particular nation or race, either over the world or over a region. The communist and fascist dictatorships differ also in their historical antecedents: the fascist movements arose in reaction to the communist challenge and offered themselves

20 *Introduction*

to a frightened middle class as saviors from the communist danger. The communist movements, on the other hand, presented themselves as the liberators of an oppressed people from an existing autocratic regime, at least in Russia and China. Both claims are not without foundation, and one could perhaps coordinate them by treating the totalitarian movements as consequences of the First World War. "The rise [of totalitarianism] has occurred in the sequel to the first world war and those catastrophies, political and economic, which accompanied it and the feeling of crisis linked thereto." (31a) As we shall have occasion to show in the chapters to follow, there are many other differences which do not allow us to speak of the communist and fascist totalitarian dictatorships as wholly alike, but which suggest that they are sufficiently alike to class them together and to contrast them not only with constitutional systems, but also with former types of autocracy.

Before we turn to these common features, however, there is another difference that used to be emphasized by many who wanted "to do business with Hitler" or who admired Mussolini and therefore argued that, far from being wholly like the communist dictatorship, the fascist regimes really had to be seen as merely authoritarian forms of constitutional systems. It is indeed true that more of the institutions of the antecedent liberal and constitutional society survived in the Italian Fascist than in the Russian or Chinese Communist society. But this is due in part to the fact that no liberal constitutional society preceded Soviet or Chinese Communism. The promising period of the Duma came to naught as a result of the war and the disintegration of tsarism, while the Kerensky interlude was far too brief and too superficial to become meaningful for the future. Similarly in China, the Kuomingtang failed to develop a working constitutional order, though various councils were set up; they merely provided a facade for a military dictatorship disrupted by a great deal of anarchical localism, epitomized in the rule of associated warlords. In the Soviet satellites, on the other hand, numerous survivals of a nontotalitarian past continue to function. In Poland, Czechoslovakia, Hungary, and Yugoslavia we find such institutions as universities, churches, and schools. It is likely that, were a communist dictatorship to be established in Great Britain or France, the situation would be similar, and here even more such institutions of the liberal era would continue to operate, for a considerable initial period at least. Precisely this argument has been advanced by such British radicals as Sidney and Beatrice Webb. The tendency of isolated fragments of the preceding state of society to survive has been a significant source of misinterpretation of the fascist totalitarian society, especially in the case of Italy. In the twenties, Italian totalitarianism was very commonly misinterpreted as being "merely" an authoritarian form of middle-class rule, with the trains running on time and the beggars off the streets. (27) In the case of Germany, this sort of misinterpretation took a slightly different form. In the thirties, various writers tried to interpret German totalitarianism either as "the end phase of capitalism" or as "militarist imperialism." (263a) These interpretations stress the continuance of a "capitalist" economy whose leaders are represented as dominating the regime. The facts as we know them do not correspond to this view (see Part V). For one who sympathized with socialism or communism, it was very tempting to depict the totalitarian dictatorship of Hitler as nothing but a capitalist society and therefore totally at variance with the "new civilization" that was arising in the Soviet Union. These few remarks have suggested, it is hoped, why it may be wrong to consider the totalitarian dictatorships under discussion as either wholly alike or basically different. Why they are basically alike remains to be shown, and to this key argument we now turn.

The basic features or traits that we suggest as generally recognized to be common to totalitarian dictatorships are six in number. The "syndrome," or pattern of interrelated traits, of the totalitarian dictatorship consists of an ideology, a single party typically led by one man, a terroristic police, a communications monopoly, a weapons monopoly, and a centrally directed economy. Of these, the last two are also found in constitutional systems: Socialist Britain had a centrally directed economy, and all modern states possess a weapons monopoly. Whether these latter suggest a "trend" toward totalitarianism is a question that will be discussed in our last chapter. These six basic features, which we think constitute the distinctive pattern or model of totalitarian dictatorship, form a cluster of traits, intertwined and mutually supporting each other, as is usual in "organic" systems. They should therefore not be considered in isolation or be made the focal point of comparisons, such as "Caesar developed a terroristic secret police, therefore he was the first totalitarian dictator," or "the Catholic Church has practiced ideological thought control, therefore . . ."

The totalitarian dictatorships all possess the following:

1. An elaborate ideology, consisting of an official body of doctrine covering all vital aspects of man's existence to which everyone living in that society is supposed to adhere, at least passively; this ideology is characteristically focused and projected toward a perfect final state of mankind — that is to say, it contains a chiliastic claim, based upon a radical rejection of the existing society with conquest of the world for the new one.

2. A single mass party typically led by one man, the "dictator," and consisting of a relatively small percentage of the total population (up to 10 percent) of men and women, a hard core of them passionately and unquestioningly dedicated to the ideology and prepared to assist in every way in promoting its general acceptance, such a party being hierarchically, oligarchically organized and typically either superior to, or completely intertwined with, the governmental bureaucracy.

3. A system of terror, whether physical or psychic, effected through party and secret-police control, supporting but also supervising the party for its leaders, and characteristically directed not only against demonstrable "enemies" of the regime, but against more or less arbitrarily selected classes of the population; the terror whether of the secret police or of party-directed social pressure systematically exploits modern science, and more especially scientific psychology.

4. A technologically conditioned, near-complete monopoly of control, in the hands of the party and of the government, of all means of effective mass communication, such as the press, radio, and motion pictures.

5. A similarly technologically conditioned, near-complete monopoly of the effective use of all weapons of armed combat.

6. A central control and direction of the entire economy through the bureaucratic coordination of formerly independent corporate entities, typically including most other associations and group activities.

The enumeration of these six traits or trait clusters is not meant to suggest that there might not be others, now insufficiently recognized. It has more particularly been suggested that the administrative control of justice and the courts is a distinctive trait (see Chapter 10); but actually the evolution of totalitarianism in recent years suggests that such administrative direction of judicial work may be greatly limited. We shall also discuss the problem of expansionism, which has been urged as a characteristic trait of totalitarianism. The traits here outlined have been generally acknowledged as the features of totalitarian dictatorship, to which the writings of students of the most varied backgrounds, including totalitarian writers, bear witness.

Within this broad pattern of similarities, there are many significant variations to which the analysis of this book will give detailed attention. To offer a few random illustrations: at present the party plays a much greater role in the Soviet Union than it did under Stalin; the ideology of the Soviet Union is more specifically committed to certain assumptions, because of its Marx-Engels bible, than that of Italian or German fascism, where ideology was formulated by the leader of the party himself; the corporate entities of the fascist economy remained in private hands, as far as property claims are concerned, whereas they become public property in the Soviet Union.

Let us now turn to our first point, namely, that totalitarian regimes are historically novel; that is to say, that no government like totalitarian dictatorship has ever before existed, even though it bears a resemblance to autocracies of the past. It may be interesting to consider briefly some data which show that the six traits we have just identified are to a large extent lacking in historically known autocratic regimes. Neither the oriental despotisms of the more remote past nor the absolute monarchies of modern Europe, neither the tyrannies of the ancient Greek cities nor the Roman empire, neither yet the tyrannies of the city-states of the Italian Renaissance and the Bonapartist military dictatorship nor the other functional dictatorships of this or the last century exhibit this design, this combination of features, though they may possess one or another of its characteristic traits. For example, efforts have often been made to organize some kind of secret police, but they have not even been horse-and-buggy affairs compared with the terror of the Gestapo or the OGPU (afterwards MVD, then KGB). Similarly, though there have been both military and propagandistic concentrations of power and control, the limits of technology have prevented the achievement of effective monopoly. Again, certainly neither the Roman emperor nor the absolute monarch of the eighteenth century sought or needed a party to support him or an ideology in the modern party sense, and the same is true of oriental despots. (389c) The tyrants of Greece and Italy may have had a party — that of the Medicis in Florence was called *lo stato* — but they had no ideology to speak of. And, of course, all of these autocratic regimes were far removed from the distinctive features that are rooted in modern technology.

In much of the foregoing, modern technology is mentioned as a significant condition for the invention of the totalitarian model. This aspect of totalitarianism is particularly striking in the field of weapons and communications, but it is involved also in secret-police terror, depending as it does upon technically advanced possibilities of supervision and control of the movement of persons. In addition, the centrally directed economy presupposes the reporting, cataloging, and calculating devices provided by modern technology. In short, four of the six traits are technologically conditioned. To envisage what this technological advance means in terms of political control, one has only to think of the weapons field. The Constitution of the United States guarantees to every citizen the right to bear arms (fourth amendment). In the days of the Minutemen, this was a very important right, and the freedom of the citizen was indeed symbolized by the gun over the hearth, as it is in Switzerland to this day. But who can "bear" such arms as a tank, a bomber, or a flamethrower, let alone an atom bomb? The citizen as an individual, and indeed in larger groups, is simply defenseless against the overwhelming technological superiority of those who can centralize in their hands the means with which to wield modern weapons and thereby physically to coerce the mass of the citizenry. Similar observations apply to the telephone and telegraph, the press, radio and television, and so forth. "Freedom" does not have the same potential it had a hundred and fifty years ago, resting as it then did upon individual effort. With few exceptions, the trend of technological advance implies the trend toward greater and greater size of organization. In the perspective of these four traits, therefore, totalitarian societies appear to be merely exaggerations, but nonetheless logical exaggerations, of the technological state of modern society.

Neither ideology nor party has as significant a relation to the state of technology. There is, of course, some connection, since the mass conversion continually attempted by totalitarian propaganda through effective use of the communication monopoly could not be carried through without it. It may here be observed that the Chinese Communists, lacking the means for mass communication, fell back upon the small group effort of word-of-mouth indoctrination, which incidentally offered a chance for substituting such groups for the family and transferring the filial tradition to them. (346a) Indeed, this process is seen by them as a key feature of their people's democracy.

Ideology and party are conditioned by modern democracy. Totalitarianism's own leaders see it as democracy's fulfillment, as the true democracy, replacing the plutocratic democracy of the bourgeoisie. From a more detached viewpoint, it appears to be an absolute, and hence autocratic, kind of democracy as contrasted with constitutional democracy. (346b) It can therefore grow out of the latter by perverting it. (30) Not only did Hitler, Mussolini, and Lenin* build typical parties within a constitutional, if not a democratic, context, but the connection is plain between the stress on ideology and the role that platforms and other types of ideological goal-formation play in democratic parties. To be sure, totalitarian parties developed a pronounced authoritarian pattern while organizing themselves into effective revolutionary instruments of action; but, at the same time, the leaders, beginning with Marx and Engels, saw themselves as constituting the vanguard of the democratic movement of their day, and Stalin always talked of the Soviet totalitarian society as the "perfect democracy"; Hitler and Mussolini (347) made similar statements. Both the world brotherhood of the proletariat and the folk community were conceived of as supplanting the class divisions of past societies by a complete harmony — the classless society of socialist tradition.

Not only the party but also its ideology harken back to the democratic context within which the totalitarian movements arose. Ideology generally, but more especially totalitarian ideology, involves a high degree of convictional certainty. As has been indicated, totalitarian ideology consists of an official doctrine that

* Lenin's Bolshevik Party was quite different in actuality from the monolithic autocratic pattern that he outlined in *What Is To Be Done?*. (205e)

radically rejects the existing society in terms of a chiliastic proposal
for a new one. It contains strongly utopian elements, some kind of
notion of a paradise on earth. This utopian and chiliastic outlook of
totalitarian ideologies gives them a pseudo-religious quality. In fact,
they often elicit in their less critical followers a depth of conviction
and a fervor of devotion usually found only among persons inspired
by a transcendent faith. Whether these aspects of totalitarian ideologies bear some sort of relationship to the religions that they seek to
replace is arguable. Marx denounced religion as the opium of the
people. It would seem that this is rather an appropriate way of
describing totalitarian ideologies. In place of the more or less sane
platforms of regular political parties, critical of the existing state of
affairs in a limited way, totalitarian ideologies are perversions of
such programs. They substitute faith for reason, magic exhortation
for knowledge and criticism. And yet it must be recognized that
there are enough of these same elements in the operations of democratic parties to attest to the relation between them and their perverted descendants, the totalitarian movements. That is why these
movements must be seen and analyzed in their relationship to the
democracy they seek to supplant.

At this point, the problem of consensus deserves brief discussion.
There has been a good deal of argument over the growth of consensus, especially in the Soviet Union, and in this connection psy-
choanalytic notions have been put forward. The ideology is said to
have been "internalized," for example — that is to say, many people
inside the party and out have become so accustomed to think,
speak, and act in terms of the prevailing ideology that they are no
longer aware of it. Whether one accepts such notions or not, there
can be little doubt that a substantial measure of consensus has
developed. Such consensus provides a basis for different procedures
from what must be applied to a largely hostile population. These
procedures were the core of Khrushchev's popularism, as it has
been called, by which the lower cadres and members at large of the
party were activated and the people's (mass) participation solicited.
By such procedures, also employed on a large scale in Communist
China, these communist regimes have come to resemble the fascist
ones more closely; both in Italy and Germany the broad national
consensus enabled the leadership to envisage the party cadres in a
"capillary" function (see Chapter 4). As was pointed out in the last

chapter, such consensus and the procedures it makes possible ought not to be confused with those of representative government. When Khrushchev and Mao talk about cooperation, one is reminded of the old definition aptly applied to a rather autocratic dean at a leading Eastern university: I operate and you coo. There is a good deal of consensual cooing in Soviet Russia and Communist China, there can be no doubt. That such cooing at times begins to resemble a growl, one suspects from some of the comments in Russian and Chinese sources. There is here, as in other totalitarian spheres, a certain amount of oscillation, of ups and downs that they themselves like to minimize in terms of "contradictions" that are becoming "nonantagonistic" and that are superseded in "dialectical reversals."

In summary, these regimes could have arisen only within the context of mass democracy and modern technology. In the chapters that follow, we shall deal first with the party and its leadership (Part II), then take up the problems of ideology (Part III), and follow them with propaganda and the terror (Part IV). Part V will be devoted to the issues presented by the centrally directed economy, while the monopoly of communications and weapons will be taken up in special chapters of Parts III, IV, and VI. Part VI will deal with certain areas that to a greater or lesser extent have managed to resist the totalitarian claim to all-inclusiveness; we have called them "islands of separateness" to stress their isolated nature. In the concluding Part VII the expansionism of these regimes is taken up, including the problem of stages of totalitarian development and the possibility of projecting such developmental models into the future.

II

Dictator and Party

3

THE DICTATOR

The idea of totalitarian dictatorship suggests that a dictator who possesses "absolute power" is placed at the head. Although this notion is pretty generally assumed to be correct and is the basis of much political discussion and policy, there have been all along sharp challenges to it; it has been variously argued that the party rather than the dictator in the Soviet Union wields the ultimate power, or that a smaller party organ, like the Politburo, has the final say. Similarly, it has been claimed that the power of Hitler or Mussolini was merely derivative, that "big business" or "the generals" were actually in charge, and that Hitler and his entourage were merely the tools of some such group. While the dictatorships of Mussolini, Hitler, and Stalin were still intact, there existed no scientifically reliable way of resolving this question, since the testimony of one observer stood flatly opposed to that of another. We are now in a more fortunate position. The documentary evidence clearly shows that Stalin, Hitler, and Mussolini were the actual rulers of their countries. Their views were decisive and the power they wielded was "absolute" in a degree perhaps more complete than ever before. And yet this documentary material likewise shows these men to have stood in a curious relationship of interdependence with their parties — a problem we shall return to further on. As for Stalin, the famous revelations of Khrushchev sought to distinguish between his personal autocracy and the leadership of the Communist Party. Even before, the large body of material which skillful research in a number of centers had developed suggested that Stalin's position, particularly after the great purges of the thirties, was decisive. A number of participants in foreign-policy conferences with Soviet leaders had already noted that only Stalin was able to undertake immediately, and without consultation, far-reaching commitments. Furthermore, the personal relationships among Soviet leaders, to the extent that they were apparent at such meetings, also indicated clearly that Stalin's will could not be questioned. A similar situation seems now to have developed in Communist China. Although our sources are quite inadequate, various indications suggest that Mao Tse-tung has achieved a personal predominance comparable to that of Stalin and Hitler. His position is enhanced by the long years during which he led the Communist Party in its struggle to survive. However, his style of leadership is different. Part of his power is based upon his capacity to inspire intellectual respect. The "thought of Mao" is a source of much of the personality cult surrounding his overweening position. (346d) It has served as a cloak by providing, in Mao's own words, the collective-leadership principle as the key to Chinese leadership. (215a)

The partisan political flavor of the argument over collective leadership and the cult of personality have obscured the basic process by which a collective leadership in any hierarchic and highly bureaucratized organization is apt to yield to the dominance and eventual rule of a single man. This monocratic tendency was noted by Max Weber and has been fairly generally recognized since. The skill and hypocrisy with which both Stalin and Khrushchev, not to mention Mao, proclaimed the "principle" of collective leadership, while each allowed the cult of their own person to go forward, can most readily be explained in terms of a desire to prevent the rise of any rivals who could always, like Kao by Mao, be accused of this "cult." (240a; also Chapter 5)

A very interesting and to some extent deviant case is presented by Fidel Castro. Basically inclined toward accepting the cult of personality and lacking any effective party organization, he found that he could not handle the Cuban situation, as it evolved toward totalitarianism. Hence a "union" with the Communist Party (PSP) had to be worked out, and Castro became its secretary general, thus providing himself with that minimum of organized support that is quintessential to the totalitarian dictator. (75) The predominance of such leaders does not destroy the decisive importance of the party, which becomes manifest at a succession crisis. But it is nonetheless very real. Stalin's autocracy was in fact made the key point of attack in Khrushchev's speech at the Twentieth Party Congress, in which he developed his points condemning Stalin's cult of personality and attendant autocratic behavior. The argument has since been toned down somewhat.

It might be objected, however, that, had Stalin's position indeed been so predominant, the transition of power following his death would not have been quite so smooth. This objection is not valid, for the transition was not altogether smooth. Stalin's death led to the attempted Beria coup, which manifested itself first of all in seizures of power by the Beria elements at the republic levels. It was only through decisive action at the very top, and almost at the last moment, that the party Presidium succeeded in decapitating the conspiracy. (37a) The fact that the Soviet system continued to maintain itself after Stalin's death is significant; however, it points not to the lesser significance of Stalin but to the higher degree of institutionalization of the totalitarian system through an elaborate bureaucratic network, operated at the top by the political lieutenants of the leader. It is they who pull the levers while the dictator calls the signals. When the dictator is gone, they are the ones to whom falls the power.

"Party ideological unity is the spiritual basis of personal dictatorship," one experienced Communist has written. (74) Ideological unity as such will be discussed later. However, it is necessary at this point in our analysis of the dictator to speak briefly of his ideological leadership. Unlike military dictators in the past, but like certain types of primitive chieftains, the totalitarian dictator is both ruler and high priest. He interprets authoritatively the doctrines upon which the movement rests. Stalin and Mao, Mussolini and Hitler, and even Tito and other lesser lights have claimed this paramount function, and their independence is both manifested and made effective in the degree of such hierocratic authority. It also embodies the dictator's ascendancy over his lieutenants. In a firmly knit totalitarian set-up, the dictator and his direct subordinates are united in ideological outlook; a breach in this unity signalizes that a particular lieutenant is no longer acceptable. "The continuance of ideological unity in the party is an unmistakable sign of the maintenance of personal dictatorship, or the dictatorship of a small number of oligarchs who temporarily work together or maintain a balance of power," Djilas has written, and at the same time pointed out that this enforced unity signifies the culmination of the totalitarian evolution. (74a) It provides the underpinning for the bureaucratization.

Bureaucracy has an inherent trend toward concentration of power at the top, that is to say, toward monocratic leadership, in Weber's familiar term. Totalitarian dictatorship provides striking evidence. Yet the bureaucratization does not exist at the outset, and hence the question of how the totalitarian dictator acquires his power must first be considered. Obviously he does not, like autocrats in the past, get it by blood descent, military conquest, and the like (see Chapter 6 for further details). Lenin, Mussolini, and Hitler first acquired their power through initiating and leading a movement and wielding its effective controls. By fashioning the movement's ideology, the leader provides it with the mainstay of its cohesion. It is in keeping with the "laws of politics" that such leaders become the dictators, once the government is seized. Having thus achieved absolute control of the "state," they then proceed to consolidate their power — a process in which they are aided and abetted by their immediate entourage, who expect to derive considerable benefits for themselves from the situation. There is nothing unusual about this process; it closely resembles that in a constitutional democracy, when the victor at the polls takes over the actual government. But under totalitarianism there now is no alternative; for the movement's ideological commitment is absolute, and its utopian thrust calls for the total marshaling of all available power resources. Hence the "structure of government" has no real significance because the power of decision is completely concentrated in a single leader. Any constitution is merely a disguise by which a "democratic" framework is being suggested, a kind of window dressing or facade for the totalitarian reality. Such groups in the Soviet Union and the several satellites as appear in the garb of "legislative bodies" are essentially there to acclaim the decisions made. Similarly, the judicial machinery, devoid of independence, is actually part and parcel of the administrative and bureaucratic hierarchy. The very shapelessness of the vast bureaucratic machinery is part of the technique of manipulating the absolute power that the dictator and his lieutenants have at their disposal. It is therefore necessary to say something more about these subleaders.

The significant role played in the totalitarian system by the political lieutenants of the dictator makes their coming and going a barometer of the system. These lieutenants wield the levers of control that hold the totalitarian dictatorship together and are instrumental in maintaining the dictator in power. There was a time when the crucial function of the subleaders tended to be ignored. The important role they played after Stalin's death changed all that. Sigmund Neumann's path-finding analysis (265a) has been amply borne out. He pointed to the four decisive elements that "make up the composite structure of the leader's henchmen." (209) These were the bureaucratic, feudal, democratic, and militant.

The bureaucratic element, in the light of Neumann's analysis, is the outstanding feature of the totalitarian leadership elite. (74) Modern totalitarianism, unlike the more traditional dictatorships, is a highly bureaucratized system of power. Without this complex bureaucracy the character of the system could not be maintained. The party organization in particular is a hierarchically structured political machine, and the efficient bureaucrat is indispensable to the dictator. In this respect the similarity between such men as Bormann and Malenkov is more than striking — they were both capable and efficient bureaucrats who held their positions by virtue not only of administrative ability but, and in totalitarianism this is more important, "because they were found worthy of the supreme leader's confidence." (265b)

The second characteristic of these lieutenants is their feudal type of leadership. It is perhaps not historically accurate to speak of the development of localized autocratic spheres of power as "feudal." (57) But there can be little doubt that such was the implication of the "principle of leadership" (*Führerprinzip*) in Germany, as exemplified by the *Gauleiter*. Comparable results can be observed in the conduct of *obkom* secretaries. (89) Such "feudal" vassals are not only territorially distributed; they also operate on the top levels, manipulating important levers of power such as the secret police. Himmler, Bocchini, and Beria were thus responsible for making sure that no internal challenge to the dictator's power arose, and the dictator at all times had to make certain that such posts were filled by men of unquestionable loyalty. In return, all of these lieutenants shared in the system of spoils, and every effort was made to develop in them a vested interest in the continued maintenance of the dictator's power.

The third feature of this leadership, called "democratic" by Neumann, might more properly be designated as "oligarchic." It is not subject to the democratic process of selection and election. The fact that these lieutenants "had better not play the boss within the circle of their associates" (265) does not produce anything like the equality of opportunity characteristic of democratically organized groups. Rather, they display the typical propensities of oligarchic groups, with their intense personal rivalries, their highly developed sense of informal rank, and their esprit de corps toward outsiders. It is this feature of the group of subleaders which found expression in the sloganized principle of "collective leadership." It is risky to become too popular within such a group, as long as the sense of collective anonymity prevails; yet it is precisely behind this facade of anonymity that the emergent dictator, be it Stalin or Khrushchev, organizes his ascendancy toward predominance within and above the group. But even after such a position has been achieved by one, the rest of the group retains the oligarchic characteristics. It might be added, though it is a separate issue, that the jealousy of the dictator of any ascendant rival helps to maintain the oligarchic character of the group of lieutenants. He can fall back upon it as a safeguard against any challenge to his power and prestige.

The final element, growing out of the revolutionary character of totalitarianism, is the militancy of the leadership. The political lieutenants must act as subleaders in the struggle for achieving the totalitarian society. Each in his particular sphere, the totalitarian lieutenant will attempt to break down all resistance to the ideological goals of the regime. He will lead the "battle of the grain," strive for higher accomplishments in "socialist competition," or encourage women to increase the number of their pregnancies. And it is through his militancy, through such battles, be they local or national, that the political lieutenants are weaned, steeled, and promoted. In short, the lieutenants have the function of providing the dictator with effective links to the vast apparatus of party and government. They also share in manipulating patronage and thereby in controlling political and administrative advancement.

The resulting clienteles are likely to play a significant part in intra-party power struggles.

The general aptness of this analysis is illustrated, with some obvious reservations, in the case of Soviet internal politics. The men who surrounded Stalin prior to his death, and who since have risen to the top, were precisely of this type. They provided the dictator with an efficient bureaucratic machine and substituted its filing indexes for many a machine gun. Men like Malenkov, who worked at the apex of the political apparat, or Khrushchev, who acted for many years as a feudal vassal in the Ukraine, produced for Stalin an efficient core of loyal supporters who were not likely to challenge his political supremacy. They came to the fore only after he died. Such internal intrigues and struggles are, of course, not limited to the period after the dictator's death. The history of both the fascist and the communist regimes shows that during a dictator's lifetime much sparring for position occurs at all levels of the party. The struggles between Zhdanov and Malenkov, among Goering, Goebbels, and Himmler, are cases in point. A dictator typically encourages and even promotes such conflicts. He thereby maintains internal mobility among his following and preserves his ascendancy, preventing any rival from endangering his own power.

Khrushchev also developed his own body of able and hard-working political assistants. The careers of men like Brezhnev and Podgorny are illustrative of the efforts of Khrushchev to surround himself with efficient and trustworthy political bureaucrats. Leonid Brezhnev is typical of the newer apparatchiki of the post-Civil War generation. Born in 1906, he joined the party in 1931, studied at a metallurgical institute, and rose through a combination of party and industrial work. From the position of regional party secretary in Dnepropetrovsk, he moved to Moldavia as first secretary and then to Moscow following the Nineteenth Congress as member of the Secretariat and candidate member of the Presidium. After Stalin's death, he was dropped from both posts and appointed head of the Political Administration of the Navy. In March 1954 he assumed the post of second secretary in Kazakhstan under Ponomarenko, became first secretary a year later, and at the Twentieth Congress in 1956 was again appointed to the top party organs. In 1957 he was elected a full member of the Presidium as a reward for his support of Khrushchev in the June crisis, and he played an important role in the industrial reorganization of 1957–58. In 1960 he left the Secretariat and became the largely ceremonial head of state. In June 1963 he returned to the Secretariat, became deputy leader of the party, and was thus put in a position to assume an important role upon Khrushchev's departure from the scene. Presumably he played a key part in the ouster of Khrushchev in October 1964, when he became head of the party.

The background of Nikolai Podgorny is in many ways similar to that of Brezhnev. Born in 1903, the son of a smelter worker, he played an active role in the creation of the Komsomol. In 1925 he was sent to study at a rabfak, a type of school established by the Soviet government to prepare workers for entry into higher educational institutions. Podgorny then went on to study at the Kiev technological institute of the food industry. He joined the Communist Party in 1930 and then held a series of important engineering positions in the Ukrainian sugar industry. In 1939 he was named deputy people's commissar of the food industry for the Ukrainian republic. In 1950 he moved into party work in the Ukraine where he rose to the position of first secretary of the Central Committee in 1957. He was elected to the Central Committee of the Communist Party of the Soviet Union in 1956, and in 1960 became a full member of the Presidium. Long presumed to be a protégé of Khrushchev's, Podgorny apparently deserted his patron in the crisis. Now a ranking member of the Presidium and secretary of the Central Committee in charge of party cadres, he is in a position to wield enormous influence in any struggle for power. Both Podgorny and Brezhnev typify the younger generation of political lieutenants who combine technical expertise with wide experience in party affairs and whose rapid promotion in recent years was largely the result of their loyalty to Khrushchev.

Their counterparts are to be found in the satellite Communist leadership of Eastern Europe. During Stalin's life, efforts were made to focus the spotlight of totalitarian propaganda on certain local leaders and to build them up in the image of the central director, Stalin. Admittedly this was only a halfhearted attempt. They were never allowed to claim the position of the dictator in such crucial matters as ideological interpretation, and they were continually expected to affirm their allegiance to the "Teacher and Leader of World Communism." Nonetheless, men like Bierut or

Gottwald or Rakosi were pictured as outstanding leaders, and they received the major share of the allotted quotas of propaganda limelight. Following Stalin's death and the temporary emergence of a nonpersonal type of leadership in the USSR, it was felt in Moscow that the prominence of a Bierut or Gottwald could constitute a threat to the unity of the Soviet bloc. It is indicative of the subservience of these Communist parties to Moscow that, within half a year of the proclamation of the principle of collective leadership in the Soviet Union, a de-emphasis of personal leadership was apparent in the satellites. However, since that time and in keeping with the emergence of Khrushchev as the personal leader, Gomulka managed to achieve a measure of independence for himself and his party. The extent to which this trend has gained force was revealed at the fall of Khrushchev. A number of leaders in the satellite states issued such clearly critical statements, and indeed insisted upon visiting Moscow to receive explanations, that it is perhaps no longer even very accurate to speak of these regimes as "satellite." There is much evidence to suggest that all this has happened not only because of changes of outlook in the Soviet Union, but also because of the Chinese challenge. The conflict between China and the Soviet Union has not only provided a shelter for such radical dissidents as Albania, but has also opened up room for maneuver for those regimes that on the whole still side with the Soviet Union. How large this room for maneuver has become is manifested by the regime of Georghiu-Dej in Rumania.

But even where the dependence of the satellite political lieutenants has been great, they have differed from their Soviet counterparts in an important respect. There is considerable evidence to indicate that decision making in the USSR is highly centralized and is the prerogative of the men at the top of the party apparat — the Presidium. The Soviet political lieutenants have little discretionary power and generally operate on the basis of either direct orders or specific instructions. Their colleagues in the satellite nations naturally also operate within the framework of general Soviet policies, but these tend to be somewhat more flexible in their local application. On the other hand, the satellite leaders tend to base their decision making to a certain extent on the anticipated reaction of the central Moscow leadership, which is not able at all times to provide policy direction. This gives the national Communist leaders a greater degree of responsibility, although also increasing their occupational risks.

Both the Soviet and the satellite political lieutenants used to fit the categories suggested by Neumann's analysis. They operated on behalf of the central leadership and in most cases were its direct appointees until Stalin's death. Since that time the situation has changed considerably, especially in Poland. It was never true in China, where Mao Tse-tung built up an independent movement. His rise to power, his leadership of the revolution, and his control over the vast masses of China puts him in a different position. Until Stalin's death, Mao Tse-tung acknowledged Stalin's ideological supremacy and in this respect appeared in the guise of an apostle. He was accordingly on an intermediary level between a political lieutenant and a totalitarian dictator in his own right. Stalin's death left Mao in unquestioned political and ideological control of the Chinese Communist Party, which until recently continued to acknowledge the common ideological as well as the power-political bonds with Moscow. He has abandoned this link now, and we shall later discuss the Soviet-Chinese antagonism. In this he has been followed and supported by Hoxha of Albania, as he was preceded by Tito who, when Moscow tried to force him into line, defied Stalin's authority in 1948 (see Chapter 27). Hence one must conclude that the lieutenancy of the satellite leaderships was a passing phase of the overreaching extension of a totalitarian dictatorial power.

With this problem of the lieutenants clarified, let us now return to the position of the leader. Hitler, in the opinion of Alan Bullock in his carefully documented biography, exercised absolute power if ever a man did. (46b) He thus confirmed a report given by the former British ambassador, Nevile Henderson, who wrote that Goering told him that "when a decision has to be taken, none of us count more than the stones on which we are standing. It is the Führer alone who decides." (142a) In support he quotes the notorious Hans Frank as writing: "Our Constitution is the will of the Führer." The Nuremberg trials produced massive evidence in support of this conclusion. The position of Mussolini, according to Ciano's diary, was very similar. (309a) Such concentration of power in the hands of a single man proved an element of decided weakness as well as strength. A number of Hitler's gravest errors of judgment, such as the attack upon Poland and later upon the Soviet

Union, were arrived at without any kind of consultation, let alone by group decision. All available evidence suggests that, had there been such group action involved, the errors would not have been made. (122b; 123) This truly absolute power of Hitler manifested itself during the war in his assumption of military tasks for which he was wholly unprepared. He came to picture himself in the position of making ultimate decisions in this field, which proved the undoing of the German army. (143; 121)

The position of overwhelming leadership that the totalitarian dictator occupies makes it necessary to inquire into the kind of leadership he wields. It is also necessary to explore more fully the relation of the dictator to his party following. The two questions are to a considerable extent interrelated, but for purposes of clarification they must nonetheless be treated as distinct. There have been a number of approaches to the problem of leadership. One of the more comprehensive schemes of classification is that offered by Max Weber. (380) Since his theories have had so much influence, it seems desirable to state that the totalitarian leader fits none of Weber's categories. However, Hitler has been described by a number of writers as a "charismatic" leader. (263b) Since Moses, Christ, and Mohammed were typical charismatic leaders, according to Weber, neither Stalin nor Hitler nor any other totalitarian dictator fits the genuine type. Arguments to the effect that the factor common to both Hitler and Moses — their inspirational and emotional appeal to their followers — is misleading in a twofold way. In the first place, Weber's conception of genuine charisma implies a transcendent faith in God, which was characteristically lacking in Hitler himself and in the typical follower of the National Socialist creed; the same applies to Mussolini and other Fascist leaders. In the second place, the believed-in charisma is not primarily an emotional appeal, but a faith of genuine religious content, metarational in its revealed source, rational in its theology. It is the gift (charisma) of God. Not every inspirational leader is a bearer of charisma in this primary sense. Leadership of the genuinely charismatic type has been enormously important in history, but it has typically been apolitical and quite often hostile to the task of organization. (421a)

The fact that Hitler was not a charismatic leader does not mean that he was therefore *either* a "traditional" leader or a "rational-legal" leader — Max Weber's other two types. For the traditional leader is typified by monarchs like Louis XIV or Henry VIII, while the rational-legal leader is exemplified by the president or prime minister of a constitutional democracy. (412b) The emergence of the totalitarian dictator proves the Weberian typology inadequate. This is part of the unprecedented, unique quality of totalitarian dictatorship, which has been stressed before. The problem of what kind of leadership characterizes totalitarian dictatorships therefore persists.

It is evident from the experience to date that totalitarian leadership is built upon metarational and emotional appeals that are cast in strongly rational terms. Analysis of ideology will show that this leadership is believed to be an executor of history, of forces that arise inevitably from the predestined course of social events. It is the consequent sense of mission that has led to the interpretation of this leadership as charismatic. Such a view entirely overlooks that this "appeal" is reinforced by factors that are totally absent in the case of genuine and even routinized charisma,* more especially the control of mass communications and propaganda and the terror apparatus (see Chapters 11 and 14). Both these features fully mature only in the course of the effective seizure of total power, but they are present from the start. The early history of the Fascist and Nazi movements is replete with the technique of mass propaganda and the manipulation of coercive violence. The notorious whippings, burnings, and castor-oil orgies of the Italian Fascists are paralleled by the *Saalschlacht* (lecture-hall battles) of the Nazi storm troopers, which led to large-scale intimidation of both followers and outsiders long before the actual seizure of power. The tactics of Lenin (see Chapter 9) also were violently coercive and made of the Bolsheviks a conspiratorial military brotherhood rather than a group competing in the market place through discussion and argument. We are not implying here that the conditions of tsarist Russia were favorable to such "bourgeois" or liberal conduct; the facts are, however, that propaganda and terror cradled the Bolshevik Party, as well as the Fascist parties.

* This analysis is not helped, but confused by introducing the category of "routinized charisma." Since totalitarian leadership was not charismatic in the genuine sense, as shown above, it could not be "routinized" evidently. But the term is of doubtful value anyway, since the concept of charisma was originally developed in an effort to cope with the problems of "routinization," with, say, organizing the church.

Still another type of totalitarian leadership, more obviously non-charismatic, is that of Stalin, who certainly cannot be discarded, although he appears in retrospect (together with Hitler) to have been an extreme type. From the period of Lenin's death to the purges of 1936–1938, there was certainly no question of a charismatic appeal exercised by Stalin on the masses. His climb to power was made possible purely by internal bureaucratic measures, augmented by firm doses of terror and propaganda, while the appeal that rationalized his claim to power was phrased in terms of collectivization, industrialization, and preservation of the Soviet Union. But this appeal was made possible only through intraparty maneuvers, and it was organization and not popularity — for Trotsky was certainly more popular — which provided the basis for Stalin's seizure and consolidation of power. Khrushchev, who also rose by means of skillful manipulation of intraparty support, saw fit to broaden the base of his legitimacy. Broadening the mass support, often misinterpreted as "democratization," constitutes a new phase in the evolution of totalitarian leadership proper, which might be called popular totalitarianism: "a diffuse system of repression more or less willingly accepted by the mass of the population." (254) It has been suggested that this is an "internalized" totalitarianism, in which most repression would be self-inflicted. Since the controls remain all-permeating and the dictator continues to have the last word, it remains a system of total power, even though the techniques are changed. The same holds true for Mao Tse-tung, except that he, like Lenin, possesses the aura of the founder of the state; he consults, he exhorts, he persuades. But his decisions are final. (228a; 215c)

As a result of the organizational interaction between the leader and his following, the peculiar nature of this leadership is inseparable from the mythical (or, perhaps more precisely, magical) identification of the leader and the led. In the early days of the Nazi movement, a book appeared that was entitled, characteristically, *Hitler — A German Movement.* (62) The concept that helped the Nazis to accomplish this feat of collective identification was the "race." The race, of course, is not to be confused with the Germans; the Aryans are to be found among a variety of peoples, and their discovery is possible only on the basis of their identification with the leader. The corresponding concept in the communist armory is that of the proletariat, which does not consist solely of those who actually work, except in a marginal sense. By introducing the idea of class-consciousness, the actual mass of the workers is transcended, just as the Germans are in the Aryan race concept, and only those workers who are ready to identify themselves with the leader, Marx, Lenin, Stalin, are truly class-conscious and hence intrinsically involved in the process of totalitarian leadership.

There is no particular reason for inventing a weird term to designate this type of leadership, other than to say that it is "totalitarian." It represents a distinct and separate type, along with the "traditional," the "rational-legal," and the "charismatic." It may be helpful, considering the pseudo-religious emotionalism of these regimes, to designate this kind of totalitarian leadership as "pseudo-charismatic." It bears certain resemblances to still another distinct type, also not adequately developed by Weber and his followers, the "revolutionary" leader. Indeed, it may be argued that the totalitarian leader is a kind of revolutionary leader. Certainly, the characteristic features of Hitler or Stalin are more nearly comparable to those of Robespierre or Cromwell. In any case, the general problem of the typology of political leadership is properly a topic of political theory. (110a)

It may be said in conclusion that the totalitarian leader possesses more nearly absolute power than any previous type of political leader, that he is identified with his actual following, both by himself and by them, in a kind of mystical or magical union, that he is able to operate on this basis because he is backed by mass propaganda and terror, and that therefore his leadership is not to be confused with tyranny or despotism or absolutism in their historical forms.

4

THE NATURE AND ROLE
OF THE PARTY

To call a totalitarian leader's following a party is quite common. And yet it is a rather bewildering use of the word, for the totalitarian following is decidedly different from the kind of party usually found in constitutional democratic regimes. The totalitarian movements outwardly adopted the forms of such parties, but their inner dynamic is quite different. They do not freely recruit their membership, as democratic parties do, but institute the sort of tests that are characteristic of clubs, orders, and similar exclusive "brotherhoods." They correspondingly practice the technique of expulsion, often on the basis of an autocratic fiat by the party leader, though formal action may be taken by a party organ. In democratic party life, the expulsion, if employed at all, is the result of a formalized judicial process. Within the totalitarian party, there is also no "democracy." The party following does not even decide if it votes or elects the leadership; it is subject to autocratic direction in matters of policy and to hierarchical control in matters of leadership. Such oligarchic tendencies are marked also in democratic parties (248), but the competition between them forces the leadership to "mind" the following.

Following Max Weber, but eliminating his normative aspect of "free recruitment" from the general definition of a political party, it may be characterized as follows: a political party is a group of human beings, stably organized with the objective of securing or maintaining for its leaders the control of the government, and with the further objective of giving its members, through such control, ideal and material benefits. (104b; 195c; 380a) It must be stably organized in order to distinguish it from temporary factions and the like; the control of the government should be understood to cover other than political government, for example, church government; and it is very important to include both ideal and material advantages, since no party can exist without some advantages of both kinds accruing to its members. The familiar distinction between parties oriented toward ideology and toward patronage is sound only if the two criteria are understood as "predominating" rather than as exclusive. But another distinction must be drawn in the light of the facts of totalitarian dictatorship, and this is the distinction which may be expressed as that between cooperative and coercive parties. The latter are exclusive (elitist), hierarchically organized, and autocratic. This too is not an absolute contrast, but a question of the prevailing tendency. (248)

These traits of the totalitarian party have at times been rationalized in terms of the fighting position of such groups. Since, generally speaking, any group organization tends to be more tightly autocratic as the group encounters more difficulty in its fight for survival, there is some ground for thus explaining the autocracy of totalitarian movements. But what concerns us primarily here is the *fact* of such autocratic leadership, not its explanation. It would, in any case, not hold after the seizure of power, for, even after the party has achieved complete control, it does not become less autocratic. On the contrary, it becomes the vehicle for transforming the entire society in its image. This well-known dynamic process shows that there are other drives involved besides the needs of a fighting group.

The first to formulate and to set in motion the operational principles of a totalitarian party was Lenin. In his fanatic insistence on strict party discipline, total obedience to the will of the leadership, and unquestioning acceptance of the ideological program (as formulated by the leader), Lenin charted the path so successfully later followed by Stalin. In his *What Is To Be Done?* (1902), Lenin outlined the centralist organizational pattern his movement was to adopt, and he rejected firmly the idea of a broad popular party with open membership. "Everyone will probably agree that 'broad democratic principles' presuppose the two following conditions: first, full publicity, and second, election to all functions. It would be absurd to speak of a democracy without publicity, that is, a publicity which extends beyond the circle of the membership of the organization . . . No one would ever call an organization that is hidden from everyone but its members by a veil of secrecy, a democratic organization." (205e) Such an open organization, under tsarist conditions, Lenin considered unworkable, and his conviction about a disciplined paramilitary party did not waver despite the split it produced in the Marxist ranks. The basis for the first totalitarian movement was thus laid. It can be seen, insofar as Lenin was right in justifying his course by reference to conditions in tsarist Russia, that the autocracy of the tsars is thus mirrored in totalitarianism. This must be borne in mind in considering the general problem of the totalitarian party.

These organizational principles have spread throughout the Communist movement. More particularly the German Communist Party was organized along strictly hierarchical lines, exclusive and autocratic. (98.1; 100.1) Its techniques were copied by the National Socialists, as its Italian counterpart had been by the Fascists. Even though National Socialism conceived of itself as a movement, gathering many different elements (*Sammlungspartei*), it soon developed the elitist characteristics of an autocratic leadership (*Kaderpartei*). This transformation is clearly seen in the successive editions of *Mein Kampf*. Hitler at first still accepted the principle of elections within the party as long as the leader, once elected, enjoyed unquestioned authority thereafter; he dubbed it "Germanic democracy." But he later abandoned this notion in favor of the strictly autocratic leadership principle.*

In the matured totalitarian society, the role of the party is a distinctive one, which bears little resemblance to the role of parties in democratic societies. As has been pointed out in the preceding chapter, it is the role of the party to provide a following for the dictator with which he can identify. According to a well-known phrase of Mussolini, the party has the function of the capillaries in the body; it is neither the heart nor the head, but those endings where the blood of party doctrine, party policy, and party sentiment

---

* "The movement stands on all levels for the principle of Germanic democracy: election of the leader, but absolute authority of him." *Mein Kampf*, 1928, p. 364f. Five years later it reads: "The movement stands on all levels for the principle of absolute authority of the leader, combined with highest responsibility." *Mein Kampf*, 1933, p. 378f. Cited as given by Bracher, 269 (translation mine).

mingles with the rest of the body politic. In a sense, the party may be pictured as the elite of the totalitarian society, if the word elite is taken in a very neutral sense.* In view of the total dependence of the party upon the leader at its head, it can be argued that the party does not possess a corporate existence of its own. It is in this respect comparable to the Hobbesian state, in which all the separate members of the society are severally and totally dependent upon the sovereign. But somehow such a view seems not to do justice to the collective sense of the whole, to the almost complete loss of personal identity that the party members suffer, or rather enjoy, as they feel themselves merged in the larger whole. This feeling seems to contradict another aspect of these movements, namely, the unquestioning obedience. Fascists and Nazis never wearied of repeating Mussolini's formula, "Believe, Obey, Fight" — these were the focal points of Fascist and Nazi education. In this kind of military subordination, the individual seems to confront the commander as an alien and wholly detached being. Fascist writers found the answer to this seeming paradox in what they conceived to be the "style" of the new life. This "style of living" was proclaimed in National Socialist Germany, as it had been in Italy, to be that of the "marching column," it being of little matter for what purpose the column was formed. (465a)

The Soviets, on the other hand, never weary of proclaiming that their party is a democratically organized movement composed of class-conscious workers and peasants. Unlike the Fascist parties, the organization of the Communist Party is thus designed to give the outward appearance of intraparty democracy, with the final authority resting in the hands of the party membership through the party congress. This concept was reaffirmed in the party program adopted at the Twenty-Second Congress in 1961. Not only is the party member entitled to "elect and be elected," but he may also discuss freely questions of the party's policies at meetings and in the press, and "to criticize any Communist, irrespective of the position

---

* Such a usage would, however, conflict with that suggested by Lasswell and Kaplan (196), p. 201, where an elite is defined as those "with most power in a group"; it is contrasted with the "mid-elite," who are those with "less" power, and with the class that has "least" power. Following such a definition, the party would be the "mid-elite." For a more extended discussion of these problems, see 110b.

he holds." It is reaffirmed that the guiding principle is democratic centralism: there is full discussion prior to the determination of policy, but once policy is determined subsidiary organizations are expected to execute it in full. The "business-like discussion of questions of Party policy" is said to be "free" and as such an "important principle of inner-Party democracy" (Sec. 27 of the program). Yet the highest principle is collectivism, that is to say, a collective leadership as conceived by Lenin. "The supreme organ of the CPSU is the Party Congress," the program states. The congress, which is to meet at least once in four years and is composed of delegates from all the party organizations, is the highest legislative body of the party. It elects a Central Committee as its permanent organ to legislate on behalf of the congress during the lengthy intersession periods.* The executive organ is the party Presidium, known until October 1952 as the Politburo, and the party Secretariat is the chief bureaucratic organ. The organization of the party parallels the structure of the government. Below the central organs there exist in all the republics, except the RSFSR,† party organizations, each with its own central committee, presidium, and secretariat. These in turn are broken down into regional (*oblast*) party organizations, and below this level there are city (*gorod*) organizations and rural production subdivided into ward (*raion*) organizations. The foundations of this pyramid are the primary party organizations of factories, farms, offices, schools, and any other institutions where at least three members can be found. On October 1961 there were a total of 296,444 primary party organizations.

The structure of the Communist Party was profoundly transformed by the reorganization of 1962, which divided the party into two vertical hierarchies, one agricultural and the other industrial,

* The relevant section 35 reads: "Between congresses the CPSU Central Committee directs the activities of the Party, the local Party bodies, selects and appoints leading functionaries, directs the work of central government bodies and social organizations of working people through the party groups in them, sets up various Party organs, institutions, and enterprises and directs their activities, appoints the editors of the central newspapers and journals operating under its control, and distributes the funds of the Party budget and controls its execution." The Central Committee is to hold no less than one meeting every six months.

† The Russian republic does not have its own party congress and central committee. The subordinate party organizations are coordinated by the Central Committee of the Communist Party itself, through its Russian Bureau.

which converge only at the republic level. This reorganization, however, is intended to reinforce rather than to dilute the power of the central organs.

We see, then, that authority and decision making are highly centralized, and during the Stalinist era the power of the dictator was such as to reduce the role of the party to a minimum after 1939. The rise of Stalin was made possible by his skillful exploitation of the position of general secretary of the party. In the internal struggle for power, he knew how to manipulate the personnel of the party organization, to put his henchmen into key positions, to demote or denounce the followers of his rivals, and generally to utilize all the resources of a large organization, including its files, as so many weapons.* During his rule, the apparat, composed of full-time party members in a position to wield the most power, steadily developed and expanded, but already by 1925 some 25,000 party members were full-time employees of the party apparat. This apparat is now estimated to number between 150,000 and 200,000. (89a) On Stalin's death a small group of individuals in the Presidium, who took over control of the party, exercised the dictatorial power together. Control over the party was for a while concentrated in the hands of this small group, but before long the first secretary of the party (and presumably chairman of the Presidium), Nikita Khrushchev, who through the Secretariat controlled the Central Committee of the party, emerged as the key figure. However, it is generally held that his power did not become as absolute as Stalin's. It is difficult to say whether this was so because of his personal preference or because of forces in the party and the government that he was unable to subdue. Certainly his power was very great, since he directed the executive sections of the Central Committee. (89b) These sections not only control the life of the party, but also supervise the functions of the respective ministries of the government. In fact, the top party leaders often assume personal direction for various phases of state activity: it was reasserted in a resolution of the Central Committee (November 23, 1962), which provided for party guidance of the national economy.

---

* Khrushchev's secret speech of February 1956 revealed that even the Politburo was broken up by Stalin into smaller committees (e.g., the "Sextet" for Foreign Affairs), which Stalin himself coordinated, and that Stalin sometimes arbitrarily forbade Politburo members to attend its sessions. (174; 209b)

This bureaucratization of power is also duplicated on lower levels. The regional party committee, for instance, also reflects through its organizational pattern both the concentration of power in the hands of the party bureaucrats and the control of the state bureaucracy by the party. The regional party committee accordingly, in addition to its own secretariat, has various sections dealing with such matters as propaganda and agitation, industry, roads, agriculture, trade unions, trade organizations, and political enlightenment. It is no exaggeration to say that the regional committee is constantly in charge of the entire life of the region, through either actual direction or supervision. As a result, the party leaders are usually swamped with work. This impairs the zeal and the revolutionary quality of the party. There is constant ambivalence in party declarations on this subject; at one point, the party warns its officials against becoming too involved in operations of the governmental bureaucracy; at another, it insists that the party must see to it that the government functions properly. For instance, the official journal of the Central Committee, in an article entitled "Raise the Organizational Role of the Party Apparat," emphasized the necessity for *supervision* and stressed that party officials should not work for others — that is, the state bureaucrats — and should guard against red tape. (434a) Yet the Central Committee explicitly urged party members "to put a decisive end to a liberal attitude toward violators of state discipline . . . to replace them by active organizers . . . to intensify the guidance of industry, to strive for concrete results in improving the work of enterprises." (419a) The division of the party into two hierarchies, intended to increase its control over industry and blurring in some sectors the distinction between government and party, will create new problems because those functionaries preoccupied with production, whether industrial or agricultural, may increasingly neglect other functions. The production committees may serve in fact to obliterate the distinction altogether. In any case, it is only natural that, if such authority is conferred upon the *party* functionary, the *government* functionary will consult him, defer to his judgment, and let him decide if he will.

The party bureaucracy is undoubtedly the hard core of the Soviet system. Without it, not only would the political regime likely crumble, but probably the entire economic life of the country would come to a standstill. In this sense, the party bureaucracy is far more important to the system than its counterparts in both the National Socialist and Fascist states. Since the death of Stalin, the apparat has become even more important as a mechanism of modern dictatorship. To quote a sound assessment of one of the foremost students of the Soviet scene: "the thrust of the Khrushchevian initiative was . . . to reinforce the authority of the Party apparatus . . . This reaffirmation of Party hegemony epitomizes the road by which Khrushchev traveled to supreme power. Embodying himself in the Party and proclaiming its right to unchallenged leadership, he raised his entourage of Party functionaries to heights of authority which they could not have dreamed of in Stalin's day." (89c)

This, however, does not mean that the individual party member is unimportant. On the contrary, the Communist Party puts the greatest emphasis on the individual eligibility, personal loyalty, and political consciousness of the candidate for membership. Indeed, a member must be virtuous. As *Pravda* once stated it: "It must not be forgotten that to enter the sacred door of the Party one must be spotless not only in his public life but in his personal life as well." (441c) The new party program has reaffirmed this norm. Although this ideal Party membership opens the way to greater career opportunities, it is not devoid of hardships and obligations. Indeed, one of the outstanding features of Communist Party membership is the pressure put on the members to make them active participants in the organization's collective as well as individual undertakings. This point was strongly re-emphasized at the Nineteenth and Twentieth Party Congresses, and Khrushchev spared no words in his castigation of those party members who fail to perform their tasks. Party members are accordingly expected to participate constantly in various study circles, reading sessions, special seminars, and discussions. They are utilized in stimulating "socialist competition" in their places of work. They are expected to proselytize among their relatives, friends, and colleagues. They must be active in setting up small study groups among nonmembers to familiarize them with the teachings of Marxism-Leninism.

At the regular party meetings, the prime concern of those attending is to report on the failure or success in meeting their *partnagruzka* (party duty or obligation). In such meetings the individual members must fully account for their activities, admit any shortcomings, and criticize themselves. In this they are assisted, either spontaneously or by prearrangement, by their colleagues, who also report their own delinquencies. (355) These mutual self-examinations are not restricted to party performance only. The party is also a paternal institution concerned, albeit for motives of efficiency, with the moral and personal life of its members. Accordingly, such meetings quite often develop into dissecting operations in which a member's personal life is scrutinized and castigated. Excessive drinking, sexual promiscuity, vulgarity, and rudeness to subordinates or family are subjects that crop up constantly at such meetings. And all of this is recorded faithfully in extensive protocols and individual *kharakteristiky* (individual personal files), which are kept in the party archives and copies of which are forwarded to upper party organs. During periods of accentuated militancy and crisis, such sessions often produce expulsions from the party and subsequent arrests, although these are not as frequent as the imposition of reprimands. (355)

Party members are furthermore obliged to participate in the special campaigns, such as elections or production campaigns. In the course of these mass operations, the party members agitate, propagandize, and work for the fulfillment of the tasks set. This they do after work, during lunch breaks, and in their leisure time. They thus set the example for the masses with their energy, spirit of self-sacrifice, and complete devotion to the Soviet state. All this, of course, is very time-consuming and physically exhausting. One of the frequent complaints of party members, expressed after they have defected to the West and evident also in Soviet materials, is that they are overwhelmed, overburdened, overused. (13) Yet, at the same time, all this generates considerable enthusiasm. The membership is made to feel part of a constructive machine, led by dynamic leaders, achieving unprecedented goals. Their personal identity is submerged in the totality of the party, and the might of the party becomes a source of personal gratification. That this gratification frequently takes the form of more rapid promotion seems further to enhance its value, while a sense of unity and integration frequently obscures the seamier aspects of the system. Popular totalitarianism has, if anything, reinforced this function of the membership as a stimulant of popular "consensus." Trends in the Soviet Union have in this respect assimilated the Communist to the Fascist and National Socialist system. The situation in Communist China appears very similar. (215d)

While such total identification of the party with the leader and its related capillary function is thus quite common to all totalitarian regimes, significant differences appear when we ask about the relationship of this organization to the government. This relationship is frequently pictured as simply one of control, but the actual situation is more complex. The divergence among the Soviet, Fascist, and National Socialist regimes is symbolized by the position of the leader in each. Stalin for many years and until World War II was General Secretary of the Communist Party of the Soviet Union. Mussolini proudly called himself for many years the Capo del Governo (head of the government), while Hitler was the Führer (leader) of the movement and president and chancellor of the Reich at the same time. The relation of the party to the government corresponded to this set of titles. In the Soviet Union, as just described, the party was and is superior to the government, and the heads of government departments were correspondingly "people's commissars." The same holds true for China and the satellites, even though different titles were and are used. In Italy the government was for many years superior to the party; this corresponded to the Hegelian emphasis on the state in fascist ideology (see Chapter 7). But, as Germino has observed, although at first Italian Fascist theorizing on the party differed notably from the National Socialist and Communist ideologies, "these contrasts became less sharp as the non-totalitarian wing of Fascism became silenced and the party, in accordance with what appear to be the imperatives of totalitarian rule, expanded to wield extensive power independently of the governmental services." He concludes that "the Fascist, Nazi and Soviet parties are of one cloth. They do not differ in kind, for each is a totalitarian single party in an advanced state of maturation." (120b) Their relation to the government nevertheless differed.

In Hitler Germany, party and government were fairly balanced in power and influence, and the same was true of Italy in the late thirties. The German situation was strikingly characterized by Ernst Fraenkel when he undertook to interpret the Nazi system as that of a "dual state" or, more properly speaking, a "dual government." One of these he designated as the "prerogative" state, in which everything was arbitrarily decided by party functionaries from the Führer on down; the other was the "legal" state, which continued to function along the lines of the established legal order. Fraenkel leaves no doubt, however, that the prerogative state was more powerful in his opinion, that it had the last word in that it could at any time break into the other, set aside its rules, or super-impose others. (102b) This situation was perhaps best illustrated at the time when Hitler is said to have exclaimed, after a court had found Pastor Niemöller not guilty, that "this is the last time a German court is going to declare someone innocent whom I have declared guilty." He had Niemöller rearrested by the Gestapo. But, precisely because it was Hitler himself who had the final say and who was both leader of the party and chief of the state, something like coequal status prevailed in the lower echelons.

It seemed at the end of war, and also under Khrushchev after he assumed the title of premier, that a similar situation was developing in the Soviet Union. As premier of the Soviet Union and marshal of its armed forces, Stalin appeared in the dual role similar to that which Hitler occupied until his death. However, the party secre-tariat and the premiership were in different hands, making it more feasible to assess their respective roles. Ever since that time and on all levels of Soviet life, from the agricultural collectives through the secret police to the foreign ministry, the role of the party has been strengthened, as we have seen. Indeed, there are no indications that the influence of the party is on the wane. Determined efforts to revitalize its militancy, such as a new ideological campaign and a membership drive for workers and peasants, suggest clearly that the party remains the political and ideological standard bearer and con-tinues to supervise the activities of the state apparatus. This outlook dominates the new party program. Among the first to bear the brunt of this attack resulting from a re-emphasis of party predomi-nance were the intellectuals, who were curtly reminded that it is the party which sets their tasks and determines their doctrinal com-pliance. Similarly, the state officialdom was attacked for its bureau-cratic attitudes and ordered to mend its ways. Symptomatic of the party's crucial role is the fact that it is the first secretary of the party who leads the agricultural "battle" for increased grain production. The resolution of 1962 cited above reconfirms this general outlook.

The administrative-political role that the party plays in the USSR, acting as a sort of superbureaucracy controlling and penetrating the purely administrative institutions, would seem to indicate that its predominance, as far as the foreseeable future is concerned, is not likely to be challenged. Periodic purges as well as new campaigns restore to the party the necessary degree of élan and consequent cohesion, while maintaining at the same time its revolutionary fervor. How to maintain this élan and revolutionary fervor was, furthermore, not nearly as acute a problem in the USSR as it was in Fascist Italy or Hitler Germany, where large numbers of people were admitted into the party by fiat. In the USSR, membership in the Communist Party still is a privilege. And while the state apparatus maintains the system in function, it is the party, or rather its leaders, which sets new goals and keeps the totalitarian grip on the population. Without it the Soviet system would become brittle and sterile and would be likely to lose its vitality. The current emphasis on *partiinost* (partyness) serves as a reminder to those who would like to forget it.

In order to work effectively, the party must be restricted in size. To belong to it must be an honor worth striving for. Neither the Bolshevik nor the Italian Fascist Party was very large at the time power was seized by its leaders — nor was the Communist Party in China, let alone Poland or Rumania. These parties were subsequently enlarged. The Nazi Party, on the other hand, while at the outset also exclusive and restrictive, eventually made efforts to increase its size as long as it was engaged in competition with other parties. The same holds true today of the Communist Party in Italy and France, among others. In such cases, one can expect the membership after the seizure of power to be reduced; the fact that this did not happen in Germany explains in part the position the party occupied. Yet, in a sense, the blood purge of June 30, 1934, was such a reduction of party membership; the storm troopers of Captain Röhm became an inferior group in the party hierarchy. Gradually, the Elite Guards (SS) took over the functions of a totalitarian political party.

The Communist Party in the Soviet Union increased its membership very gradually during the twenties, then grew rapidly between 1928 and 1933, reaching a high of 3.5 million in 1933. It declined sharply during the purges of the thirties, although by 1941 it again reached its 1933 level. During the war there occurred a rapid step-up to about 6 million, as the leadership tried to secure greater support for the war effort by conferring the coveted party membership on a large number of people. During some of the war months, the party actually was growing at the rate of 100,000 people per month. Since the end of the war, there has been increased concern shown by the leaders over the low political literacy of the membership and a number of local purges have occurred, particularly in the national republics. The over-all party membership remained rather static, growing slowly by the end of 1952 to 6.9 million and by the end of 1956 to about 7.6 million. It was approaching 10 million by the time of the Twenty-Second Party Congress. At present, the party constitutes almost 5 percent of the total population of the Soviet Union.

The Italian Fascists similarly represented only a small percentage of the total population. There were about a million members by 1927, somewhat over 2 percent of the population. Up to that year, the party had remained formally open. Recruitment was "free," in Weber's sense, which was logical enough, considering that not until some time after 1926 did the Fascists achieve absolute totalitarian power. Soon afterwards the ranks were closed. But they were opened again for some months in 1932–33, and some groups, such as government officials, were actually forced to join. After 1932, membership became "more than ever a necessary condition not only for government employ," but also "for all positions of any importance in industry, commerce, and culture." (309b)

The growth of the Fascist Party was due to yet another circumstance. Mussolini liked to stress youthfulness, and therefore an annual contingent of several hundred thousand members were admitted from the youth organizations. By October 1934, the party had reached 1,850,777, and by October 1939, 2,633,514, according to official figures issued by the party. This figure would still be only 5 percent of the population, but it constituted about 17.5 percent of the total electorate. Actually, during the war, membership rose even more rapidly, and by June 10, 1943, had reached 4,770,770. This was a result of the removal of all restrictions for soldiers after the outbreak of war. The Fascists, like the Soviets, soon realized their mistake and in 1943 attempted to reverse this trend, once again trying to make the party a selective one that would be composed of "fighters and believers," the custodian of the revolutionary idea. (446a) In any case, the Fascist militia, with its half million mem-

bers, was the real heart of the party, reinforced by the "old guard"
and some of the more zealous youth. This militia, characteristically,
always contested the secret police's monopoly of terroristic procedures.

The German party, the Nationalsozialistische Deutsche Arbeiter
Partei (NSDAP), went further, both in enlarging its size and in
developing a hard core of fanatics. For one thing, it was a mass
party at the time of Hitler's accession to power; it had reached
approximately one million by 1933. Financial as well as general
political considerations led Hitler to build it into the largest political party ever built in Germany until that time, measured not only
by votes but by membership as well. There was a rush into the
party immediately after the seizure of power in 1933; a further
expansion took place in 1937, when all government officials were
forced into the party by "law." Since the Nazi Party was thus
watered down into a fairly nondescript agglomeration, hardly ani-
mated by genuine enthusiasm, the inherent need for such an elite
corps reasserted itself in the SS (Schutzstaffeln) of Heinrich Himmler. The SS were at first merely a part of the brown-shirted storm
troopers, but after the eclipse of the latter in 1934, the SS became
separate and predominant. Indeed, this closed order, rather than the
National Socialist Party, must be considered the dynamic core of
the Nazi system. The SS remained always quite restricted, even
though during the war the organization of the Waffen-SS (see
Chapter 14) diluted it somewhat. (465b)

Generally speaking, these facts show that the party and the special cadres within it will be highly selective and elitist in a totalitarian dictatorship. This tendency toward elitism reinforces the
strictly hierarchical structuring of the totalitarian parties we have
noted above. (240b; 209g) The rigid hierarchy and centralized
power are the result of an evolutionary process; everywhere there is
at first considerable impact from below; later the party following
becomes more and more subdued, until finally its influence is neg-
ligible. This is part of the maturing process of totalitarian regimes.
Whether it would be accurate to describe this development as the
formation of a new ruling class, as Djilas and others have done,
seems arguable (74a); but there can be little doubt that a gradual
stratification is now occurring. Rotation of party leadership becomes a very real problem in connection with this solidifying of the

hierarchy. Both in Italy and in Germany, the fact that the same leader remained in control throughout the existence of the dictatorship undoubtedly inhibited this rotation. Yet a purge occurred in both regimes by which some of the older subleaders were eliminated. Others no doubt would have followed after the war, if several confidential statements to that effect by Hitler, Himmler, and others are allowed to stand. In the Soviet Union and the satellites, the purge has become a regular institution, while in Communist China brainwashing, that is, systematic thought control, has been substituted. But such crises notwithstanding, the party constitutes the mainstay of totalitarian dictatorship. (209a) Without his party's support, the dictator would be inconceivable; his unquestioned leadership gives the party its peculiar dynamic, indeed fanatical, devotion to the dictatorship, and the spineless attitude of subjection of its members toward the man at the top is merely the psychological counterpart to the party's ruthless assertion of the will and determination to rule and to shape the society in its image.

5

YOUTH AND THE FUTURE
OF THE PARTY

Modern politics is much concerned with youth. Political parties are inclined to organize youth movements, thereby encouraging the sprouting of political interest and concern at the earliest possible moment. In constitutional democracies, such party indoctrination is quite separate and apart from publicly supported "civic education," though it surely contributes to the "making of citizens." (242) In totalitarian dictatorships the two tasks are largely merged. The organized efforts to indoctrinate youth are begun at a very early age and are used for the discovering of political talent among children.

The totalitarian dictatorship, because of its sense of mission, is vitally concerned with the transmission of its power and ideological program to the younger generation. Indeed, it is upon the young that the hopes of the dictatorship are focused, and the totalitarian regime never tires of asserting that the future belongs to the youth. Feeling little or no commitment to the past, the totalitarian regimes are unrestrained in emphasizing the failures of yesterday and the utopian quality of tomorrow. Stalin put it in a way that would fit Hitler and Mussolini just as well: "The youth is our future, our hope, comrades. The youth must take our place, the place of the old people. It must carry our banner to final victory. Among the peasants there are not a few old people, borne down by the burden of the past, burdened with the habits and the recollections of the old life. Naturally, they are not always able to keep pace with the party, to keep pace with the Soviet government. But that cannot be said of our youth. They are free from the burden of the past, and it is easiest for them to assimilate Lenin's behests." (337d) The imaginations and the energy of the youth, the leadership hopes, will thus be harnessed to aid, and later carry on, the program of totalitarian reconstruction launched by the party. The intensity of the efforts to convert and discipline youth have no parallel in the recent traditional dictatorships, which were much more concerned with the problem of immediate political and social stability. Only some philosophic utopias like the Platonic republic come close to matching the totalitarian myths for, and indoctrination of, the young.

All of the totalitarian movements have been concerned with the indoctrination of the young. *Giovinezza* was one of the key slogans in Mussolini's rhetoric. Both the Italian Fascists and their German imitators organized youth before their advent to power. When Hitler said that the National Socialist state would have to take care that it obtained, through an appropriate indoctrination of youth, a generation ready to make the final and greatest decisions on this globe, he was merely echoing views that Mussolini had expounded from the beginning. The Italian Balilla organization (ONB), although formally embodied into the governmental apparatus by the law of April 3, 1926, formed the training ground for the Fascist Party. (120c) The law establishing it declared that Fascism considers the education of youth one of the fundamental tasks of the revolution, in an "atmosphere of discipline and service to the nation." Hitler, when he came to put forward the National Youth Law on December 1, 1936, could do little better than paraphrase these sentiments, stating that on the youth depends the future of the German people (Volkstum). The age groups in the Hitler Youth (Hitlerjugend) were somewhat higher than in the Balilla, but otherwise the story was largely the same.

All Fascists stress the training of youth outside family and school for the tough life of warriors and conquerors who are continally on the march and must be ready to endure all the hardships of such an existence. Hitler proclaimed dramatically at the party meeting of 1935: "The German youth of the future must be as hard as the steel from the plants of Krupp. The development of mental capacity is only of secondary importance." Both the Balilla organization and the Hitler Youth (365) were considered essential branches of the party, even though the Balilla remained within the framework of the government until 1937, when the secretary of the Fascist Party personally assumed the leadership of the organization. But from 1926 onward Fascist youth was actually led by a key member of the party directorate, who also directly reported to the Capo del Governo. In Germany, the Reich youth leader likewise reported directly to the Führer. However, the German youth organization always remained much more definitely a distinctive party organization. Both organizations aspired to and eventually largely achieved the total control of youth. The German law of 1936 explicitly stated that "the totality of German youth must be prepared for its future duties," but only in April 1939 was membership made obligatory for all German youth. The Balilla did the same in 1937. We do therefore find a close parallel in objectives: they are stated for the Balilla as military, physical, technical, spiritual, and cultural — a significant ranking of priorities. In keeping with this stress on the warrior task and the warrior virtues, both organizations engaged in a great deal of paramilitary activity. It is a melancholy thought that much of the idealism and love of adventure which is perhaps the best part of boyhood was thus channeled by these organizations into activities that stimulated the lower instincts. The free organizations of the democratic countries, whether boy scouts or religious or artistic groups, and even those connected with political parties, though at times outwardly resembling these youth organizations are yet very different; even when the slogans they use are similar, when they stress character and sports and the benefits of outdoor life, the purpose is individual improvement and a finer personality rather than the brute objectives of war and conquest.

The growth of these youth organizations under the inducements and pressures of the fascist regimes was striking: in January 1924, the membership of Italian youth organizations was 60,941, while in July 1937 it was 6,052,581. In Germany, the total at the end of 1932 was 107,856, while early in 1939 it was 7,728,259. Considering the relative populations of Italy and Germany, it can be seen that the Italian organization was even more successful in its effort to absorb the entire youth of the country. However, in the course of the war, the Germans caught up, and their total by 1942 approached 10 million.

Within the context of these vast organizations, a rigid selective process was organized. Boys and girls were put through various tests before they could graduate into the next higher group, and these graduations, in Italy called *Leva Fascista*, were accompanied with solemn ceremonies and highly emotionalized totalitarian ritual. Of course, the final test was whether a member of one of the youth organizations qualified for membership in the party, or better, the SS or the Armed SS (Waffen-SS), Himmler's military formations (see Chapter 13). Indeed, within the Hitler Youth, by the year 1939, an inner core of superior fellows was organized, known as the Stamm-HJ, or trunk of the Hitler Youth. Members of this nucleus were presumably carefully selected and had to fulfill the same racial conditions that the Nazi Party insisted upon for its members. Thus was the total enlistment of youth made a key factor in the long-range maintenance of the fascist regimes. But since these regimes did not last, we cannot be sure whether these programs would have succeeded — there are some indications that they might not. But for a more conclusive story we must turn to the USSR.

According to an official Soviet interpretation, the powerful appeal of the Communist Party is derived from the fact that "it is linked with the broad masses by vital ties and is a genuine party of the people, that its policy conforms to the people's vital interests. The role of such mass organizations as the Soviet Trade Unions and the Young Communist League has greatly increased in rallying the working people around the party and educating them in the spirit of communism." (441d) This conviction again found explicit expression in the new party program of 1961. It devotes a special section (VII) to the party and the Young Communist League (Komsomol). It is described as a "voluntary social organization of young people." Evidence in support of this claim has not been produced; most young people like to "run with the gang," and nonparticipation would therefore be intrinsically improbable. The party no doubt takes advantage of such willing participation, even exploiting it as a first step in selecting the more promising. For such a regime, it seems essential that the process of selection begin with the young to whom the elite character of the organization has a special attraction. The youth are made to understand that membership in the organization involves a special state of communion with the Soviet body politic, and the official acceptance of a young boy or girl into the Young Pioneers (ten-to-fourteen age group) is accordingly a ceremony celebrated with pomp and solemnity, and marks the first step in their career. That career began with membership in the Octobrists, comprising the very young children under ten years of age, from which they are graduated into the Pioneers.

After this initial period, the abler Pioneers are recommended for promotion into the Komsomol. Entrance into this organization is more difficult and hence presumably exercises all the attraction that results from competition. (89d) The Komsomol today is a mass movement embracing the great majority of the Soviet youth. It is so organized as to provide planned direction for young people from the time that they begin their education. At the age of fourteen, if considered qualified, the Pioneer is allowed to join the Komsomol proper, where the actual training for ultimate party membership begins. In fact, both in organization and in operation, the Komsomol is a younger replica of the party. The party relies heavily on it in its various propaganda and agitation campaigns, in its political controls over the military, and in educational drives. Those who are most able become party members; in the words of the Komsomol statutes, "a Komsomol member considers it the greatest of honors to become a member of the Communist Party of the Soviet Union and in all his work and studies prepares himself for Party membership." (423b) Like the Fascist organizations, the Komsomol has increased steadily through the years: in 1936 it numbered 3,800,000; in 1949, 9,300,000; in 1951, 13,380,000, and in 1962 it had reached 19,400,000. (89; 86; 423c) Thus the party has ample reserves to draw upon, and only those considered most able, or, as it happens sometimes, those with the best connections, can hope to become members.

The emphasis placed on indoctrinating the young follows quite logically from the position of the Communist Party that the people, in order to be "liberated," must be made "conscious" of their role and position. The process of making them conscious ought to start at the earliest possible time, and for this reason the party, through its affiliates, must pay special attention to the young. However, unlike the Fascists, the Communists could not operate a mass youth movement prior to the seizure of power. The tsarist oppression made necessary a conspiratorial formation, and in that situation any form of organized activity for Russian youth was out of the question. Most of the conspirators were young men anyway. The first steps in organizing a youth movement were taken a year after the

Bolshevik seizure of power. In November 1918, the First Congress of what later came to be called the Komsomol was held. It was, however, not until the Second Congress, in October 1919, that the youth movement was made, in terms of both program and organization, into an affiliate of the Communist Party, a relationship continuing to this time.

The history of the Komsomol, in many respects, is a reflection of the problems and difficulties that the party faced. (89e) There was a period of disillusionment during the NEP when many young stalwarts thought the revolution was being betrayed; there was a time of considerable Trotskyite support in the ranks; then came the enthusiasm and the challenge of the First Five-Year Plan and the collectivization of agriculture. The party employed the energies of the young in combating inertia, old traditions, and the peasants in pushing through its program. The industrial center, Komsomolsk, far in eastern Asiatic Russia, was built under most difficult climatic conditions by the young Komsomolites. Then came the purges and the decimation of the thirties, particularly those of the Yezhov period. The Komsomol suffered great losses, like the party (see Chapter 15), but at the same time the purge opened up new career opportunities. When the world war came, Stalin once again relied heavily on the youth for the partisan battle and for ideological leadership in the armed forces. (208) The young Komsomolites became guerrilla leaders and political officers; many were promoted into the party membership. And after the war, they were called upon to help in the task of reconstruction.

Since 1956, the party has harnessed the Komsomol for yet another task: to combat the growing juvenile delinquency in Soviet cities. This problem, common to all urbanized societies, has become a source of major concern to the Soviet leadership, and the Komsomol is called upon to show the way to "Soviet morality." Nonetheless, there are signs that some of the revolutionary qualities of the Soviet youth are on the wane, and that even among the Komsomol there are those whose interests tend more toward jazz and good living than to efforts "to build communism." The following harangue, which was published recently in the Soviet Union, illustrates the difficulties: "A playboy is recognized by his special style of slang speech and by his manners; by his flashy clothes and impudent look . . . the female of the playboy species wears tight-fitting clothes which reveal her figure to the point of indecency. She wears slit skirts; her lips are bright with lipstick; in the summer she is shod in Roman sandals; her hair is done in the manner of fashionable foreign actresses." (454) The Soviet press has been forced to acknowledge that even Komsomolites have been guilty of criminal activities. During the fifties, the agricultural campaign in the virgin lands (see Chapter 20) gave the Komsomol an opportunity to appeal again to the imagination of Soviet youth and to channel the energies of the younger generation into tasks that benefit the Soviet state. The Soviet press since 1955 has been full of accounts of young Komsomolites leaving the cities and going east, to build new state farms in Kazakhstan and Central Asia. This movement, although officially inspired, doubtless has occasioned enthusiasm among some of the young; many young people see in this kind of work a new opportunity for heroic struggle on behalf of communism.

That the party continues to expect the Soviet youth to lend its energies to the many and continuing tasks of building "communism" was demonstrated by the following words of Khrushchev, addressing in April 1956 the All-Union Conference of Young Builders:

Comrades! Hundreds of thousands of new workers will be required for the major construction projects of the Sixth Five-Year Plan. To provide the personnel for these construction projects the Party Central Committee and the Soviet government will appeal to Soviet youth to send their finest comrades to build the most important enterprises.

The Y.C.L. [Young Communist League] has 18,500,000 members. Will the Y.C.L., then, not be able to assign 300,000 to 500,000 members from its ranks? I believe they will be quite able to do so. (*Stormy applause.*) We believe in the energy of the Y.C.L. and the young people; we believe in their militant spirit. We know that our young people aren't afraid of cold weather or the Siberian taiga. (*Applause.*) (441q)

The situation in Communist China closely parallels the Soviet setup. The Communist Youth League is to the Chinese party what the Komsomol is to the Soviet party. It too serves as an instrument for the political and ideological indoctrination of young people, as an organization for channeling youthful energies and enthusiasms into economic and social projects useful to the party, and as a recruiting ground for future leaders. The Chinese Communist Party throughout its history has had a variety of youth groups

closely associated with it. In 1949 the New Democratic Youth
League was established on a national basis as a broad organization
requiring of its members only that they accept the basic principles
of the "new democracy." Paralleling changes in the Chinese political scene and in the role of the party itself, the NDYL gradually
became more restrictive, and its evolution was completed by the
change of its name in 1957 to the Communist Youth League. Its
membership rapidly increased during these years, from 3 million in
June 1950 to 20 million in 1956, and by 1959 had reached 25 million.
Below the CYL, as in the Soviet Union, there exists the Young
Pioneer organization, grouping children under the age of fourteen.
This organization has grown even more rapidly than the CYL. Its
membership of 1.9 million in 1950 had soared to 50 million by 1960.

Those who have had contact with the youth of today's Communist totalitarian regimes testify that the regimes appear to have been
successful in making many young people identify their future with
that of the system. (240d) In view of the magnitude of the efforts
just described, this is hardly surprising. However, such identification may take different lines, which are sharply in conflict
with each other. Speaking generally, there is a conflict between two
sets of values, both of which in some sense serve the purpose of the
regime but which are also mutually exclusive. On the one hand,
there is the mystique of collective life and activism and social obligations, which emerges most clearly in the notion of volunteering for
work in the virgin lands. On the other hand, there is the mystique
of science and technology and expertise. This tends to have indi-
vidualistic implications — it is accompanied by demands for less
political interference. Meetings and political activities are seen as
interference. But the defenders of both points of view claim that
theirs is the best way to build communism. Even so, totalitarian
regimes may, given time, succeed in transforming the thinking and
the attitudes of an entire society — and thus perpetuate themselves
for a long while to come.

There is one further aspect of the Communist approach to youth
that has assumed increasing importance in recent years. It is the
world-wide cooperation of the youth groups. An international
youth movement, paralleling the internal totalitarian youth organization, was set up as early as November 1919. This organization,
known as KIM (Communist Youth International), after the fail-

ures of revolutionary upheavals in Germany, Poland, and Hungary did not assume world-wide importance until 1945, when the old KIM apparat was reorganized into the World Federation of Democratic Youth (WFDY) under the control of its Soviet affiliate, the Anti-Fascist Committee of Soviet Youth, which is the foreign branch of the Komsomol. The close link existing between this organization and the Soviet Communist Party illustrated by the fact that in East Germany the WFDY organization was first set up in 1945 by Ulbricht and Hiptner, old Comintern agents. At present, the WFDY claims 83 million members, which includes the 19 million Komsomolites and many more millions in the satellite and Chinese youth organizations. Its activities, be it "anti-germ-warfare" agitation or the Stockholm peace appeal, used to follow closely the foreign-policy propaganda line of the USSR. Little is known about how the split in the world Communist movement has affected this organization. The split has brought on a crisis and its future is uncertain.

Even this cursory review shows how keen is the interest of totalitarian dictatorship in the development of youth. As such a regime succeeds in capturing the minds and the energies of the young, it will be able to build a solid foundation for an ideological consensus. It was very recently put forcefully by a Chinese leader who addressed the Ninth Congress of the Communist Youth League as follows:

The Youth of our country must carry forward the great spirit of arduous struggle of the predecessors of our revolution. They must do their utmost and make themselves the shock force of socialism . . . At the Tenth Plenum of the Eighth Central Committee of the Communist Party, Chairman Mao, our beloved leader and teacher, pointed out with great emphasis that it is necessary to strengthen the class education of youth to ensure that the revolution in our country will not be perverted in generations to come . . . It is a great strategic task of the proletarian dictatorship and also a fundamental aim of the work of the Communist Youth League to hold aloft the red banner of the great thinking of Mao Tse-tung, so as to help turn the young people of the coming generations in our country into proletarian revolutionaries. (435)

In all the totalitarian regimes, the party has assumed full responsibility for the ideological training of the younger generation and has used the youth movement both as a training ground and as a recruiting device for ultimate party membership. Only the USSR, however, has had the opportunity to maintain its system for a longer time-span than one generation. Over this period, the Soviet leadership has devoted ceaseless efforts to assure itself of the loyalty and support of the youth. Indications are that, given the complete monopoly of communications, with constant, unremitting, and simultaneous appeals to the future through grandiose projects, it is difficult for the young to resist the totalitarian temptations.

6

THE PROBLEM OF SUCCESSION

The history of government as a formal scheme of organization tends to obscure the problem of what happens when those who hold effective power disappear. The problem can be stated also as that of establishing a convincing identification between the departed ruler(s) and the newly instituted one(s). In the modern West, two schemes have predominated: that of the traditional monarchy and that of the constitutional republic; constitutional monarchy, which from the late seventeenth until the middle of the nineteenth century was seen as a happy synthesis of the schemes of Locke and Benjamin Constant, proved to be an unstable transitional form. In a monarchy of the traditional Western type, the problem of succession is solved by a law which provides that legitimate blood descent should be, as in private property, the basis of succession. This law persisted throughout the absolutist period. So strongly held were the convictions upon which it rested, that wars were fought over successions. In earlier autocracies legitimation by blood descent, implemented by the approval of a priesthood, was common. Often elaborate rituals had to be observed. In the later Roman empire, the actual control of military power, epitomized in the acclamation by the Praetorian Guard, became decisive. In a constitutional republic, the problem of succession is, in a sense, eliminated because the rulers are periodically changed as the result of constitutionally organized elections, while the constitutional order is considered as self-perpetuating under an amending procedure that the constitution itself provides for. In totalitarian dictatorships, on the other hand, the problem of succession presents itself anew with real insistence. (110c; 37c)

Insofar as totalitarian dictatorship retains the outward, formal features of a constitutional republic, it may be able to fall back upon certain procedures in the crisis necessarily precipitated by the death of the leader. In a way, this may be the most important aspect of the retention of "constitutions" in totalitarian dictatorships, apart from the propaganda value which the making of such constitutions has for pressing the claim that the totalitarian dictatorship is a democracy. But it would be folly, indeed, to assume that the succession to Lenin or Stalin was actually settled in a democratic process "from below," since all the dynamics required for the functioning of this process, like freedom of expression and competing parties, are nonexistent in the totalitarian state.

The action of the larger, more popular bodies, like the Supreme Soviet, is purely acclamatory. This still leaves open the question of how succession is to occur. The build-up of adulation for the totali-leader and the development of the vacuum around him create a most dangerous hiatus the moment this mortal god dies. In the nature of things, the leader has not been able to designate a successor of his choice; even if he had, it would leave such a person without real support after the leader is dead. Indeed, such a designation might well be the kiss of death. As we have seen, persons close to Stalin were "eliminated" by the group of lieutenants that found itself in control of the actual source of physical power after the death of the leader.

The documentary evidence we have on the subject of succession is rather scanty. Besides the story of Stalin's rise to power after Lenin's death, when the Soviet Union was not yet fully developed as a totalitarian state, we have only the somewhat controversial data concerning Khrushchev's rise and fall. There is also some documentary evidence regarding potential successors to Hitler and Mussolini. This evidence allows a tentative conclusion: the problem of succession was unsolved, the question of who might take over was an open one, and there is little doubt that in Germany there would have taken place a sharp struggle between the military men and Himmler and his SS. Who would have won is hard to say. If the Soviet Union gives any clue, the army might have made common cause with certain key party leaders, such as Goering, and eliminated Himmler. That a military man took over from Hitler did not constitute a succession; the totalitarian regime was in an advanced state of decomposition. In the case of Mussolini, the army's attempt to supersede him was foiled, but it was foiled by Nazi intervention, and so that case is even more inconclusive. It is rather interesting that earlier in his career Mussolini had sought to dictate his successor. After 1929, it was to be the Grand Council's task to pick a successor; various leaders, like Ciano, Italo Balbo, Bocchini, and Buffarini, as well as the party secretary, Starace, were mentioned from time to time. In any case, all signs point toward the conclusion that in Italy, too, a bitter struggle would have ensued among various contenders. All this is speculation, however. In fact, the case for both Hitler and Mussolini is vitiated by the fact that they were defeated in war; their successors were the victors.

Returning to the Soviet Union, it now seems pretty clear that the hiatus left after the death of Lenin was at first filled by no one. Into the breach stepped a party clique of top leaders who immediately proceeded to compete with one another for ultimate control. In light of the evidence that Fainsod and others have sifted (89f; 253b; 49b), it seems that Trotsky, who considered himself entitled to the succession, immediately aroused the mute antagonism of Stalin. The fight was focused on a disagreement of policy; whether this disagreement precipitated the antagonism or whether the antagonism begat the disagreement in policy is an idle question — the two were obviously part of the same total situation. Stalin, after isolating Trotsky and destroying his power, as well as that of his associates, then turned on those who had assisted him in this task and in turn isolated and destroyed them. At the end of three years, he emerged as the omnipotent leader in full control of the regime.

Stalin's emergence in control of total power was facilitated by the absence of an established and well-functioning state bureaucracy and by his ability, as party secretary, to manipulate the party organs. The local party organs had by the twenties already assumed important administrative functions. These functions were not infringed upon either by the secret police or by the army, then weakly organized on a territorial militia basis. (387) And insofar as the party was greatly involved in local administrative-operational problems, a central headquarters — the Secretariat and the secretary — tended to assume paramount importance in questions not only of patronage but also of occupational loyalty. Stalin's vital capacity for such work, as well as his actual position, was hence crucially important to his seizure of power.

The situation after Stalin's death turned out to be the same as after Lenin's: a group of insiders took over control and proclaimed themselves collectively in charge.* The fluid character of the situation thus created was demonstrated by the change which occurred in the top Soviet leadership circles after March 1953. Five distinct phases of development in the succession struggle may be distinguished between 1953 and 1956. The first stage, lasting only a few days, resulted in Malenkov's inheriting most, if not all, of Stalin's power. During this brief interlude, Malenkov basked in the sunshine of Soviet press acclamation and, more concretely, held the crucial posts of premier and party secretary. In a notorious photomontage *Pravda* portrayed him in an intimate huddle with Stalin and Mao Tse-tung; all other participants were eliminated from the original photograph. This stage, however, was short-lived. The other lieutenants quickly gathered together to prevent the emergence of a new dictator who subsequently might wish to promote his own lieutenants. Malenkov was forced to concede one of his power posts, and Khrushchev replaced him as party secretary. The principle of collective leadership was proclaimed, and *Pravda* declared that "collectivity is the highest principle of party leadership" and that "individual decisions are always or almost always one-sided decisions." (441e)

This second stage, however, was also short-lived. For obscure

* Those readers interested in the possibilities and risks of political prediction may find it illuminating to compare what follows with the discussion in our first edition, written in 1955, on pp. 49–50: "This experience, while of course not conclusive, suggests that it would be rather risky to draw any inferences from the present state of affairs in the Soviet Union. It is too soon, presumably, to know what is going to be the outcome of the struggle over succession. But we are, in the light of the foregoing analysis of totalitarian dictatorship, justified in doubting that anything like group control or collective leadership has been permanently substituted for monocratic leadership. It is, as we have seen, at variance with the inner dynamics of the system." There is no apparent reason to suppose that it will be different this time, even though two men, Brezhnev and Kosygin, have been entrusted with the leadership of party and state. Prophets have of course once again appeared, proclaiming the emergence of a nontotalitarian system in the Soviet Union, but the sequestering of Khrushchev indicates how far from such a change the Soviet system remains. It seems more likely by far that from the group which unseated Khrushchev there will in time emerge a true successor to his autocratic preeminence.

reasons, Beria, the head of the secret police, felt it necessary to
assure his own safety through further acquisition of power. (37d)
The third phase was thus one of a power struggle between Beria
and the other leaders, apparently headed by Malenkov. Despite
initial successes, mirrored particularly in increased control over
some of the national republics (notably Georgia and the Ukraine),
Beria and his colleagues were finally arrested and liquidated. Beria's
lack of prudence, possibly because of circumstances beyond his control, probably united the other leaders against him and led to his
fall. His removal from the "collective leadership" necessarily involved an internal reshuffling, which inevitably produced subsequent shifts. The pattern as seen in the fourth phase brought a
polarization of power between Malenkov and Khrushchev, in the
respective capacities of premier and first secretary of the party,
especially in view of the former's commitment to a consumer-goods
policy and the latter's emphasis on agricultural and heavy industrial
expansion. The fifth phase began early in 1955. Khrushchev's control of the party apparat proved decisive, and the January 1955
session of the Central Committee fully endorsed its boss's position.
Malenkov resigned early in February and Bulganin, backed by
the military but a willing collaborator of Khrushchev's, became
premier. At that point, the highly developed and bureaucratized
state administration and the party seemed like two Greek columns
supporting the edifice of the Soviet state, with collective leadership
providing the arch that kept them together.

There followed the anti-Stalin campaign. (209c) This campaign
began in fact a few days after his death. References to Stalin soon
became quite scarce; greater emphasis began to be placed on
Lenin; * collective leadership was contrasted with the harmful
effect of one-man rule. The open attack came in February 1956. At
the Twentieth Party Congress Mikoyan frankly criticized a number
of Stalin's basic tenets while also referring to some purged victims
of Stalinism as "comrades." Then a few days later, at a secret night
session of the congress, Khrushchev came out with a detailed and
highly emotional attack on Stalin, charging him with a variety of
offenses. These ranged from inept leadership in the war against

---

* References to Lenin soon became idolatrous. At the Twentieth Congress he was
constantly referred to as "the immortal teacher" and "the source of all the successes
of the Party."

Hitler to charges of terrorism and murder. The stage was thus set for the disintegration of the idol. (174; 209b)

Reports of the speech spread rapidly throughout the Soviet orbit, and special meetings were held with party members to whom a Central Committee letter on this subject was read. In some places, particularly Georgia, convinced Stalinists reacted very unfavorably. There were reports of demonstrations and shootings in Tbilisi. An even greater stir occurred in the satellites, where the attacks on Stalin were more energetic. One of the secretaries of the Communist Party of Poland (United Workers' Party), Jerzy Morawski, openly wrote in the party paper of the terror and damage wrought by Stalin and of his paranoiac tendencies. In some cases past grievances were denounced and previously purged (and hanged) Communists rehabilitated.

Insofar as succession is concerned, this development makes the emergence of an absolute ruler an unlikely prospect in the immediate future. It certainly excludes the possibility of anyone's claiming the mantle of Stalin, although one cannot exclude entirely an alternative of this type. The more likely prospect, however, is that the present leadership will continue to claim that it has returned to true Leninism and has abandoned the cult of personality. But Leninism does not, as the record shows, exclude the possibility of one-man rule, and it would be possible for a new ruler to claim that he is enforcing a Leninist policy while in fact maximizing his own power. That is precisely what Khrushchev did. In the final phase of the succession crisis he succeeded in effectively strengthening his own power in the party apparat. The Twentieth Party Congress resulted in an extensive purge of the Central Committee (about 40 percent of its members were dropped) and was preceded by similarly thorough purges of the republican central committees. At the congress Khrushchev delivered the political report in which he severely criticized some of his colleagues. He increasingly took the initiative in international affairs, while the other Soviet leaders followed. But apparently opposition gradually crystallized among them. This opposition culminated in a dramatic but abortive effort to remove Khrushchev from his key position in 1957. Why did it fail? because Khrushchev in a skillful maneuver succeeded in mobilizing the lower echelons against the top leadership. It failed because Khrushchev's rivals did not fully appreciate the decisive role of the party as a corporate whole in determining the succession. The conflict was, as in the twenties, not merely one of personal rivalries, but also one of issues. Khrushchev favored conciliatory gestures in foreign policy, such as the re-establishment of friendly relations with Tito, while insisting on the continuing importance of heavy industry and linking both with a renewed emphasis on the world revolutionary goals. Molotov favored the Stalinist course abroad, while Kaganovich and Malenkov advocated the need for consumer goods at home. The showdown came in the summer of 1957. In June of that year the opposition, having grown to seven of the eleven members of the Presidium of the Central Committee, demanded the resignation of Krushchev. He countered by refusing to resign unless the Central Committee itself joined in the request, counting on the solid following he had in the Central Committee. A substantial delegation from the latter demanded that a meeting be held, maintaining that the Presidium as its executive had no right to effect a change in the top leadership without its assent. Khrushchev as general secretary quickly summoned a gathering and achieved a stunning victory, 251 of the 312 members present voting to retain him. The tables were then turned on the opposition. The key oppositionists, Molotov, Malenkov, and Kaganovich, were removed from the Presidium and this body, after being enlarged to fifteen, was packed with Khrushchev followers. Then various other rivals, including Marshal Zhukov who had supported Khrushchev, were eliminated in the sequel, and the succession was settled. During the next two party congresses (the Twenty-First and Twenty-Second) such fulsome adulation was bestowed upon Khrushchev that he himself had to protest: his style remained different from Stalin's, built as it was upon the emphasis on the role of the party and its unity. As Fainsod has commented in concluding his review of these developments: "Embodying himself in the Party and proclaiming its right to unchallenged leadership, he [Khrushchev] raised his entourage of Party functionaries to heights of authority which they could not have dreamed of in Stalin's day." (890) It is as yet hard to know whether his failure to show corresponding skill in 1964 was due to ill health, to the participation of his intimates in the plot, or to other causes, perhaps in combination with these. Many of his innovations had been opposed inside the party, and this may have led to a "ganging up" against him, although the continuation of his key innovations renders this explanation rather unsatisfactory.

In view of the inconclusive nature of the empirical evidence on succession, it may be worthwhile to consider the question from the standpoint of the inherent rationale of the totalitarian system. For it would seem that succession necessarily rests upon the legitimation of a government's power. It exposes a regime's authority to its greatest strain, since the passing away of the ruler calls not only his but the system's authority into question. The broad problems of authority go beyond our present purpose, but it should be noted that authority may result from brute force; it may also be the consequence of rational persuasion or effective participation in the choice of its wielder. Authority of the kind resting on force is most readily transferred, because all that is needed is to pass on the means of coercion. (110d)

It would seem that, since the dynamic focal point of the totalitarian dictatorship is the leader-party interdependence, the party would provide the key to the succession problem, not as a democratic and cooperative group of more or less equal individuals, but as a bureaucratic apparatus with an hierarchical structure whose decisions are reinforced by a ritual of acclamation. Hitler himself spoke of a body of his lieutenants acting like the Vatican Council. (150c) With all due allowance for the fundamental differences, the doctrinal cohesion of the faithful, upon which the legitimacy of hierarchical leadership in an ecclesiastical organization rests, allows for some analogical questions. Is not the election of a spiritual head of such an organization by a group of senior members of the hierarchy an indication of how succession in totalitarian dictatorship may become formalized, if totalitarian dictatorship lasts as a governmental organization? Is not the authority of such a leader legitimized by this very choice made by his peers in the hierarchy of believers? Is not such a procedure "convincing" in terms that fit both the ideology and the power structure of the totalitarian dictatorship? Against such a hypothesis, weighty arguments have been advanced in support of the contention that the police, having gained the upper hand in the totalitarian dictatorship, will manipulate the succession. (112a; 5c) But what is the basis of such claims? Must not the police seek to demonstrate its orthodoxy, and how is it to accomplish this task, except by appealing to the party? There may be much cynical mockery among actual power holders in such a system, but do we find even a Himmler ever abandoning the key ideological framework of the party-in-being? *

It would seem that there is a rather simple explanation for this phenomenon. The "commissars" ruling within such a totalitarian system are eminently practical men; they are as far removed from contemplative, theoretical studies as they can be. This would predispose them to avoid ideological controversy or even reflection upon party slogans. Changes in these slogans will become necessary from time to time, but these are never a total rejection or even a rejection of the major part of the established set of formulas which have been learned by all the adherents. It would make little sense to appeal to others, to the inert and intimidated masses who are not adherents and organized in the dominant party. In short, the party would seem to fill the breach, bridging the hiatus created by the death of the leader, and only he who fully understands its role has any chance of succession. And who will win in the ensuing struggle is a question of personality, of effective control over the apparat, and of skillful manipulation of the various competitors. The succession that involves rejuvenation at the very top of the hierarchy cannot be managed except in interaction with and support by the apparat.

It is thus from this inner sanctum of the system, this apparat that is its mainspring, that a new leader will finally emerge. This process of emergence may be brief or long, depending on the interaction of the many variables involved. During the interregnum of determined succession, effective leadership is provided, symbolically, by the party — as the personification of ideological unity and continuity — and, actually, by the top levels of the apparat. Within this apparat the fight for power, as already seen in the Soviet experience after Lenin's and Stalin's deaths, is likely to be fierce. This much it is fairly safe to predict, and it applies not only to Soviet leaders, but also to Mao Tse-tung, Tito, Gomulka, and others. In all these situations, it will be well to follow closely the maneuverings in the party, and more especially its top echelons (this generalization probably applies as well, *pari passu,* to nontotalitarian one-party regimes).

* When he finally did, in his secret negotiations with Count Bernadotte, it was only to save his skin in the face of imminent defeat.

However, the struggle for succession is not likely to disintegrate the totalitarian system, as so many have been inclined to hope, even though the conflict is intense. For the party remains, with its cadres and its hierarchy. The appeal to party unity is a powerful one, and failure in such a struggle is apt to be fatal and consequently will be waged with caution. All of those concerned in the succession have a vested interest in the continued maintenance of the regime and are not likely to tear it apart recklessly. The closing of the ranks that occurred after Stalin's death is an illustration in point. In the initial period after the dictator's death, then, compromise and mutual adjustment are likely to be the policies followed. A political principle of mutual "no trespassing" is to prevail, with due warnings and penalties for those who trespass against their colleagues.

This, in a sense, tends to produce a frightening Orwellian image of an entire system that embraces millions — politically controlled masses, being ruled by an impersonal collective, without individual faces and individual voices. The masses have no real indication of internal relationships and developments within this closed circle. They know only what they read and see in the official newspapers, which dutifully publish on every state holiday a somber photograph of the "collective leadership" — a group of stony-faced men. Changes within that group become apparent only after they have physically manifested themselves—through fall from the apparat and subsequent liquidation. A careful reader is then able to plot, *ex post facto,* the internal web of intrigue. But even within a few years all references to the fallen colleague are expunged from the record and he ceases to have existed.

This element of secrecy and total separation from the masses is precisely what makes unlikely the disintegration of a totalitarian system through a struggle for succession. Political struggles will occur within the apparat as they must among men wielding power and wanting more. But no leader will be able to break out and make a mass appeal. No ideological conflict of the pretotalitarian scale of Trotsky against Stalin will be possible. Totalitarian monopoly of all communications and all weapons will make it unfeasible. The intricate system of cross-controls will make it difficult for any one leader to gain the uncontested support of a power structure, like the army, for his cause. The internal struggles are apt to be resolved within the apparat, and only its aftermath is likely to reach the masses, as was the case with Beria and Khrushchev. By this time the question of disintegration will be meaningless. (112b)

Political power, however, is never static. The collective leadership of a totalitarian system is likely to be subject to gradual elimination of its fringe elements, and a tendency toward the emergence of central contestants in time is likely to manifest itself. The logic of power points toward its monopolization, and the history of the three Soviet successions seems to confirm this. The process of decision making, and consequent accountability, unavoidably leads to internal inequalities in the "collective leadership," and true leadership again begins to assume a personal veneer, even if still contested by two or more competitors within the closed circle of the apparat. But it is within the apparat, and not on the barricades of ideological conflict, that new totalitarian leaders are begotten, destroyed, or eventually made triumphant. This conclusion is sometimes contested in terms of the 1957 struggle, which was settled by an appeal to the Central Committee rather than within the Presidium. In this connection it is said that the appeal to special interest groups was more overt than ever before: Khrushchev's proposals clearly benefited the party and threatened the state bureaucracy, and his opponents represented the interests of the threatened groups. *Pravda* and *Izvestiya* occasionally took sides in the struggle. What then is to prevent a widening of conflict in the future and public appeals on behalf of the conflicting parties?

It seems that one of the major reasons why this will not occur is because no one leader will align himself exclusively with a single interest, but will attempt to conciliate or at least neutralize the others. In connection with Khrushchev's ouster in October 1964, many speculations and various interpretations have been advanced, stressing the role of the managerial bureaucracy, or the party bureaucracy, or the military, or sections of these groups. But what seems, in terms of succession, the most important point is that the ouster was manipulated by men who utilized the established party machinery, much as a dissident group in a British party might use this formation to overthrow the government. Lest false analogies be drawn from such an observation, it should be noted that the decision about the successor was secretly planned and that no part in choosing a successor was assigned even to the party membership at large, let alone the electorate, which might well have opted for Khrushchev. Indeed, Khrushchev was kept virtually incommunicado, which suggests that his successor feared his or a broader challenge of their decision.

III

The Totalitarian Ideology

7

THE NATURE OF TOTAL IDEOLOGY:
ITS SYMBOLS AND MYTHS

It has of late become fashionable to proclaim the "end of ideologies" and to engage in speculation about the consequences. (189) At times, wishful thinking is involved, but a marked sophistication concerning ideological positions and tenets has undoubtedly occurred in this century. The critique of conventional ideologies by the revolutionary movements has given rise to general assessments, such as Karl Mannheim's well-known *Ideology and Utopia*. In this overrated work he goes so far as to describe ideologies as "utterances" that "structurally resemble lies." (227a) The increasing sophistication, however, has by no means ended the function and role of ideology in contemporary society. Quite the contrary. The process of "ideologizing" the ideas prevalent in various polities is still going forward at a rapid pace, as traditional and conventional notions are transformed into action programs of particular movements, groups, and parties. (240c)

A special case of the argument that ideologies have lost their significance is the contention that ideology is not a significant feature of a totalitarian regime, but merely a weapon of the rulers. Even if that were true, ideology would be important, and in any case there cannot be any doubt that ideology is a weapon not only in the hands of totalitarian rulers, but of power seekers and power wielders everywhere. Nor is ideology any the less serviceable for this purpose, if it is passionately, fanatically believed to be true. There are in any event clear indications that the ideology shapes the behavior of the totalitarian leaders as well as of the mass following. Djilas is quite right when he says that ideological unity is the mainstay of the Communist Party, which makes obligatory for its members "an identical concept of the world and of the development of society." (74b) A purely manipulative attitude on the part of the leaders would not work.

This conclusion forces itself upon the observer not only in regard to such major policies as the collectivization of agriculture in the Soviet Union, Communist China, and the satellites, but also in many minor policies. The discussions during recent party congresses as well as the Soviet conflicts with China, Albania, and Yugoslavia become hard to understand if ideology is discarded. The same holds true for the Fascist regimes, notably Hitler's. His "final solution" of the Jewish problem by mass extermination was clearly ideological in motivation. We need not depend upon public declarations in this respect. His comments to confidants are quite convincing evidence (150), and we have further signs that this motivation continued powerful to the end. On February 14, 1945, he said to Bormann: "I ought to have had twenty years for leading the new elite to maturity, an elite of young men who would have been bathed in the philosophy of national socialism from infancy." (153a) The world-revolutionary posture of totalitarian movements is unthinkable without the ideological thrust from which they spring.

Marx and Engels described the whole range of ideas as "superstructure." Religion, law, and other systems of ideas were seen by them as nothing but camouflage, surrounding the bare and brute facts of economic controls, the "control of the means of production." They served as weapons in the class struggle, by which the ruling class buttressed its position of power. Thus Marx and Engels wrote: "The ruling ideas of each age have ever been the ideas of its ruling class" (231), and later Marx again: "every historical period has laws of its own . . . as soon as society has outlived a given period of development, and is passing over from one given stage to another, it begins to be subject to other laws." (230) Clearly, according to them, the prevailing ideology of any particular epoch was both the outward rationalization of that epoch's economic organization and the tool used by the dominant class to stop history from continuing on its inevitable path. For, as Marx and Engels saw it, history was a perpetual progress through time, propelled irresistibly by the class struggle, though at varying rates of advance. The struggle produced the historical momentum and established the economically dominant classes in a position of power and then toppled them from it. "All history is the history of class struggles," the *Communist Manifesto* declares. Throughout this unfolding pattern of dialectical change, combining revolution and evolution, ideology served both to mask and then to unmask "objective reality."

Though we can readily see that this communist approach to history and the ideas at work in it was the product of a specific historical period, Marx and his followers believed its unique quality to be that it was more than an ideology. To them, this approach embodied the science of history and as such constituted an unprecedented insight into the true course of development. It provided those who fully grasped it with a key for understanding not only the past and the present, but also the future. And because its view of the future was said to be scientifically accurate, and because it asserted that the future would be better than the present, it readily became a compelling call to action. The future, thus clearly perceived and rightly valued, must be hastened; its advent must be assisted with all available means. Dialectical materialism (or *Diamat,* in Soviet parlance) offers, according to the communists, not only an infallible perception of the meaning of the interrelationship of social forces, but also a clear guide to the character of inevitable social change. It combines moral indignation against the Today with a fiercely fanatic conviction that the Tomorrow, which is bound to come, will be a higher, indeed a near perfect, state of society. (277)

Marx and Engels, by making ideas depend upon the economic system, raised the issue of what has come to be known as the "sociology of knowledge" — or the study of the social conditioning that causes and thereby explains the rise and growth of ideas, of notions regarding values, of scientific discoveries, and of practical programs of social reform. By claiming that all such knowledge is essentially superstructure, of which the substructure is the system of economic controls, the Marxist makes knowledge a dependent variable that changes with the economic system. This is a sweeping sociological generalization, and it was natural that scholars, and not only they, should question it and ask in turn: how true is this proposition? To what extent is the economic system primary, the first cause of all other changes in the intellectual field? Indeed, the obvious query suggested itself: is this true of the Marxist system itself?

We are not now going into this vast problem of intellectual creativity and its relation to environmental conditioning, but we wish to make quite clear at the outset that these issues are involved in the problem of ideology and its role in the totalitarian dictatorships of our time. The Soviet dictatorship, more particularly, rests upon this belief in the instrumental nature of ideas and ideology. Far from reducing the role of ideology, this conviction has led to its explicit cultivation and to the large-scale indoctrination of the masses. An intense concern with ideological conformity is the paradoxical consequence of the doctrine that ideas are nothing but weapons.

But before we further elaborate a typology of totalitarian ideology, it is necessary to determine what is to be understood by it. The problem of totalitarian ideology must be seen as a special case of the role of ideology in the political community. Ideology is often too broadly taken simply as a set of ideas prevalent in a community. (273a) Or it is too narrowly seen as a political "myth." (195a) Ideologies usually contain myths, but that is not all. Before this element is explored, one question needs an answer: what is an ideology? Ideologies are essentially action-related "systems" of ideas. They typically contain a program and a strategy for its realization, its operational code. (201a) Their essential purpose is to unite (integrate) organizations that are built around them. (110d)

An ideology is, therefore, a set of *literate ideas* — a reasonably coherent body of ideas concerning practical means of how to change and reform a society, based upon a more or less elaborate criticism of what is wrong with the existing or antecedent society. Where such reformist ideologies become potent, an ideology may also be developed to defend a society; such defensive ideologies contain a correspondingly elaborate criticism of the reformist or revolutionary ideologies. Finally, a totalitarian ideology would be one that is concerned with total destruction and total reconstruction, involving typically an ideological acceptance of violence as the only practicable means for such total destruction. It might accordingly be defined as "a reasonably coherent body of ideas concerning practical means of how totally to change and reconstruct a society by force, or violence, based upon an all-inclu-

sive or total criticism of what is wrong with the existing or antecedent society." * This total change and reconstruction in its very
nature constitutes a "utopia," and hence totalitarian ideologies are
typically utopian in nature. (110e) Totalitarian ideologies, in this
perspective, are a radical form of a development which, although
there are precedents, is typically modern; they must not be confused
with traditional notions, beliefs, and customs prevalent in more
mature societies.

A significant aspect of such ideologies is their symbolism, invented for the purpose of effectively competing with the symbols of
the rival ideologies. The donkey and the elephant, the red and the
green flag, and the like illustrate this. In the case of totalitarian
ideologies, their symbols are typically invented to undermine the
symbolism of the political order to be overthrown. (110f) Hammer
and sickle, swastika and fasces, are the familiar symbols of the
totalitarian movements. They are well known to many who have
no clear conception of the movements for which they stand. Each
of these symbols embodies an element of its ideology that has central importance, and its importance to the totalitarian order deserves consideration. The symbol gives concrete form and focus to
an abstraction, while the abstraction serves to illumine for the faithful the "meaning" of the symbol. (110e) The hammer and sickle
stand rationally enough for the workers and peasants who together
constitute the new society that the USSR aims at. The swastika and
fasces (the bundle of sticks that the Roman lictor or police officer
used to carry) symbolize the ancient tribal world to which Nazism
and Fascism wished to be linked, the barbaric heathens in the
woods of pre-Christian Northern Europe and the Romans of early
times. While the swastika is a ritual symbol of uncertain origin,
quite common in primitive societies, the fasces are an image of the
harsh discipline of sober and archaic Rome, which presumably provided the basis for the city's eventual greatness. It is probably not
an accident that the symbol of the Soviet Union and its satellites is

---

* Brzezinski has recently restated his position with particular reference to "revolutionary" ideologies as follows: "Modern revolutionary ideology is essentially an
action program derived from certain doctrinal assumptions about the nature of
reality and expressed through certain stated, not overly complex, assertions about
the inadequacy of the past or present state of societal affairs. These assertions include an explicit guide to action outlining methods for changing the situation, with
some general, idealized notions about the eventual state of affairs." (38a; also 39)

a constructed symbol, invented by the leaders of the movement and pointing to the future, while the Fascist and Nazi symbols are ancient and inherited forms relating the movement to a mythical past.

An inclination to identify the living person of the dictator with the symbolism of the regime became very marked in the USSR toward the end of Stalin's life. His seventieth birthday, for instance, became the signal for a veritable orgy of celebrations, gifts, panegyrics, and declarations of faith. This symbolism proved a considerable embarrassment for his successors after they had decided to attack him. But the difficulties did not prove unsurmountable. Khrushchev decided to fall back upon the prestige of Lenin and to re-emphasize the role of Lenin (whether he did so instinctively or deliberately is not important). Such glorification of a dead man leaves the Soviet leadership ample room for defining what Leninism is; at the same time, a living leader can constantly define his own premises and policies, which may differ considerably from those of his immediate predecessor. In that sense, the Soviet collective leadership strengthens its own broad appeal while not limiting its manipulative capacity in policy formulation. Thus Lenin could much more effectively serve as an effective symbol than Stalin could.

An additional important symbol for all the totalitarian regimes is negative: the stereotyped image of the enemy. For the Nazis it was the fat rich Jew or the Jewish Bolshevik; for the Fascists it was at first the radical agitator, later the corrupt and weak, degenerate bourgeois; for the Soviets, it is the war-mongering, atom-bomb-wielding American Wallstreeter; for the Chinese Communists, it is the Yankee imperialist and the Western colonial exploiters. In these negative symbols, the ideological basis of all such symbolism is even more evident. It is also found to some extent in the competitive politics of constitutional regimes. (224)

As it is with symbols, so it is with myth. The rise and development of reformist ideologies is a feature of the democratic age, associated with the development of parties. Parties of reform fashion ideologies that they propose to put into practice after their assumption of power. In this process, adaptations take place and some of the more utopian aspects of the ideology are eliminated as a concession to reality. (8a) Totalitarian parties are an extreme instance of this general trend. By their elimination of all rivals, they monopolize the field and convert their group ideology into a governmental one. But the process of adaptation to "reality" still takes place, even though a persistent effort is made to maintain the myth that the ideology is intact and that concessions are temporary. It is at this point that ideologies are to some extent transformed into myths. A myth is typically a tale concerned with past events, giving them a specific meaning and significance for the present and thereby reinforcing the authority of those who are wielding power in a particular community. (110f) They may carry a lesson, explicit or implied, for the future course of events. Such myths may be invented or they may "just grow," but they play a vital role in totalitarian dictatorships. Though myths are certainly found not only in totalitarian dictatorships, (4) the question arises as to whether totalitarian myths have a special quality. This is indeed the case: they are pseudo-scientific. The communist myth rests upon the notion that its view of history is beyond criticism, while the Nazi myth claims biological superiority for a particular race.

Naturally, considerable difficulties arise when such notions are confronted with reality. This process has been ridiculed by George Orwell in *1984,* where a Ministry of Truth is staffed with officials who are always at work shaping and reshaping the record of the past to bring it into consonance with the particular situation and the exigencies in which the dictatorship finds itself. There has been enough of this actually happening to make the caricature significant. When, after Stalin's death, it became important to highlight certain new men, pictures appeared associating them closely with the deceased. In fact, some of these were forgeries manufactured for the purpose of establishing a firm link between the new rulers and the old. Stalin himself, at an earlier date, had engaged in similar tricks to establish the myth of Lenin's appreciation for him. (49a; 391) But such frauds should not blind us to the important and very real place that the myth has in totalitarian as in all political societies. It is the result of a spontaneous response of men who possess power and seek authority and who wish others subject to that power to accept it as legitimate.

The myths that have played an important role in the dictatorships are numerous. For the Soviets they are in part at least embedded in Marxist writings. As tales, myths tell stories about the past or the future. Dialectical materialism provides the key myth of the communists. In the laborious words of Stalin, "if the passing of slow quantitative changes into rapid and abrupt qualitative changes is a law of development, then it is clear that revolutions made by the oppressed classes are quite a natural and inevitable phenomenon. Hence the transition from capitalism to socialism and the liberation of the working class from the yoke of capitalism cannot be effected by slow changes but only by a qualitative change of the capitalist system, by a revolution." (337c) That all past history is a history of class warfare is part of this general myth of the communist world; that Lenin detested Trotsky and was anxious to rid the movement of his counterrevolutionary plots is a specific myth; both are related to the past; they are historical myths. That there will eventually be established an anarchic paradise of freely cooperating individuals is a similar general myth referring to the future; another, but more specific, futuristic myth is that the Soviet Union will liberate peoples falling under its sway, that it will abolish class distinctions, and so forth.

In the case of the Nazis, the role of myth was specifically proclaimed as basic to the movement and the regime. Harking back to certain notions popular since the days of the Romantics, Alfred Rosenberg expounded in his often mentioned but seldom read *The Myth of the Twentieth Century* (298; 266a) a rather confused racial doctrine. To this myth is related the other that the Germans as a nation of culture stand guard against the Slavic barbarians who, for some unexplained reason, are denied the status of a race with a historic function. The abysmal hatred of all things Slavic, which was also such a strong impulse of the Austrian Hitler, produced in the Baltic German Rosenberg an attitude that made him mystify the mythos. Although Hitler himself admitted that he had never read this book (150b), "the German mission" was rooted in this same race myth. His wordy generalities about India, Persia, and the rest of the Nordics and Aryans, in the manner of Stewart Houston Chamberlain, culminate in the proposition that honor and spiritual freedom are the metaphysical ideas which are shaping the Germanic myth.

In Italian Fascism we find a similar conscious stress on myth. One early interpreter went so far as to misunderstand this to the extent of writing that "fascism represents a religious revival." Having a pragmatic view of religion, this writer immediately added, however, that he did not mean that fascism had developed a new theology, but only "that it has given to thousands of Italian youths an ideal for which they are ready to sacrifice all." (318) If this were a valid criterion for determining whether or not a movement were a religious one, it would only be consistent to conclude that all totalitarian movements are religious movements, for they certainly make their youthful members ready to sacrifice all. In point of fact, it is crucial to distinguish clearly between religion and a political myth. Later (Chapter 23) we shall deal with religion and the churches, but the political myth of fascism is the idea of "the grandeur that was Rome," sometimes seen as a synthesis of the Roman empire at its glory, reinforced by the Roman Catholic Church as its spiritual guardian, but more typically divorced from the latter. The love all Italians feel so passionately for their country was projected in terms of conquest and imperial violence, which were sanctified by the memories of a historical past. History itself was, as in the case of the Germans, "spiritually conceived," that is, similarly distorted and seen as revolving around Italy: the Latin nation par excellence, the center of all civilization, the "light of the world."

That Mussolini's stress on the creative force of the myth goes back to the inspiration he derived from Georges Sorel and Vilfredo Pareto is apparent in all his utterances. Sorel, in his *Reflexions sur la violence* (334; 83), had argued that the general strike is or should be "the myth in which socialism is wholly comprised." He had defined such a myth as "a body of images capable of evoking instinctively all the sentiments which correspond to the different manifestations of the war undertaken by Socialism against modern society." Heroes and martyrs are woven into the general myth to give concreteness and consequent appeal to the masses.

This viewpoint had been put into the broader perspective of a general view of society by Pareto (270), who stressed "nonlogical conduct" as characteristic of such political, and other social, life and assigned to myths, of which he examined many historical variants, an essential role in organized mass activity. Although practical applications were rather far removed from Pareto's scientific interests, he was obviously implying that a man who wants to build a political movement would do well to create myths calculated to satisfy the human craving for transrational beliefs in terms of which man's emotions can be organized for action.

The role of the myth in totalitarian ideological patterns, intimately intertwined as it is with symbolization of persons and ideas, serves to show that an ideology can be more or less "rational" in its elaboration. The Soviet ideology, based as it is upon the allegedly scientific findings of Marx and Engels, as elaborated by Lenin and others, appears to be more rational than that of either Fascist Italy or Hitler Germany. In the latter instances, the ideology was distinctly "personal." It rested, in the case of Mussolini, upon his journalistic writings and more especially his article on fascism in the *Encyclopedia Italiana* (1932) (268a); in the case of Hitler, it is expounded in *Mein Kampf* (148), written in 1923–24 during his sojourn in jail and maintained ever after as the gospel of National Socialism. An analysis in terms of antecedent intellectual influences and the like would incline one to differentiate further and call Mussolini's creed more rational than Hitler's. (266b) The degree of "rationality" here involved is that of a rationality of means rather than of ends. For the values in all three ideologies are of a transrational sort. This may not make much difference to the skeptic who considers all value judgments beyond rational discourse, but in any case there are differences of degree, and it is certainly permissible to assert that the value judgments at the base of Thomism, Confucianism, and modern constitutionalism are more rational than those of the totalitarian creeds, even if they are not wholly rational.

These totalitarian ideologies can also be classified according to their ultimate values, and this is the more usual and conventional procedure. Apart from the obvious classification suggested by the terms "communist" and "fascist," the degree of universality is of prime significance here. The Soviet ideology is universal in its appeal — "Workers of the world, unite!" — whereas the fascist ideologies address themselves to a particular people in terms of their grandeur, power, and historical role.* In the Soviet ideology, the place of the national group is taken by the proletariat, which is invested with the historical role of liberating mankind from the shackles of industrial capitalism, but Marx and Engels make it very

---

* Even so sophisticated a writer as Ernst Forsthoff speaks repeatedly of the specific historical mission of the German people, e.g. on p. 17, where he mentions a "truly national constitution." (101a)

clear that this proletariat, by overthrowing the existing class structure, ultimately eliminates itself and ceases to exist as a proletariat. From this standpoint, in communism social justice appears to be the ultimate value, unless it be the classless society that is its essential condition; in fascism, the highest value is dominion, eventually world dominion, and the strong and pure nation-race is *its* essential condition, as seen by its ideology. Since there are many nations and races, there can theoretically be as many fascisms, and this has actually proven to be the case. Wherever fascism has raised its head, whether in Germany or Italy, in France, England, or the United States, the strength and the purification of the particular nation involved has been at the center of ideological attention. This aspect is an element of weakness in fascist ideologies, as contrasted with the communist ones. The latter have the advantage of an inherent universalism and the consequent ability to cope more readily with the extension of power to other nations. The Soviet Union more especially has benefited from this position in its dealings with Poland, Czechoslovakia, and Germany, China in dealing with Korea, Indochina, and so forth (see Chapter 27).

It is precisely this doctrinal catholicism that makes communism an effective weapon of combat, not only between nations, but also, and generally unlike fascism, within nations. Fascism, when a spontaneous product of local agitation, by necessity tended to accentuate national distinctiveness and national sovereignty. It emphasized frequently the biological superiority of the given community. Fascism, when imposed on foreign nations, produced, as it did during World War II, vigorously hostile reactions. Universality based on a restricted nationalist appeal is a contradiction in terms. Even so, Italian Fascism had a good deal of appeal beyond Italy. Similar movements cropped up in Austria, Hungary, Rumania, Spain, France, and Great Britain, and one must not forget that Italian Fascism was, after all, the inspiration for many of Hitler's followers as well as for Hitler himself. Peron also followed the basic line of Italian Fascism. There is a very interesting item in the Italian Fascist catechism used in the youth organizations: "Question: Is Fascism exclusively an Italian phenomenon? Answer: Fascism, as far as its ideas, doctrines and realizations are concerned, is *universal,* because it is in the position of saying to all civilized people *the word of truth without which there cannot be lasting peace in the world; therefore it is the sustainer and creator of a new civilization."* (120a) It should be noted, however, that this kind of "universalism," while it may be able to arouse imitators, will have the result that each fascist movement will itself seek world or regional dominion, and hence create obstacles to the extension of effective control by the "creator." Presumably, a fascist France or England would have been at least as vigorous a rival of Italian aspirations to dominion in the Mediterranean as the democratic regimes of these countries were.

Communism, on the other hand, has been markedly successful in operating on a national base for the sake of supranational goals. For communism, unlike fascism, works simultaneously on two levels: one is the universal, "orthodox," and philosophical plane, which until recently was the exclusive domain of the Soviet leadership; it has since been challenged not only by Tito but more significantly by Mao Tse-tung, who earlier had made some modest theoretical contributions. The basic issue now is the Chinese view of war as an essential element in world revolution. The other level is the practical, the tactical. On this level communism may vary, temporarily at least, from country to country. Thus the nature of the communist appeal is markedly dissimilar in, let us say, France and India. Similarly, even in the captive nations of Eastern Europe and in China, great stress was laid on the distinctive nature of their communist development. In Poland, for instance, in the immediate postwar years, the official party declarations stressed the fact that communism in Poland was to be implemented in "the Polish way." (432a) Indeed, it became the standard weapon of the parlor communist in Eastern Europe to emphasize the distinctive, allegedly more democratic, character of the development of a communist society in Eastern Europe as contrasted with past Soviet history. Nevertheless, significant local variations of a practical nature are to this day evident, such as in the treatment of the Catholic Church or the farmers in Poland, or in the redefinition of the concept of the elite in China. The crucial determinant of ideological loyalty is the ultimate implication of the local variation: if it serves to further the over-all goals of the universal ideology, without fragmenting the power bloc on which the ideology rests, the practical deviation is tolerated. If not, it is excised.

We conclude that ideology constitutes an operative force in totalitarian political orders, as it does in nontotalitarian ones, that its symbolism and its myths are among the significant elements of the contemporary political scene, and that there is every prospect that this situation will remain so. This does not mean, however, that the substantive content of ideology is not undergoing a continuing evolution, as do all institutions and processes in totalitarian regimes. Besides, there are types of totalitarian ideology to be distinguished which significantly affect the pattern and the operations. New types may emerge in the future. Now we can say that so far two primary typologies of totalitarian ideology have appeared, one distinguished by the degree of rationality, the other by the factor of universalism. No doubt other typologies could be elaborated. But what should be avoided is the adoption of typologies derived from the totalitarians' own ideological premises, such as calling one revolutionary, the other reactionary, or one progressive, the other conservative. For not only do such classifications have themselves a propagandistic effect, but they imply an acceptance of the directional premise of the particular ideology. Both of the types suggested here are explicitly related to the doctrinal aspect of these ideologies. It has been suggested that "deductions based on behavior," leading to an "operative social theory," should be included. But unless these deductions are themselves absorbed into the doctrinal context (see Chapter 9), they do not become ideological in a precise functional sense, such as the one here employed. To be sure, a view of ideology as *consisting* of the original texts, the scriptures, so to speak, would be too rigid and artificial. At the same time, reference to these basic texts constitutes a vital part of the controversies in this field, and the texts do therefore in some measure define the frame of reference.

In any case, there is to be observed a continuing evolution in ideology, as in other realms of totalitarian reality (260). Before we turn to an analysis of this evolution, however, the historical roots need more detailed exploration. For the adaptations of ideology to the exigencies of political life are undertaken in ideological terms inherited from the past. What are the roots of these ideological movements? And what is the importance of "ideas" as such in an ideology? Should certain groups or thinkers be "blamed" for the rise of totalitarian ideologies in the sense that, if they had not written, the ideologies could not have been fashioned?

8

THE HISTORICAL ROOTS
OF TOTALITARIAN IDEOLOGY

In seeking to trace the roots of totalitarian ideology, every kind of link has been argued. (5; 180; 181; 126) Marx and Hegel, Nietzsche and Hobbes, Kant and Rousseau, Plato and Aristotle, Augustine, Luther, and Calvin — all have been charged with having forged the ideas that became weapons in the arsenal of the totalitarians. Since all these thinkers are in turn related to many other intellectual trends and views, it is not too much to suggest that the sum of all the arguments is plainly this: totalitarian ideology is rooted in the totality of Western thought, and more especially its political thought. To be sure, the key points of emphasis, such as equality, justice, freedom, are of so general a nature that they do not lend themselves to very precise analysis in this context. But even more specific points, like the stress on democracy or the state, are similarly elusive. This situation should not surprise anyone, for the programs of action the totalitarians proclaim are programs cast in terms of the antecedent states of European and American society (with interesting variations introduced in such cases as China), and they must therefore be related to the patterns of ideas associated with these antecedent states. Moreover, since ideology has an instrumental function, as we have seen, totalitarian leaders will fashion their ideological tools to fit the states of mind of the masses they are addressing. For example, the idea of progress, so peculiar a product of the Western mind, is embedded so deeply in totalitarian thought that such thought would collapse if this idea were eliminated.

It should be clear that this entire discussion of the roots of totalitarian ideology rests upon what answer is given to the question:

what is the role of ideas in history? Do ideas have demonstrable effects, or are they merely incidental to reality, like the froth on top of the waves of an agitated sea? Many of the writers who have placed major emphasis upon the ideological background of totalitarian movements have failed to realize the full implications of this view. For if ideas are assumed to have significant causal effects upon the course of events, a spiritualistic interpretation of history is apt to be implied. A stress upon religious ideas is most especially prone to carry this implication. The common argument that men act in accordance with the ideas in their minds does not settle the question of where such ideas come from. If some such notion as inspiration is introduced — Trotsky wrote that revolution is the mad inspiration of history — then one must ask: whose inspiration and by whom inspired? Some of the totalitarian ideologies are basically trite restatements of certain traditional ideas, arranged in an incoherent way that makes them highly exciting to weak minds. That was particularly true of National Socialism. By contrast, the Soviet ideology is based upon the rigorous, if erroneous and dated, historical and economic analysis of Karl Marx — which he would probably be the first to alter, if not to reject, in light of the reality, both economic and political, that has developed since his day.

The roots of not only so capacious a thinker as Marx but even of Mussolini and Hitler are as varied as the backgrounds of the people who expound them and who listen to them. One might illustrate this by the recurrent references in Hitler's *Mein Kampf* to the notion that the end of national glory justifies any means appropriate for its achievement. To call this "Machiavellism" means to attribute to it what was in Machiavelli, at least for his time, a novel and fairly sophisticated doctrine. In Hitler's treatment it becomes a crude and banal thought.*

In other words, any effort to relate totalitarian ideology more specifically to antecedent thought reveals that the antecedent thought is either distorted to fit the proposition or completely misrepresented. Thus Hegel is made an exponent of the doctrine that "might makes right," when as a matter of fact he explicitly and sharply rejected it. Or Hobbes is claimed to believe in the "state's

---

*These remarks do not mean that Machiavelli's notions should, in historicist fashion, be condoned. See Leo Strauss, *Thoughts on Machiavelli*, 1958, for an acute restatement of the moral objections; also 108a.

regulating everything," when it is quite evident to any careful but unprejudiced reader that Hobbes was inclined to restrict the sovereign to the police function, that is, to the function of maintaining peace in a given society. If one were to argue all the various statements that have been set forth in thus distorting the history of ideas to "explain" totalitarian ideology and practice, he could fill volumes. Such arguments may have a certain value in the market place, where the fighting about these ideas takes place; but on the whole, it is an arid enterprise, devoid of convincing results. It should be remembered that the history of ideas is a particularly difficult field of scholarship, fully measured by few. In any case, the problem of what an author actually said, and what he meant in the saying of it, calls for a never-ending search, and the more comprehensive the author, the more divergent the answers. Only when an author is an official source of ideology is such inquiry vital to the study of totalitarianism. Thus an understanding of the discussion of whether or not the activities of the Soviet Union fit the ideas that Marx and Engels expounded is a source of continuing controversy. This debate has now assumed explosive character in the dispute between the Soviet Union and Communist China.

There is no doubt that Marxism owes a great intellectual debt to the traditions, and particularly to the modes of thought, of the French Revolution. The intellectual climate of Europe in the first half of the nineteenth century was very much formed by the slogans but also by the philosophic content of that great enterprise. As a result, though surely not for the first time in the history of Europe, the intellectual, in his role of interpreter of the past and present, reached out to shape the realities of tomorrow. To acknowledge that Marxism is part of that stream is not, however, to establish a causal relationship, for to do so, as some have, is to engage in ex post facto attempts to interpret the ideas and even motivations of eighteenth-century thinkers in terms of categories imposed by nineteenth- and twentieth-century realities. Nonetheless, it can be shown that the Rousseauistic concept of total democracy can easily degenerate into total dictatorship when the "legislator" ceases to be a transient educator and becomes a permanent ruler acting in behalf of the people. Such concepts as "knowledge" are not far removed from such "consciousness" as that of a class, and both need to be instilled in those "who are born free and yet everywhere are in

chains." The emphasis on unity, unanimity, and ceaseless participation is suggestive — but no more than that — of the twentieth-
century "passion for unanimity" characteristic of the totalitarian
systems (see Chapter 13). And, what is more, it was the French
Revolution which gave an outlet to the feeling of rationalistic revolutionaries that society must, and can be, remade in its totality to
assure man the liberty that is inherently his. Indeed, a dialectical
relationship to the religious zealots of the past suggests itself. Like
Saint-Just in the French Revolution, such individuals become the
self-appointed guardians of virtue and truth; genuine conflicts of
opinion are excluded, and disagreement is condemned as absolutely
wrong.

Similarly, the Marxist dialectic derived not only from Hegel, but
from Babeuf and his primitive notions of class struggle. At the
same time, Marxian doctrine divorced the utilitarian emphasis on
self-interest from the individual, welded it to an economic class, and
made it the focal point of the historical movement. Thus various
antecedent notions, borrowed from different writers and movements, were fitted to the requirements of the industrial age and the
peasant reaction to the machine. One need not linger, however, on
the relationship of Marxism to preceding thought in the Western
political heritage to prove how complex is the task of establishing
meaningful intellectual causation. Within Marxism itself, which developed, as we shall see later, through schismatic clashes, there are
continual disputes over whether a certain interpretation is an elaboration or a distortion. For instance, the formation of the new
Communist regimes in Central Europe and Asia, bringing with it
the problem of transition from a bourgeois or feudal society to a
communist one, has perplexed Soviet ideologues in recent years. For
various practical reasons, the theory of the dictatorship of the proletariat, mentioned only once by Marx in his *Critique of the Gotha
Program*, though developed by Engels and made by Lenin into
something of utmost importance, has become unsuitable for these
regions. A new terminology and interpretation, evolving around
the term "people's democracy," have been coined. The relationship
between this view and Marx's own about the postrevolutionary
situation is open to dispute.

Disappointed believers in some of the ideas contained in a particular ideology recurrently constitute very strong opponents of the

regime based upon such ideology. This is a phenomenon familiar from the history of religion. After all, the story of Christianity is to a considerable extent the story of successive disagreements over what Christ meant, and over the true import of his message. From these disagreements have resulted the successive dissents leading to new sects and churches. Considering the relatively short time that totalitarians have been actively at work, it is surprising how many divergent interpretations have already been expounded and made the basis of schismatic movements.*

And yet it is these schisms which provide a real clue to the meaning of the term we have been using — totalitarian ideology. The splits and disagreements on the basic tenets of Marxism, for instance, have served to accentuate the democratic and nondemocratic aspects of that theory. Through a process of political adaptation, differences in degree have become differences in kind, despite the original uniformity of view. Are not then social democracy and communism possibly the products of the same intellectual roots? Do they not claim ancestorship of a common family tree? Are not their basic assumptions to be found essentially in the same body of writings? Despite the necessarily affirmative answers, the distinction between the two schools of thought, when translated into actual practice, becomes fundamental and far-reaching — one is totalitarian, the other not.

The translation of an ideology into practice usually serves to reveal certain inadequacies inherent in human foresight. Attempts to picture the future and to prescribe the methods of achieving it clearly cannot conceive of all eventualities, of all possible situations, and communism is further handicapped by the general looseness of its philosophical structure. Consequently the schismatic movements that developed immediately as attempts were made to put Marxism into political practice were, apart from pure power factors, the inevitable product of such an attempted implementation. When theory is applied to a real-life situation, there are usually only two alternatives: one is to modify theory so as to make it more compatible with the prerequisites of practice, and the other is to attempt to force reality to fit the theory. The totalitarians, by their almost complete rejection of the status quo, are inclined to attempt to force

* A reading of such a classic account as Harnack's (133.1) constantly reminds one of present-day situations, when it discusses the doctrinal controversies, especially the great and intrinsically senseless debate over the various alleged heresies.

history to fit their conception of it.* And when such a conception involves a far-reaching idea of the desirable, that is, historically inevitable, scheme of social organization, the efforts to mold society to fit it, and the consequent measures to break down the resistance to it, call for such a massive deployment of organized force that the result is totalitarianism. At the present time, the conflict between the Soviet Union and Communist China is basically over such a deployment of force in the international arena, China taking the position that even the violence involved in nuclear war should be accepted in promoting the revolutionary aims of communism (see Chapter 26).

Not all the original supporters of such an ideology, however, are willing to go quite so far. This is particularly well demonstrated by the Marxist schism on the issue of evolution versus revolution. Marxism embodies both concepts, which are said to be historically inseparable. "Revolution is the midwife of every society," said Marx, but before the midwife sets to work, a lengthy evolutionary process precedes the climactic spasms of the revolution. The inner contradictions of capitalism have to ripen lest the revolution fail by coming too soon. And it is precisely on this time element that conflicting interpretations have clashed. What is the precise moment for revolutionary action?

The so-called Revisionists felt that precipitate revolutionary action would merely revive the blood flow in the corroded veins of capitalism and thus prolong its life. The key to success, according to Bernstein and the Social Democratic school, was the ability to wait, while exacting concessions through participation in the democratic process. Socialism would in time supplant the capitalist order, and the revolutionary stage would, in effect, become merely the technical act of taking over. Capitalism would die of old age, and so it need not be slaughtered. The revolutionary act would consist in burying it, not in killing it. (18; 169; 170; 190a) The Social Democrats have therefore been unwilling to engage in drastic measures to destroy the capitalist society. Their optimism in the certainty of their success has made them patient and willing to work within the framework of the constitutional order. Having accepted the perspec-

---

* The totalitarians are particularly vehement and violent in their criticism of "existing" (antecedent) societies. Their effort to change history does not, however, prevent them from making specific concessions in their ideology when such are necessitated by expediency. See Chapter 9.

tive of an inevitable historical victory, they are content with the thought that the status quo is not going to last.

The totalitarians, on the contrary, having announced that the status quo is doomed, proceed to prove the correctness of their analysis through measures to effect it. To them, willingness to wait is sheer treason. "Reformism . . . which in effect denies the Socialist revolution and tries to establish socialism peacefully . . . which preaches not the struggle of classes but their collaboration — this reformism is degenerating from day to day, and is losing all marks of socialism." (336) Lenin and the Bolsheviks, accordingly, emphasized that revolutionary action was the key to historical salvation, and that only direct measures aimed at overthrowing the capitalist order would produce its fall. "Great historical questions can be solved only by *violence*," exclaimed Lenin (205b), calling upon the revolutionaries to act as the gravediggers of history and to help place the remnants of capitalism in the dustbin of antiquity. For, unless a revolutionary party acting as the vanguard of the proletariat acts firmly, the working classes will develop a pacifist trade-union mentality and become the unwitting tools of capitalist measures of self-preservation.

In the Nazi movement, the socially more radical elements were strongly represented in the storm troopers, the brownshirts. These men, under the command of Captain Röhm, liked to suggest that all they needed to do was to turn their swastika armbands around to make them red. To be sure, all this argument remained on a very low level, as did the ideological discussion in the Hitler movement generally, but it nonetheless represented a characteristic ideological conflict pointing to the divergent strands in the official creed. There developed also a "leftist" deviation in Italian Fascism, headed by Giuseppe Bottai, Edmondo Rossoni, and Ugo Spirito. Giovanni Gentile was eventually prevailed upon to make common cause with this group, and his last work (118; 266) expounds the group's general theory. Two journals expressed these views in a veiled fashion, but it should be noted that these ideas had no support in the inner circles of the party.

In both the Fascist and the Nazi movements, actually, the physical presence of the men who formulated the programs prevented the emergence of major splits. The essential postulates of both movements — stressing the leadership principle, the traditional and historical values of the people as contrasted with "bourgeois" degeneration, the *Etatismo* of Italy and the *Volk* veneration of Nazism, state corporatism but private ownership, the mystic quality of the soil, and last, but not least, the race principle — generally remained unchallenged during their relatively brief existences.

Both communism and fascism are characterized by their insistence on the revolutionary fulfillment of the "truths" of their doctrines, and it is this insistence that leads to the further conclusions on the necessity of a disciplined party — the elite of the proletariat of the nation. Its infallible leadership, through science or intuition, was to effect the conditions which, according to the ideology, are considered necessary for the achievement of its utopian apocalypse. It is precisely this attempt to impose on society a rationally, or rather pseudo-rationally, conceived pattern of distinctly novel forms of social organization that leads to totalitarian oppression. And since this oppression is justified in terms of the ideology, this ideology is totalitarian.

The fact that totalitarian ideology is rooted in the totality of Western ideas raises the question of its relation to democracy and Christianity. On the face of it, these two bodies of thought are the patent antitheses to fascist and communist ideology. The conflict with Christianity was highlighted in the Soviet Union by the Movement of the Godless; in Germany it led to protracted struggles to establish control over both Protestant and Catholic churches (see Chapter 23). With regard to democracy, the situation is somewhat more confused, since both communists and fascists like to consider themselves true democrats. Only if democracy is defined in constitutional terms, characterized by a genuine competition between two or more parties, a separation of governmental powers, and a judicially enforced protection of individual rights, is the conflict fairly obvious on both the ideological and the practical levels. Yet in spite of these sharp conflicts between totalitarian ideologies and the Christian and democratic heritage, it is only within the context of this heritage that the ideologies can be fully understood. Communism is not Christian, but it could not have taken root without the foundations laid by Christian belief in the brotherhood of man and social justice. Perhaps even more important than these substantive links are the habits of mind established by Christianity and the other religions with a formal theology, such as Buddhism and Mohammedanism, for they establish the cultural habit or trait of relating action programs and norms to elaborate rationalizations. These rationalizations are then elaborated into a theology that is in turn secularized and made the basis of rival ideologies. There is, to put it another way, a style of living involved that calls for transcendent explanations of what is right. When the theological explanations become untenable as a result of the decline of religious faith, these "secular religions" then fill the vacuum. (319; 5a; 110d) When seen in this perspective, it becomes evident why a totalitarian ideology has become potent even in China, which is not a Christian country. The argument is reinforced by the consideration that China inherited, but did not invent, the communist ideology. It seems more than doubtful that Chinese thought would have produced this kind of ideology, and all of Mao's presumed originality in interpreting the Marxist-Leninist heritage is little more than an attempt at applying it to specific Chinese conditions. (141; 320a) It may be well to add that communist ideology has, in a sense, a similar relation to Chinese traditional culture as Christian creeds have had: it is a missionary body of alien thought.

It must be pointed out finally that the relation of the totalitarian ideology to Christian and democratic ideology is a "dialectic" one — that is to say, the relation is antithetical. But just as antithesis in logic cannot be conceived except in juxtaposition to its thesis, so also in the movement of ideas the root is often the thesis of which the idea or ideology in hand is the antithesis. The importance of this kind of relationship lies not only in the consequent "consanguinity," enabling human beings to shift back and forth between these ideologies, but it also may provide a clue for the next step in the dialectic.

All in all, our discussion has indicated that the roots of the totalitarian ideologies, both communist and fascist, are actually intertwined with the entire intellectual heritage of Western man and that all specific links should be seen, not in terms of causation — of this or that thinker or group of thinkers being "responsible for" the totalitarian ideologies — but as strands of a complex and variegated tapestry. However, the specific totalitarian ingredient — the employment, even glorification, of violence for the realization of the goals that the ideology posits is largely absent from the thought of those whose ideas these ideologies have utilized and, in utilizing them, distorted.

9

THE CHANGE AND CORRUPTION
OF IDEOLOGY

In the discussion of the role of ideology in totalitarian societies, some deny, as we noted, that ideology plays any significant part in the thinking of the leaders. Those who so argue usually dwell upon the changes in ideology that they feel are in fact corruptions, proving the insincerity of the leaders. The key leadership groups are said not to take the ideology seriously, but to manipulate it, to change it arbitrarily to suit their shifting policy lines. (5) But change need not be corruption; it can be genuine adaptation and meaningful alteration. It must, however, be admitted that in the case of Hitler a strong case can be made for such an interpretation, because of Hitler's own cynical statements about the matter. Certainly, several well-known passages in *Mein Kampf*, as well as remarks by Rauschning in *The Revolution of Nihilism* (289), lend color to the proposition that Hitler's attitude toward ideology was "manipulative." On the other hand, Hitler's secret talks (150a) give a different impression; in these monologues he clearly stays within the framework of his racist ideology.

Whatever may be the conclusions concerning Hitler's opinions, it appears quite clear that Soviet leadership, and Communist leadership generally, has continued to attach considerable importance to ideology. Indeed, it would be impossible to write a meaningful history of the USSR without giving sustained attention to ideological issues. But, of course, the ideology has undergone a steady evolution, as the leadership confronted novel situations and fashioned policy to cope with the issues as they arose. There is a constant interaction among the changing environment, the policy responses to it, and the ideological setting for these responses. This is not a mechanical determinism, but a live, organic process. "For if ideology," a thoughtful student of these matters recently wrote, "influences Soviet policy via the minds of the policy-makers, it also is demonstrably true that policy influences ideology, that official interpretations of Marxism-Leninism develop and change in response to policy needs, political interests, and changes in the policy mind." (360b) In short, ideology is decisively important, as was already pointed out in discussing the party, and hence the leaders are sincerely exercised over ideological issues. The recent Chinese-Russian clashes that have been mentioned several times reinforce this conclusion. All that the ingenuity of those opposed to this view has actually been able to prove is that there are important *changes* in the ideological pattern employed by the leaders.

Some of the key controversies in the earlier ideological clashes revolved around the questions of the spread of the revolution, the issue of democracy versus dictatorship, and the nature of the party's organization and operations. (66a; 190b) The first controversy, that of world revolution versus socialism in one country, was resolved for the Bolsheviks more by necessity than by doctrinal decision. Still, the issue gave rise to most vehement arguments and bitter disagreements.

Originally, most of the revolutionary leaders were hopeful that the revolution would spread from Russia to the West. Trotsky spoke glowingly of how "the working class of Russia, by leading in the political emancipation, will rise to a height unknown in history, gather into its hands colossal forces and means and become the initiator of the liquidation of capitalism on a global scale." (356; 71) The Treaty of Brest-Litovsk, dictated by German bayonets, clearly implied, however, that the revolution was territorially limited to Russia proper. This gave rise to a serious intraparty crisis. Bukharin declared it to be a blow aimed at the international proletariat, which caused him and his supporters to "turn aside with contempt." Lenin's reply was characteristic: "Yes, we will see the international world revolution, but for the time being it is a very good fairy tale, a very beautiful fairy tale — I quite understand children liking beautiful fairy tales." (205c)

Nonetheless, Bolshevik hopes soared high for a brief period after the Armistice and the consequent collapse of Austro-Hungarian and German imperial power. Central Europe became a political vacuum, torn by social and political strife. The situation seemed ready-made for communism. By January 1919, the commander of the Red Army, Leon Trotsky, was proclaiming: "It is no longer the spectre of communism that is haunting Europe . . . communism in flesh and blood is now stalking the continent." (359) He was re-echoed, albeit in a less ringing fashion, by Lenin, who observed hopefully that the "revolution has begun and is gaining strength in all countries." (203c)

Yet this was not to be. The revolution failed to spread, but still succeeded in Russia. Its failure as an international movement led to the birth of the theory of socialist victory in one country at a time. This view was at first propounded cautiously and halfheartedly, and Soviet leaders continued to emphasize that it was merely a transitional point in historical development. In one of his earlier statements Stalin expressed it as follows: "While it is true that the *final* victory of Socialism in the first country to emancipate itself is impossible without the combined efforts of the proletarians of several countries, it is equally true that the development of world revolution will be the more rapid and thorough, the more effective the assistance rendered by the first Socialist country to the workers and laboring masses of all other countries." (337b) The Soviet Union accordingly became the base of world communism. This issue was somewhat overstressed by the struggle between Trotsky and Stalin which, because it operated within an ideologically oriented setting, necessarily took the form of a theoretical clash. (312a)

Later on, the issue shifted to that of stages of development, Stalin claiming that there was one road, that of the USSR. At the Twenty-First Party Congress, Khrushchev gave the issue a new twist when he announced that the Soviet Union, having consummated the program that signalized the stage of "socialism," was then ready to enter the transition leading from socialism to communism. But there would not be "any particular moment" when socialism would end and communism begin. Oddly enough, he suggested that such familiar aspects of advanced capitalism as free lunches for schoolchildren, free nurseries, pensions, and scholarships at institutions of higher learning marked this transition. And he added that not luxuries, but "the healthy requirements of a culturally developed man" was meant when communism spoke of "satisfying the needs of the people." Such pragmatic goals seem far removed from the early ideological controversies. Yet they are involved, as the argument with the Chinese shows.

The situation is similar in the discussion over democracy versus dictatorship. It has repeatedly been charged that the Bolsheviks here again had abandoned true communism. In a sense, it was out of this conflict that the Bolshevik Party was conceived. It is not idle, however, to re-emphasize that Marxism is subject to varying interpretations, and the divergent lines developed by the Bolsheviks and the Mensheviks offer a striking illustration. Lenin stressed that during the revolutionary period it is pointless to talk of democracy because "broad democracy in party organization amidst the gloom of autocracy . . . is nothing more than a useless and harmful toy." (203d) And once the revolution has been achieved, terror is needed to eliminate the remnants of the bourgeoisie. The dictatorship of the proletariat, therefore, will not tolerate any restrictions on its freedom of action against the fallen, but still not liquidated, foes. Lenin put this quite flatly: "Dictatorship is power based directly upon force and unrestricted by any laws. The revolutionary dictatorship of the proletariat is power won and maintained by the violence of the proletariat against the bourgeoisie, power that is unrestricted by any laws." (205d)

The question of dictatorship is inherently related to the conflict over the nature of the party that was to lead the proletariat. The issue is again as old as the Bolshevik movement itself. The split between the Mensheviks and the Bolsheviks was precisely on this crucial issue, and some of the severest attacks ever launched by fellow Marxists against Lenin were uttered during the development of this schism. Trotsky's famous charge, often erroneously cited as aimed at Stalin, was to reverberate over and over again, whenever this question came to be discussed by Marxists: "Lenin's methods lead to this: the Party organization . . . at first substituted itself for the Party as a whole; then the Central Committee substituted itself for the organization; and finally a single 'dictator' substituted himself for the Central Committee." (358) But since all this vituperation failed to prove that Lenin's insistence on a disciplined, paramilitary party organization was un-Marxist, it is not surprising that in view of the political reality of tsarist Russia it was the

Leninist view that prevailed, and it was the Leninist party that seized power in 1917. Political events proved Lenin to be right, and among the first to acknowledge this was Trotsky himself.

If one considers this range of ideological conflict, one is struck by the fact that the issues are political rather than economic. This is at least in part because Marx and Engels were inclined to minimize the political problem that arises once the proletariat has "seized power" (see Chapter 7). The *Communist Manifesto* seems to envisage a purely cooperative living together, without any government. "The state withers away," Engels wrote, and he meant, of course, the disappearance of the bureaucracy. Marx and Engels concentrated their ideological effort on the criticism of the existing state of society — that is to say, on the second aspect of ideology defined here — and as proud students of economics they dealt in detail only with the analysis of economic reality, treating political problems incidentally. This is in a way curious, considering that the two men had been harshly critical of earlier socialists as "utopian" because they did not give due attention to political realities and, more especially, "the state." Likewise, Marx's controversies with the anarchists focused upon the latter's failure to appreciate the power of existing states and the effort required to overthrow them. (246) His latter-day followers have been much troubled by the anarchic implications. This doctrine of the withering away of the state is maintained to this day, in spite of the obviously different reality. Khrushchev offered a rationalization to the Twentieth Congress, when combatting the notion that the future communist society would be "a formless and unorganized, anarchistic mass of people," by stating that it would be "highly organized" and that "within it everybody will have to fulfill . . . his work function and his social duty."

One might further add that the gigantic task of industrialization which confronted the Soviet leaders in Russia called for state planning on a comprehensive scale, regardless of any doctrinal positions. The Marxist doctrine, economically speaking, is elaborate only in regard to "capitalism"; to say that Marxist dogma is "closed" or finished on the economic side is certainly incorrect. Such generalities as "to each according to his need, from each according to his ability" are general social slogans, not economic theory. (88a)

Generally speaking, the ideological changes in the Soviet Union need not be seen as corruptions of ideology, as they have been by socialist and, more especially, Marxist opponents of the USSR. They may be interpreted as adaptations or modifications and thus may be seen as a sign of vitality, as suggested by cultural comparison in other spheres. Adaptability and flexibility are virtues, provided they do not lead to empty opportunism. There are a number of passages in Marx and Engels suggesting such adaptations. On such fundamental issues as equality, authority, nationality policy, or foreign relations, striking adaptations to the imperatives of political reality have been made. To take one further example only, the Soviet Union is today, as it has been said correctly, "a system of organized social inequality" despite its almost fanatic fulminations against capitalist inequality. (252a) This Soviet inequality involves not only a highly differentiated scale of rewards, which creates distinct classes of haves and have-nots, but, even more, distinct levels of opportunities for advancement on the social scale. (252b)

The problem of adapting the communist theory of equality to fit the Soviet reality could not, because of the importance of this doctrinal facet, have been evaded. But neither could this principle of equality be repudiated. The Soviet rationalization accordingly runs along the lines of the *Pravda* article on socialism and equality, which states in part: "The idea of equality is not an unshakeable eternal truth. It was born of certain definite social relationships. Its content changes with changes in the latter. The sense of the demand for equality lies only in the abolition of inequality. With the disappearance of inequality, the content of the demand for equality is lost." (441a) It is no accident that the concept of equality occupies no significant place in the constitution of the USSR, nor in the Rules of the Central Committee, as adopted in 1961. It is simply taken for granted that the elimination of class oppression and class struggle eliminates inequality. The countless manifestations of inequality in the USSR are accordingly, in the light of this Soviet analysis, not indications of inequality at all, but the necessary concomitants of a complex industrialized society.*

A steady elaboration of Marxist, or rather Soviet, doctrine occurred at the Twentieth, Twenty-First, and Twenty-Second Congresses. These changes illustrate the plasticity of Bolshevik

---

* It is of interest to note in this connection the considerably greater pay variation between officers and men in the Soviet army and comparable scales in the "capitalist" United States army.

ideology, a virtue which the Soviet leaders frequently comment upon. At the Twentieth Congress Khrushchev jettisoned the Leninist concept of the civil war as a *necessary* stage in any society's transition to socialism; he declared that the necessity for civil conflict depends upon how determined and strong the oppressing classes are. If these classes are weak and are faced by powerful, united labor masses, then "the winning of a stable parliamentary majority backed by a mass-revolutionary movement of the proletariat and of all the working people could create for the working class in a number of capitalist and former colonial countries the conditions needed to secure fundamental social changes." Since then, the Soviet regime has repeatedly reaffirmed similar views — and this especially in its conflict with the Chinese Communist leadership, which inclines toward the older notion that a violent revolutionary overthrow of the existing political order is necessary and inevitable.

Why do we not find any comparable pattern of ideological change in the fascist states? Apart from their shorter life spans, it might first of all be suggested that both Mussolini and Hitler were able to "interpret" their own thought. The situation resembles that of the Socialist International at the time when Marx and Engels were still alive and could be consulted. Certain alterations in their own views were nevertheless acknowledged by the fascist dictators. (266d) Changes could be claimed as a natural sequel to what the leader himself asserted had been his purpose and intention all the time. In fact, on certain subjects, sharp differences of opinion developed over ideological questions. Thus Mussolini's concordat with the Catholic Church was felt by a number of fascist subleaders to be a betrayal of fascist ideology; no less an ideologist than Gentile took this view. The varying attitudes adopted by Hitler toward the Protestant churches led, on the one hand, to sharp conflicts with Protestants, who had accepted his leadership on the strength of his alleged purpose of revitalizing the Christian religion, and, on the other, alienated some of his more decidedly pagan followers (see Chapter 23). We have already alluded to the potential conflict with brown-shirted "socialists," whose rebellious spirit was quelled in the blood purge of 1934. The difficulties in this sector of relations between "capital" and "labor" never ceased to plague the Nazis; a series of uneasy compromises were struck.

Even more perplexing is the anti-Semitic aspect of National Socialist ideology. It was, of course, central to Hitler's early ideological position, as developed in *Mein Kampf*. According to Hitler, it was his "studies" on the Jewish question that transformed him "from being a feeble world-citizen" into a "fanatical anti-Semite." (149a) To Hitler, anti-Semitism was inherently linked with anti-Communism, and he firmly believed that "if the Jew, with the help of his Marxist creed, conquers the nations of this world, his crown will be the funeral wreath of the human race, and the planet will drive through the ether . . . empty of mankind." (149b) Hitler himself has attributed his own conversion to certain Austrian leaders and acknowledged their inspiration — more especially the then mayor of Vienna, Dr. Lueger. While Hitler found ready responses to this anti-Semitism among the peasantry of Germany, it was a double-edged sword. At least one investigator (1) has offered striking evidence in support of the proposition that Hitler gained his adherents not because of, but in spite of, his anti-Semitism. Considering this fact, as well as the extent to which anti-Semitism proved a handicap in his foreign policy, it is striking with what radical determination Hitler pursued this "ideological" goal to the bitter end. The wholesale extermination of Jews during the war was, no doubt, in part motivated by Hitler's belief that the Jews were responsible for British and American opposition to him and his policies, and hence it was an act of revenge. However, the ideological aspect remained of central importance; in the secret talks recorded at the height of his power and triumph, he expounded it with fanatical zeal. (150a; 122a) It appears, in some ways, the inner rationale of his entire conduct.

It is possible, especially in the light of the catastrophic end of Hitler's enterprise, to argue that his failure to adapt his ideology to the realities of both German and international politics was a source of weakness, perhaps even the greatest source of weakness. Timely "corruption," such as was argued at times by Goering and others of his subleaders, might have saved him. (122b) He was not a complete purist; for he enunciated the curiously paradoxical doctrine that no one whom he proclaimed an Aryan could be a Jew. Several men of his immediate entourage were, according to the available evidence, non-Aryan in Hitler's sense of having some Jewish ancestry. This fact did not only provide the opponents of the regime with occasions for mockery; it also troubled the race purists. But since the issue was not worked out ideologically, but put in terms of a fiat of the Führer's godlike will, the believers in the Third Reich could argue that such Aryan non-Aryans were purified by the "divine touch."

It might finally be suggested that a certain flexibility lends an appearance of infallibility: positions which are brought forward as developments of an underlying theme, no matter how illogical, can be made to reinforce this theme. As long as the ultimate goal remains pure, the adaptations appear to strengthen it.

Since both communism and fascism are "success philosophies," built upon the confident assumption that history is on their side, ideological factors are weapons in the struggle for men's minds. In the past, the role of ideology in strengthening the body politic had always been played by religion and tradition, and by the symbols and myths in which religion and tradition were embodied. In modern totalitarian societies, the leaders must carefully create and control the ideological weapons useful to their political existence; ideological adaptations and corruptions are ultimately tested by the role they play in the propaganda and education of totalitarian societies.

10

THE CONSTITUTION, THE LAW,
AND JUSTICE

Every constitution contains strong ideological elements. Not only any bill of rights it may contain, but also the organizational fixation it undertakes, are ideologically oriented. This ideological element is sometimes a severe handicap to anyone who would seek to understand a system of government by means of reading its "constitution." (1041) It cannot therefore come as any great surprise to recognize this element in the constitutions of totalitarian dictatorships of the communist type. Characteristically, the Fascist and National Socialist regimes did not fashion a constitution, although Hitler allowed the Weimar constitution to remain "in force." He thereby expressed his contempt for a "system" that had proven a house of straw, once the strong winds of National Socialist ideology began blowing. (317) The Bolsheviks, on the other hand, undertook to fashion a fairly elaborate constitution, which bears the ideological stamp in its very opening: The Union of Soviet Socialist Republics is a socialist state of workers and peasants, the first article proclaims. It then proceeds to speak of its political foundation, the soviets or councils that sprang up "as a result of the overthrow of the power of landlords and capitalists and the conquest of the dictatorship of the proletariat." Landlords, capitalists, workers, peasants — the constitution conjures up their image as engaged in a vigorous class struggle.

Orthodox accepted scholarship in the Soviet Union and elsewhere in the Communist world projects this picture of the class warfare back upon the constitutions of the "capitalist" world. In a recent paper, a leading Soviet scholar, after reviewing a number of conventional conceptions of the constitution from Jellinek to Greaves, commented: "Ignoring the political (class) essence of a constitution is an important demerit of the above-mentioned general definitions of constitutions." (210) He argued that a constitution expresses the will of the ruling class, as indeed it must according to Marx's view of law and the state. It would follow that in a mature communist order there would be no need for a constitution. Yet so far there has been a constitutional evolution not only within the Soviet Union (and a new constitution is presumably in the making), but also in other Communist states, notably Yugoslavia (which recently completed a new constitution). (448)

In the Russian constitution of 1918, the function of the constitution as an instrument of class warfare, and hence its ideological function, was even more forcefully put thus: "The basic task of the Constitution . . . is the establishment of the dictatorship of the city and village proletariat and the poorest peasantry in the form of a powerful All-Russian state authority." The concept of the constitution implied in such a statement is not at all that of the Western tradition with its protection of the individual against the state and its division of power, but rather the opposite: no one has any rights and all power must be concentrated in the hands of the victorious proletariat, that is to say, its leaders. The new constitution of 1923, while seeming to establish representative government, by no means abandoned the ideology of class warfare, but rather institutionalized it. In retrospect, its democratic features may appear like mere "facade," (402a; 312) but the constitution actually epitomized the pretotalitarian phase of the Soviet Union's evolution, a phase when vigorous ideological debate was still carried on (88b) and before the totalitarian breakthrough occurred. This was genuine "revolutionary legality." By contrast, the constitution of 1936, promulgated at the height of the physical terror of the Great Purge, had a more clearly ideological function. When it was referred to in the Soviet Union as "that genuine charter of the rights of emancipated humanity," it was clearly seen in this light. Constitutional law, and with it all law, was made a key feature of the Soviet system, the crowning phase in the development of law. As it was put by the leading authority on Soviet law: " 'Revolutionary legality' was redefined as the strict observance of those laws which the Revolution has established: from a symbol of flexibility the phrase was converted into a symbol of stability." (19b; 374a) As such, it was by no means merely facade; it was the fixation of the ideological setting of Soviet totalitarianism.

In a way, this problem is related to a more general one in the theory of constitutionalism, which concerns what has been called the "living constitution." Ever since Howard Lee McBain published his well-known study in 1927 on the American constitution, seeking to identify its living corpus as contrasted with obsolete formulas, there has been discussion about it.* This is really a special case of the "living law" argument; for there has always been and always will be the problem of how much of the formal law, as set down in constitutions, statutes, and ordinances as well as in judicial decisions, is the operative law by which a legal community lives. (110e; 105c) The school of legal realists in the United States went to an extreme in the direction of arguing that only operative law is "real" (105d), but such a position creates great difficulties when it comes to interpreting radical changes in constitutional interpretation, such as have recently occurred in the United States. Such changes are usually put forward in terms of the existing constitution and must therefore be presumed to have been incorporated there as some kind of law, even though not operative. There is also the well-known range of "rights for which there is no remedy." Such rights presumably are law, even though not enforceable.

Autocratic legalism, however, must not be confused with the totalitarian distortion of the notion of law in what is spoken of as the "laws of movement." These are presumably "laws of nature" or "laws of history" (but history understood as a part of nature); they contain an existential, rather than a normative, judgment. The interrelation of existential and normative law has been a central problem in the long history of the natural law. (105) The totalitarian ideology tends to dissolve the normative in the existential realm and to consider all ordinary laws merely as expressions of laws of nature and history. "All history is the history of class struggles," for example, would be such a law in terms of which the positive legal order must be structured; it provides the standard by which to measure positive laws, to interpret and if necessary to alter and break them.

---

* Dolf Sternberger has used this notion in analyzing constitutional practice in the Federal Republic of Germany, apparently without knowing McBain's work — see his *Lebende Verfassung,* 1956.

All laws become fluid when they are treated merely as the emanation of such laws of movement, and their very multiplicity testifies to their normative weakness. (447a) Such fluidity makes them incapable of serving as standards of responsible conduct, since every violation can be argued away by the rulers as merely an adaptation to the higher laws of movement. A similar difficulty attached to the law of nature when it was intended to serve as a restraint upon absolute rulers, who in the past were allowed to contravene it whenever "reason of state" required it.

A comparable, though distinctive, complication is presented by the Chinese distortion of the traditional conception of *li* or *li-mao,* the rules of personal conduct evolved on the basis of Confucianism. The party leadership in Communist China has "endeavoured to re-structure the social obligations [arising from the Communist credo] by selectively pressing certain useful habits drawn from the *li-mao* pattern." (215j) The basic meaning of the *li* is thereby distorted.

Bearing in mind these general positions on constitutions and law, it seems only fair to interpret totalitarian and more especially Soviet constitution and law in this perspective. It then would appear that the Soviet Union, as well as Hitler Germany, Fascist Italy, and other totalitarian regimes, have maintained a legal system that is suitable for the nonpolitical reaches of interpersonal relations. But not only that. A very considerable range of highly political activities are subject to constitutional and other law, as long as the party or rather its leaders — the effective powerwielders — do not wish to interfere with it. In this respect, totalitarian dictatorship resembles many older autocracies. The great corpus of Roman law was developed after the disappearance of the Roman republic, under emperor-autocrats who became increasingly despotic as they claimed the "divine right" of an imperial prerogative: *quod placet principem, legis habet vigorem* (what pleases the prince, has the force of law). This central principle was resuscitated by the exponents of royal absolutism in sixteenth-century Europe and became the core of the Western doctrine of sovereignty. It did so at the very time that the legal systems of continental Europe were becoming ever more elaborately refined, culminating eventually in the great codifications. It should therefore not occasion any special surprise that the Soviet Union has promulgated codes of law in various fields, and that there has been a considerable amount of regional diversification. Indeed, some Soviet jurists would make this diversification the mainstay of an argument in support of the reality of Soviet federalism. One might even argue that there is an inherent tendency of autocracy to proliferate legal norms, as long as the ultimate authority is retained by the autocratic ruler, the reason being that through law the authority (as contrasted with the power) of such a ruler is enhanced and his legitimacy buttressed. (110f) In both Italy and Germany, as well as in Poland, Czechoslovakia, and even Russia, a large body of law has remained in force because it is expressive of folkways and cultural traditions that the totalitarian leadership sees no reason to alter, because it does not affect the political goals of the regime. The presumed claim to total manipulation (*Erfassung*) of those subject to such a regime does not exclude the possibility of accepting a good deal of the law that exists. Specialists have argued with convincing evidence for a "specific Russian component of Soviet law." Though there are numerous other illustrations, the procuracy, criminal law, and the law of the peasant household provide excellent illustrations of the specific Russian component of Soviet law. (19c; 240e)

The same argument applies, of course, a fortiori to the Hitler regime. Great sections of German law remained, as a matter of fact, completely intact, having come down from the nineteenth century and indeed continued into the Federal Republic. This situation gave rise to the theory that there existed a "dual state" in Germany under Hitler (102d), the "legal state" and the "prerogative state." It is unfortunate that the important insight into the dualism of two conflicting orders was obscured by the term "state"; for a state is presumably all-encompassing so that only one state can exist in one territory. The state, therefore, was Hitler's, and what remained of the pre-existing legal order was not a state, but a complex of norms expressive of numerous aspects of human relations with which National Socialism was not or not yet concerned. There is every indication that, after a successful conclusion of the war and a further stabilization of the regime, various fields of law that had remained untouched until 1945 would have been subjected to radical alteration in light of the National Socialist ideology. But just as in the Soviet Union, those alterations would still have been "law" in the sense of being valid rules of conduct. As defined by the authoritative Vyshinsky: "Law is a combination of rules of conduct which express the will of the ruling class and are established by legislative procedure, and also of customs and rules of community life sanctioned by state authority, whose application is secured by the compulsory force of the state for the purpose of protecting, strengthening and developing relations and procedures advantageous and convenient for the ruling class." (374b) It is evident that this definition is virtually identical with that given by such theorists as Hobbes, except for the introduction of the class concept. But if the meaning of that concept in Soviet reality is borne in mind, even that addition cannot be considered very much of a deviation. The will of the ruling class as represented by the rulers of the Soviet Union is in fact the will of those rulers: Lenin, Stalin, Khrushchev, and the party apparat that they led.

The Fascists and National Socialists were more candid about this predominance, though from a Communist viewpoint they failed to face the class influence reflected in the dictator's legal will. The strongly ideological ingredient of totalitarian law is thereby made manifest. As a National Socialist jurist, confronted with the legal reality, put it: "Law is the formed plan of the *Führer,* and therefore expression of the folk order of life (*völkische Lebensordnung*). The formed plan of the *Führer* is the highest command of the law." (232) In such a statement, both the voluntaristic and the compulsive aspects of law are submerged in the inspirational representativeness of the Führer's intuition and plan. In place of the class as the determining factor, the folk or nation has become the reference point. As a result, the notion of law in the fascist mind is associated with such ideas as the *Volksgeist,* which had been developed by the Romantics and the historical school of jurisprudence. But the former conservative flavor of a doctrine, which tied legal development to and restricted it by the traditions and folkways of a particular people, has been turned into a revolutionary thrust by dint of the will of the dictatorial representative.

It is in keeping with this revolutionary thrust that totalitarian law greatly expands the area of penal and criminal law. This is accomplished both by the extension of such conceptions as treason and subversion and by the broad interpretation of the "national interest" and the "security of the state." With their help, many legal conceptions are perverted and at times turned into the opposite of their original intent. (147) Matters that in constitutional systems are the subject of a suit between individuals become the concern of the state and are permeated by the ideological concerns of the regime. While the Germans and Italians had to abandon their former traditions of a legal order, the Soviet Union was greatly aided by the tsarist tradition, which was autocratic though not totalitarian.

One of the institutions of this ancient autocracy had been the office of the public prosecutor, or procurator. (19d) In the constitution of 1936, this official's functions are stated thus: "Supreme supervisory power to ensure the strict observance of the laws by all Ministries and institutions subordinated to them as well as by officials and citizens of the USSR generally, is vested in the Prosecutor General of the USSR"; he is "appointed by the Supreme Soviet of the USSR for a term of seven years" (articles 113–114). The prosecutor general himself appoints a host of lesser prosecutors throughout the Soviet Union; the system is completely centralized in his hands, since he also confirms the appointment of the local prosecutors, who have been proposed by his own subordinates. One leading scholar has summarized the varied functions as follows: the prosecutor sees to it that the vast administrative apparatus acts according to the law; he participates in local affairs. Whenever a prosecutor considers an act or proposal to be contrary to the constitution or the laws, he may "protest" to the next higher administrative organ; in the case of a ministry, this would be the Council of Ministers. He is supposed to supervise the operations of the security offices, the police, criminal investigations, and the corrective labor camps. Only the Council of Ministers as a body is beyond his control.

Besides these functions of an administrative kind (reminiscent of the French Conseil d'Etat under Napoleon), the prosecutor's office has comprehensive tasks in conjunction with the courts. It orders the arrest of those suspected and appoints the investigators of crimes who conduct pretrial examinations — a system generally found in Europe, but in constitutional regimes elaborately circumscribed by legal protections for the accused. It also prosecutes at criminal trials, supervises all civil proceedings, and may intervene in any civil suit. This is part of the extension of criminal law we pointed out above, although not formally recognized as such in the

Soviet Union. The prosecutor may request that any proceeding, civil or criminal, be reopened and tried again in a higher court. In short, the Chief Prosecutor's Office combines in one vast operation the functions of the American Attorney General's office, congressional and other legislative investigating committees, grand juries, and public prosecutors. We have in this office one of the most striking instances of the concentration of power, characteristic of autocratic regimes, as contrasted with its division under constitutionalism. The prosecutors in the Soviet Union are an adaptation of an institution of the old autocracy to the needs of the totalitarian order, with its vast administrative system.* It has been copied in the satellites, including the German Democratic Republic, where its operation has assimilated the National Socialist practices of people's courts and prosecutors, which in the minds of many Germans symbolize the end of the rule of law (*Rechtsstaat*). And yet, in a very real sense, the system of the procuracy represents the totalitarian method of securing some kind of legal order, under the sway of revolutionary legality. It may sound grotesque to claim that "the principal contribution of the Russian Revolution to the development of constitutional law is the adaptation of autocracy to twentieth century industrial society" (19e), but within the context of Soviet ideology it is a meaningful statement. A vast amount of law, including that of the constitution, is being maintained by this system. It stands behind this otherwise almost incredible statement by a leading Soviet jurist:

Great is the role of the Soviet Constitution in securing the rights of Soviet citizens. It secures the basic rights and duties of Soviet citizens, that is, such rights as enable them to take an active part in state activities, in exercising state power. To these rights and liberties the constitution refers the right of all people to have reached a certain age to elect and be elected to all Soviets of Working People's Deputies, the right to education, freedom of speech, freedom of the press, freedom of assembly including the holding of mass meetings, street processions and demonstrations and other rights and liberties. (210)

Such a claim is not a bad joke, but is meant to possess real content. Whatever content it has is due to the prosecutor general's willing-

---

* Berman, ch. 16, has interpreted the Soviet system in this respect as a "parental" system which treats the litigant as a ward of society. It would be more in keeping with established usage to call such a system paternalistic.

ness to support a particular person or office in his legal claim to the right. It is true that "bills of rights, under such regimes as the popular democracies, become purely declaratory and unenforceable; they constitute essentially declarations of the principles and goals which the regime wishes the world at large to believe them to be dedicated to" (403b); but it is true only in the sense that a ward cannot seek the enforcement of his rights, though his warden can. The constitution *is* a weapon in the armory of the prosecutor general, when he wishes to protect a particular right or individual against the encroachments of a state or other office. It all is subject to the warden's typical concern: the welfare of the ward, as he sees it, or "the material conditions necessary for the realization of such rights." It is primarily a matter of protection against arbitrariness and prejudice. Vis-à-vis the state (and party) itself, the Soviet citizen does not and cannot have any rights. There can be no question that protection against administrative abuses is a legal protection of some sort. Its totalitarian limits were rather well stated by a satellite minister of justice: "The real task of those employed in the administration of justice is to be the realization of every word of party and government resolutions, but particularly the consolidation of the socialist legal structure and the modeling of our courts on the shining example of the courts of the Soviet Union." (450)

It is clear from the foregoing that the ultimate issue is an ideological one which turns upon the meaning of justice. What is to be understood by this basic value that has been central to the discussion of law and legal philosophy through the ages? (110g; 111) It is undeniable that the totalitarian autocracy, like monarchical absolutism in Europe, the Roman empire, and oriental despotism before it, operates in terms of its peculiar concept of justice. In this respect, these more permanent forms of autocracy contrast sharply with the tyranny of the Greek city-states, which Plato and Aristotle considered "devoid of justice" and hence the most unstable forms of government. If justice is considered in its political dimension, that is to say, in terms of the just political act, "An action may be said to be just, and hence likewise a rule, a judgment or a decision, when it involves a comparative evaluation of the persons affected by the action, and when that comparison accords with the values and beliefs of the political community." Justice, in brief, is the comparative evaluation of persons and acts according to the prevailing values and beliefs of a political community. Such comparisons are valid only if the facts upon which they are based are not untrue, if the relation between facts and values is not arbitrary, and if the norms derived from such comparisons do not ask the impossible. It is evident that justice thus understood has a distinct and meaningful application to the handling of a large number of human relations in these totalitarian orders. It is evident also that the growing consensus makes the enlargement of the area within which justice prevails quite feasible. But such a widening scope of justice does not by any means signify the end of autocracy. Consensus and justice have been characteristic of much autocracy in the past. A secret police may still be needed, because the rigid limitations upon public criticism of the official exercise of power oblige such a regime to search out potential enemies by other means. Yet no autocratic regime, even that of a tyrant, would endure long without providing a measure of believed-in justice. Modern totalitarianism has sought to facilitate its task by providing an ideological consensus that is manifested and symbolized in constitution and law, as it has been traditionally in the constitutional democracies of the West.

IV

Propaganda and the Terror

11

PROPAGANDA AND THE MONOPOLY
OF MASS COMMUNICATIONS

The psychic fluidum — that is, the peculiar atmosphere — of totalitarian dictatorship is created by two closely related phenomena, propaganda and the terror. Terror may be a rather strong word, but it focuses attention upon an objective reality, as contrasted with the subjective response to that reality. Terror may be crude or subtle; it may work with the threat of execution or with defamation and social shame. Its chief characteristic is the deliberate effort to intimidate. Governmental terror seeks to frighten those under its sway into conformity and obedience. It therefore may create a measure of consensus and willing cooperation. Any realistic account of prison life, like Brendan Behan's, provides ample illustrations for such "consensus" in response to intimidation. A pervasive atmosphere of anxiety and a general sense of insecurity are the subjective concomitants of such terror. Often the victims of such terror are quite unaware of their own psychic states. That is the reason why simple interviews, especially by casual travelers, rarely disclose its presence. (238d) Because the terror reinforces the monopoly of mass communication, and indeed a good part of all communication, totalitarian propaganda can be understood only within this context. And conversely the terror assumes its all-pervading quality because it is spread about through the continuous repetition of official propaganda lines. This linkage of propaganda and terror distinguishes them from all comparable phenomena in other systems of government.

The nearly complete monopoly of mass communication is generally agreed to be one of the most striking characteristics of totalitarian dictatorship. It is also one of the features which clearly differentiates it from earlier forms of autocratic rule, as we have noted. Modern mass-communication media, the press, radio and television, and the film, have been developing gradually and have, under competitive conditions, been looked upon as an essential condition of large-scale democracy. For, without the possibility of communicating a great deal of information that is beyond the reach of the immediate community, even the casual participation in policy determination which the citizen of the modern state is called upon to perform would be impossible.

In totalitarian dictatorships, all these means of communication are centrally controlled by the government, regardless of whether they are also actually owned by the government, as in the Soviet Union, or continue under "private" ownership, as in fascist countries. Hence they are not available for the expression of criticism or even adverse comment. This monopoly of the channels of mass communication is reinforced by the control of the means of private communication, the postal services and more especially the telephone and telegraph. Wire tapping is a common practice, and there is of course no such thing as "privacy" of the mails. In the interest of combatting counterrevolutionary plots, the government claims the right to open all mail. What this means is that only word-of-mouth communication remains for those who wish to carry opposition beyond the point permitted by the government — surely a rather inefficient method under the conditions of modern mass society. All effective control over the content of communications is vested in the state," which in fact means the top party functionaries who usually possess, as a result of previous revolutionary agitation, considerable know-how in the field of propaganda.

Propaganda as such is not a peculiarity of totalitarian dictatorship. It has become increasingly recognized as an integral part of all organizational activity in a highly literate society. (104k) Propaganda has been defined in different ways, depending in part upon what it was to be distinguished from. It should be pointed out here that the Soviets make a clear distinction between propaganda and agitation. Some of what we mean here by propaganda would, in Soviet terminology, more accurately be called agitation. To the Soviets, propaganda is restricted to a more refined, rational, documented appeal, designed to convince rather than to induce. Agitation tends to be more vehement, striking, and generally aimed at the masses.

It has been said that "propaganda is the other fellow's opinion." In line with such a superficial notion, many people think of propaganda as essentially untruth. But no propagandist worth his mettle will prefer an untruth to a truth, if the truth will do the job. This is the vital test of all propaganda activity: does it do the job? and what is the job? The needs, interests, and requirements of the organization for which the propagandist works determine the answer to this question. If it is the Red Cross, the "job" may be to secure contributions; if the *Ladies' Home Journal*, it may be subscriptions. The latter example shows that propaganda, under competitive conditions, resembles advertising; both are often soft-pedaled as "public relations." In short, propaganda is essentially action-related; it aims to get people to do or not to do certain things. That action focus may be either very visible or hidden away. But it always is there and needs to be inquired into, if propaganda is to be understood. And since propaganda is carried on in behalf of an organization, it is equally important to inquire into who finances it. Many propagandists are reluctant, therefore, to reveal the source of their funds. (107a)

In totalitarian dictatorships, virtually all propaganda is directed ultimately to the maintenance in power of the party controlling it. This does not mean, however, that there are not many sharp conflicts between rival propagandists. As will be shown later, the maintenance of totalitarian dictatorship does not preclude the occurrence of many internecine struggles; on the contrary, it lends to these struggles a fierceness and violence which is rarely seen in freer societies. This issue of the rival component elements in the totalitarian society poses very difficult problems for the over-all direction of propaganda. The chief propagandist often has to opt between such rival groups. (In the National Socialist Ministry of Propaganda and Public Enlightenment, these rival claims to some extent found expression in the organization of the "desk," that is to say, of different bureaus which would report on different sections of the society and would thus mirror the conflicts.) (73a)

The documentary evidence that has become available since the war tends to support earlier views regarding the inner workings of Goebbels' propaganda organization. (331a) There is no need here to go into details of the organization, but some outstanding features deserve brief comment. Perhaps the most important aspect of this "monopoly" control was the dualism of government and party. Each had its elaborate propaganda setup, both headed by Goebbels, who succeeded in maintaining a measure of effective coordination. But on the whole it would seem that the Ministry of Propaganda and Public Enlightenment and the party office of propaganda were in a coordinate position. However, key officials of the ministry who stood in sharpest antagonism to Goebbels, like Otto Dietrich, the press chief of the Hitler government, also occupied pre-eminent posts in the party's propaganda machine, and this "personal union" extended fairly far down the line. The relationship has been described as follows: "The task of the Propaganda Ministry in the whole machine for controlling and creating public opinion might be compared with a Ministry of War. It coordinates, plans, and is responsible for the smooth carrying out of the whole propaganda effort of the German government. The Party Propaganda Department, on the other hand, is comparable to the General Staff of an army which actually directs operations and musters and organizes the forces and their supplies and ammunition." (331b) It is seen from this and other evidence that the two organizations had different functions within the regime, comparable to the difference between party and government. The aggressive boldness of a leader of the National Socialist movement was as much a quality required of Goebbels as was the forceful caution of a leading government official. It is generally agreed that the most important instrument of Goebbels in planning and coordinating all the far-flung activities of his two organizations was the Coordination Division of the ministry. Here was centered the conflict between the rival requirements of the two organizations; here, if possible, such difficulties were solved by the key officials of the division or, if necessary, by Goebbels himself. But it was never an easy task to draw together the various divergent strands of the propaganda apparatus, and the difficulties experienced by the Ministry of Propaganda reflected the tensions of the moment. It is an ever present problem when total monopoly control exists.

The same problem, often in aggravated form, confronts the totalitarian propagandist in the field of foreign relations. While he gains the advantage of controlling all channels of information to other countries, he suffers under the distinct disadvantage of having little chance to secure the confidence of people abroad, including the foreign governments themselves, about any information reaching them. Hitler showed considerable awareness of these difficulties. At one time, talking among intimates, he noted that a sharp distinction must be made between handling the domestic and the foreign press. Radio messages for foreign countries must similarly be differentiated. Such messages, if intended for Britain, should contain musical offerings, since they would appeal to English taste and accustom the British public to tune in to German broadcasts: "As regards news-bulletins to Britain, we should confine ourselves to plain statements of facts, without comment on their value or importance . . . As the old saying has it, little drops of water will gradually wear the stone away." (150d) Goebbels added that the opinion of people who have confidence in their leadership can be effectively swayed by pointed and unequivocal value judgments. He therefore recommended that, in messages to the German people, reference should be made again and again to "the drunkard Churchill" and to the "criminal Roosevelt."

This attempt to create stereotype images of the enemy has been developed to a fine point in Soviet propaganda. All discussions and pictorial representations of the enemy stress some specific feature suggesting the enemy's alleged criminal nature and evil intent. Operating on a huge scale and addressing its appeal to the great masses of the Soviet people, Soviet propaganda strives to present a simple, unrefined, and strikingly negative portrayal, so as to create the politically desirable conditioned reflex in those to whom it is directed. (For further comment on "enemies," see Chapter 14.) It is to some extent in terms of these negative symbols that the "consensus" develops. As a matter of common observation, shared hostilities are an effective source of political association. Indeed, some political analysts have gone so far as to assert that political parties essentially rest on these shared animosities. The totalitarian dictatorships have built upon such negativist positions a good part of the popular loyalty to the regime.

During the war, Soviet anti-Nazi propaganda usually associated "Hitlerite" with such terms as "vermin" or "beast," frequently with corresponding illustrations. The anti-American campaign has similarly employed certain words over and over, such as warmongering and imperialist, in speaking of American leadership. *Krokodil,* the humor magazine, has become a real rogues' gallery of various criminal types, with beast-like faces, dressed either in U.S. Army uniforms or in top hats and morning coats, their fingers dripping with blood and threateningly grasping an atomic bomb. In external propaganda, the Soviet Union never fails to draw a distinction between the people as such and the leaders, who are the ones who fit the stereotype.

The nearly complete control of all means of mass communication gives the totalitarian dictatorship the very great advantage of being able to shift its general line of propaganda rather radically over short periods of time. This is especially helpful in the field of foreign affairs. After the Hitler-Stalin Pact of 1939, Communist and Nazi propagandists were stressing all of a sudden the common features of these "popular" regimes and their contrast with the "Pluto-democracies" of the West. Various points were brought forward in this connection — such as that the Russians and Germans were both young and vigorous as contrasted with the decadence of the West. Even more striking is Russia's recent turn in regard to Communist China, as indeed has been the change in China itself. Such reversals in official propaganda lines are inconceivable under competitive conditions.

But while these shifts may work in the Soviet Union, they certainly tend to bring on a crisis in the Communist movement in other countries. Many Communist followers, including important men, have changed sides in the past and may do so again. After the Hitler-Stalin Pact twenty-one French Communist deputies out of a total of seventy-two abandoned the party. (28) Similarly, Nazi sympathizers in a number of countries, especially the United States, were deeply disturbed, and anti-Nazi activities were assisted by this change. Even deeper were the fissures caused by Khrushchev's denunciation of Stalin. In fact, the repercussions of that move are still audible in the way Communist parties have been affected by the conflict between the USSR and China.

But even internally the alteration in an official line may have subcutaneous reactions, which the leadership fails to appreciate. When Hitler suddenly decided to invade the Soviet Union in the summer of 1941, he was much pleased with his success in accomplishing this *salto mortale.* "I am proud that it was possible with these few men [himself, Goebbels, and a few aides] to shift course by 180 degrees. No other country could do the same." (152b; 150c) In this instance, we know from postwar documents that the effect on German public opinion was quite mixed. For, while some men who had previously stood aloof decided that in a life-and-death struggle with communism they must support Hitler, others concluded that the game was up and joined what became a dangerous and large-scale opposition movement. Detached analysis suggests that it was not so much the propaganda as the very facts themselves which had the greatest effect. (302a; 76a)

This instance serves to illustrate what is probably a very important aspect of all totalitarian propaganda. The fact of monopolistic control gradually causes in the general public a profound distrust of all news and other kinds of information. Since people do not have any other sources of information, there develops a vast amount of rumor mongering as well as general disillusionment. And since a man cannot think without having valid information upon which to focus his thought, the general public tends to become indifferent. This in turn leads to a phenomenon we may call the "vacuum," which increasingly surrounds the leadership. Comparable problems have beset autocracies in the past. Well known is the tale of Harun al-Rashid, who stalked Baghdad at night disguised as a commoner to find out what was going on. Harun al-Rashid, so the tale goes, was wise enough to realize that his subordinates were prone to abuse their great power and, instead of employing it for the good of the community and the commonwealth, would oppress and exploit the people. He had no reliable way of ascertaining the common man's views through regular channels, since all of these were controlled by the very subordinates he wished to check up on, so the great Caliph disguised himself from time to time and mingled, in the dark of night, with the people in taverns and streets to listen to their tales of woe. On the basis of what he had heard, he would bring those to trial who had been talked about as vicious and corrupt. This problem of checking up occurs, of course, in all human organizations, but under orderly constitutional government (and the corresponding patterns of responsibility in private organizations), such checking occurs readily and continuously as a result of the open criticism that is voiced by members not only in formal meetings, but informally through press, radio, and all the other channels. Under the conditions of totalitarian dictatorship, the check-up becomes exceedingly difficult, if not impossible.

This failure to communicate effectively, both within the hierarchy and with the rest of the people and the world, we have called the "vacuum." There develops within the totalitarian regime a kind of empty space around the rulers, which becomes more and more difficult to penetrate. A slow disintegration affecting all human relations causes mutual distrust so that ordinary people are alienated from one another; all the bonds of confidence in social relationships are corroded by the terror and propaganda, the spying, and the denouncing and betraying, until the social fabric threatens to fall apart. The confidence which ordinarily binds the manager of a plant to his subordinates, the members of a university faculty to one another and to their students, lawyer to client, doctor to patient, and even parents to children as well as brothers to sisters is disrupted. The core of this process of disintegration is, it seems, the breakdown of the possibility of communication — the spread, that is, of the vacuum. Isolation and anxiety are the universal result. And the only answer the totalitarian dictatorship has for coping with this disintegration of human relationships is more organized coercion, more propaganda, more terror.

We know today that the SS of Himmler made extensive check-ups on the attitude of the German population during the war. Many of these reports show a remarkable candor about the faltering and eventually vanishing support for the regime. (371) But there is every reason to believe that these reports never reached Hitler, even in abbreviated form. It is not even clear how many of them became available to Himmler. The terror that permeates the party and secret-police cadres, no less than the general population, operates as an inhibition to truthful reporting. Block wardens falsify their reports, in the hope of currying favor with their superiors. We shall see later how this tendency to pretend that results are better and more favorable to the regime than the facts warrant and to make adjustments, not only in reports about attitudes, but also in those about production and maintenance of industrial plant, interferes with industrial planning (see Chapters 17, 18).

A similar situation arose in Italy. We learn from Leto's *Memoirs* that only Rocchini among Mussolini's lieutenants had the courage to tell him that the Italian people were bitterly opposed to entering

World War II; Starace even claimed that almost all Italians would unite behind the Duce. The Duce was similarly misinformed about the state of Italy's military preparedness; his subordinates preferred to flatter their chief by presenting rosy estimates, suggesting the prowess of his regime. (212)

In the Soviet Union, the vacuum became most pronounced at the height of the Stalin terror. It has now become greatly reduced as a consequence of the policies of "popular totalitarianism." But even under the current regime, there is a good deal of it—as shown by the recurrent efforts of stimulating "letters to the editor." It also is operative in the world Communist movement and thereby affects the USSR's intelligence work in its foreign relations. It appears that Soviet intelligence is also handicapped by the fact that, in some respects at least, it must work with and through local Communist parties. If it tried to do without them, it would soon find itself in difficulties, particularly with reference to the problem of recruiting agents and contacts, as well as penetrating the government institutions of foreign powers. (305) But when the intelligence service employs the local party organization, it is exposed to the effect of this process of falsification, rooted both in fear of the Moscow center and in ideological blindness. Local Communist leaders, fearful of Moscow disfavor and subsequent purges, easily develop a tendency toward overestimating their strength and the degree of inner disintegration in the capitalist order. Soviet miscalculations in France and Italy are among many examples, dating back to the days of the Comintern and the unsuccessful Soviet venture in China. Also at the time of the blockade of Berlin, undertaken by the USSR in June 1948 to counteract the currency reform that the Allies had instituted after lengthy Soviet obstruction (56; 404a), it became clear that the Soviet Union, on the basis of East German information, had confidently counted upon the Germans in Berlin to abandon the Allied cause and submit to the Soviet position; even elementary intelligence work could have informed them to the contrary. In fact, there is reason to believe that the entire Soviet policy in Germany was, to some extent, the result of such a failure of intelligence, because of excessive reliance upon German Communist information.

It would be a mistake, however, to conclude that the Soviet intelligence agency, both at home and abroad, operates like a man wearing red-colored blinders. Soviet leadership makes special efforts to develop alternate channels of information and control in order to eliminate precisely this element of coloring and distortion. Soviet espionage, apart from collaborating with the local Communist parties, also operates independent networks, which report directly to Moscow. Espionage revelations show that there are normally at least five such networks in a country subjected to intensive Soviet espionage: one working through the local Communist party, another run by the MVD, a military intelligence network, a commercial espionage network, and finally the foreign-service intelligence network. Excessive discrepancies can thus be more easily detected when all such reports are processed in Moscow and submitted to the policymakers. Similarly, in their domestic surveillance, the Soviet rulers are careful not to make themselves dependent on only one source of information. Apart from the secret police and the ordinary channels of the party, there exist the Party Control Commissions, which investigate party activities in all walks of life, the Ministry of State Control, which is specially concerned with keeping in touch with administrative functions and making independent reports on their operations, and the prosecutor general and his subordinates, who have recently been given additional investigating powers. (463) There is also the technique of *samokritika,* or self-critique, according to which Soviet officials and functionaries as well as the people in general are encouraged, besides examining themselves, to criticize the operations, but *not the policy,* of the party, the state administration, or the economic enterprises.* This not only serves as a vent to pent-up aggression, but is also useful to the rulers in detecting current weaknesses, abuses, and public attitudes. As a result of this, the Soviet regime can, when it wants to, judge the responsiveness of its population to its propaganda with a surprising degree of accuracy. Also, besides these sources, there are the press and the letters to the press and party headquarters, which have, at least for Smolensk, been analyzed thoroughly. (90a) One is bound to wonder whether the recent changes in the Soviet Union were not, at least in part, motivated by such evidence about dissatis-

---

* "Self-critique" is preferable to the more frequent translation of "self-criticism." There is a Russian word *krititisizm* which means criticism. *Kritika* means critique, and the Soviet regime is interested in promoting the technique of critique, but not in encouraging a critical attitude through criticism.

faction with the regime. There is one major problem, however: as the totalitarian regime maintains its internal coercion and indoctrination, the degree of apparent consensus will in time increase, and the secret police will find it much more difficult to do its work. There is no doubt that the Soviet population is today much less divided in its opinions and reactions than it was a generation ago. This naturally makes information gathering less reliable. But it also makes it less urgent, since such consensus means that the regime's ideology has been "internalized" (see Chapter 15). And propaganda is thereby greatly facilitated.

Such consensus, such internalizing of the ideology, did not occur to any extent in Germany under Hitler (except within the party). Goebbels was by no means unaware of the difficulties he was confronting. In his diaries, published by Louis Lochner after the war (125), the problem is a recurrent theme. They also show how well he knew how to exploit the clumsy views which were being aired by the Allies regarding the German people as a whole, particularly the demand for unconditional surrender. As the plain facts of the Allies' successful air war against Germany mounted, the unconditional-surrender formula remained as one of the few propaganda weapons to fall back upon. Another one was provided by the Morgenthau Plan put forward at Quebec in September 1943. But not only did the Allies provide desperately needed propaganda weapons; the Soviet Union, by repeatedly demanding that ten million Germans be furnished for reconstruction purposes in the Soviet Union, allowed Goebbels to note: "Demands like that are wonderful for our propaganda. They stir German public opinion deeply. The idea that our soldiers might not return home at all but might have to remain in the Soviet Union as forced labor is a terrible thought for every woman and every mother. The German people would prefer to fight to their last breath." (125a) Incidentally, this is an illustration of the fact noted above that a propagandist prefers a good fact to the best lie. But in spite of such aids, the task of propaganda became ever more desperate as the war continued. What evidently kept Goebbels going was that he himself believed, at least until the end of 1943, in the Führer's ability to avert disaster.

That critical views printed in the press need not have any significant effect in a totalitarian regime, unless the leadership sees fit to take them into account, is demonstrated by Hitler. Great difficulties resulted from his hostility to the German press. This contrasted curiously with his avid interest in reading press reports from abroad. (73b) But although they were brought to him almost hourly, they failed to influence his modes of expression and his basic propaganda lines. Nor did he receive sound information about the probable course of British and American policy, nor about the trend of opinion in both countries. When he arrived at his decision to go to war with Poland, he did not seem to have expected the British to do much more than make a gesture of protest, and he hoped until the last to be able to keep the United States out of the war. The efforts of certain qualified persons, especially in the Foreign Office, to furnish Hitler with more adequate data were thwarted by the predominant party cadres. (321; 391) This circumstance shows the catastrophic effect of the factor we are here analyzing: an unintended consequence of totalitarian terror is an almost complete isolation of the leader. At the time Hitler decided to go to war, in the fateful August days of 1939, he isolated himself, and no advisers, not even Goering, let alone foreign diplomats — according to Sir Nevile Henderson's pitiful account — could secure access to Hitler. (142b)

Not the vacuum specifically, but the effect of it on the totalitarian ruler has caused one leading student of these problems to make the following comment: "Where the instruments of public enlightenment are wholly under the domination of the active elite of power, the controllers of the media develop a fantasy world in which the images communicated to the people have little relationship to reality. The stream of public communication becomes dogmatic and ceremonial to such a degree that it is inappropriate to think of communication management as a propaganda problem. It is more accurate to think of ritualization than propaganda." (112e) Undoubtedly this kind of ritualization exists to some extent. On the other hand, repeated shifts in the actual lines of communication, involving the leadership in serious self-contradictions, suggest that large amounts of propaganda as such continue to be issued. The "fantasy world" in which the dictator lives, and which is a product of the vacuum that the terror has created around him, plays its role in competition with the real world that he seeks to master.

The lieutenants of a dictator are often more clearly aware of the complexity of the issues and the risks involved in a particular course of policy. It is interesting that a key German official believed that Hitler's unrealistic propaganda lines were decidedly detrimental to the regime. His comments indicate a typical clash of views between the professional propagandist and the ideologue, whether educator or party fanatic, who is preoccupied not with the survival but with the advance of the totalitarian movement. This man's comments are so revealing that they deserve quoting in full:

I was of the firm conviction at that time that a national socialist Germany could live in peace with the world, if Hitler had been restrained in his actions, had bribed the radicalism internally, and had externally an objective which took account of the interests of other nations. The provocative demonstrations, unnecessary in their extent . . . the anti-semitic excesses, the inciting and tolerating of violence, and the world propaganda of Goebbels as embodied in the tone and content of his Sportpalast demonstrations were psychologically unsuited to gain support abroad for national socialist Germany and to cause other nations to recognize the good side of national socialism. These tactless and offensive outbursts decisively influenced world public opinion against Germany immediately after 1933. (73c)

That the propaganda was unwise probably is right, but it overlooks the fact that Hitler was not primarily interested in the German people and was basically motivated by his totalitarian mission, as he conceived it; for this the German people were merely the tool.

As in nature, so in society, the vacuum is relative. And since totalitarian dictators, as already mentioned, to some extent at least realize their isolation, various efforts are made to reduce the "thin air" around them. We have shown some of the techniques employed for increasing the intake of popular reactions; totalitarian regimes have also developed techniques for increasing the outgo. Apart from the party members' continuing function as spreaders of propaganda lines, there has been developed the technique of whispering campaigns. A high party official will call in some of his friends a little further on down the line in the party and, in strict confidence, tell them something highly startling or secret. He knows perfectly well that they will go and tell somebody else, in similarly strict confidence, and so on. This technique was and is employed also for the purpose of reaching and misleading foreign correspondents. The technique is, of course, not unknown in other societies; but in them it serves a purpose radically different from that in a totalitarian dictatorship. It is the means of penetrating a fog rather than reducing a vacuum.

The vacuum has another curious effect, as far as outgo is concerned. As already mentioned, people under totalitarian dictatorships become so suspicious of all communication, suspecting every news item of being propaganda, that even paramount facts are disbelieved. Thus it appears that, as late as September 12, 1939, the Germans professed not to know, or rather not to believe, that Britain and France had declared war upon Germany. To the blatant headlines of Goebbels' propaganda press, their reaction evidently was: "Another of Goebbels' propaganda stories." At the time of the Franco rebellion, when the papers reported, quite truthfully, that the British navy was demonstrating in the western Mediterranean, a widespread public reaction in Germany created a genuine war scare, because people were convinced that the British navy was threatening instead the North Sea coast of Germany. (125b) Goebbels in his diaries reports a number of other instances of this kind, and the entire collection provides a striking illustration for the vacuum theory; as the war went on, the problem of reaching the German populace became more and more perplexing.*

In the Soviet Union, the war also gave rise to many rumors, which swept the population by means of the OWS news agency — a translation of the popular and symptomatic abbreviation for the Russian phrase, "one woman said . . ." During the period of initial Soviet reverses, many exaggerated accounts of Soviet defeats, flights of leaders, and so forth were passed from mouth to mouth, contradicting the official radio broadcasts and newspaper communiqués. Later on, by 1943 and 1944, as a corollary to the many promises of a happy future made during the war by the Soviet leaders, rumors circulated that the Soviet government had decided to end collectivization of agriculture and to release all political prisoners. Possibly such rumors were even originated purposely by the regime itself in order to gain public support for the war effort. In any case, some interviews with former Soviet citizens suggest that these rumors

---

* Actually, this problem also plagued the people in charge of wartime propaganda in the Western democracies, for during the war "constitutional dictatorships" were instituted, and the controls over news resulting from this temporary concentration of power caused the public to become increasingly suspicious.

were widely believed, and the population was quite disappointed by the postwar harshness of the Stalinist policies. A similar instance is the extensive misrepresentation of figures on the grain harvest in the late fifties, which so gravely affected Khrushchev's agricultural efforts.

It would seem from all the evidence at our disposal that the vacuum works like a cancer in the totalitarian systems. This means that its growth endangers the continued existence of the totalitarian scheme of things. It may even catapult such a dictatorship into a calamitous foreign adventure, such as Hitler's wars. Stalin's ignorance of the agricultural situation similarly made the food problem in the USSR very much more acute, according to Khrushchev's revelations. Reality is hard to perceive in a vacuum created by fear and lies, buttressed by force — hence the Khrushchevian policy of reducing the vacuum by greater popular participation.

An important feature of totalitarian propaganda is its all-pervasiveness, the direct result, of course, of the propaganda monopoly. Not only the members of the party and the more or less indifferent masses, but even the more or less determined enemies of the regime fall prey to its insistent clamor, to the endless repetition of the same phrases and the same allegations. A general pattern of thought, almost a style of thinking, proves increasingly irresistible as the regime continues in power. This is the basis of the consensus formation in the USSR. "It is clear," we read in one thorough study of these problems, "that there are people in all ranks of life who believe implicitly what they read and hear." Arguing from a presumably hostile sample, these analysts say that despite this "it is striking how the more implicit aspects of Soviet official communications, the mode of thought and the categories in which events are grouped, are reflected in the thought patterns and expression of our informants." (161b)

It has been, as a matter of fact, the frequent experience of interviewers of former Soviet citizens to find that even those who profess the most violent hostility to the Soviet system tend to think in patterns instilled into them by that regime. Their attitudes on such matters as freedom of the press or the party system are often inclined to mirror, even by contradiction or negation, official Soviet propaganda. Similarly, in such matters as word usage, words laden with propaganda-derived value judgments are used as part of their daily vocabulary. They thus serve unconsciously as unwitting propagandists for the regime they abhor.

This singular success of totalitarian propaganda is the result of constant repetition. Soviet press, radio, oral agitation, and propaganda operate ceaselessly, supplementing the party and Komsomol activities and the ideologically oriented training system. (160a) Soviet newspapers, controlled centrally, repeat day after day the political themes set by *Pravda,* the organ of the party Central Committee, and *Izvestiya,* the central-government organ. *Pravda* itself, with a circulation of well over three million, is read and studied throughout the Soviet Union, particularly in the party cells, where it is compulsory reading. Local newspapers, many with circulations of several hundred thousand, such as *Pravda Ukrainy* and *Leningradskaya pravda,* re-echo the essential points of the Moscow daily, often reprinting its editorials and commentaries. The local press is also sometimes given special instructions about the handling of the news and the sequence in which the various statements of the leaders are to be presented. For instance, after Malenkov's "resignation" in February 1955, Radio Moscow issued such special instructions to all the provincial papers. In addition to *Izvestiya* and *Pravda,* there are a large number of specialized papers for youth, the trade unions, the military, and others, published centrally and distributed throughout the USSR. All these newspapers, with a combined circulation of over forty-seven million in the 1950s, play an important role in the Soviet process of indoctrination. (422a)

This process is backed by the other two basic media of propaganda and indoctrination: the radio and personal agitation. The radio, with an estimated listening audience of about forty million, quite naturally devotes a great deal of its time to political matters. (160b) A reliable estimate places the amount of time devoted to political and scientific broadcasts at 28 percent of the central program time. One of the most important Moscow radio broadcasts is the morning reading (7:00 A.M.) of the *Pravda* editorial, which is relayed simultaneously by all other Soviet stations. (409a) Soviet radio publications openly admit the political importance of radio broadcasting, as seen in the following statement: "Radio helps considerably in the Communist education of the workers. It is one of the most important means of disseminating political information, of spreading the all-triumphant ideas of Marxism-Leninism, popu-larizing the most advanced industrial and agricultural techniques and the achievements of socialist culture, science, and art." (445) News and editorial programs particularly are designed to comple-ment the press propaganda coverage and highlight the important points in the current propaganda themes. Foreign news is rarely given prompt treatment, and it is usually presented as a commen-tary. Furthermore, the use of radio-diffusion speakers, which work on the basis of wire transmission and are therefore useless for listen-ing to non-Soviet stations, is promoted. This, of course, insures complete monopoly for Soviet broadcasting, and about 70 percent of all sets in the USSR are of this type. (160c) Similar sets are now being introduced in the satellite regimes of Central Europe.

The third and, in some ways, the most important device is that of direct, personal agitation. This involves literally millions of agita-tors, some full-time, some part-time during special campaigns, who organize mass meetings, give lectures, visit families in their homes, distribute literature, set up study and discussion groups, and, in general, attempt to draw everyone into active participation in the indoctrination process. The estimated number of regular agitators is around two million, thus providing one agitator for every hundred Soviet citizens (including children). (160d) In a sense, this mass indoctrination constitutes an effort to conduct a nationwide process of brainwashing, which only a very few succeed in completely avoid-ing. It is on these propaganda processes, as well as on the educa-tional training system, that the regime depends for the achievement of total ideological integration of its people. It is these instruments of mental molding that are used by the administration to produce a generation of convinced followers, thinking and acting in disci-plined unison.

The technique of personal agitation has been elaborated by the leaders of Communist China. Based upon their experience during the long period of incubation when they were struggling to survive — a time they speak of as the "low ebb" — they have evolved, sys-tematized, and tested what they call the democratic "mass line." As early as 1934 Mao charged the party cadres with mobilizing the broad masses to take part in the revolutionary war. (228) Although the situation has radically changed, since Mao and his party took over the government of all mainland China and established a totalitarian dictatorship, they have retained, adapted, and elaborated these techniques. "The mass line is the basic working method by which Communist cadres seek to initiate and promote a unified relationship between themselves and the Chinese population and thus to bring about the support and active participation of the people." There is nothing particularly novel about the mass line; it is the propagation of the party line, applied under primitive technical and intellectual conditions, to millions of illiterate followers. To vulgarize and in the process distort and corrupt Marxist economic and social analysis was and remains no mean task. The detailed methods are in each case molded naturally by the folkways of the particular people. "This method includes the two techniques of 'from the masses, to the masses,' and 'the linking of the general with the specific,' the basic formulization [*sic*] given by Mao Tse-tung in 'On Methods of Leadership' (June 1, 1943)," writes the most penetrating student of Communist Chinese leadership methods. (215)

Fascist propaganda techniques placed a similar emphasis upon the spoken word. Both Mussolini and Hitler were powerful orators who served as examples to many of their subleaders. Both also explicitly favored the technique; Hitler had supported this method emphatically in *Mein Kampf,* and it became a key policy of the Goebbels operation. One whole section of the party's propaganda apparatus was dedicated to the training of speakers, and there was a deliberate effort made to cultivate oratory rather than written communications. Thousands of men were thus trained to emulate Hitler in developing the technique of rousing the mass assembly, with its emotional outbursts and its vague longings, to violent action against the Jew, the Marxist, and the November criminal.

All in all, the system of propaganda and mass communication developed in the totalitarian systems is of crucial importance for the maintenance of the regime. It may be doubted whether it could function so well without the terror, but it cannot be doubted that as it actually functions it is highly effective. If manipulative controls are carried beyond a certain point, the system becomes self-defeating. Hence the loosening up after Stalin's death was intended to make the anti-Stalin propaganda effective. Now that there has developed a distinguishable "Soviet style of thinking" (161c), there can be some easing of the controls. But "it would be unduly optimistic to assume that the Soviet leadership is to any major degree moving toward the establishment of free discussion." (161c) The principles of thought control, as maintained by Lenin and other Communist leaders, are merely more flexibly applied. In a sense, such thought control dehumanizes the subjects of the regime by depriving them of a chance for independent thought and judgment.

12

EDUCATION AS INDOCTRINATION AND TRAINING

When discussing the nature of the party, we showed how the totalitarian organization extends to the young and even the very young. Octobrists, Pioneers, and the Komsomol seek to organize and indoctrinate the child at the earliest possible age, as did the Hitler Youth and the Ballila. But besides engaging in this party activity, the totalitarians also transform a large part of the educational process itself into a school for their particular ideology. The entire educational process is utilized for the propaganda efforts of the regime and is part of this purpose in ever larger measure as the totalitarian nature of the dictatorship unfolds. (161d) As such, it is a mainstay of the process of consensus formation, as in turn the growing consensus obscures the propagandistic nature of the instruction. This is true even though the educational system, especially on its higher levels, provides an important haven for dissidents and serves as an "island of separateness" from which a certain amount of opposition emanates. We shall discuss this aspect of education in another place (see Chapter 24). Here we wish to consider its operation as a technique for "making" fascists or communists.

In considering totalitarian activity in this field, however, it is important to remember that a certain amount of such "civic education" is found in all political societies. In a well-known study, Charles Merriam explored this problem in its various ramifications and undertook to formulate certain generalizations. (242) It is quite evident that all societies must instill a love of the country and its institutions in its citizens in order to generate that degree of loyalty without which there cannot be effective cooperation. And since no political regime can last without a certain amount of effective cooperation from most of its members, the development of loyalty has been the concern of all governments. This was emphasized by Aristotle, who devoted some significant pages of his *Politics* to the "making of citizens." But there is a vital difference between employing the educational system to develop in youth the ability and inclination "to think for themselves," as the conventional phrase goes, and using education for the purpose of making all those who come within its grip think alike. There can be no question that time and again civic educational programs in free countries have tended to overstep the boundary suggested by this contrast. Patriotic organizations often seek to pervert education into some kind of propagandistic indoctrination, "to develop a burning faith," or in some other way to restrict free inquiry and confine it within the bounds of a particular political (or religious) orthodoxy. But such activities are fairly generally recognized for what they are and, even though they may temporarily prevail under the impact of a war or other crisis, they are at length repudiated by the citizens at large.

In the nature of the case, almost no criticism is possible under totalitarian dictatorship. Teachers and pupils alike are continually exposed to the pressures emanating from the totalitarian party and its associated mass organizations. And when, in the course of the dictatorship's development, more and more teachers become absorbed into the movement, often by formal recruitment into the party itself, the distinction between education and propaganda becomes increasingly blurred, as far as broadly moral and social fields of study are concerned. (58) Education, like ideology, becomes an instrument in the hands of the regime that takes upon itself the definition of the truth. This process reached its extreme point in Stalin's celebrated concern with language. In his *Marksizm i voprosy yazykoznaniya,* Stalin completely rejected the hitherto official Soviet doctrine of linguistics, branding it as "un-Marxist." Until Stalin's 1950 statement, the official line, enunciated by academician N. Ya. Marr, was that language was part of the superstructure derived from the economic basis. As such, it was subject to the same process of dialectical development. Stalin declared that, on the contrary, language was an independent phenomenon, not to be confused with the superstructure. Party propagandists, quickly taking the cue, declared that the Russian language was the international language of the age of socialism, just as Latin, French, and English had been the common languages of past epochs. Similarly, in the case of the now discredited Lysenko theories, it was through the official intervention of the regime, particularly of Zhdanov, that an obsolete environmental approach to biology was proclaimed to be in keeping with Marxism. The attempt to force various fields of culture into line with the party orthodoxy, of course, had very serious deleterious effects upon the educational system. The same was true of the Nazi claim that the theory of relativity was a "Jewish" deviation from truth, and that certain trends of modern mathematics and physics, not to speak of biology, must be rejected because they were in conflict with the race myth of the official ideology.

In order to be able to direct an educational system to respond to such metarational directives, it is necessary to organize it in strict subordination to the official hierarchy. Beyond the general bureaucratization characteristic of all modern society (see Chapter 16), it becomes necessary to force all teachers into membership in the party or into related organizations, such as the National Socialist Union of Teachers, the Fascist Association of Teachers, or the Soviet professional unions for academic workers. But what is even more important is that the entire educational system be permeated by the "spirit" of the movement. From the elementary school to the university, the system must be responsive to the propaganda appeals at the top, as they elaborate and adapt the official ideology. At the same time, it must be geared to creating the "new Soviet man," who would be an idealizing projection of certain key features of the ideology, such as the class-conscious worker in the Soviet regime or the "warrior" in the Fascist regimes. (130; 12; 201b) This notion of the infinite pliability of human beings is, of course, an important premise of the totalitarian emphasis on education as the long-range arm of propaganda. (107b)

The organization of the educational system of the Soviet Union underwent considerable change after the first postrevolutionary phase. The original ideologues, more especially Lunacharsky, were fired with a genuine enthusiasm for educational reforms, which bore a resemblance to what has become known throughout the

West as "progressive education." They believed in freeing the child of the fetters of traditional authority and hoped that a system of complete freedom in the schools would be suitable to the molding of the future Soviet citizen. Sidney and Beatrice Webb, themselves committed to this Western progressivism, have written movingly of this early phase of Soviet educational effort. It was combined with a vigorous attack upon analphabetism, which had been so doleful an aspect of tsarist autocracy. (379b) It is evident, in retrospect, that this phase of Soviet education predates the consummation of totalitarian dictatorship in the USSR.

Marked by a spirit of revolt against the disciplinarian traditions of the tsarist schools, this reform resulted in the shattering of school authority. Pupil self-government was considered the best method of instilling a sense of responsibility in the young; the authority of the teacher was minimized, homework and examinations were abolished, and, in short, it was "child-centered." This somewhat destructive phase ended, however, as early as 1923 and was followed by a similarly unsuccessful era of organized experimentation designed to develop a uniquely Soviet educational process. The new Soviet education was to be a manifestation of the class relationships prevailing in the USSR, and hence was to favor the laboring masses. Discriminatory practices became widespread against the children of white-collar workers, ex-aristocrats, and others. At the same time, efforts were made to give the children the benefits of political education at the earliest possible age. Even kindergarten children were expected to participate in discussions involving, for instance, the relationship of the military to the bourgeoisie. In short, it was "ideology-centered." Traditional subjects, on the other hand, were neglected. (134; 354; 388)

The big change occurred in the early thirties. It was a part of the general process of totalitarianizing the system, marked by the party purges, collectivization, and the suppression of the opposition. It occurred also in the midst of a tremendous expansion of educational facilities, as the following figures for primary- and secondary-school attendance indicate: 1914: 7,800,000; 1928: 11,952,000; 1939: 32,000,000; 1950: 33,000,000; 1954: 29,000,000; 1962–63: 38,500,000. (72)

The number of teachers also grew rapidly: 1914–15: 23,007; 1938–39: 1,270,162; 1962–63: 2,199,000. (464a) By 1932 the regime

had acknowledged the failure of its experimental educational policies, and an about-face was made. For it had been discovered that
the educational system failed to produce the skilled manpower
needed in an increasingly industrialized society. As a result, profes-
sorial ranks were re-established in an effort to give the academic
profession more prestige; salaries were rapidly increased; traditional
subjects (such as history and literature) reappeared; the Komsomol
was called upon to help assert the authority of the teacher; and the
process of political education was rationalized. On the youngest
levels it was abandoned altogether, while it received growing emphasis in the upper academic classes. In 1938 the official, short-
course history of the party, a remarkable falsification of the past,
was made obligatory study matter for the older students. The
purges removed from the scene many nonparty teachers, and the
others were made fully subject to party control through the professional teachers' unions. The internal atmosphere of the schools
became characterized by the strictest discipline and great respect for
the teacher as a representative of the state. Indeed, an American
high-school student would be surprised by the regulations which
bind his Soviet counterpart according to the RSFSR decree of August 2, 1943, which we quote in full. Every student is bound to:

1. Stubbornly and persistently master knowledge in order to become
   an educated and cultured citizen as useful as possible to the Soviet
   Fatherland;
2. Duly learn; attend classes regularly; not be late at the beginning of
   school occupations;
3. Obey unquestioningly the directives of the director of the school
   and of the teachers;
4. Come to school with all required textbooks and writing materials;
   be completely ready for the class before the entry of the teacher;
5. Come to school clean, with hair well-groomed, and tidily dressed;
6. Keep his place clean and orderly;
7. Enter the classroom immediately after the ringing of the bell and
   take his place (one may leave or enter the classroom during class only
   with the teacher's permission);
8. In the classroom sit erect, not lean on his elbow, not sprawl, listen
   with attention to the teacher's explanations and to the answers of
   other students, not talk and not indulge in any extraneous matters;
9. When the teacher or the director of the school enters the classroom
   or leaves it, greet him by rising;

10. While answering the teacher, rise, keep erect [this and no. 9 are also true of university students], and sit down only with the teacher's permission; raise one's hand when wishing to give an answer or ask a question;

11. Enter in a notebook the exact notation of the assignments made by the teacher for the next day and show this notation to his parents; do the entire homework by himself;

12. Show respect to the director and the teachers; when meeting the director of the school or a teacher in the street, greet him by a respectful salutation, the boys by taking off their headwear;

13. Be courteous with elders, behave modestly and decently at the school, in the street and in public;

14. Not use swear or rude words, not smoke; not play any games for money or any objects of value;

15. Take care of the school property; take care also of his own and his colleagues' property;

16. Be attentive and obliging with old people and children, with weak or sick persons, let them pass and give them one's seat, assist them in every way;

17. Obey parents and help them in taking care of small brothers and sisters;

18. Keep one's room clean, and one's clothes, shoes, and bed linen in good order;

19. Always carefully keep the student's card, not give it to other persons, and produce it at the request of the director or a teacher of the school;

20. Cherish the reputation of the school and of one's class as much as one's own.

Students are liable to be punished, including expulsion from the school, for violation of these rules. (65; 189a; 15a)

The internal atmosphere of the school was thus made to correspond to the general emphasis on discipline so characteristic of authoritarian societies.

More recently, increased emphasis has been paid to technical and vocational training, at the expense of literature and the humanities. (15b; 462) At the same time the regime has made it clear that not all high-school students can expect that their studies will lead them to higher institutes of learning. On the contrary, in keeping with the swing initiated in 1940, admission to higher institutes is becoming increasingly difficult, not only through the introduction of fees, but also through the raising of admission standards. This trend has continued; and while fees have been abolished once more, standards of admission have remained high. The striking achievements of the Soviet Union in the field of technical education were highlighted by the sputniks and have since become a familiar argument in the West, cited by all those who seek to improve scientific and technical education in the United States and elsewhere. There has in fact grown up something that has been rightly called a "mythical image" of education in Communist countries. The idea that education is equally accessible to all and that all take as much as they possibly can is hardly a realistic description of Soviet education. (161a) Careful statistical analysis has revealed that educational opportunities are definitely related to the rank of the parents, and as these rank groups (classes) are fairly stable, the differentiation is marked.

Partly as a consequence of this situation, and partly because of the high opinion of education that Communist ideology promotes, the USSR has no shortage of candidates for higher education, and it has become dangerous for all pupils to orient themselves purely in terms of higher academic training. The schools are to instill in the pupils "a desire to join the ranks of the toilers" (430a), and high-school graduates are now being sent directly into industry or agriculture. This is particularly true in the agricultural regions, where many pupils complete their education at the age of eleven and are allowed to work. In the urban areas the minimum working age is fourteen. Basically, it is a matter of getting ahead. "The only substantial opportunity for advancement," a leading authority has said, "is within the framework of the Soviet bureaucracy, which like all bureaucracies rewards skills which are ordinarily obtained through formal education." (161f) For a while there was even a trend toward looking down upon manual work. Khrushchev made vigorous efforts to counteract this trend. Soviet education is widely appreciated by the public, and even escapees have expressed the view that much of this education should be kept. The same sort of reaction has been noticeable among East German refugees. The propagandistic, regime-oriented aspects are evidently not felt to be sufficiently important to outweigh the availability of education for all.

The administration of the educational system is highly centralized, despite the formal autonomy of the republics in the field of education. Textbooks, educational programs, and the ideological line emanate from the center, and the intellectual activity of scholars is closely supervised. Recent years, for instance, saw repeated attacks on many historians in the various Soviet republics for their alleged "nationalist deviationism." On the whole, however, it would be erroneous to conclude that, because of the emphasis placed on political indoctrination, the Soviet school fails in the function of training and preparing specialists, technicians, and generally alert Soviet citizens. Indeed, the conclusion is that Soviet totalitarianism seems well on the way to achieving a fairly high level of schooling as well as an educationally reinforced general consensus.

The National Socialists, although they almost immediately attacked the educational task in totalitarian terms, did not really have sufficient time to mature such a system. Even though they were vigorously aided by the Hitler Youth (see Chapter 5) from the very beginning, schools and more especially universities maintained a degree of passive resistance (see Chapter 24). Nevertheless, the liberal and humanistic educational system, which had been the pride and glory of Germany in the past, was revamped. Physical education was placed in the center, and the kind of personality in which the Nazis believed, where loyalty and honor were invoked to cultivate an unquestioning obedience to the Führer, was not only encouraged but coercively imposed. This unquestioning obedience was given a meaningful underpinning by inducing the pupils to identify themselves completely with the Führer and his regime. The process of building such an identification meant, where it succeeded, that education was completely politicized. Not only the content of various subjects, such as history, literature, and biology, but also their range of priorities of preference were determined by such political considerations as could be derived from the party ideology. The key concept in this connection became action (*Tat*), expressive of a thoroughly pragmatic attitude which may be indicated by paraphrasing an old American saying: "We don't know where we're going, but Hitler does and anyhow we're on the way." This education for action and active obedience appealed, in a sense, to an older strand of passive submission to traditional authorities which the few years of the Weimar Republic had not succeeded in uprooting, despite the efforts of the men then in charge. But it must not be confused with the older concept, as was done by wartime propaganda. For the new activist outlook committed the person who accepted it to the values and beliefs of the National Socialists, in many respects sharply at variance with traditional German views. The identification it asked for could have become the stepping stone for a more independent viewpoint, once the identification had disintegrated; but, while it lasted, the mystique of "service" and "loyalty" made the submission to the "will of the people and of the state," as personified by Hitler, and to the orders of functionaries and officials appear not only as naturally right, but also as "morally obligatory." (192a) This mystique or ideology possessed, of course, strongly militaristic and imperialistic overtones, which helped to convert the entire educational system into a school for aggressive war and conquest.

The Nazis made short shrift of the former local autonomy in the field of education. They at once organized a Ministry of Education, in which all educational authority was centralized. This Reich ministry did not, however, succeed in completing a revolution of the methods and organization of education, which merely became again somewhat more authoritarian and rigid. But it imposed upon the schools a welter of politically oriented subject matter that even in its headings is revealing: family sociology, race theory and practice, genetics, population policy, ethnography, prehistory, current events, colonial politics, planning, civil defense, aeronautics, social aid. (472) It will be recognized that some of these subjects may well be useful additions to the curriculum of a modern school, if taught in the spirit of experimentation and free inquiry. By the Nazis they were made vehicles for the transmission of their ideology of "blood and soil."

The situation in Fascist Italy, though resembling that of Hitler Germany, was characterized by the struggle between the government and the church over the control of the schools. The Fascists actually sought to counterbalance the continuing influence of the Catholic Church in the schools by a compulsory service in the Fascist youth organizations (see Chapter 5). In the course of this struggle, they developed approaches which the Germans never improved upon; indeed in the entire field of education, the Italians were the originators, led as they were by a man of unusual learning and ability, Giovanni Gentile. It must be said at once, however, that his "reforms" were perverted by the needs of the totalitarian dictatorship. One commentator has written that Gentile's reforms were "designed to reduce the domination of the textbook, and of learning by rote, and to bring the tang of actual life, and the problems of conduct, into the schools." And he comments rightly that "this is the crucial issue in education all over the world." (95d) But what the totalitarians did was exactly the opposite. They substituted for the scholarly text of the humanist tradition the domination of the programmatic party textbook, the learning by rote of rituals and propagandistic formulas, all seemingly unbookish — to bring the tang of life and conduct, as seen by totalitarians, into the school-rooms. In short, they revealed the great danger to all education implicit in these well-sounding phrases. Time and again the theme song was repeated: "The School is life, and Italian life is the enthusiasm of faith and Fascist discipline."

The wearisome details of teacher regimentation and pupil indoctrination in Fascist Italy need not be described further. The story is essentially the same as in the other totalitarian regimes. The schools were permeated by the party, dedicated to the task of "making Fascists." (319) There were pictures of the Duce everywhere, commemorative altars, tablets, celebrations, songs, parades, and the ever repeated slogans of Fascist propaganda. The Teachers' Association issued guides to help the teachers keep up the continuous barrage, and the textbooks were full of the same slogans. A learned investigator at the time summed up his impression of these texts in a rather effective manner:

Why are you a Balilla? Why are you a "Little Italian girl?" It is not enough to have a membership-card and the uniform! You must be sincere in heart and educated to Fascism! For example, you must learn to obey. What is the first duty of a child? Obedience! The second? Obedience! The third? Obedience! The Fascist celebrations are explained. The Flag and the rods are illustrated . . . The life of the Duce is retold under the caption: "The Child Prodigy" . . . An entire legend of Mussolini as a war hero is created. The impression is given that the war was fought at his wish and under his direction. (95e; 225a; 367)

The same theme song was repeated over and over again throughout the years from elementary and high school into the universities. And although much rigorous intellectual training of the formal continental sort continued in Italy's schools, the essential framework was provided by this typically totalitarian adulation of leader, party, and system. It seems astonishing, in view of this record, that further reforms in this direction were envisaged by the proposed school reform (Carta della Scuola) of 1938 (225b) put forward by Giuseppe Bottai. Bottai called for an "organic union of party and school through the youth organization" which would "finish forever the age of the agnostic school . . . we decisively want a Fascist school, a Fascist pedagogy — Fascist teaching to create the Fascist man, by the thousands upon thousands." (446b)

How nearly alike in method and effect the communist and fascist approaches to school education are is dramatically shown by developments in the Soviet zone of occupation in Germany. Only the controlling elite cadres and the ideology differed — and these not as much as was pretended. The development of educational reform started with a genuine impulse toward democratization. A number of former teachers and school officials, mostly members of the Social Democratic Party and committed to the progressive educational idealism of the Weimar Republic, were put to work and produced the "law for the Democratization of Education," in 1946. Rejecting the traditional concepts as those of a *Standesschule* (class school), and professing a sharply antifascist outlook, the law provided: "The German school must be organized so as to guarantee the same right to education, according to their abilities, to all youth . . . regardless of the estate of their parents." And, consequently, it demanded that "the form of public education is a system of schools which is equal for boys and girls, is organically structured and democratic." (192b) So far, so good. But as the evolution of the Soviet zone of Germany veered toward totalitarianism, the interpretation of the term "democracy" became increasingly that of the Soviet Union. Democratic school reformers left or were ousted, and the entire school system was permeated with the spirit of the class struggle, that is to say, it became politicized and was made into an arm of the propaganda machinery of the dictatorship. All teachers were enrolled in the official organizations; the students were exposed to a variety of strictly pragmatic subjects related to the tasks of the dictatorship; and loyalty was made part of the test of admission to the higher ranges of the educational system. At the same time, the students were subjected to rigid and doctrinaire discipline. Today education on all levels in East Germany is rated inferior to that in the Federal Republic, and the trend toward predominantly technical work is viewed as educationally doubtful. (192; 257) The continuous flight of technical and scholarly personnel, which reached disastrous proportions before the building of the wall in Berlin, served not only as a striking reminder of the intellectual limitations of the regime, but also provided outsiders with much detailed information.

The experience of East Germany is part of a general process, undertaken in all the European satellites of the USSR, of politicizing education and relating it to the indoctrinating function of the party. In all these regimes, the schools have been subjected to intensive purges designed to weed out both the recalcitrant teacher and the hostile student. The most notorious, but certainly neither unique nor extreme, example was that of the Communist Action Committee in screening and expelling professors and students of the ancient Charles University in Prague, after student demonstrations on behalf of the Benes government. In all of the satellite systems, political loyalty was made the prerequisite for admission to higher institutes of learning. Candidates have been screened in an oral examination designed to test their political consciousness and to ascertain the level of their ideological maturity. A candid description of these practices was given in a short story published in 1955 in *Nowa Kultura,* the official literary organ of the Communist regime in Poland. The author describes the emotions and experience of a peasant boy facing the examining board. Prior to departure from home, his mother pins on him a holy picture, which his father silently removes just before they arrive in town for the examination, and his uncle warns him — "our times are political; remember to say everything as you should, just like we read in the papers." (433)

But admission was made to depend not only on the ability of the candidate to convince the examiners that he is suitable for higher education in the "people's democracy." (457) A special system of priorities was set up, designed to keep out of the higher institutions those whose class origin might make them potentially enemies of the new system. In that discriminatory spirit, Anna Jungwirthova, a member of the Czech parliament, suggested that "if the children of bourgeois origin are healthy enough, they should choose manual work, the kind of work in mines and factories which their class

gladly left to the proletariat . . . There, deep underground, applying the drill to the coal, or in the harsh glare of the foundries near
the molten iron, they will see a new world, a world of versatile
work. There they will find their new higher schools and colleges:
there we will be able to mould and re-educate them into builders of
socialism." (425; 45)

In conclusion, it can perhaps be said that the profession of teaching is profoundly different under a totalitarian dictatorship. In
terms of the ideals of teaching in a free society, this profession may
be said to be totally incompatible with the totalitarian conception of
education. As in so many other fields, totalitarianism totally alters
the meaning of the terms used. The teacher becomes the long-range
indoctrinator, the instiller of an ideology that is intended to subju-
gate the students intellectually and to commit them for the rest of
their lives to a doctrinal orthodoxy. But, unlike quite a few other
features of totalitarian dictatorship, this is not a new notion. Plato
expounded it in his *Laws* and argued that a stable community
depended upon such firm indoctrination (279; 284; 128), and various churches, including the Roman Catholic, the Greek Orthodox,
and the Moslem, have taken this view with varying intensity over
the centuries. But so have the Confucians and Buddhists, and the
Mandarin bureaucracy of the Chinese empire was built upon the
doctrinally fixed teaching of virtue in a manner strictly analogous
to Plato's views. It is evident that the totalitarians in their approach
to teaching and education have returned to what has been the
predominant tendency of the past. Where they differ is in asserting
that these ideological doctrines are "scientific" rather than transcen-
dentally inspired by religious experience. They allege them to be
rational and hence in keeping with the modern world. Unfortunately for them, true science is forever on the move, and even those
genuinely scientific insights that were involved in the totalitarian
movements' original positions have since been superseded by new
ones. It is difficult to forecast what this will do to the stability of the
totalitarian structure in the long run, but it cannot be doubted that
it contributes to their long-range difficulties.

13

THE TERROR AND THE PASSION
FOR UNANIMITY

Totalitarianism is a system of revolution. It is a revolution which
seeks to destroy the existing political order so that it can subsequently be revolutionized economically, socially, and culturally. Totalitarian movements, motivated by the general goals that their
ideologies outline, have, like the great revolutionary dictatorships of
Cromwell and Napoleon, not been content with taking over the
government. But other, earlier, dictatorships have been only concerned with the maintenance of the status quo. Such dictatorships,
after seizing power, usually have devoted their energies to the preservation of the existing order, without setting in motion any further fundamental changes. And when such changes did occur, as
the result of the logic of counteraction, they were more often than
not produced in spite of the efforts of the dictator.

By contrast, the totalitarian movement, having seized power,
seeks to extend this power to every nook and cranny of society.
Thus change becomes the order of the day. This change, which is
not meant to stop with the fulfillment of a five-year plan, is intended to be the task of generations. The process of building communism is not finished with the mere physical liquidation of the
capitalists. The revolution continues, as Soviet leaders still emphasize, with each accomplished task giving birth to another. Similarly,
victory in World War II was not to be the signal for Hitler to sit
down and contemplate the "Thousand-Year Reich." It was to be
followed by gigantic schemes of reconstruction for the whole of
Europe, of vast resettlements, of constant colonization, of a relent-
less struggle for the worldwide extension of Hitler's Reich. The

present is never good enough — the totalitarian movement is always concerned with the future.

This futuristic orientation, to repeat, is based firmly on the totalitarian ideology, with all its pseudo-scientific doctrines and all its actual twists. Whether it be the "inevitable" laws of Marxism-Leninism or the equally inaccurate "intuition of the Führer," the totalitarian movement goes ahead confident in the blissful thought that it is marching in step with history. The constant rejection of the present for the sake of grandiose schemes of social reconstruction and human remolding thus provides the basis for the total extension of totalitarian power to all segments of society.

It is this determination to achieve total change that begets the terror. (401a) Change always entails opposition; in a free society total change cannot occur, because it would bring forth massive resistance from a variety of groups and interests. In a totalitarian society, opposition is prevented from developing by the organization of total terror, which eventually engulfs everyone. Yet total change remains a utopian goal. The spreading vacuum around the leader prevents, as we have seen, a total fulfillment, since the alienation of even the party cadres multiplies that of the population at large. Nonetheless, the totalitarian schemes for the destruction of the existing society are indeed total. In every respect, human life and the nature of social existence are to be profoundly altered. What the ideology originally provided is supplemented by the subsequent operational requirements of the regime. Revisions need not be embarked upon all at once — indeed, the history of totalitarian systems shows that usually a step-by-step program, with considerable oscillations in the use of violence, is adopted. Yet violence that leads to terror is almost inevitable within this context. For life in society is composed of closely interlocking and overlapping groups. It is almost impossible to subject one social group to punitive, or as totalitarians would call it, "re-educative," measures without producing a hostile reaction not only from the group concerned, but also from connected groups, whose vested interests dictate this response. The totalitarians really have no choice but to intensify their efforts.

Thus the repressive measures of the totalitarian regimes, which aim first at eliminating their open enemies, are gradually extended to other sections of society. Totalitarian terror grows until it reaches the limit where it becomes self-defeating. The vacuum, indifference of the populace, and apathy among the workers all operate to set these limits. Actually, these shifts and oscillations are in themselves in line with the terror as process: unpredictability is an essential part of it. It not only becomes a political prophylaxis of the regime, aimed at anticipating political resistance — it becomes the fundamental method of achieving the total goals of the regime and of maintaining the permanent revolution without which the regime would lose its character and probably also its power. (112c) Totalitarian terror broadly understood is, therefore, the vital nerve of the totalitarian system.

This system, because of the alleged ideological infallibility of its dogma, is continually tempted to increase terror by a violent passion for assent, for unanimity. Since history tells the totalitarian he is right, he expects all others to agree with him, thereby vindicating the correctness of his historical insight. This passion for unanimity makes the totalitarians insist on the assent of the entire population to the regime's outlook and activities. Such assent, which finds expression in coerced plebiscites and elections, must not be passive; on the contrary, the totalitarian regimes insist that enthusiastic unanimity characterize the political behavior of the population. Thus periodic elections in the USSR consist of more than the act of depositing a single-name ballot in the electoral box. For weeks before the election, intensive agitation is conducted by millions of party members and Komsomol youths. The population is expected to attend mass meetings, pass appropriate resolutions, and approve the past and future policies of the regime. The election day itself becomes a joyful event — a holiday — in which the masses are expected to celebrate the 99.9 percent support they give to the regime.

Plebiscites are not an invention of the totalitarians. It was an important feature of the dictatorial rule of Napoleon and even of Cromwell. The practice grew out of the revolutionary consultations of the people, which were supposed to embody Rousseau's ideas on direct democracy. But Napoleon went further. At certain crucial moments in his career, such as his election for life as first consul and his assumption of the emperorship, he called for popular plebiscites. These were held openly, with much coercion. Even so, the French proved too independent, and therefore Napoleon personally "corrected" the result to improve on what local intimidation and fraud had failed to accomplish. (104c) The practice was revived by

Napoleon III with comparable results, though there was even greater leniency allowed those who were determined to register their opposition.

These plebiscites of the Napoleons and their imitators resemble the practices of the contemporary totalitarian regimes, perhaps inspired them. However, the official sources show a difference in approach. According to a National Socialist authority, "the meaning of such 'consultation' of the people by the Führer was to be seen in the fact that the relation of confidence between the leader and the people as followers receives tangible political expression on the occasion of important political decisions." Not only is the decision made by the leader, the people merely "registering" their agreement, but the magical unity of leader and led receives its symbolic consecration. Here is one of the roots of the passion for unanimity. Any dissent is like an act of desecration, which must be "stamped out" if it cannot be prevented by terrorization beforehand. Mussolini stated this quite frankly, before the 1929 plebiscite, saying that even if the majority voted no, the Fascists would not step out, that a plebiscite could consecrate but not overthrow a revolution.

The National Socialists used the plebiscite repeatedly to demonstrate a thoroughly metarational state of affairs: a people completely in the grip of passion, the passion of self-assertion and self-realization. They talked of the "boiling soul of the people" (*Kochende Volksseele*) as one might talk of an erupting volcano — a force of nature at once formidable and irresistible. When Hitler, in the autumn of 1933, decided to leave the League of Nations and the disarmament conference, he appealed to the people to express their feelings. The move was designed to prove to the whole world that this demand for "equality of treatment" was backed by the boiling folk soul. But it was also, and even more importantly, intended to commit as many Germans as possible to the folk community of the Nazis by making them feel united in their national passion. The referendum, held on November 12, 1933, produced the desired results: of 45,176,713 qualified voters, 43,491,575 or 96.39 percent participated in this ballot, and of these 40,622,628 or 95.1 percent were reported as voting in the affirmative; 2,101,191 or 4.9 percent as voting in the negative; the remainder as invalid. We spoke of the "desired result"; actually this result was still far from the 99.9

percent figure which was eventually achieved after the technique had been applied again and again. When Hitler, after Hindenburg's death in July 1934, took over all the powers of the presidency, when he occupied the Rhineland (1936), when he forced the Anschluss of Austria (1938), the decision was "submitted" to the people for "ratification" in a "free plebiscite." (104d) Elections served the same purpose in Fascist Italy. There, too, the desperate search for a magic unity through patent uniformity exemplified the totalitarian passion for unanimity. Basically, the Italian electorate at large remained indifferent, while the cadres of the party organization were gripped by a veritable frenzy to seek support. Their "capillary action," to use Mussolini's phrase, became intensified at such times to the point where terroristic acts of violence, large and small, were the order of the day. (95f)

But why should the leaders of such all-powerful regimes invariably demand the support of more than 99 percent of the population? What causes this passion for unanimity? Could it be that this is itself a propaganda weapon? Does a Goebbels consider that a feeling of apartness and loneliness in those who are not satisfied with the regime should be fostered as an effective means of discouraging and eventually completely disorienting them? Such an effect would presuppose that opposition elements believed the results of such plebiscites and accepted the figures as bona fide. Yet why should they, when they distrust all official news?

Such concern for unanimity could, however, be explained in other ways. There is the totalitarians' concern with the judgment of history. It is satirized in Orwell's *1984*, where the totalitarian propagandist of the Ministry of Truth finds himself rewriting history by manipulating the reports, but the satire is quite real. There is the further probability that this urge for unanimity results from the rulers' desire to delude themselves about the actual extent of their support. Furthermore, with overwhelming support the totalitarian leadership may feel justified in committing the most outrageous crimes. They hide, so to speak, in the womb of a solid collectivity. Another, at least partial, explanation of the passion for unanimity is the totalitarian belief in the big lie as a propaganda technique. Hitler, Goebbels, and others are on record as believing that, if you have to tell a lie, tell a big one — the mass of the people will be more ready to believe it because it appeals to their superstitiousness.

Thus the 99.7 percent ayes in a plebiscite compel belief in a highly favorable result, even though the actual figure is assumed to be exaggerated. Evidence from the Soviet experience seems to indicate that the compulsive emphasis upon total support of the regime may actually have succeeded in convincing many, even those who are highly suspicious.

But in the last analysis, the passion for unanimity seems to spring from the pseudo-religious fervor of the totalitarian ideology. The great universal religions conceive of their mission as that of converting all mankind to their faith as the only means to salvation in the world to come. The totalitarians similarly believe in the universal validity of their secular mission. The drive toward unanimity manifested itself in the Middle Ages in the persecution and extermination of sectarians and heretics, such as the Waldensians and the Albigensians, and the later recurrent pogroms instituted against the Jews. Their dissent, indeed their very existence, was felt to be an intolerable offense to the majesty of the divine order that all the faithful accepted. The dissenter in a totalitarian dictatorship is in a similar position; he too is an intolerable offense to the grandeur of the totalitarian enterprise and must be liquidated because, according to the ideology, he has no place in the world the totalitarian movement is bent upon building. The terror involved in these enterprises, though partly intended, may prove self-defeating. Yet in spite of all his awareness of such possibilities, Khrushchev continued in the familiar pattern. Votes in the Supreme Soviet and other bodies were unanimous and acclamatory; dissidents were thrown out of the party, arrested, and in every way harassed; and the atmosphere of terror, though tempered, was in essence maintained. However, it does not seem to have prevented a plot against him. His successor may well consider this experience a lesson to be heeded.

We can see clearly why totalitarian terror and total unanimity are thus interdependent. The passion for unanimity, characteristic of a mass movement, demands tools to enforce it. And according to totalitarian ideology, all "normal" members of the society will naturally be part of that unanimity. Only scattered social misfits — be they bourgeoisie (historically doomed) or non-Aryans (racially deformed) — remain outside that unanimity, possibly joined by a few traitors. The terror makes certain that the masses are not infected, while the social misfits are liquidated. In this way, all the brutal, premeditated violence of the terror becomes rationally justified to the totalitarian.

Totalitarian terror has not only this negative function to perform. Operating within the context of enforced unanimity, it becomes a stimulant to more enthusiastic expressions of support for the regime. It classifies men's behavior according to degrees of dedication, and mere absence of opposition to the regime becomes insufficient as proof of devotion to it. Positive action is demanded, and men compete in loyalty. It is no accident that secret-police files in the USSR stress, first of all, whether a given individual is passive or active. One can of course be active in a totalitarian society only on behalf of the regime. Hence the unanimity desired of all is particularly required of party members. A remark on someone's file that he is passive represents a major question mark as to his dedication. The Communist Party of the Soviet Union particularly stresses the fact that *partiinost* demands active, very active, support of the regime, measured by concrete achievements.

The same was true in the Fascist and Nazi dictatorships. In the election campaign after the murder of Matteotti, there was a great deal of pressure, of violence, of the parade of uniformed force. Whether or not one agrees that these "secured the triumph of the party," there is no question that it is right to stress the extent to which party activity was made the test for membership after the victory had been won. "No compromise, no quietism, no cowardice in the face of the responsibilities imposed by the party" — that sums up the party member's role. (95g) Outward conformity to certain changes in style of speaking and eating were made the test of party enthusiasm, and members who did not conform were not only rebuffed, but at times expelled, beaten, or imprisoned.

In National Socialist Germany, the party was so large that its membership failed to display some of the characteristics of complete dedication just described. As a consequence, the SS increasingly stepped into the role of unquestioning, enthusiastic supporter of the regime. It was the SS in its three distinct formations that embodied, for the masses of the subject people, the terroristic apparatus of the regime, symbolized by the dagger that every member received upon his initiation into this "elite." From one careful analysis (465c), it becomes clear that the SS possessed a more satanic outlook on life and politics than was represented by the ordinary Nazi and SA men. There was at work a distinctly anti-intellectual and antirational trend in the SS which was fully shared by Himmler, their boss. These anti-intellectuals infiltrated the government, the military and economic cadres, and the party, which they sought to control. (202) After the abortive putsch of the underground opposition, the SS even succeeded in taking over the key controls of the armed forces. Its style of "the marching column" triumphed. The SS was essentially an "order." Its attitude was pointedly summed up in the already quoted demand, "Believe, Obey, Fight!" All ideas were reduced to the sloganized framework of an ossified ideology to be enunciated, and perhaps restated, by the Führer at his pleasure. Any dissent, whether in the party or the people at large, must be ferreted out and crushed with ruthless terror. (43; 465c; 261; 191)

Information about Communist China is quite inadequate in this matter of terror, as in so many other respects. But the technique that has come to be known as brainwashing appears to be a particularly vicious form of terrorizing people inside and outside the party. (217a) In any case, the mass flight into Hong Kong, which could only be stopped by violent measures comparable to the Berlin wall, would seem to suggest, and interviews with the escapees confirm, intensive terror on a vast scale. China, like Russia, has of course known terror intermittently in connection with its autocratic past. As one leading scholar has put it: "Terror is the inevitable consequence of the ruler's resolve to uphold their own and not the people's rationality optimum." In all oriental despotism, terror has been employed regularly, sometimes extensively, at other times with circumspection. But this terror was not linked with propaganda and ideology. It is in Communist China, of course, and the hundred flowers soon withered in its hot blasts. (389b) Recurrent statements by Mao and his lieutenants about education, persuasion, and "the light" ought not to deceive one about the psychic terror involved. (217a; 215f)

In both Stalinist Russia and Hitler Germany, the totalitarian terror increased in scope and violence as the totalitarian system became more stable and firm. But it would appear now that this was due to special factors, more especially the character of the leader, rather than to any inherent trait of totalitarian dictatorship.

The degree of terror appears to be oscillating, with a return to the extreme always possible, depending upon personal and situational conditions. (400) But let us review the development in both these regimes. In the initial period after the seizure of power, the major energy of the machinery of terror was directed at the obvious enemies — such as the Social Democrats in Germany, the Mensheviks or bourgeoisie in Russia, the democratic parties in Eastern Europe (see Chapter 14). Only when such enemies are destroyed is the sword of the regime turned against the masses; only then does mass terror gradually develop. Hannah Arendt observes:

The end of the first stage comes with the liquidation of open and secret resistance in any organized form; it can be set at about 1935 in Germany and approximately 1930 in Soviet Russia. Only after the extermination of real enemies has been completed and the hunt for "potential enemies" begun does terror become the actual content of totalitarian regimes. Under the pretext of building socialism in one country, or using a given territory as a laboratory for a revolutionary experiment, or realizing the *Volksgemeinschaft,* the second claim of totalitarianism, the claim to total domination, is carried out. (5)

This proposition exaggerates, for what is a potential development is stated as a universal law. But it is probably true to say that, at the stage where violence becomes capricious, totalitarian terror reaches an extreme. It aims to fill everyone with fear and vents in full its passion for unanimity. Terror then embraces the entire society, searching everywhere for actual or potential deviants from the totalitarian unity. Indeed, to many it seems as if they are hunted, even though the secret police may not touch them for years, if at all. Total fear reigns.

A different and less extreme form has prevailed in the Soviet Union in recent years. It is directed against "antisocial" elements, variously denounced as "hooligans" as "parasites," whose behavior deviates markedly from the forms approved by the party and its leaders. Such behavior is seen as possibly amendable, and hence instrumentalities of social pressure and other forms of psychic intimidation are more promising than physical violence, though this is not excluded and may be quite arbitrary. It remains to be seen how permanent this "stage" turns out to be.

The total scope and the pervasive and sustained character of totalitarian terror are operationally important. By operating with the latest technological devices, by allowing no refuge from its reach, and by penetrating even the innermost sanctums of the regimes (see Chapters 14, 15), it achieves a scope unprecedented in history. The atmosphere of fear it creates easily exaggerates the strength of the regime and helps it to achieve and maintain its facade of unanimity. Scattered opponents of the regime, if still undetected, become isolated and feel themselves cast out of society. This sense of loneliness, which is the fate of all but more especially of an opponent of the totalitarian regime, tends to paralyze resistance and make it much less appealing. It generates a universal longing to "escape" into the anonymity of the collective whole. Unanimity, even if coerced, is a source of strength for the regime.

Of course, it would be a gross oversimplification to claim that in all places and at all times the citizens of a totalitarian regime are subject to immediate arrest and live in a spine-chilling fear for their lives. First of all, terror can become internalized; the people become familiar with a pattern of conformance; they know how to externalize a behavior of loyalty; they learn what not to say and do. Second, reliance on force can decrease as a new generation, brought up in loyalty and fully indoctrinated, takes its place in the totalitarian society. But terror as a last resort is always present in the background, and the potentiality of its uninhibited use does not disappear. "The strain may well be less now," a close and long-time observer of the Soviet scene has written, "than in the harshest times under Stalin. But nobody can be certain that there never will be a reversion to Stalin's methods." (238b)

Terror is not restricted, of course, to totalitarian regimes. Under the more despotic tsars terror had been recurrent in Imperial Russia. So it has been in other autocratic regimes throughout history. It also occurs in nonautocratic regimes where it may prevail in particular "zones of terror," such as that constituted by a racial minority. (403c) But the totalitarian regimes of the twentieth century have brought the skills and insights of modern technology to the terroristic enterprise; they have perfected the "process of terror." The preceding analysis has shown the terror to be a process in which activities of deliberate violence are undertaken by the power wielders to strike general and undefined fear into anyone who dissents. The clearest indication of the nonexistence of terror is the presence of organized groups that criticize the powers-that-be publicly and continually. Where this sort of opposition is lacking, under modern conditions, terror is at work, whether it be crude and open or subtle and disguised.

14

THE SECRET POLICE
AND THE PEOPLE'S ENEMIES

"When the old society dies, the corpse of bourgeois society cannot be nailed down in a coffin and put in the grave. It decomposes in our midst, this corpse rots and contaminates us," warned Lenin. (394) To the totalitarian, this "rotting corpse" of the *ancien régime* is still a mortal enemy from whom the people must be protected. It makes no difference whether the people desire such protection or not. The totalitarian is convinced either that the masses are with him or that they ought to be. And in both cases, they have to be defended from the enemy who makes every effort to impede the process of indoctrination — to teach people to perceive the totalitarian "truth" — and even to overthrow the totalitarian system. This struggle against enemies is a constant one and, as suggested in the preceding chapter, often grows in intensity as the totalitarian regimes become more stable. The regime can then afford greater violence, and initial patience and expediency give way to unbridled terror.

Who are the enemies? A list would include the several categories of enemies, spies, saboteurs, and traitors that the totalitarian regimes pursue continuously. Each totalitarianism, or pseudo-totalitarianism, has its own special major enemy and a whole cast of additional foes who appear and disappear from the scene, depending on the given political and international climate. Thus the Hitler regime had one arch foe: "the international, capitalist, Jewish conspiracy." This conspiracy was said to include Jewish Bolshevism, except for a brief interlude during the Stalin-Hitler Pact. In addition, the enemies of the Nazis were the various non-Germanic races: the Slavs who were to be destroyed; the Latins who, except possibly the Italians, were said to be generally lazy and effeminate; the Americans who were said to be Semitic, negroid, and so on. Domestically, the enemies were the Communists, the Social Democrats, the racially impure (partly Jewish), and the churches, which acknowledged a higher deity than the Führer. This by no means exhausts the list, but it does suggest that the "enemies" are numerous, and constant means to remove them are therefore needed.

In Communist China, the imperialists and colonialists have been in the center of attention, Americans serving as the prime illustration of such hideous aberrations of humanity. This singling out of the Americans is, of course, due to the United States's support of Chiang Kai-shek on Taiwan; since he is unabashedly counterrevolutionary, the argument appears unanswerable. Khrushchev and his lieutenants have also come in for their measure of abuse; not only have they been dubbed traitors to the sacred cause, but also revisionists, imperialists, and so on. The totalitarian propaganda becomes difficult with such shifting of fronts; not only the United States and China but Yugoslavia as well illustrate the point of sudden transformation from friend to enemy, and the consequent transfer of hostile symbols and terms.

But probably the most imposing roster of "enemies of the people" is provided by the history of the struggle of the Stalin regime against its many and varied foes. The entire capitalist order, with its countless satellites, is said to be the enemy of the Soviet Union. On the international plane, it supposedly organizes successive systems of capitalist encirclements and plots, ringing the Soviet Union with air bases and military establishments, planning war and destruction. It is sufficient to read the daily Soviet press to perceive a most terrifying picture of warmongering and conspiracies against the USSR. This, the Soviet leaders assure their people, has internal repercussions also. The last remains of the bourgeoisie, they say, take heart and proceed to sabotage "the great socialist construction," endangering the people. In this field, Khrushchev and his regime were as thoroughly totalitarian as its predecessors. Not only has the abuse of the non-Communist powers (and especially the United States and Germany) continued unabated, with such new terms as "revanchists" being added to the list; there has also been added abuse of members of the internal opposition, as Stalinists, dogmatists, and counterrevolutionaries.

"Enemy of the people" is a familiar phrase in Soviet terminology. It appears in the press, in speeches, in secret archives. At various stages of Soviet development it has embraced former Mensheviks and liberals, disaffected elements in the Communist Party, supporters of the opposition against Stalin, local nationalist leaders, unsuccessful Soviet industrial managers, defeated generals, purged party, police, and military leaders. And as Soviet influence has expanded westward, the former leaders, political, intellectual, and professional, of the satellite countries have also become enemies of the people. Anyone in contact with the "bourgeois international conspiracy" is an enemy, and it is symptomatic that, among the orders issued to the NKVD at the time of the occupation of Lithuania in 1940, one was to arrest all Esperanto students and foreign-stamp collectors.

The totalitarian regimes, however, do not proclaim the total destruction of all their enemies. In the case of some of them, the totalitarians' official purpose is to "re-educate" them, though the National Socialists seem to have been less hopeful than others about their capacity to do this. The enemies of the people have sinned, it is true, but once the totalitarian regime is firmly in power and the environmental situation is different, some of them may actually be redeemed and re-educated. Such a process, of course, demands sacrifice from those concerned, and it was because of this cynical spirit that the inmates of the Auschwitz and Dachau death camps were met by signs proclaiming "Arbeit macht frei" (Labor makes free).

In general, however, the enemies of the people are found to be "incorrigible." Their liquidation becomes the standard practice and may be decreed for large groups of people as well as for individuals (see Chapter 15). The liquidation of individuals is particularly characteristic of the initial totalitarian period, after the seizure of power or the takeover with foreign help, when such individuals still stand out. Much more typical, and indeed unique in its scope, is the liquidation of vast masses of people, categorized in an arbitrary fashion as enemies of the people and therefore unsuitable for further existence in the totalitarian system. Such was the fate of the Jews killed by Hitler's henchmen in the death camps, or of the

Polish officers murdered by the Soviets in Katyn, or of the Chechen-Ingush peoples deported in 1944 to Siberia for allegedly having fought against the Soviet Union.

All of this, of course, demands an elaborate machinery of terror, and the history of the totalitarian regimes is to some extent mirrored in the gradual evolution and perfection of the instruments of terror. In the Soviet Union one of the early acts of the regime was to organize a special body with the task of stamping out its enemies. This All-Russian Extraordinary Commission, or Cheka, was set up in December 1917 and was charged with combatting counterrevolution and sabotage. (441g) The bourgeoisie, it was said, aided and abetted by the Entente, was plotting a comeback, and constant vigilance was therefore required. The abortive attempt in August 1918 by the Social Revolutionaries to assassinate Lenin gave the Bolsheviks an excellent practical justification for the intensification of terror. Mass arrests followed, and the shooting of hostages became widespread. Terror did not cease with the conclusion of the Civil War but grew with the growing stabilization of the regime. The official label of the secret police was changed occasionally, as political circumstances made it expedient: first Cheka, then GPU (State Political Administration) and OGPU, then NKVD (People's Commissariat of Internal Affairs), then MGB (Ministry of State Security) and MVD (Ministry of Internal Affairs), and in 1954 MVD and KGB (Committee for State Security). (89g)

The greatest impetus to the expansion of the Soviet secret police was provided by the collectivization of the early thirties and the purges of the Communist Party and the state apparatus, which operated almost incessantly for a decade, until the Eighteenth Party Congress in 1939. The opposition of the peasants to the collectivization program resulted in the adoption of stringent repressive measures. The GPU, in cooperation with local party organizations, arrested and deported literally millions of so-called kulaks, some of whom were merely resettled in the distant regions of the USSR, and some of whom provided the backbone for the developing network of NKVD labor camps. Police organization naturally expanded in proportion to the demands of this task. The importance of the secret police was similarly maximized by the mass purges, launched by Stalin, to clean up the party and the state bureaucracy by removing former deviationists and potential opponents. These great purges accounted between the years 1933 and 1938 for some two million of the three and a half million party members in 1933. (37e) As the purge became more hysterical and violent, it ceased being merely a party operation, and the secret police became the prime agent. Indeed, the period 1936–1938 is known in common Soviet parlance as the Yezhovshchina, named so after Yezhov, the head of the NKVD. By 1938 the situation had become so strained that, if it had not been for the timely liquidation of Yezhov and his close associates, the secret police might have swallowed up the party.

Between 1939 and 1953 the Soviet secret police was headed by Lavrenti Beria. During his rule its forced-labor operation expanded tremendously and included mass deportations from Poland and the Baltic States. At the same time, the NKVD carried out the "pacification" of territories acquired through the Ribbentrop-Molotov pact, particularly by eliminating the local intelligentsia in the newly acquired territories. After the war, similar policies were carried out in the Central European areas controlled by the USSR. The satellite police forces were then closely linked, through personnel and direct supervision, with the Soviet MVD.

After Beria's arrest in 1953, the role of the secret police diminished somewhat. Since then the secret police has not had a personal spokesman in the highest party organ, the Presidium. The administrative organ for meting out sentences, the Special Board, was quietly abolished. Another change was the division of functions between the MVD and the newly established KGB. This measure, however, was probably made necessary by considerations of administrative efficiency. The vast functions of the secret police were split into two separate entities, very much like the former division between the MVD and the MGB. Under the existing arrangement the MVD is charged with the broad functions of policing the interior and maintaining its elite troops. The KGB performs the more specialized tasks of investigation, espionage, counterintelligence, and the like. Needless to add, this change not only might result in greater administrative efficiency, but certainly makes the emergence of a state within a state — as some have called the secret police — more unlikely. "Informed visitors to the Soviet Union," we are told, "agree that most Soviet citizens appear far less fearful of the KGB than they were of its predecessor organizations under Stalin, but they also report that the KGB continues to be active, subjecting the politically suspect to careful surveillance and relying as of old on networks of informers to report disloyal utterances or conduct." (89p)

As a further safeguard and also to prevent excessive abuse of power, a special division in the Chief Prosecutors' Office (see Chapter 10) was set up in April 1956 to supervise and investigate the activities of the secret police. This Office has since provided considerable protection for Soviet citizens. Cases of such protection have been greatly on the increase in recent years — only time will tell how regularized the situation will become. As of now the secret police continues to play a great role in Soviet life. Khrushchev explicitly underscored this in April 1956 — two months after criticizing the "Stalinist terror" — by declaring in a speech to the Komsomol: "Our enemies are hoping that we will relax our vigilance, that we will weaken our state security agencies. No — this will never happen! The proletarian sword must always be sharp." (441r)

In both fascist movements, the original instrument of the terror, designed to intimidate opponents as well as eventually the governments, were uniformed armed bands, the blackshirts or squadristi in Italian Fascism, the brownshirts or SA (storm troopers) in National Socialism. They committed various acts of violence: broke up meetings of opponents, administered castor oil to their leaders, beat up persons whom they considered undesirable, and so forth. Both movements eventually became concerned with these "revolutionary" elements and sought to subdue them. The Nazis were more successful in this than the Fascists, the reason being that Heinrich Himmler succeeded in replacing the SA with his Elite Guards (SS or Schutzstaffeln) and in turn assumed the control of the police and eventually superseded it, using the SS to do so. At the beginning, the Secret State Police (Gestapo or Geheime Staatspolizei) was the key arm of the government and was under the control of Hermann Goering as head of the Prussian government, but Himmler succeeded in taking it over on June 17, 1936. Just before the war the Gestapo and the SS became two branches of one office under Himmler, by a decree of May 26, 1939, although distinct tasks were presumably assigned to them. The police at that time contained two organizations: the Ordnungspolizei (ordinary police) and the Sicherheitspolizei (security police); both were headed by immediate subordinates of Himmler and key SS men. The Gestapo, which formed an integral part of this complex organizational whole, had by 1936 become part of the prosecutor's office, was removed from judicial control, and assumed theoretical control and operation of the concentration camps. But it actually had little to do with the operation of the concentration camps, which in 1939 were placed under the Economic Office of the SS. The Gestapo perverted the notion of "protective custody" and used it for any-one's arbitrary arrest and confinement in a camp for as long as it wished; it thus became the most dramatic symbol of the terror and of totalitarian dictatorship at its worst. Cooperating closely with it and soon exceeding it in arbitrary violence was the Security Service (SD or Sicherheitsdienst) of the SS. Many of the worst excesses, such as the management of the slaughter houses at Auschwitz, were placed in their hands. (43; 261; 291)

The Italian development was quite different from the Nazi. As we said, the party activists or squadristi remained a factor in the Fascist dictatorship, committed to and committing violence. The secret police, on the other hand, was run as a *state* service, and on the whole tended to oppose the more extreme party elements. The party, in fact, continued to maintain its own investigatory services, while the secret police, organized after 1926 as Opera Volontaria per la Repressione Antifascista (OVRA), operated as an arm of the government not even exclusively staffed by Fascists. It was headed until his death in 1940 by Arturo Bocchini, who never achieved anything like the position of Himmler in the Councils of Fascism (213), thereafter by Carmine Senise. Throughout, the relations be-tween party and police were fraught with tension. Actually, the party continued to operate its own secret-police units and to try and control the political aspects of the OVRA. Its special service of Political Investigation was lodged with the militia, which contained the party stalwarts. It had direct control of the Special Tribunal, which took charge of the cases of anti-Fascists. It also administered, together with the state police, the *confino* or confinement, the Italian version of protective custody, by which persons who had incurred the displeasure of the party or the regime would be confined either to a locality or (in more serious cases) to the penal islands, which took the place of Hitler's concentration camps.

Though conditions were not as serious, they were surrounded by the same air of terrifying mystery and, when combined with the common practice of beating up individuals at random, sufficed to create the characteristic atmosphere of totalitarian terror. Ciano tells in his diaries of the beating of an individual merely because he had used *Lei* (he) instead of the Fascist-decreed *Voi* (you). The police, remaining independent of the party, as well as of the Ministry of the Interior, illustrated well the relation between government and party in Fascist Italy (see Chapter 4).

Germino, in his discussion of the police (120e), draws attention to a passage in Ignazio Silone's *Bread and Wine* which describes the all-pervading tentacles of the terror:

It is well-known [says Minorca] that the police have their informers in every section of every big factory, in every bank, in every big office. In every block of flats the porter is, by law, a stool pigeon for the police. In every profession, in every club, in every syndicate, the police have their ramifications. Their informers are legion, whether they work for a miserable pittance or whether their only incentive is the hope of advancement in their careers. This state of affairs spreads suspicion and distrust throughout all classes of the population. On this degradation of man into a frightened animal, who quivers with fear and hates his neighbor in his fear, and watches him, betrays him, sells him, and then lives in fear of discovery, the dictatorship is based. The real organization on which the system in this country is based is the secret manipulation of fear.

In Italy as elsewhere, party and police shared in this manipulation of fear, though on the whole the system was less total, less frightful, and hence less "mature" than in Germany and the Soviet Union, and in China and the satellites today.

The machinery of terror, defending the "people" from their "enemies" and glorified in totalitarian publications for its heroism and efficiency, relies on a rather elastic criminal code which makes the category of political crime a broad one. As we saw earlier, there occurs in all totalitarian regimes a great proliferation of criminal (penal) laws (see Chapter 10). Thus even industrial failure frequently becomes a political offense for which the guilty ones must be found.

Soviet press articles have continually tended to emphasize the dangers of subversion and to stress the merits of constant vigilance.

In one article, "On Political Vigilance and Watchfulness" published in *Partiinaya zhizn*, the party membership was exhorted to remain ever vigilant against foreign plots to undermine the Soviet Union. Because of the activity of imperialist agents and spies, party members were warned to observe all security regulations carefully, to beware of gossiping, and to guard themselves against drunkenness and greed which would make them susceptible to the offers of enemy agents. But the article also warned against "creating an atmosphere of suspicion against honest Soviet people." (434) Careful scrutiny of the Soviet press also reveals that in all regions there are now operating, parallel to local MVD offices, plenipotentiaries of the KGB. The degradation of judicial procedures, which formerly was the result of all this secret-police activity, has now been somewhat reduced. Yet the Law on Criminal Liability for State Crimes (December 25, 1958) reaffirms a set of very elastic general provisions concerning "counterrevolutionary" activity. When one then considers that Khrushchev himself believed that one should not wait in punishing a thief until one has caught him, but should indict and try him in anticipation (89q), the courts' role still appears — in the political sphere — that of a handmaiden to the secret police. (15)

In serious political cases, the principle of collective responsibility has been frequently adopted by the totalitarians. In 1934 it was officially made a part of Soviet law with respect to cases involving deserters to foreign powers. The totalitarian secret police is furthermore given a free hand in political cases, and the Soviet NKVD and the German Gestapo dispensed "justice" through administrative processes from which there was no appeal. Confinement in concentration camps, or even execution, was the way most political cases were handled. The Soviet secret police often exercised its prerogative of forcibly resettling suspected "enemies of the people" in outlying districts of the Soviet Union, from which they were not allowed to depart. This method was used particularly frequently with those who are condemned en masse in a hostile category, such as the Volga Germans in 1941. These methods have by now greatly attenuated. Recently it was even reported from Moscow that a Soviet court had propounded the principle of the "presumption of innocence" of an accused man. The terror has assumed increasingly subtle forms.

In terms of the development of totalitarian terror techniques, the

Soviet secret police has generally been more sophisticated in its operations and more effective in eliminating opposition than the Gestapo was, especially in relation to foreign peoples. The MVD has been able to penetrate the subject population much more thoroughly with networks of police informers, and consequently the experience of underground movements in Communist nations has been altogether unhappy. Relying more on local cadres than the Gestapo was able to, the MVD has been generally successful in nipping in the bud any organizational moves by incipient opposition elements. And unlike the practices of the Gestapo, in recent years there were no more mass street arrests, shootings of hostages, or public-square executions, which serve only to intensify resistance. Soviet arrests were quiet, usually by night; liquidations were performed in secluded death chambers or other discreet spots.

Besides the enemies of the people inside a totalitarian society, there are, of course, the even more formidable enemies who are suspected to operate beyond the frontiers of the system. Apart from the foreign policy of the regime, there are many activities which the terroristic apparatus of the totalitarian regime engages in to cope with these enemies. First, there are the activities, usually criminal in nature, by which a totalitarian regime seeks to remove, through murder or abduction, outstanding individual enemies of the regime. The Soviet secret police eliminated, so it is generally believed, Leon Trotsky by the hand of a murderer in Mexico. Other notorious cases involve two deserters from the Soviet secret service: Ignace Reiss and W. G. Krivitsky. Reiss deserted the NKVD network in Western Europe because of the purges in Russia, reacting particularly to the execution of Marshal Tukhachevsky in June 1937. He succeeded in evading NKVD murderers until September, when his body was found riddled with bullets on a lonely Swiss road. Swiss police established the fact that he was killed by an NKVD liquidation squad. Krivitsky, an NKVD general and head of its Western European spy network, deserted soon afterwards and succeeded for four years in evading repeated attempts at assassination or kidnaping, but finally died a mysterious death in an American hotel.

A second, and in many ways more dangerous, method is that of organizing subversive groups which, since the Spanish Civil War, have been known as "fifth columns." These became particularly notorious in connection with the Hitler conquest of Europe. In all the countries that Hitler eventually attacked, movements sprang up and were supported by the Nazi secret police, whose avowed aim it was to organize their country on a fascist model and to cooperate with Hitler to the point of surrendering national independence, if necessary, to accomplish this goal. (348a; 165) By this growth of fifth columns, the concept of the "people" is really extended to include a worldwide population of sympathizers. This process of "universalizing" the people is evidently more easily consummated when the ideology itself is universalist and rests upon such a slogan as, "Workers of the world, unite!" But it was also at work in the case of the Nazis, and on a considerable scale. Its psychological effects upon the "enemy" of the Hitler regime were very much greater, however, than was warranted by the actual strength of the movement, and the same terrorizing effect can at present be observed in connection with the Communist cells in the United States. A careful student of this entire fifth column activity has shown that only in the instances of Czechoslovakia and Austria were the Nazi activities a genuinely effective factor in the conquest of the country. But their effectiveness in terrorizing the "enemies of the people" was phenomenal. In Holland, in Belgium, in France, in Norway, in Denmark — everywhere, the "enemy within" was believed to be the real explanation of the sudden collapse of a country that had been believed defendable. (69) This enemy, who when seen from the Nazi side was "the people on the march," consisted of German soldiers and officers, police agents and saboteurs, disguised as every imaginable kind of native, aided and abetted by quislings, as they came to be called. The atmosphere soon acquired under such conditions the eerie quality of a novel by Kafka.

Unfortunately, the case is more serious when the ideology is universalist and when genuine native movements provide a transmission belt for the "strategy of deception." (172) Infiltration by Communist agents is facilitated by the availability of individuals and groups who have become thoroughly alienated from the national community and indoctrinated with ideological notions that make them a ready prey to such approaches. What is even more serious, in the long run, is the atmosphere of anxiety created by such activities and the corresponding mass hysterias and witch hunts they engender. Only a firm and temperate policy of "constitutional reason of state" can provide the desired security. (108)

15

PURGES, CONFESSIONS, AND CAMPS

The purge, which the totalitarian terror has fashioned into a special instrument, may be understood in the distinctive sense of rejuvenating the movement, its cadres and the apparat. In this sense the purge is limited in its application to members of the totalitarian movement. Such purges are consequent upon the imperatives of power and the dogmatic dictates of the ideology as interpreted by those in control. It is the interaction between these two factors which produces the purge as a unique instrument of totalitarian governments. It must be recognized, however, that the purge also occurs at the beginning of a totalitarian dictatorship, when it is directed against those not associated with the movement but occupying positions of power, or against nontotalitarian collaborators of the movement whom it wishes to eliminate as it consolidates its power. Such was the purge of the German bureaucracy in April 1933; such the purge of liberals and socialists in the Soviet satellites after 1946; such was the elimination of most of the liberal and democratic followers from Fidel Castro's ranks, as he turned Cuba into a dictatorship. In what follows we shall deal primarily with the specifically totalitarian purge that recurrently cleanses the ranks of a totalitarian movement, for the other kind of operation is also found in nontotalitarian systems of government.

As we have seen, totalitarian terror maintains, in institutionalized form, the civil war that originally produced the totalitarian movement and by means of which the regime is able to proceed with its program, first of social disintegration and then of social reconstruction. The pulverization of the opposition, both actual and potential, makes room for a coerced public enthusiasm for the official goals and introduces into the system a vigorous competition in loyalty to the regime. The purge, however, is more restricted in scope. Jews or capitalists cannot be purged because by definition they are not part of the system. The purge can be applied only against those who are already anointed, who have accepted the totalitarian ideology, and who are, directly or indirectly, associated with the movement.

The purge, furthermore, is a manifestation of the resilience and energy of the totalitarian movement; though it may be related to and an indication of its corruption, it is not, as is sometimes said, a sign of its forthcoming disintegration. Soviet leaders have at times claimed that the party strengthens itself by purging itself, and the unity of the party has indeed often been strengthened through recourse to a purge. Elements that might challenge the will of the leadership are removed, often brutally, and inner cohesion re-established. The party records of Smolensk down to the late thirties suggest these aspects. (90b)

Purges have generally not occurred when the totalitarian parties are either weak or engaged in internal power conflicts. They have taken place during periods of relative political stability, when the leadership could afford to engage in such an operation. Also, when the purge has been part of an inner struggle for power, its extreme, explosive, and more widespread manifestations appeared only as an aftermath of that struggle and signified the victory of one of the competitors. Being then essentially a clean-up operation, the purge is by no means a manifestation of weakness.

Soviet totalitarianism is much more fully developed in this connection than its Nazi or Fascist counterparts. Because of its longer life span, Soviet totalitarianism has had time to undergo a considerable internal revolution, and it has passed through phases of totalitarian development that were forestalled in Germany and Italy by the outbreak of the war. The Fascist institution of the "Changes of the Guard," however, was a mild form of purge and served the same purpose. In contrast, the Soviet regime has been able to revise radically its ambitious schemes of social reconstruction and has already been faced with three crises of succession. The shift in direction that such successions have entailed naturally increases the likelihood of purges. Clearly, all this did not happen in the Fascist (120f; 24; 37f) and Nazi dictatorships, which to a large extent maintained their original teams intact, though there were of course shifts in influence among the several lieutenants. There was, however, the Roehm purge by which Hitler smashed the smoldering opposition of his leftist following in the storm troopers, incidentally eliminating a number of prominent enemies of the movement, such as General Schleicher. But this purge did not possess the functional characteristics that we have just indicated as those of the developed totalitarian purge. A similar observation applies to the large-scale executions following upon the attempt, on July 20, 1944, to kill Hitler. The extensive resistance movement which had been developing among Germans in all walks of life — trade unionists, businessmen, government officials, university professors, as well as army officers — was a natural consequence of the defeats Hitler had suffered in the war he had provoked and of the certain loss of the war and the large-scale destruction of German cities by bombing. (302b; 76b; 295a; 100) But that those implicated in an armed revolt, especially in wartime, should be executed is an event in no way peculiar to a totalitarian dictatorship, although the cruelty, ruthlessness, and savagery with which the punishments were administered are truly totalitarian. All things considered, the sequel to July 20, 1944, would seem not to be a purge, in the sense here defined as an "institution" of totalitarian dictatorship, but rather a punitive action against a resistance resulting from the rapid disintegration of the regime. Consequently, we have to conclude that no real purge technique developed under the Hitler regime. The explanation may partly be in the personal traits of Hitler, but there are two other factors of major importance involved. On the one hand, Hitler kept a large part of the German bureaucracy in office, forcing them to join the party and thus committing them to the regime. Since such formal commitments could hardly be expected to produce ardent National Socialists, there was no sense in trying to differentiate among them by the typical purge criterion of loyalty to the party and its ideology. (103a) On the other hand, Hitler really substituted the SS for the party as the hard core of his regime, and it is in this sector that eventually a purge might have proved necessary and desirable.

Another significant deviation is China. Once again, it may be too early to tell, because Mao is still in power and operating largely with his original associates. A minor purge occurred in 1955, but it does not seem to have been followed by others. Instead we find party followers and others quite ready to make confessions of ideological aberrations and thereupon to be restored to confidence. One is tempted to speculate whether we do not have to admit here a certain influence of older Chinese traditions, especially the anti-ideological pragmatism. It would seem that "deviations" do not play the role they have in the Soviet Union and some of the European satellites. (217b; 215g) Even so, there have been several purges, and it has rightly been said of the Kao-Jao purge (1954) that it comes closer to the Soviet model for eliminating challenges to the ruling clique. One author writes: "It places the Chinese approach to party organization and leadership squarely in line with orthodox Communist thought and practice," and he adds: "Once the Communist party gains power in a country, it would seem, resort to the purge as the ultimate weapon for maintaining internal leadership solidarity becomes almost inevitable." (346a) There is a difference, but it is a difference in degree rather than in kind. This difference is suggested by another student's observation that "party members are reared in a climate of sin . . . In time all must be expected to be exposed for errors . . . Ideology stipulates that right prevails in the party and in the objective process . . . An individual must be blamed for every failure." (215i) Hence the purge is truly a purification process: "The purged are vilified . . . and are repudiated as the source of failure in entire periods or organizations." (215i) The functioning of the purge, as here set forth, seems to be very general in the satellites, however, and in each of these countries — Poland, East Germany, Hungary, Bulgaria — purges have been a persistent occurrence. Not only were major figures eliminated, such as Gomulka, Slansky, Llaslo Rajk, all prominent Communists, in the early fifties, but massive purges cleansed the rank and file. One in four party members was purged in each of these countries. (38b) This kind of purge, of course, broadly parallels that of the Soviet Union. It all suggests not only that the more accentuated manifestations of the purge are essentially an indication of the resilience of the totalitarian movement, but also that there is a continuity in the purging operations. The history of the Communist Party of the USSR indicates that the leadership of the party, operating in a context devoid of the democratic devices for assuring efficiency through open electoral competition, is faced with the dilemma of resolving the problem of efficiency, while maintaining the elite status of the party. Since the latter aim excludes any open political competition, the problem has to be resolved internally by the device of the purge. This purge then operates continually, on the basis of constant interaction of personal motives, group manipulation, and power pressures. The purge is in this sense permanent. (37) However, it continues to be in part motivated by a genuine fear of actual revolts, as has been shown. (38b)

In specific crises, the purge may be utilized for the achievement of particular power objectives and may, if need be, become quite violent and far-reaching. Thus the period of transition of the Soviet dictatorship into a modern industrial totalitarian regime made the thirties a period of extreme purges. It is not within the scope of this chapter to set forth a detailed account of this period. Suffice it to say that, from the time of the assassination of Kirov in 1934 to the liquidation of Yezhov in 1938, some one million party members were purged, and many of them, particularly the higher officials, were executed. By such means the consolidation of the Stalinist dictatorship was achieved. Stalin was not boasting idly when he declared that, after the party had smashed the enemies of the people, it became still more united in its political and organizational work and rallied even more solidly around its Central Committee. (325a) However, the Central Committee itself lost about 75 percent of its membership. Another very important aspect of the Great Purge was the elimination of a large part of the top army personnel. This final act came toward the end, in 1937, after much of the purge of the party had already taken place. Schapiro has argued convincingly that this delay may have been a deliberate design on the part of Stalin, since it would have been impossible for him to survive without the support of the armed forces. (312f) This author, in keeping with prevailing thought, cannot find any evidence for a plot on the part of the military; but that does not mean, of course, that Stalin did not believe there was one, especially since evidence to this effect was reportedly "manufactured" by the Soviet secret police in collaboration with the Gestapo. (312g)

The overshooting of the mark in the course of the Great Purge led to consequences that were at variance with the purge's real functions. "In the atmosphere of fear and indecision which the purge engendered, it was becoming increasingly difficult to restock the party and the administrative apparatus with replacements, made necessary by the many removals," one authoritative scholar has written. (312c) This experience taught the Soviet rulers a permanent lesson, it is believed. Subsequent purges have not been allowed to go to such extremes. Mao, too, had to call a halt to the upsurge of violence, but even his calling it "a product of feudal society" did not prevent the Chinese peasants from engaging in orgies of bloody revenge during the year of violence, 1952. However, less extreme conditions have prevailed since that time, and, after all, the liquidation of the landlords and other enemies of the people was not a purge in the technical sense. (215h; 376)

Nonetheless, in the Soviet Union after the conclusion of the hostilities in 1945, a series of quiet purges swept the party apparat, as well as the intellectual circles, and reached, after Zhdanov's death in 1948, people of such stature as Voznesensky and other close collaborators of the deceased heir-apparent. Such purges continued on the republic levels until Stalin's death in 1953, which immediately gave them a more specific political connotation. The most striking purge after 1953 followed the aftermath of the struggle for succession between Beria and the other members of the collective leadership. It now appears clear that Beria felt himself to be in an insecure position, probably because of the original implications of the "doctors' plot" of January 1953. At that time, it was clearly hinted in the Soviet press that the "Jewish doctors' conspiracy" against the leading personalities of the Soviet regime was tolerated by the secret police. Beria probably felt that he had to buttress his position in the power hierarchy by placing his own men in key positions throughout the USSR. In this manner he would be able to neutralize the elements which sponsored the January intrigue aimed apparently at him. But efforts to do this provoked a reaction from the other leaders, who in turn felt endangered by Beria's maneuvers. The situation was brought to a climax in June 1953, and Beria was arrested. During the summer and early autumn, many of his supporters were removed from office, and a number of them were imprisoned. Beria and six of his closest associates were executed in December 1953. This episode illustrates both the continuing nature of the purge and its link to the aftermath of a crisis situation.

Let us repeat: the purge appears to be endemic to some forms of modern totalitarianism. It is produced both by the existential conditions of these systems and by the subjective motivations of its leadership. The purge serves to invigorate the movement, which often is clogged with careerists and flatterers. It restores some of its original revolutionary fervor. It ensures what Pareto called a "circulation of the elite." It releases the inherent tensions of a closed system. And it has been noted that the purge evokes from the masses a grim feeling of satisfaction at the sight of the downfall of frequently oppressive bureaucrats and party officials. This "equalization" of suffering makes the burdens of political oppression somewhat more palatable to the average man.

At the same time, the purge is utilized to prevent the stabilization of political forces around the totalitarian leadership and to prevent the development of local autocrats in the provinces, which could weaken the central control of the leadership. An artificial instability is accordingly created among the upper levels of the party, and existing deficiencies are transferred from the shoulders of the leaders to convenient scapegoats. This, in turn, allows the totalitarian leadership considerable freedom of action, not hampered by established group interests. No potential alternatives to the leadership are allowed to mature, while the institutionalized competition in loyalty ensures the perpetuation of unchallenged supremacy of the leadership.

The purge is thus an important and unique instrument of totalitarian government. But it has to be handled carefully; Soviet experience in 1937 shows that it can get out of hand. The purge, as a political instrument, operates with the human element, and the forces of hysteria, the drive for power, and sheer brutality can easily get hold of it. The purge can develop a momentum of its own and reach such proportions as to endanger the system itself. Its supporters may be swept away by panic and their loyalty may wane. This is precisely what happened in the Soviet Union during the years 1937 and 1938, and ever since then the Soviet leadership has been careful to avoid using the purge on a total scale.

To sum up: since the purge operates within a political context, the changing nature of that context influences the character of the purge. Originally, during the first decade of Communist rule, the purge was restricted to the party alone and was handled by party procedures. (395) With the growing totalitarianism of the system and the fundamental social and economic changes of the thirties, the purge increased in scope and violence and became, at the same time, primarily a secret-police function. After World War II, during the period of consolidation, the purge operated quietly in cleansing the party of undesirable elements admitted during the conflict, and it did not erupt violently until the struggle for succession. But even then it tended to be restricted to the upper levels of the apparat. The public learns of such conflicts only after they are over, when official announcements are made about who was purged.

Whatever the future character of the purge may be, many totalitarian regimes will continue to find the purge useful for maintaining operational efficiency, and one of the indictments of the system may be the fact that it cannot operate efficiently without it.

A curious sequel to the purge has been the confessions. "I do not want clemency. The proletarian court must not and cannot spare my life . . . I have only one desire, to stand with the same calmness . . . on the place of execution and with my blood to wash away the stain of a traitor to my country." So pleaded a former Bolshevik revolutionary before a Stalinist court in 1937. (293) And the state prosecutor mused: "Time will pass. The graves of the hateful traitors will grow over with weeds and thistle, they will be covered with eternal contempt . . . But over our happy country, our sun will shine with its luminous rays as bright and as joyous as before." (292)

The confessions, the vulgar abuse by the prosecutor, the verdicts of death, and the announcements of execution — all made for a fearful pattern that dominated Soviet life during the notorious years of the Great Purge. The confessions were particularly mystifying and troublesome. Here were men who had spent their lifetimes in danger, who had faced death on innumerable occasions, but who were now cringing, admitting their guilt, beating their breasts. And yet none of them *appeared* to have been tortured, drugged, beaten. Why did they confess, and why did the Soviet regime want them to confess?

Before an attempt is made to answer this, it must be pointed out that the Soviet techniques of obtaining confessions and staging public trials evolved gradually toward the stage of refinement reached by the mid-thirties. It is also noteworthy that the emphasis on the role of confession in public trials parallels closely Stalin's rise to a dominant position in the party. Thus the first large trials which received considerable publicity and in which the defendants pleaded guilty and cooperated with the prosecution occurred only at the end of the twenties and the beginning of the thirties. In 1928 a political conspiracy against the Soviet regime was "unmasked," and the accused confessed to having hatched crude plots to seize power. A much improved version of such a confession trial came two years later with the so-called Industrial Party trial. In it leading Russian technicians confessed to elaborate schemes of sabotage, designed to upset the Soviet economy. But even here the secret police slipped up on occasion, as in the instance involving two alleged contact men for the conspiracy, who in fact had died five years earlier. Another setback occurred in 1933 at the Metro-Vickers trial when some of the accused foreign technicians repudiated their confessions, taking courage in the intervention on their behalf by the British government. Their Russian colleagues, completely at the mercy of the regime, remained faithful to their confessions.

A number of other trials occurred before the "big shows" of 1936–1938. The growing competence of the prosecution, the more elaborate nature of the confessions, and the instances of dramatic confrontation and confirmation displayed in the trials testified that the secret police was mastering its art. This process generally paralleled the further totalitarianization of the political system and the consequent need to eliminate the last possible alternatives to Stalinist rule. It is this developmental factor which probably explains why similar large public trials were not staged in Hitler Germany. The Germans entered the war within six years of the Nazi seizure of power. It was only after the unsuccessful July coup of 1944 that the People's Courts were let loose with full vengence on actual or potential opponents of the regime, and show trials, with all their terroristic qualities, were staged.

In dealing with the general problem of confession in the totalitarian public trial, it ought to be noted, first of all, that not all of the political prisoners are actually brought to trial. Many of them perish, and only their alleged admissions of guilt are actually brought to trial. This was the case with some of the leading Soviet officials purged both under Stalin and under Malenkov and Khrushchev. The military leaders, notably Marshal Tukhachevsky, were executed after a trial in camera in June 1937, and such was also the fate of Beria and his henchmen in December 1953. The possibility that they may have refused to confess clearly suggests itself. Admittedly, however, a great number of the accused do confess. And they include men who, by normal standards, could not be considered weaklings, cowards, or fools. Therefore the question of why they confessed still demands an answer.

Any attempted explanation of this phenomenon must be, quite naturally, both speculative and inconclusive. It should be obvious that these confessions in a criminal proceeding are a radical extension of the technique of "self-critique," mentioned when we discussed party membership and its personal obligations (see Chapter 11). Such a technique is frequently self-incrimination, at least potentially, and it is therefore easy to see how it might be extended and elaborated where a member is accused of crimes. (238e) State and party can never be wrong, or at any rate not the party. There are sufficient data, furthermore, from former prisoners as well as secret policemen to suggest the basis for at least a partial analysis. (343; 269; 255) It appears that confessions are brought about by two parallel and overlapping processes: the wearing down of the prisoner both physically and mentally. The former technique tends to be more important with non-Communists, the latter with Communists. But both are used simultaneously, differing only in degree of application. They may also be explained in terms of a "circularity of belief." (282a)

The wearing-down process, on the basis of available evidence, consists of four main methods. First, there is sleeplessness, induced by such devices as night-long lighting of the cell, the prohibition against keeping one's hands under the blanket, and the obligation to lie, when trying to sleep, flat on one's back, with the face upwards, toward the electric light. Sleep, under such conditions, is not easy. A second physical discomfort is coldness, caused by poor heating. The cell is never really cold, but always chilly and sometimes somewhat damp. This again makes relaxation unlikely. Third, systematic undernourishment keeps the person above starvation level, but never gives him enough. Food becomes an obsession, obscuring all other thoughts. Finally, there are endless examinations, lasting often for ten hours without interruption and conducted by relays of investigators, all expressing their belief in the prisoner's guilt. These interrogations may often include beating and torture of the prisoner.* Added to this are such devices as the tomblike silence prevailing in the prison, solitary confinement, the occasional screams of those led to the execution chamber. All of these clearly tend to break down the prisoner's physical resistance.

The other aspect, much more important in terms of the actual trial, involves the technique of intellectually pulverizing the prisoner. Through a process of intellectual attrition, the prisoner is gradually induced to question his own judgment, his own memory, even his own motives. He is confronted with witnesses who repeat in detail alleged conversations with the prisoner, attesting to his evil intentions or acts. In time, with the physical factors also playing their role, the prisoner either begins to realize the futility of further resistance or may actually begin to accept the interpretations pressed upon him by the secret police. Once this happens, he is ready for public exhibition at the trial.†

This intellectual distortion of reality is much more likely to be effective with believing Communists than with non-Communists. The communist way of thinking, operating on the basis of the dialectical process, generally tends to make no differentiation between such elements as prediction and preference. Thus, for instance, to predict Soviet collapse is to favor it, as the following exchange between Vishinsky and Radek, at the latter's trial in 1937, clearly shows:

Vishinsky: Were you in favor of defeat in 1934?
Radek: In 1934, I considered defeat inevitable.
Vishinsky: Were you in favor of defeat in 1934?
Radek: If I could avert defeat, I would be against defeat.

* The use of physical torture, according to Khrushchev's secret speech of February 24–25, 1956, was specifically ordered in the mid-thirties by Stalin himself as a method of interrogating "obvious enemies of the people."

† Psychological studies that have been conducted in conjunction with the National Institute of Mental Health give a more scientific validation for the above hypothesis. These studies involved experiments in which the subject was placed in a water tank face down (with an oxygen mask) and left there to float. At first this created a sensation of great delight and relaxation. After a while, however, his mind began to go blank and his thinking became disorganized. At that point, the subject was ready for a process of "feed-in" of information from those in charge of the experiment, and the subject would absorb this information as his own thinking, without being able to distinguish truth from falsehood. The parallel between this and the material described above suggests a most striking and frighteningly real explanation for the pattern of confessions.

Vishinsky: You consider that you could not have averted it?

Radek: I considered it an inevitable fact.

Vishinsky: You are answering my question incorrectly. Did you accept the whole of Trotsky's line given to you in 1934?

Radek: I accepted the whole of Trotsky's line in 1934.

Vishinsky: Was defeat part of it?

Radek: Yes, it was a line of defeat.

Vishinsky: Trotsky's line included defeat?

Radek: Yes.

Vishinsky: Did you accept it?

Radek: I did.

Vishinsky: Hence, since you accepted it you were in favor of defeat?

Radek: From the standpoint . . .

Vishinsky: You headed for defeat?

Radek: Yes, of course.

Vishinsky: That is, you were in favor of defeat?

Radek: Of course, if I say yes, that means we headed for it.

Vishinsky: Which of us, then, is putting the question rightly?

Radek: All the same, I think that you are not putting the question rightly.

Vishinsky: In 1934 you were not against defeat, but in favor of defeat?

Radek: Yes, I have said so. (294)

The prisoner is thus forced to admit that the situation he expected to come about was the one he desired. And having desired it, he was working for it. Therefore, it would not do to explain that one wanted precisely to avoid such a situation, for as Lenin said, "it is not at all a matter of your wishes, thoughts, good intentions . . . What matters is the results." (203e)

All of these factors together, plus the likely elements of threats and promises of deals, made the prisoners confess or, as often was the case, cooperate with the prosecution while attempting to evade some part of the responsibility. (200) But why was the regime so anxious to have them confess? The answer probably lies in the mass character of modern totalitarianism, which operates on the basis of mass slogans and simple explanations. The trials and confessions are accordingly very useful devices in the "educational" programs of the regime; they give the masses easy explanations for all the existing evils, while justifying the might and wisdom of the leadership. To permit the prisoners to defend themselves, to deny the accusations, to permit crossexamination would only complicate matters, would create heroes, would confuse the public. The confession, buttressed by subsidiary testimony, eliminates such an eventuality and makes the public trial into an important educational function of terror. The trial of Gary Powers at Moscow in 1960 presumably fits into this pattern. It has also been extensively used in Communist China. (376)

Confessions have been generalized in the most extraordinary fashion in China. In a way that would have been abhorrent to Karl Marx, the Chinese Communists have invested the class situation with a moral significance. Now to some extent this has always been a tendency in vulgarized Marxism, and it has played its role in the Soviet Union, but never has it been allowed to occupy the center of the stage. "Sin" and "guilt" are not key words in the Marxist vocabulary; they make little sense in a philosophy of materialist historical determinism. But in Chinese Communism they have become the core of "thought control" — the infamous brainwashing that is the heart of the Chinese terror. Once again, we are face to face with the basic issue of terror, namely that it is by no means limited to the dimension of physical violence, but has an economic and a psychic dimension as well. Indeed, Chinese thought control is organized psychic terror. For we have here a conscious manipulation of the environment. It has been called the "psychology of the pawn" — a manipulation by which the victim "has been deprived of the opportunity to exercise his capacities for self-expression and independent action." (217c) It is, as has been shown, by no means limited to the Chinese totalitarians, but they have pushed it far beyond the limit observed in the USSR, Hitler Germany, and elsewhere. It is by all odds the most dangerous form of terror because it dehumanizes the victim.

Confessions are the key to this psychic coercion. Nowhere else has totalitarian terror so perfected this instrumentality. It is practiced in two contexts: the prison and the revolutionary university. In both, the inmate is subjected to a constant barrage of propaganda and ever repeated demands that he "confess his sins," that he "admit his shame," and so on, coupled with enforced exhibitionism. Based upon the notion that only the believers in the official ideology are human, whereas their opponents and even doubters are subhuman, that there are people and nonpeople, such coercion goes to the length of pronouncing the death sentence upon a victim unless he becomes a "new man." But physical death is actually less formidable than the constant questioning and reprimanding, inquiring and condemning that goes on day and night under the direction of the thought controllers. Confession becomes a cult, based upon a demand that the victim "confess to crimes he has not committed, to sinfulness that is artificially induced, in the name of a cure that is arbitrarily imposed." (217d) Such confessions involve a total exposure by forcing a man into a "symbolic self-surrender." Thus, the terror-induced confession embodies the "claim to total ownership of each individual self" and is the penultimate projection of totalitarian "totalism." Confessions — and an elaborate confession completes the process of "reform" in both prison and university — serve the purpose of destroying the individual and his sense of identity. "Individualism" in the sense of any attempt to retain a limited feeling of self-identity is in fact looked upon as one of the worst crimes. To sum up the whole gruesome process in the words of its most penetrating analyst: "Combining personal anecdote, philosophical sophistication, and stereotyped jargon, the confessions followed a consistent pattern: first, the denunciation of one's past — of personal immorality and erroneous views; then a description of the way in which one was changing all of this under Communist guidance; and finally, a humble expression of remaining defects and a pledge to work hard at overcoming them with the help of progressive colleagues and party members." (217e)

Similar confessions are notably lacking in the case of the fascist dictatorships. It is a subject of speculation why this should be so. Do they belong to a later phase of totalitarianism? Are they part of the peculiar dogmatic fanaticism of the Bolshevik creed? These and other explanations have been given, but all we know for sure is that they did not take place under fascism, but have occurred in the European satellites, though less frequently. An interesting case has been advanced for the proposition that something analogous happened in Tudor England. (420)

The concentration camp is another significant and familiar feature of totalitarian terror. It is one of the unique aspects of these systems, not paralleled in the traditional coercive institutions of constitutional or absolutist regimes. In a sense, one of the tests of the "totalitarian" character of a regime is the presence or absence of concentration camps. These camps are designed to accommodate those social elements that, for one reason or another, are allegedly incapable or unwilling to adjust themselves to the totalitarian society (see Chapters 13, 14). In the concentration camp they are to be given an opportunity to redeem themselves and to make themselves useful again to society. That most of the victims perish in this process is, according to the totalitarian point of view, merely incidental.

According to Eugen Kogon, who has written much the most penetrating study of the Nazi concentration camp, these camps (called Kazett, from *Konzentrationslager*) were the sharpest expression of the system of terror, and at the same time its most effective method. (178; 304) He believes that their purpose was to eliminate all actual, potential, and imagined enemies of the regime, by first separating them, then humiliating, breaking, and destroying them, killing ten innocents rather than allowing one "guilty" one to escape. He allows that there were a number of collateral purposes; among these he notes that the camps were intended to provide a training ground for the Himmler "elite" — men who would learn how to be hard and ruthless, specialists in brutality, whose instincts of hatred, domineering, and exploitation would thus be developed. There also was the purpose of providing the SS leaders themselves with readily available slaves who would serve their masters in cringing terror as long as it pleased them to keep them alive.

The camps started from relatively modest beginnings, some dozen of them, with no more than about one thousand inmates each. The acts of revolting torture, sufficiently attested to even at the very outset, did not constitute a system at first. They were the result of brutality of individual guards, but Heinrich Himmler and his SS soon caught on and began to systematize these practices into an elaborate ritual. They were administered from one center, under the direct control of Himmler. Eventually, there were three layers of camps, the labor camps, which were relatively the mildest, a much more severe second group, and finally those that bore the name of "bone mills," which very few people survived. But these distinctions are really not of very great importance. For example, Dachau, which always remained in Group I as a labor camp, actually was among the worst.

It is still not possible to be at all definite about the number of persons placed in camps over the years. Kogon is convinced that millions went through the camps in the course of the Nazi regime.

Since at least 3.5 to 4.5 million were killed in Auschwitz alone, 8 to 10 million does not appear to be a fantastic figure. But probably there were never more than about one million in the camps at any one time, considering that even the large original camps, such as Dachau, Buchenwald, and Sachsenhausen rarely had more than 100,-000 inmates. It seems that toward the end, Himmler at one point mentioned a figure of about 600,000 in a decree, at a time when approximately half a million inmates had already been liberated by the Allied armies.

What were the main categories of human beings placed in these camps? According to the SS conception, there were four main groups: (1) political enemies of the regime, (2) members of inferior races and persons who seemed biologically inferior, (3) criminals, and (4) asocial persons. It is evident that these were quite flexible categories, which were by no means interpreted by courts or judicial bodies but simply by discretion of the SS leadership. Under (2) we find, until 1939, largely Jews and people related to Jews. Criminals were not necessarily men who had committed crimes, but also those who might commit or had in the past committed crimes. Among the "asocials" there were, besides tramps, drunkards, pimps, and the like, many who had done nothing worse than being late for work and offending some Nazi. Among the political enemies of the regime, a great variety of people, including dissident Nazis, clergymen (especially Catholics), and Jehovah's Witnesses were found.

Kogon, Rousset, and others have shown that the SS camp directors and their minions depended to a very considerable extent upon the inmates themselves for the running of the camps. They developed the art of setting one group against another: communists were encouraged to maltreat socialists, and the criminals more especially were given frequent opportunities to practice their various "arts" upon fellow prisoners. In response to this system, a variety of secret organizations developed among the prisoners, and extensive defensive mechanisms were worked out to cope with the gruesome realities of camp life. Compensating, in a higher sense, for the depravity of the SS and its helpmates in the camps, there developed opportunities for selfless comradeship and heroic sacrifice. The world of the camps, so incredible from the viewpoint of a liberal and civilized society, reduced human beings to their ultimate essence; unspeakable viciousness, corruption, and debauchery were counterbalanced by acts of saintliness and a display of the finest and most noble qualities in man.

Soviet labor camps began to develop on a large scale during the thirties in order to accommodate the hundreds of thousands of deported kulaks. These dispossessed peasants were herded together into large-scale makeshift camps and were used as cheap labor in the construction of such projects as the Stalin canal in the semi-Arctic north. Needless to say, the mortality rate was high. Parallel to this came the gradual increase in the number of political prisoners, starting first with the oppositionist elements in the party and then embracing the many thousands arrested during the purges of the thirties. Soviet concentration camps gradually took on more of a political character and became the main repositories for imprisoned alleged enemies of the Soviet system. During the war, these prisoners were joined by hundreds of thousands of arrested Poles, Balts, Finns, and — later on — other Central Europeans, and even a sprinkling of Americans and Britons. The only exceptions to this practice were those executed outright, such as the four thousand Polish officers massacred in the Katyn Forest, and those considered important enough to be put into solitary confinement in the main secret-police prison, Lublyanka, in the center of Moscow. (185)

In theory, Soviet concentration camps were styled "corrective labor camps," designed to "purify" the prisoner and to train him for acceptance as a Soviet citizen. All accounts of former prisoners, however, emphasize that the mortality rate was very high and that few political prisoners were released. (144; 124) As a consequence, consignment to camp meant for most victims a dragged-out death sentence. The camps themselves were run by the Main Administration of Corrective Labor Camps (GULAG) of the MVD. It was the MVD that set the work quotas, standards of living, internal regulations, and disposition of prisoners. GULAG also made an important contribution to the Soviet state economy. According to the Soviet "State Plan of Development of the National Economy of the USSR for 1941," captured by the Germans, the secret-police share of the projected capital investment amounted to about 18 percent of the total planned. (89h) This did not include such well-known MVD undertakings as the lumber industry in the north or goldmining in Kolyma. Clearly, such vast enterprises demanded many prisoners, and the various estimates of forced labor used in the USSR range in the millions. (393) Greatly reduced in number and size, and renamed "corrective labor colonies," they are now administered by GUITK.

Another striking feature of the Soviet forced-labor system was the fact that not infrequently the secret police hired out its prisoners to local agencies for the purpose of carrying out some local project. When this happened, elaborate contracts were drawn up between the two parties, specifying all the details and setting the rates at which the secret police is to be paid. At the conclusion of their task, the prisoners, or more correctly the slaves, were returned to the custody of the secret police.*

After Stalin's death in 1953, and particularly after Beria's arrest in June of the same year, a wave of unrest swept the camps, culminating in a serious outbreak in the Vorkuta coalmining camps in the north. The regime successfully quelled the revolts, or strikes, but viewed them with sufficient seriousness to warrant some reforms. The administration of the camps was then taken over by the Ministry of Justice, and efforts were made to improve their internal conditions. The criminal prisoners were no longer allowed to terrorize and suppress the political prisoners, and those prisoners who overfulfilled their work norms had their sentences shortened accordingly. That in turn, of course, helped to raise the productivity of the prisoners, a matter not alien to the interests of the regime.

In the fall of 1955 the post-Stalin regime engaged in the first large-scale releases of political prisoners. The scope of this amnesty is not certain; it did not, as far as is known, result in the complete liquidation of the labor camp, and that odious institution still plays its role in the Soviet arsenal of terror. Nonetheless, a number of political prisoners arrested during the purges regained their freedom. Some of them included old Bolsheviks, who had spent twenty years behind barbed wire. Also many foreign prisoners were released. Among the leading groups were two very dissimilar ones: Polish underground fighters seized by the Soviet secret police in 1945 and 1946 and who, after fighting the Nazis for five years, spent their postwar years doing forced labor; and about 10,000 German prisoners, classified by the USSR as "war criminals." The number

---

* A vivid picture of life in these camps is given in Solzhenitsyn's *One Day in the Life of Ivan Denisovich*.

of people released is, however, small compared to the hundreds of thousands of prisoners who probably perished.

Purges, confessions, and camps are thus part of the equipment of a developed totalitarian system. Camps represent the great and fearful unknown. The occasional public trial, with the mystifying spectacle of the confession, further enhances this feeling. These devices have been developed to the highest point in the Communist dictatorships, where social changes, mass elimination, and succession struggles within the party went the furthest. But available evidence suggests that, had the Nazi regime endured beyond Hitler, the succession struggle and ideological conflict among Bormann, Goering, and Himmler would also have produced large-scale purges in their aftermath. For the totalitarian system, the purge provides the mechanism of elimination and stimulation within the movement; the confessions are useful to vilify the opposition and to underline the infallibility of the leadership; the camps provide cheap labor and a tool for the liquidation of the "enemies of the people." All three make their contribution to the terror by which the totalitarian regime reinforces the propaganda that in time produces the consensus any government requires in the long run, whether it be democratic or autocratic, constitutional or totalitarian.

As we pointed out at the start of our analysis, such consensus, while providing a basis for the authority of a totalitarian leadership, need not be a sign of democratization, as is often assumed. It is better to think of it in terms of "sources of support" in contrast with "lessening of hostility." (161m) Obviously, there is bound to be a certain amount of consensus, at any one time, among the populace of any government; even the Allied military government achieved some "consensus" among subject Germans. Such consensus is likely to be shifted in content and in degree. It is subject to considerable oscillations, even among party members. There was, for instance, much more consensus behind Hitler's regime among Germans before he started his war, more when he was victorious than when he was encountering defeat. Oscillations of this sort have been observed in the Soviet Union; it was greater when Khrushchev could announce the sputnik exploits than when he had to inform the people of rising food prices. Similarly in Communist China the euphoric consensus among party men when the regime first entered upon the building of communes has given way, according to their own reports, to much resentment and apathy. Besides these shifts, there are marked differences between regimes in this respect. The consensus is greater in the Soviet Union than in China, greater in Bulgaria than in Poland.

Indeed, consensus in some of the satellites is limited to very specific issues: Gomulka's nationalist posture presumably was applauded by most Poles, even those who were sharply opposed to his regime. Similarly, consensus in Yugoslavia clearly supports Tito's policy of national independence, but how far it extends beyond that is debatable. The fact that the regime considered it necessary to jail a dissenter and opponent, Djilas, because he took a critical view of its "class character" suggests that consensus cannot be very great. Generally speaking, consensus permits moderation and even tolerance. The great Balfour once put it very succinctly when he said of Britain: "We are so fundamentally at one, that we can safely afford to bicker." This saying applies equally to other mature democratic societies, but it does not mean that, when a political community is fundamentally at one, it will permit bickering; it means even less that the degree of actual dissent is roughly proportional to the degree of consensus or oneness. On the contrary, if the consensus is dogmatically based and ideologically rationalized, widespread consensus may manifest itself in popularly acclaimed witch hunts. The year of violence in Communist China (1952) was based upon a presumed widespread consensus, and this is as paradigmatic for such a situation as Hitler's "boiling folk soul," even though both may have been largely a figment of the leader's imagination. The kind of manipulated consensus that the totalitarians are able to create is a far cry from the sort of basic agreement that allowed Lincoln to counsel a friend to put his trust in the people.* But it is a useful means of ensuring support for the regime, enhances its legitimacy, and is apt to increase as long as the regime is successful in raising the standard of living. Indeed, the passion for unanimity discussed earlier is undoubtedly in part motivated by the desire to achieve a minimum of consensus. Purges, confessions, and camps are the tools of coercion by which the recalcitrant are brought into line and made to acknowledge the claims of the regime.

* "Remember, Dick, to keep close to the people — They are always right and will mislead no one." Carl Sandburg, *Abraham Lincoln: The War Years* (1939), III, 384.

V

The Directed Economy

16

TOTALITARIAN BUREAUCRATIZATION

Whether the battle cry is "expropriation of the exploiters" or "the common good before selfishness," * the totalitarian dictatorships develop a centrally directed economy as the sixth feature in their syndrome of traits. This economy calls for an increasing number of public officials to attend to all the various functions which such an economy needs. But in addition to the appointment of all the actual public officials, there takes place a bureaucratization of large segments of organizational activity beyond the formal government system. The Germans proclaimed *Gleichschaltung,* that is to say, coordination and subordination of all organizations, as one of the goals of the regime. By this they meant that, in accordance with the leadership principle, the "leaders" of all organizations should be appointed by the government and these chosen leaders should then wield the same kind of absolute authority within their organization that the leadership principle called for all up and down the line of the official hierarchy. The idea of the corporative state served a similar purpose in Italy, as far as the economy was concerned; all organizations, whether business corporations or labor unions, were made part of one hierarchical structure with the Duce at the head. It is evident that by such a setup the functionaries of almost all organizations do in fact become public bureaucrats; the difference between them and government officials is not one of formal prerequisites, such as pension rights and status, but rather of actual political function. When looked at in this perspective, the functions of a business manager in a fascist-controlled corporation and a

---

* *Gemeinnutz geht vor Eigennutz* is not, in its alliterations, readily translated; "common benefit goes before (precedes) individual benefit," though literal, is weak.

factory manager in a Soviet trust are very similar. They are both dependent functionaries of a vast governmentally controlled apparatus. In short, we have before us what may be called total bureaucratization. (74c)

And yet there are conflicting trends. In terms of a dynamic concept of bureaucracy, such as is implicit in Max Weber's well-known analysis (308b; 274; 381; 244a), the conclusion is suggested that totalitariansim, while extending bureaucracy, also changes and perverts it. The six aspects or elements that recur in a developing bureaucracy of the modern Western type are centralization of control and supervision (hierarchical aspect), differentiation of functions, qualification for office, objectivity, precision and continuity, and secrecy (discretion). The first three are organizational aspects or criteria, the last three behavioral ones. We can speak of them as criteria when we employ them as measuring rods for determining the extent of bureaucratization; for all of them may exist to a greater or lesser degree, and it is this that determines the degree of bureaucratization. They are never fully attained, of course; in the nature of the case, in actual administration there could not be complete centralization, complete differentiation, and so forth.

What we find under totalitarian dictatorships is, however, a marked deviation and a retrogression where previously a higher degree of bureaucratization existed. Centralization of control and supervision yields to a conflict between the bureaucracies of party and government; centralization is superseded by local autocrats, like the Gauleiters; and party loyalty replaces professional qualification for office, though from the totalitarian regime's standpoint such ideological commitment constitutes a kind of qualification for office. (256a)

In terms of such a concept of developed bureaucracy, then, totalitarian systems do appear to be retrogressive. The subjection of the bureaucracy to party interference and controls, the insistence that not only those in key policy posts, but officials up and down the line, and in the fascist case those in the "coordinated organizations," be active members of the totalitarian party (see Part II and Chapter 24), all argue that totalitarian dictatorships are less rational and legal and hence less fully developed from a bureaucratic standpoint than, for example, the governmental services of some absolute monarchies in the eighteenth century.

In the Soviet Union, the supremacy of the party, described earlier, had created parallel governmental and party bureaucracies. It has been succinctly stated that "the development of the Communist Party apparatus as an extension of the long arm of the dictator constitutes one of the most impressive and formidable organizational achievements of modern totalitarianism." (89i) Its members become the apparatchiki. Ever since Stalin's appointment as secretary of the party, its inner apparatus has expanded at a steady pace, so much so that today the Secretariat of the Central Committee constitutes an imposing superbureaucracy, with its tentacles reaching into every aspect of Soviet life. It was by skillfully manipulating the appointing organs of the Central Committee that Stalin succeeded in outmaneuvering his opponents and solidifying his hold on power. Under Stalin's management the apparat became the key instrument of political power in the USSR. It is indeed significant that the Soviet leaders, who have come into prominence since Stalin's death, Khrushchev, Bulganin, Malenkov, Brezhnev, Kosygin, all came up through the apparat. And, again, it was by virtue of his control of this apparat as party secretary that Khrushchev emerged after 1955 as the top man in the Soviet hierarchy.

The apparatchiki, then, are the important bureaucrats of the Communist Party. Their counterparts, more numerous as time goes on, exist also on the lower levels of the party bureaucracy. At the top there are the heads and workers of the various sections of the Central Committee that supervise the ministries and control the party operations; then there are the republic party secretaries with their staffs and workers; there are the secretaries of the provincial and regional party committees and their staffs; there are the secretaries and staffs of hundreds of city party committees; there are the secretaries and staffs of thousands of district party committees (441h; 89j); there are finally the tens of thousands of party workers who head the primary party organizations on the collective farms, in government institutions, and in military units. A calculation made in 1956 put the number of party secretaries on all levels (and it is to be remembered that each party committee above the primary level has more than one secretary) at about 327,000. (409c) This figure would have to be increased appreciably if the sizable number of committee members were added to it. They are all part of the web spun around the Soviet Union by the Secretariat in Moscow.

The party bureaucracy operates parallel to, and also penetrates, the state bureaucracy, and its rapid extension has created the characteristic problems of bureaucratization, including status rigidity and privileges. Already by 1926 the *Large Soviet Encyclopedia* gave the total governmental service as 2,500,000 people. By 1939, it had grown to some 10,000,000. (252c) This process of expansion, however, was not without its growing pains, and the history of the Soviet bureaucracy is one of constant attempts to adjust to the theoretical and political requirements of the regime.

Prior to their seizure of power, the Bolsheviks proclaimed their violent determination to smash the existing state machinery. The state as an instrument of class oppression had to go, and the bureaucracy, being its most direct manifestation, bore the main brunt of the attack. Lenin soon found himself attempting to rationalize the need not only for a state (see Chapter 7), but also for a bureaucracy. He did so both by denying that the Bolsheviks had a bureaucracy and by admitting that they had bureaucrats but, of course, bureaucrats devoted to and recruited from the people: "Soviet power is a new type of state, in which there is no bureaucracy, no police, no standing army, and in which bourgeois democracy is replaced by a new democracy — a democracy which brings to the forefront the vanguard of the toiling masses, turning them into legislators, executives and a military guard, and which creates an apparatus capable of re-educating the masses." (205f) Trotsky was one of the first to attack this trend, but he did so without comprehending its long-range significance. He thought of it as a temporary development, something that was attributable to Stalin and other malefactors. Once they were removed, he said, the movement would return to its original spontaneity (357a; 312d). This analysis was mistaken; bureaucratization was inherent in the Communist totalitarian conception of party, government, and state. Indeed, as the Lenin quotation shows, it long antedated the controversy between Stalin and Trotsky and it outlived it.

The setting up of this Soviet bureaucracy created immediate problems. Personnel recruitment was the obvious one. A large number of tsarist civil servants had to be kept, lest the machinery crumble, until new cadres were trained. The commanding positions were, of course, taken over by party zealots, but the regime remained uneasy, and it was not until two decades later that the bureaucracy became fully sovietized. The second problem, at that time seemingly more urgent, was how to maintain the egalitarian facade, an intrinsic part of the doctrine, in the face of the requirements of bureaucratic organization and, more especially, of the hierarchical principle. Workers of the newly set-up People's Commissariat of Foreign Affairs at first thought that now they would decide collectively on the conduct of foreign affairs. Such idle dreams, however, were soon dispelled. Lenin, using Engels as his authority, blandly stated that "any demand for equality which goes beyond the demand for abolition of classes is a stupid and absurd prejudice." (203a) Centralization of command and hierarchy, therefore, were not deemed to be incompatible with equality.

The problem inherent in these contradictions was not easily solved. Sizable segments of the party opposed the rapidly developing tendencies toward centralization of power, and the early party congresses became forums for frequently violent discussions on the merits and theoretical orthodoxy of unity of command (*edinonachalstvo*) versus collegiate management, the latter being a concession to the demands for collective decision making. Collegiate management, although the principle was disavowed at the Ninth Congress in 1920 and although the practice was dropped quite rapidly on the lower levels, persisted until the thirties, when the Stalinist drives made necessary the complete centralization of command. (88c) For two decades and a half after that, the Soviet bureaucracy operated in an atmosphere of strict discipline and as a highly stratified hierarchy. Only in the post-Stalin era, and more especially under Khrushchev, was the trend reversed and a deliberate effort made to decentralize; but the difficulties encountered have not allowed it to go very far. (89aa)

During the early years of Soviet power, the party bureaucracy remained suspicious of the state bureaucracy, particularly of its former tsarist civil servants. As a safeguard, the Party Control Commission, set up by the Tenth Party Congress in 1921 as a check on the operations of the party bureaucracy, began to look into the operations of the state bureaucracy too. Efforts were also made to promote into it, as rapidly as possible, loyal party members to replace the tsarist holdovers kept purely for expediency. For instance, in 1930, out of some 450,000 civil servants screened for security, about 30 percent were dismissed. (419b; 37h) As late as 1932,

however, some Soviet administrations still had staffs about 50 percent of which were made up of former tsarist bureaucrats. (252d) It
was not until the purges of the Yezhovshchina that this cleansing
process could be considered complete. At that time, a large number
(running into hundreds of thousands) of young technicians and
students were promoted to responsible state posts. (325b)

Since that time the Soviet bureaucracy has been staffed essentially
with loyal party members or individuals screened by the party and
considered to be sympathizers. Yet even this "reliable" type of
bureaucrat remains subject to intensive control. As one leading
authority has described it: "The typical Soviet administrator functions in an environment in which every major decision is subject
to the possibility of check, recheck, and countercheck." (89k)
Whether it is planning, or staffing, or finance, there is a control
body to supervise and control him. His efficiency, his legality, his
loyalty are subject to constant surveillance.

Political loyalty is the primary criterion for assessing a governmental bureaucrat's competence. This is not to say that other more
objective standards are entirely ignored, but the political assessment
is the primary and fundamental prerequisite to a favorable report
on the performance of such a bureaucrat. The fact that such assessments are made primarily by outside party organs necessitates constant readjustment between the party and the state bureaucracy.
There has always been a tendency, which the party officially com-
bats, for the government bureaucrats to "pass the buck" to party
officials and thus avoid responsibility for decision making. (90c)
The party organs as a result were swamped with minutiae. Some of
the proceedings of party committees indicate that even the most
obviously bureaucratic concerns were being usurped by party organs. Local party leaders, instead of attending to party affairs,
found themselves involved in such matters as gasoline for tractors,
leaves of absence for bureaucrats, and housing conditions. Party
officials also decided on local bureaucratic appointments, which had
to be cleared with the party committee. The party leadership, even
in Stalin's day, could not help being concerned over this trend and
made repeated efforts to minimize such tendencies. The party organizations were exhorted not to intervene directly in governmental
operations, but merely to set an example by maintaining and insisting upon high standards of performance. Party functionaries were

to lead and to check but not to usurp the functions of duly constituted governmental bodies. The problem continues to the present
time. The increased role of the party under Khrushchev, in combination with the desire to decentralize and to buttress the autonomy of managers, intensified the issue. In a publication of the
Central Committee a typical article demanded: "Raise the organizational role of the Party Apparatus." The article specifically attacked
the tendency of some members "to work for others" and to turn
party workers into office clerks, instead of keeping them on the
level of organizers. (434c) The problem seems to be inherent in the
system itself, and it is doubtful that it can ever be resolved by a
totalitarian system, which puts a premium on a politicized bureaucracy. In 1961, the secretary of a district party committee published
the following reflections: "Looking at it from the outside you
would never make out what I am — the secretary of the party
committee or the chairman of the Ispolkom [Soviet executive com-
mittee] or an employee of the Sovnarkhoz. Really, I am a kind of
multiple tool! Of course one has to take part in economic affairs,
but surely there ought to be a difference in the approach, in the
style of work of a district committee and a factory, of a district
committee and a sovnarkhoz? But somehow or other, the boundary
lines have disappeared." (456b)

A further problem that besets the Soviet bureaucracy is the tremendous expansion of its functions and scope. Given the totalitarian nature of the system, the Soviet bureaucracy reaches every
organization, every institution, every collective farm, and indeed
anyone connected with any activity involving a group of people. As
a result, there is an apparent tendency in the state apparatus to
respond to every urgency by creating a new body to deal with it.
This is as true of the lower levels as of the ministerial hierarchy,
where the number of ministries currently is over fifty. From time to
time, a drastic curtailment is made, as after the death of Stalin, but
then a new expansion occurs. As a result, paperwork and division
of responsibility continue to plague the Soviet bureaucracy. One
regional agricultural administration, for instance, reported that during 1953 it received from the Ministry of Agriculture no less than
7,569 letters; in 1954, 8,459, and on the average about 30 instructions
per day. (434d) The Ministry of Agriculture itself was, as of December 1954, organized into 422 administrations. (453) Determined

efforts have been made in recent years to reduce this welter of administration, to rationalize as well as decentralize it, but the complexity is still formidable.

Such a situation affects the bureaucrats adversely. They are still expected "to deliver," but they can do so only by operating in a manner not prescribed by regulations. A complex system of evasion accordingly develops. Managers minimize in their reports the capacity of their organizations to produce so that the production plans will be set lower; they maximize their achievements by taking shortcuts on standards or by actually falsifying records; they organize informal arrangements among themselves, based partially on bribery, to avoid control and to exchange necessary items. (18c)

There was, accordingly, a continuing game of hide-and-seek played between Soviet bureaucrats and the Ministry of State Control, whose task it was to detect such happenings. To combat such procedures as described above, "the Ministry of State Control has been given the right to impose disciplinary penalties on officials guilty of not fulfilling the government's instructions and orders, of neglecting accounts, of wasteful management, wasteful spending of supplies and funds, and also of giving incorrect information to state control agencies." (453b) Power of removal and of turning over the guilty to prosecution was included in this grant. A series of decrees, beginning with one in 1957, have been issued to remedy this state of affairs (18a), but with limited success.

Such a situation naturally affects not only efficiency but also morale. There seems to have been a steady decline in the ideological élan of Soviet bureaucrats. The party journals have become increasingly concerned with the low level of political consciousness among the Soviet civil servants, and examples of bureaucrats ignorant of the basic works of Marxism-Leninism have been reported. The party does not want the Soviet bureaucrats to develop an esprit de corps purely their own, with their own standards of efficiency and performance. The Soviet bureaucrats are exhorted to remember that "the Soviet executive is a representative of the socialist state, a leader in whom is invested the people's trust. He must approach problems politically and work creatively and with a purpose in view. A communist ideological outlook and the ability to organize in practice the carrying out of Party and government decisions and to create conditions for increasing the initiative and creative activity

of the masses are inseparable features of a Soviet executive." (422b)
In spite of these difficulties, the Communist Party of the Soviet
Union continues to strive to create an ideologically conscious and
politically loyal yet efficient state bureaucracy. All three qualities
have, to some extent, been achieved. It is difficult, however, to reach
and maintain all three at their optimum.

All in all, it is evident that the trend in the Soviet Union is a
mixed one. We observe a rapid bureaucratization, if this term is
taken to mean an increase in the role of the bureaucracy. But this
bureaucratization has occurred in two distinct spheres: the government and the party. In a sense this trend may be compared to the
dual development of bureaucracy in democratic capitalist countries,
where we can observe a steady expansion of bureaucracy in both the
government and nongovernmental spheres of group life, especially
business and trade unions. But, whereas in these democratic countries the bureaucratization in both spheres continues to be subject
to a variety of controls, such as elections, representative bodies,
and the like, the rival bureaucracies of a totalitarian dictatorship,
though they may to some extent check one another, are free from
control from below. The bureaucracy of the democracies is responsible; the bureaucracy of the Soviet Union is not. And the
same is true, of course, with minor variations in the satellites and in
China.

A similar trend could be observed in the Soviet zone of Germany
after the war. It is particularly interesting from our viewpoint,
because the bureaucratic developments there were superimposed
upon the bureaucratization process built under the Nazi dictatorship. Because of this setting, it may be well to turn first to the
problems that the bureaucracy encountered after Hitler took over
the government.

Hitler's advent to power was soon followed by a law, rather
oratorically described as intended to "cleanse the civil service of
political favorites"; its official title was the Civil Service Restoration
Act. Passed on April 7, 1933, it was followed by another act in June,
which addressed itself to making sure that a civil servant "gives a
guarantee that he will at all times fully identify himself with the
state of national resurgence." (31b) These initial assaults upon the
professional bureaucracy, which Max Weber had once believed "un-
shatterable," were consolidated and extended in 1937 by a compre-

hensive civil-service "reform." By this reform, the traditional standards of the governmental bureaucracy were perverted; the standards of the party bureaucracy, such as loyalty to the Führer and to Nazi ideology, were made the ultimate tests of official conduct. This process is the cue to that debureaucratization of which we spoke at the outset. (244b; 103b)

In terms of the concept of bureaucracy as defined above, we find developing under Hitler a dualism of governmental and party bureaucracies, which found symbolic expression in the fact that Hitler was both chancellor and leader of the party. This is not an unfamiliar situation in constitutional systems, such as Britain and the United States. But since in these systems the party and its leader are only "in power" as long as the electorate supports them in free elections, the government functionaries are largely independent in their day-to-day operations; the party's control finds expression through the adoption of laws which the official is, of course, bound to obey, that is, to execute and to apply. Under Hitler, the party had come to stay. With its various branches and extensions, such as the Security Police, the Hitler Youth, the National Socialist Civil Servants' League, and others, it permeated and infiltrated the government service. This meant, as we have already said, that the governmental bureaucracy was debureaucratized in the following ways: the centralization of control (the hierarchy) was continually subject to challenge by party functionaries; the functions of various government officials were impinged upon by party offices (for example, the Foreign Office interferes with the Office for Foreign Policy Questions of the Party and with its branch dealing with Germans abroad, as well as with another such office in Himmler's SS — 31c); recruitment into and promotion in the government bureaucracy depended more and more upon positions in the party and its formations rather than upon qualification for office; objectivity was denounced in favor of ideological conformity; neither precision nor continuity was permitted when it conflicted with the exigencies of the moment, including the Führer's whims; official secrets were continually leaked with impunity to party functionaries who made such use of them as they saw fit, including the publishing of articles in ideologically oriented publications.

Behind these disturbing influences we find, of course, the terror. Any attempts on the part of an official to maintain former standards of legality and objectivity were seen as endangering the security of the people, its party, and its government, and correspondingly were punished by removal from office, concentration camp, and death. At first these cases were rare but, as the Hitler regime became more totalitarian, such actions became more numerous, until after 1942 they were the order of the day. The result was, of course, that the average official adopted an attitude of ready compliance with party directives of the most arbitrary kind. (102c) It is easy to picture a government councilor — timid though devoted to his task, conventional though well educated and professionally competent, secure in his routine and trembling for his job, the security of which was in his youth one of the main reasons for becoming a government official — yielding to a party official strutting back and forth in the full battle regalia of, say, an SS major, demanding in the name of the party the alteration of a decision that the hapless official had made in accordance with existing law. One needs to recall in this connection that Hitler had, at the time of the blood purge of 1934, proclaimed himself the "supreme law lord" (*oberster höchster Rechtsherr*) of Germany.*

The position of the courts, traditionally considered separate from the executive and hence the bureaucracy, deserves further comment. Under Hitler, the judges were at first slow to yield to Nazi pressure. Having played a rather conservative, not to say reactionary, role under the Weimar Republic, they prided themselves on their independence from "democratic" influences. Like the army, they believed in thir "neutrality," that is to say, their remoteness from politics. But the National Socialists could not, of course, permit such an independent judiciary. They rapidly transformed the judiciary, and more especially the criminal bench, into organs of the terror. (31e; 34) By the beginning of the forties, when the regime had become thoroughly totalitarian, a prominent jurist could write: "In the field of crime prevention the judge no longer merely administers justice. His . . . activity approaches that of an administrative official. He no longer looks for justice alone, but also acts in accordance with expediency. Judge and administrator, judiciary and police, often meet . . . in the pursuit of identical objectives. This change in the character of some judicial activity has led to a decline

* In his speech before the Reichstag, July 13, 1934; see also the detailed discussion in 31d.

[in importance] of the judiciary." (232) The United States military tribunal at Nuremberg brought suit against one such set of judges in the case of *U.S. v. Josef Altstötter et al.,* in which the whole range of the perversion of the judiciary was laid bare. It is clear from this record, as well as many records in German denazification courts, that the judiciary had essentially become a branch of the administrative service, subject to continuous interference by the party. But this was not enough. In order to handle certain kinds of criminal prosecutions, which even this kind of judiciary would not attend to, the Hitler regime organized the Volksgerichte, or people's courts, special tribunals resembling the revolutionary tribunals under the French terror as well as institutions in the USSR, in which only expediency in terms of National Socialist standards served as a basis for judgment. (147)

If we turn from these developments under the Hitler dictatorship to the East German regime (113), we find that basically the SED (Socialist Unity Party) has continued, or revived after it turned totalitarian, the techniques and practices of the Nazis. The officialdom in the government offices is subservient to the party bureaucracy to an even greater degree, in accordance with Soviet practice. Administrative law provides for a strict subordination of the governmental to the party bureaucracy. One of the main agents of this ascendancy is the attorney general of state, who has become the whiphand of the secret police. Divorced from all court control, he operates on the basis of a vastly expanded concept of security, hunting down deviationists in the complex bureaucracy, not only in the government proper but in the network of enterprise of which the socialized economy is composed. The courts themselves have become appendages of the administration. In the statute establishing the new court system, the SED completed the process initiated by the Hitler regime of depriving the courts of their independence and of superimposing upon them the notion of administrative and political expediency, as contrasted with the constitutional principle of *nulla poena sine lege.* Indeed, the East German jurists have gone one step further, in keeping with Soviet conceptions of "law"; they have introduced the notion that decisions of courts which have already been pronounced with legally binding effect may be annulled by judicial decree within a year. It is by perversion of the French concept of cassation, or review, that the attorney general (as well as the president and vice-presidents of the Supreme Court) can request cassation if the decision "violates a law," if it is "decidedly in error" in the penalty it inflicts, or if it "decidedly contradicts justice." Clearly political considerations can be, and have in fact been, the basis of this cassation. (299; 364)

In Italy, the problem of bureaucratization presented itself in a somewhat different form. As we have seen, the Fascists proclaimed the doctrine of the strong state. Such ideologues of Fascism as Gentile insisted that the party was subordinate to the state and should serve as its conscience. Mussolini stressed the point when, in his article on Fascism (268b), he asserted that "everything is in the State, and nothing human or spiritual exists, much less has value, outside the State. In this sense, Fascism is totalitarian, and the Fascist State, the synthesis and unity of all values, interprets, develops and gives strength to the whole life of the people. Outside the State there can be neither individuals nor groups (political parties, associations, syndicates, classes)." In terms of such a concept, the governmental bureaucracy, and more especially the high civil servant, assumes an independent role vis-à-vis the party and the corporate bureaucracy of business. In rejecting the view that Fascism was the arm of big business, one historian has written that there were no less than three bureaucracies: the officers of the regular army, the civil service, and the officials of the Fascist Party. He estimated that the members of these three bureaucracies constituted about one twelfth of Italy's adult males. (310a) He then proceeded to describe vividly the attitude of the civil-servant bureaucrat toward the big businessman who seeks government aid, and he added, "When a disagreement arises between a big business man and a high civil servant, Mussolini's immediate inclination is to favor the high civil servant. The person who repeats to him that the state must 'discipline' private initiative is sure of awakening a sympathetic echo in his soul. For what is the state if not Mussolini?" (310b)

When it came to clashes between the party and the governmental bureaucracy, Mussolini's inclination was likewise to favor "the state," but this might mean now the high civil servant, now the Fascist "spiritual conscience of the state." In any case, it is evident that the Fascist emphasis on the state tended to foster genuine bureaucratization. The symbolic expression of this was the "train on time" of which the Italian Fascists made so much in the early years. Yet, in spite of Mussolini's greater emphasis on the state, it would be a mistake to underestimate the continuous impact of the party bureaucracy on the governmental bureaucracy. Through its control of the associations of civil servants, and through the requirement of party membership for advancement in the governmental bureaucracy, the party wielded a powerful influence, reinforced by a system of spies. In 1932 it succeeded in effecting a purge of the entire top layer of officialdom in the Ministry of the Interior. It also managed to secure representation on the Consiglio di Stato (Council of State), which was not abolished by the Fascists and continued to adjudicate problems of administrative law involving the conduct of officials. (159) The corporate state, which extended the rule of officialdom or bureaucracy to all phases of economic life meant, therefore, total bureaucratization in the light of Mussolini's conception of the state as the all-engulfing guardian of the national life.

In conclusion, it might be said that whether in the name of the state, of the party, of the nation, or of the proletariat, the totalitarian dictatorship steadily expands the role of bureaucracy. Yet totalitarianism is not alone in this trend: it is paralleled by a steady expansion of bureaucracy and bureaucratization in all industrial nations. The trend appears to be connected with the growing size of organizations. It has found its ironic expression in "Parkinson's law," which suggests that the growth of bureaucracy is cancerous, unrelated to function. (271) What is distinctive in totalitarian dictatorship, apart from the lack of any institutional pattern of responsibility, is the sharp dualism of governmental and party bureaucracy. Hence, expansion creates serious problems of conflicting bureaucratic cadres fighting among themselves for supremacy and thereby debureaucratizing the governmental service in those countries where this service had already achieved a high degree of bureaucratization. The extension in size is bought at the price of a deterioration in quality, at least temporarily. What all this implies for the economic life of the country is the problem to which we must next turn.

17

PLANS AND PLANNING

A totalitarian economy is centrally directed and controlled. In order to execute such central direction and control, there must be a plan. Since the economy has become one gigantic business enterprise, and yet an enterprise that does not get its incentives from the desire to make a profit or from the consumers' needs and demands as expressed in the price system, its managers must be told what measuring rods to apply in determining what should be produced, and consequently how the scarce resources available for production should be distributed among the various branches of productive capacity. The slogan, "Guns rather than butter," is only a crude indication of the vast range of decisions that have to be made. The decisions involved in arriving at such a plan are the most basic ones a totalitarian regime has to make. Hence the five-year plans of the Soviet Union, the four-year plan of Hitler Germany, the two- and five-year plans of the Soviet zone, and so on, are focal points of political interest.

Characteristically, in a totalitarian dictatorship, the leader or leaders at the top, men like Stalin, Hitler, or the party Presidium, make the basic decision in terms of which the plan is organized. This basic decision was, in the case of the Soviet Union, originally that of industrializing the country; in the case of Nazi Germany, that of eliminating unemployment and preparing for war; in the case of China, again industrialization but combined with "land reform"; and in the case of the Soviet zone of Germany right after the war, that of providing the large-scale reparations the Soviet Union demanded. (88; 32; 113) These goals of planning are the most decisive issues to be settled in a totalitarian society. In the

Soviet Union, more particularly, in recent years there has been extended discussion in the top hierarchy over the question of mass consumption and consumer-goods production, as against heavy machinery, basic raw materials, and preparation for war, including nuclear arms and space control. Any such basic decision provides the starting point for a system of priorities which can be utilized in allocating raw materials to the different sectors of the producing economy.

It is the absence of such a basic decision, and indeed the impossibility of securing it, that has led many to conclude that constitutional democracy is incompatible with planning or, to put it in another way, that any attempt to enter upon planning constitutes in effect the "road to serfdom." (104f; 137) This is true if planning is understood in a total sense, and it is often so defined, especially by economists. Actually, the planning process in a democracy is very different; it is contingent upon the democratic process as a whole, whose outstanding characteristic is the continuous review of all decisions, including basic ones, by the people and their representatives. (109) In autocratic systems, and more especially in totalitarian dictatorships, the purpose of the plan is determined by the autocratic leader or ruler(s). The plan implements their basic decision. It is carried forward by a bureaucracy that has the full backing of the terrorist and propagandist apparatus of the totalitarian dictatorship. Consequently, little if anything can be learned from the planning procedures of totalitarian societies when one comes to assess the planning process in democratic societies. But an understanding of the process, of course, is essential for an understanding of totalitarian dictatorship. The great advantage that a fixed goal or purpose possesses from a technical standpoint is counterbalanced by the disadvantage of not having the planning respond to the reactions of those affected by it. Which is the greater disadvantage only experience can tell.

A comparison of the planning experience in totalitarian dictatorship brings to light some very striking contrasts, as well as similarities. In the Soviet Union, a number of years passed before the central importance of planning was fully realized. Prior to the revolution, Russia had been far behind Western Europe in industrial development. Marx and Engels, believing that the Communist revolution would take place in an advanced industrial society, had not been at all concerned with the problem of planning industrialization. They had stressed control of the economy rather than industrialization and an increase in production; indeed, the revolution was to be the culminating point of capitalist development, after the means of production had, through trusts and vast monopolies, become concentrated in "fewer and fewer hands," and this shrinking group of exploiters would be confronted by an ever larger proletariat. All that the proletariat would have to do, consequently, would be to take over and run this gigantic productive apparatus. But in Russia, over 80 percent of the population lived on farms at the time of the revolution, and a similar situation prevailed in China at the time of the Communist seizure of power. This fact was so completely at variance with Marxist anticipations that novel approaches had to be developed.

This question preoccupied the Bolsheviks throughout the twenties and gave the post-Lenin struggles for power a marked theoretical flavor. A number of solutions were advocated, ranging from left-wing emphasis on immediate efforts to increase industrial output, even at high cost and considerable coercion (expounded most clearly by Preobrazhensky), to right-wing advocacy of adjustment to a temporary, transitional capitalist stage (as, for instance, voiced by Bukharin). The ensuing policy, based more on the requirements of the situation than on ideological dogma, was one of compromise and postponement of the radical solution. (88)

Planning, accordingly, developed slowly and modestly. On February 22, 1921, the State Planning Commission (Gosplan) was set up. It was charged with the task of working out an over-all state economic plan and preparing the technical and managerial staffs and know-how necessary to its success. (438a) In fact, however, Gosplan's immediate tasks were more restricted and concentrated on developing the state plan for the electrification of Russia (Goepro), which had been prepared some time earlier and was to serve as the basis for further centralized planning. In addition, Gosplan assumed control over some sectors of the economy which were subject to crises and vital to economic survival, like the railroads. Thus, depite the very broad grant of planning and controlling power, Gosplan during the NEP period did not vitally influence the Russian economy. It concerned itself rather with collecting statistics, studying existing economic trends, and laying the groundwork for an over-all plan.*

The big impetus to centralized state planning came with the political decision to launch a large-scale industrialization and agricultural collectivization program. The era of the five-year plans began in 1928. Since then Soviet economic life has been revolving around these broad, comprehensive schemes, developed in keeping with the policy decisions of the leadership by the planners of Gosplan. Indeed, the inauguration of the First Five-Year Plan can be described as the breakthrough of full-scale totalitarianism in Russia. Stalin's program, borrowed in many respects from the left-wing opposition, notably Preobrazensky, inevitably encountered resistance from the established peasantry and other groups. As resistance mounted, so did coercion. As pointed out earlier, the totalitarian regime matured in the struggle to put into practice what theory and ideology had preached. The launching of the plan, however, despite certain initial failures (camouflaged by scapegoat trials of engineers), fired to a great extent the imagination of the more youthful party members and raised the sagging morale of the whole party. Its results, therefore, were politically important.

From then on, the Gosplanners were in their element. The coercive powers of the government and party were put at their disposal, and the process of rapid industrial development, concomitant with the collectivization of agriculture, was pushed ahead at great speed. (For further treatment, see Chapter 20.) The planning apparatus expanded accordingly. By 1938 it had grown to a central staff of 1,000 planners organized in 54 departments of Gosplan. (21) Today planning officials are to be found on every subordinate level, from the republics down to the regions and even districts and towns. The plans that they prepare include not only the over-all five-year plan, but the economic plans for all levels of the Soviet economy, from that of the RSFSR to even a small plant in Yakutsk. (90d) Gosplan is organized into departments dealing with regional planning and finally into departments charged with integrating the work of the national and regional planning departments. Gosplan committees are also attached to regional executive committees, which in

---

* The first comprehensive plan, which was not implemented by the government, appeared in 1925 as *Control Figures of National Economy for 1925–1926*.

their turn supervise the work of the district and town-city planning committees. Gosplan goals are worked out through lengthy processes of estimating requirements and needs; in the process, extended controversies with subordinate organs ensue.

There has, in fact, in recent years been a good deal of oscillation between centralizing and decentralizing tendencies. Gosplan has been employed to counteract some of the excesses of localism (*mestnichestvo*). The situation has been complicated by the conflicts between short-range and long-range planning, with Gosplan primarily now concerned with the long-range plans. Challenges have been heard, such as those of the economist Liberman and others, which would transfer managerial planning to the enterprise and re-establish a kind of market mechanism. (89cc; 267b) Basically, this would limit central direction to the broader aspects of over-all production planning and resource allocation. For Gosplan is concerned also with the problem of allocating resources. This is an important matter, since Soviet managers operate constantly in a situation of scarcity, and adequate allocation is the prerequisite to plan achievement and resulting bonuses. Indeed, one of the primary reasons for evasion is to be found in the unending competition among managers for scarce materials. In 1948 an effort was made to divest Gosplan of the allocating function and to assign it to a separate body. Apparently, the experiment was not successful, and in 1953 Gosplan again took over the allocation function.

Supervision of the execution of the plan is becoming an increasingly important aspect of Gosplan work. This supervision essentially involves the twin tasks of detecting failures and evasions and checking on the general development of the plan and analyzing the portents. A great deal in recent years has been said in the USSR on the urgent need to uncover the growing number of managers and officials who, having learned the game, have become skillful both in keeping their quotas down by underestimating the capacity of their plants and in lowering quality for the sake of achieving quantity. (89 l) However, equally important if not more so, is the task of keeping in touch with the development of the plan in order to make the necessary adjustments. Soviet leaders were at first unwilling or unable to perceive the necessity of elasticity, and many of the failures of the earlier periods can be ascribed to a rigid insistence on plan fulfillment. In 1955 measures were taken to give lower eche-

lons a greater say in planning and to make a meaningful distinction
between long-range and short-range planning, but these were revised in 1957, 1960, and 1962. The party program of 1961 suggested
a bare outline of a twenty-year "plan" for economic as well as social
progress. The pretense, however, that this plan was democratic
because of its wide discussion — 500,000 meetings involving some 70
million people — was idle. It represented the conceptions of Khrushchev and his immediate entourage. (296b) It is conceived in
terms of rapid further progress in industrialization, with an annual
growth rate of 10 percent confidently envisaged. The goal of overtaking the industrial West, and more particularly the United States,
is already proving utopian in the mid-sixties, not to mention the
agricultural debacle. (355a) Decentralization and the separation of
agricultural from industrial planning did not work out as well as
was hoped, although some improvement seems to have been
achieved. Since then, a vigorous debate has been going on over the
issue of centralization and related issues. There are those engineers
and technocrats who would intensify centralization by means of
computers and other advanced technical methods, and, in their
view, "ultimately, the computers are to take over more than just the
planning near the top: the lower echelon of the economy is to get
dehumanized as well." (442f) As against them, economists like
Liberman would leave only the decision on production goals, such
as the composition and volume of output, to the central planners, while each manager would maximize his own plant's
"profitability," computed on the basis of the capital he works with.
"Profits would become the sole success indicator." (442f) Even
more radical voices have been heard from time to time, and one
may begin to wonder at what point decentralization will go beyond
the limits set by a totalitarian dictatorship.

The principles of Soviet economic planning have also been
adopted by the Communist nations of Central Europe. The satellite
parties did not go through the preliminary stage of controversy that
the fight between Preobrazhensky and Bukharin had highlighted in
Russia, but as soon as the consolidation of power was completed,
they proceeded to launch economic planning on the Soviet model.
In Poland the State Commission for Economic Planning (PKPG)
operates as a superministry which supervises and coordinates the
economic life of the country, with the right to issue directives to

individual ministries. It has been charged with nationalization of private enterprise. The PKPG is also in charge of the Main Statistical Administration, the Central Administration of Professional Training, the Patent Office, and the Main Administration of Measures. (413; 429) Polish planning, on Soviet insistence, has been coordinated in recent years with that of Czechoslovakia and Hungary, and industrial development in these countries is to result in complementary and mutually dependent economies. In particular, the development of the Silesian basin in terms of electric energy and coal output has been made subject to close Polish-Czech cooperation. Also, as a reaction to the Marshall Plan, the so-called Molotov Plan resulted in a coordinating committee, made up of the heads of the planning boards of all the satellite regimes and of the USSR for the purpose of working out joint plans. That such plans are not devoid of political significance is seen, for instance, in the development of a new industrial town in Poland, Nowa Huta, constructed next to the old and highly conservative city of Cracow, to a great extent according to Soviet plans. Later, the Council for Economic Mutual Assistance (CEMA) was formed, which sought to coordinate bloc members in a pattern of specialization in particular fields of production. "Integration, involving greater technical specialization, offered opportunities for more rapid development of technological skills"; at the same time, the dependence on the Soviet Union was increased. (38c) As a consequence, there has been a growing inclination to secure trade ties with other countries.

The Communist Party of China faced, upon its seizure of power, an economic situation less favorable than that of the USSR in 1928 or of any of the satellites in 1946–1949. However, after totalitarian control of the regime was firmly established, a decision to industrialize rapidly followed, and a somewhat vague five-year plan was announced in 1953. Apparently a series of regional plans was gradually evolved into an over-all national plan, with the aim of rapid industrialization at all costs. That there might have been some opposition within the party to such a drastic collectivist solution is indicated by the virulence of Liu Shao-chao's attack, in February 1954, on party factionalism. (300a) Unlike the situation in the USSR in the twenties, however, no open voice has been heard in China urging a go-slow policy. In the words of Hsiueh Mu-chiao, a member of the State Planning Committee, the party must "suppress all intrigues of imperialists and class enemies within the country. Only in this way can we successfully accomplish the task of socialist industrialization in China." (441i) Communist China tried to speed this process of industrialization with what has come to be known as "the great leap forward," undertaken in connection with the Second Five-Year Plan. The plan, like the first one, gave priority to the development of heavy industry, especially steel, but there was also involved a huge water-conservation project in the agricultural communes. The core of the plan was a drive "to build small factories and open small mines using available means of production." Some sixty million persons were thrown into this "backyard blast furnaces' drive." (54a) Along with the "furnaces," hundreds of thousands of other kinds of plants were set up. After initial claims of success, the leaders had to admit that the "leap forward" had landed them in a ditch, and the entire approach has by now been abandoned. Chaotic conditions were created by the misuse of manpower and a misdirection of scarce resources. The great leap forward also had serious emotional aftereffects, comparable to those of Stalin's great purges. (415)

The situation was very different in Nazi Germany. In keeping with what we have already said, one commentator wrote in 1942: "National Socialism has coordinated the diversified and contradictory state interferences into one system having but one aim: the preparation of imperialist war." (263c) The documentary evidence that has come to light since 1945 amply supports this statement. As it has been summed up more recently: "First [there was] establishment of absolute rule internally and the building up of a sufficient military fighting apparatus, protected by a defensive and cautiously maneuvering foreign policy; then violent expansion with concentrated power." (31f) For after his protestations during the early days of his regime, Hitler soon made it clear that he intended a policy of preparation for large-scale war. It has been authoritatively described how very definitely Hitler planned the war that by 1937 he considered "inevitable." (46c) The entire Four-Year Plan, so-called, initiated in 1936, was geared to this objective. In a council of ministers, Hermann Goering, whom Hitler had put in charge of the plan, declared in 1938 that the plans and planning "start from the basic thought that the showdown with Russia is inevitable — all measures have to be taken just as if we were actually in a state of imminent danger of war." (46d)

It was essentially a matter of shifting production to war needs, and doing this not by throttling the consumption and standard of living of the masses, but by increasing production. At the same time, the memory of the blockade of 1916–1918 was still vivid enough to make it seem desirable to have Germany become as independent as possible from outside supply sources. This objective was highlighted in the slogan of "autarky," which in turn was reinforced by the notion of "living space." Such living space, related as it was to aggressive designs against Germany's eastern neighbors, was to round out the Greater German Reich into a self-supporting and independent polity. It had been a key idea, amounting to an obsession of Hitler's even when he wrote *Mein Kampf*. (148d) The course of the war showed that this objective not only was not obtained, but was indeed unattainable. The preparation for war under the Four-Year Plan was quite inadequate (46e; 162); after a transitional period Hitler, in 1942, made Albert Speer the key planner, but it was too late for "planning." All in all, one is obliged to conclude that, owing to the incompetence of Goering and to Hitler's lack of understanding of economic problems,* the planning of the Nazi dictatorship never became effective. But to argue that for this reason the Hitler regime was not a totalitarian dictatorship (260; 112f) is going too far; the measures it took in subordinating business and labor to the Führer's war policy were decidedly totalitarian, and the failure of the central plan was a result of lack of time. It is well known that the five-year plans of the Soviet Union also involved great failures at the outset.

It is interesting to see how planning developed in the Soviet zone of Germany after the war. We find here, in contrast to the Hitler regime, a plan originally directed toward a predominantly economic objective — securing reparations for the Soviet Union. This objective was supplanted by the goal of fitting the economy of the GDR into the Soviet bloc. (38d) Of course, in a way the entire enterprise of the military occupation of Germany was one gigantic "plan," a plan

---

* It has been argued convincingly that it was not simply a matter of lack of understanding, but that Hitler disregarded economic arguments because he considered them superficial in relation to his deeper aims. (31g)

for the demilitarization, deindustrialization, and democratization of Germany. (135) But this plan remained in a very primitive state, as far as the effective planning procedures were concerned, and it soon broke apart as the policies of the Allies began to diverge. Eventually it was made obsolete by the emergence of the Federal Republic of Germany as a self-directing policy. Here the liberal, free-enterprise policy of Adenauer and Erhard developed in sharp hostility toward all forms of planning, except for the purpose of freeing the economy from wartime and postwar restraints.

In East Germany, the development has taken the opposite course. Here the entire economy is subject to planning. As mentioned, the central Planning Commission was directly coordinated by Gosplan in Moscow until 1955. It is clear that the state's Planning Commission operates directly under the Presidium of the Council of Ministers and is therefore in a position to give orders to all ministries and other administrative organs of the government. (377; 341a) Actually not only the Planning Commission itself, but the Presidium and the so-called Coordination and Control Offices directly attached to it are involved in the planning process. On the whole, this process follows Soviet precedents and practice. The orders, ordinances, and regulations of the commission have, after approval by the respective control office, the "force of law." Failure to obey these orders constitutes an "economic crime," punishable by such penalties as long prison sentences. The control office has a right to demand arrests and therefore works closely with the Security Office (secret police).

In connection with this control, statistics become an instrument, since they are based upon an elaborate system of reporting all up and down the line. But the work proper of the Planning Commission, like that of Gosplan, is surrounded by secrecy; only top-level personnel have access to its findings; the statistical information furnished, usually in terms of percentages, is misleading, to say the least, since the basis of comparison is continually shifted. The middle and upper personnel staff is entirely composed of members of the SED and systematically trained along party and ideological lines. It runs into many hundreds, in large part very young men and women who have been specially indoctrinated and who are better paid than personnel in industry.

In summary, then, we may observe that totalitarian planning is formulated on the basis of ideologically determined goals; that its scope, in the final analysis, is total; and that effective time limits are absent, the usual four- or five-year periods being mere accounting devices. Totalitarian planning is a necessary concomitant of the total revolution that these regimes set in motion — without it they would easily degenerate into anarchy — and it is this *political* quality that sets it apart from democratic economic planning.

18

THE BATTLE FOR PRODUCTION
AND INDUSTRIAL EXPANSION

Within the context of a total bureaucracy and of total plans, the battle for production has so far been seen as the decisive test of the totalitarian economy. If the plans call for conquest and war, the pre-existing system of production for peacetime consumption must be revamped to provide the essential transformation. If the plans call for industrialization, controls must be set up and maintained for forcing a substantial part of the social product into capital goods, even when the standard of living and level of consumption of the people are quite low. In either case, we have what has been aptly called a "command economy." In the case of the Soviet Union and its satellites (267a), this command economy consists of a vast combine of state enterprises, each competing with the others to some extent, but devoid of the profit motive as known in other economies. Lately there has been reported an experiment to take a few plants out of this set-up and to give them the autonomy of independent, or at least quasi-independent, enterprises — a situation which would resemble that under Fascism (see also below). In Fascist countries, and more especially in Germany, industry was largely cartellized and subject to much monopolistic or oligopolistic control. The achievements of the command economy under either of these arrangements have been impressive, as far as the realization of the announced goal is concerned. The failure to satisfy consumer needs and demands cannot, strictly speaking, be held against these systems, since they have not operated with the purpose of satisfying the consumer.

Industrial progress in the Soviet Union since 1927–28, the date of the First Five-Year Plan, is indicated by the accompanying table. (156; 441t)

Soviet Industrial Development since 1927–28

	1927–28	1932	1937	1941	1963
1. Coal (1,000 m.t.)	35,510	64,664	127,000	171,160	532,000
2. Electric power output (mil. kwh.)	5,007	13,540	36,400	53,957	412,000
3. Steel (ingots, castings) (1,000 m.t.)	4,250	5,927	17,729	22,400	80,200
4. Aluminum (m.t.)	0	855	46,800	–	–
5. Crude oil extracted (excl. natural gas) (1,000 m.t.)	11,472	21,413	28,501	34,602	206,000
6. Passenger cars, half-ton trucks	580	7,511	137,016	131,000	–

The war, of course, resulted in a considerable retardation of Soviet industrial development. Destruction was particularly heavy in the industrial areas occupied by the Germans, which were subjected, first, to Soviet scorched-earth policies and then to German looting and destruction prior to evacuation. After the war, the Stalin regime made rapid industrial recovery its priority goal and, despite its many sacrifices and sufferings, the Soviet population was called upon to devote all its energy to new industrial drives. The figures of the second table, covering the same items as those of the first, testify eloquently to the scale of these efforts and to their undeniable impressiveness. (404b; 441j; 409b; 167a) Thus, in six years of admittedly intensive efforts, Soviet production, in terms of the items cited, not only made up for the war losses, but in some cases even doubled the top output of 1941.

Item	1945	1951	1953	1955	1958
1.	148,000	282,000	320,000	390,000	496,000
2.	44,900	102,900	133,000	166,000	233,000
3.	12,200	31,400	38,300	45,000	54,900
4.	–	–	–	–	–
5.	19,500	42,300	52,000	70,000	113,000
6.	83,000	364,000 (in 1950)	–	445,000	–

Since then Soviet industrial expansion, especially in heavy industry and weapons, has continued unabated, despite the temporary consideration given in 1953 to the increase in output of consumer goods. (441k) Such concern for the consumer has been a recurrent theme with Soviet leaders, but over the years producer goods have retained their primacy. Steel, a good indicator, has remained at the center of attention, although speeches by Khrushchev and the party program have given almost equal attention to "overtaking" the capitalist countries — also a Stalinist theme, as has been pointed out. (36a) Industrial expansion, but more particularly producer-good production, remains the dominant goal of the Soviet system and as such has great appeal to the underdeveloped countries of the world.

Soviet industrial achievements, as seen above, are indeed imposing. From an industrially backward country, the Soviet Union has, through unprecedented deprivation and terror, pushed itself to the forefront of the world's industrial powers. It did so by sacrificing the human freedoms to which it allegedly aspired. It did so also without foreign capital and, after the mid-thirties, with relatively little outside technical assistance. Soviet capital investment has been largely supported by the national budget (the average ranging from about two thirds to three fourths of the funds for capital construction). This "enforced" saving is continuing. It is estimated that the volume of state investment under the present seven-year plan is substantially higher than in the previous septennium. (36a) The resulting rate of industrial growth — a decisive figure for advanced industrial systems — has been very high, more than 10 percent in some years though now leveling off. Capital investment has been significantly higher than in the United States and Western Europe. This higher rate of investment has been made possible by various forms of enforced savings that cut down consumer purchasing power, most important among them low wages and high taxes.

The turnover tax has been the most important source of revenue, accounting on the average for somewhat more than half of the budget receipts in the USSR. The turnover tax is borne largely by the consumer, since each commodity price has an unspecified turnover tax included in it, and the tax is particularly high on consumer goods, for some items amounting to 75 percent or more of the sale price. The second, but much less important, source is the profit tax levied on those enterprises which actually make a profit in excess of their quotas.

Soviet industrial output is still lagging far behind that of the United States, but the swift increases in the volume of production and the general emphasis of the regime on technical achievement are accompanied by a vast and intensive training program for young engineering talent. From a meager 26 higher educational establishments offering engineering training in 1928, Soviet training facilities had expanded by 1955 to 175 with some 300,000 students, as compared to the former 52,000. (The United States at that time had about 194,000 students taking engineering in 210 colleges.) Between the years 1928 and 1955 the Soviet Union produced 630,000 engineers of all types, or the equivalent of 25 percent of the graduates of its higher institutions. (406) In the sequel the trend has continued. There were 191 institutes for training engineers by 1959, and the number of graduates has been expanding rapidly since. Such figures indicate a great capacity for further industrial expansion.

Soviet industrial expansion has, as suggested earlier, important political and social consequences. It destroys traditional bonds, creates a situation of great social mobility, and results in population shifts and the weakening of nationality lines. An important aspect of industrial development has been the deliberate effort, motivated partially by geopolitical considerations, to shift the industrial concentration from the regions of the Donbas and Moscow to other areas, relatively untouched by industrialization. A close observer of Soviet economic developments a decade ago summed up the situation thus:

The Russians in their current plans are still pursuing a policy of differential economic development, strongly favoring the central regions (Central Russia, Ukraine, Volga and Urals). Within this industrial heartland, hydroelectric power and water transportation would reduce the need for close conjunction between industry and mining. The decision to emphasize the central regions is clearly based on political and strategic considerations, rather than purely economic; for both the western regions of European Russia and Soviet Asia afford major opportunities for industrial growth. (417)

The thousands of novice workers who come to the newly constructed factories, torn from their traditional moorings and thrown into the mass barracks of the new construction sites, find themselves in an environment of strict discipline and centralization of command. Since all the factories are state-owned, the managers who run them are state officials, long subordinate to the ministry controlling their particular branch of industry. With the expansion of the Soviet industrial machine, there occurred a great proliferation of such ministries; as early as 1940 there were the following People's Commissariats dealing with industry: Heavy Industry, Oil, Coal, Power Stations, Electrical Engineering, Shipbuilding, Heavy Metallurgy, Nonferrous Metallurgy, Chemical, Building Materials, Heavy Engineering, Medium Engineering, General Engineering, Defense, Aviation, Armaments, Munitions, Food, Meat and Dairy, Fisheries, Light Industry, Textiles, Timber, Cellulose and Paper. In 1953 a drastic reorganization reduced the number of economic ministries, but by 1955 the number had again grown to about thirty. A radical change was effected by Khrushchev in 1957, which was linked to his defeat of the "antiparty group" (see Chapter 6). The reform of the economy was, as a matter of surmise, itself a major bone of contention between the rivals. In any case most of the industrial enterprises passed from the control of the central ministries to newly created regional economic councils (*sovnarkhozy*) dominated by party functionaries. The Soviet Union was divided into 105 regions. In each, a regional council was set up to plan and to operate all industrial enterprises and construction within the region; it was made subject to the council of ministers of the particular republic — this meant 70 economic councils for the RSFSR and 11 for the Ukraine — with central coordination secured by the party and Gosplan. Much more effective supervision, improved cooperation between plants in each locality, and deployment of specialists from the center to the local councils were the three desired improvements. "It is not easy to measure the degree to which these hoped-for benefits have been realized," is the recent judgment of a leading authority. (89r) Another account tells us: "the history of the reform since 1957 is one of a steady increase in the powers of the central coordinators and a decline in the effective importance of the sovnarkhozes, since the government and Party strive to implement the central plan and to combat such regionalist tendencies as obstruct the uninterrupted functioning of at least the priority sectors of the economy." (36b) Indeed, the sovnarkhozes themselves have been recentralized. Their number was first reduced by combining several into one, and finally, in November 1962, their number was reduced to about forty by the Central Committee and some of their important powers were transferred to state committees, all of them also being reintegrated through the establishment of some nineteen "natural" regions (in 1961), thereby checking the localism that had sprung up under the original reform. (89s) In the last analysis, whatever the over-all structure, the operational effectiveness of the economy as a modern industrial system depends upon the work of the enterprises it comprises.

These enterprises, or factories, are run by government-appointed directors. The director is responsible to the regional council. The various shop heads and foremen are subordinated in turn to the factory director. The principle of *edinonachalstvo* (unity of command) is thus firmly followed, and the director is fully responsible for his factory. This, in cases of accident, failure to achieve quotas, or technical inefficiency, can have rather serious consequences for a director. Indeed, the practice has been to consider serious accidents as evidence of failure or sabotage, and cases of directors going to trial have been frequent, particularly during the purge periods. In recent years, there has been a tendency toward less stringent punishments (financial penalties, restitution of damage, demotion), but the director still remains liable whenever anything unforeseen happens. This broad responsibility is hard, since the director is hamstrung by control from above. As one highly placed manager put it: "Now about the powers of the directors. Formally they are very broad, but on many questions, even minor ones, the manager of an enterprise is under petty tutelage. Can I, the director of an enterprise, hire even one economist . . . ? Can I hire one engineer for the mechanization of production . . . ? To all these and tens of similar questions there is one answer: I cannot. All this prescribed for the plant from above." (89r)

The director, however, is not only driven by fear. Productive success has very tangible attractions for him, for he is given a sizable share in the profits that follow from an overfulfillment of quotas. Large bonuses are given to those directors who have been successful, and interviews with former Soviet managers indicate that they attach the greatest importance to such premiums: "the difference between 99 per cent of plan fulfillment and 100 per cent means a difference of up to 30 per cent in income." (444b) The workers also share in these premiums, but the percentage is considerably scaled down on their level. Such incentives, however, result in a phenomenon known as *shturmovshchina* — a last-minute attempt at breakneck speed to meet the quota and share in the dividend. In the 1954 annual report on Soviet industry, we read

One of the chief shortcomings in industry was that, as a result of unsatisfactory management, many industrial enterprises were not working rhythmically. They were turning out much of their production at the end of the month and permitting a fall-off in activity at the beginning of the following month. The absence of a rhythmic work schedule led to workers and machinery being idle at certain times, to an increase in personnel beyond the planned number of employees, nonproductive expense on overtime work, overexpenditure of the wage fund, a higher percentage of scrapped production, and an increase in cost of goods. (441 l)

The temptation to share in the premiums has led those directors whose plants failed to meet their quotas to falsify results, or even to bribe state control officials. A number of incidents of this type have appeared in the Soviet press and have been confirmed by interviews with former Soviet officials. (419d) Whether the decentralized system has ended such practices is hard to say, but it seems rather doubtful in the light of some recent cases. Instead of corrupting central ministry officials, the manager now will seek to do so on a local basis. If it were not for the ideological zeal of party men, this might be even easier, if past political experience is any guide.

In his efforts to maximize production, the factory director is assisted by the factory party organization, by the secret police (the Special Section), and by the local trade union (see Chapter 19). The party organization, encompassing all the party workers in the factory, holds regular meetings at which production levels are discussed, encourages self-critique on the part of the workers and the administration, attacks laggards, watches the political morale of the personnel, and supervises the director himself. The Special Section makes certain that sabotage is prevented, that disloyal elements are ferreted out, and that enemies of the people are exposed. It organizes regular networks of informers among both the workers and the managerial staff. Occasionally it may serve as a stimulant to increased efforts by arresting known slackers or those expressing antiparty opinions. In its combination of autocratic control from above, party stimulation and police informers, acclamatory participation and popular ritual, the factory in a sense is a small-scale replica of the pattern of controls and of the hierarchy of decision making characteristic of the Soviet Union in general.

The rise of Communist regimes in Central Europe and China has resulted in similarly drastic efforts to push industrial expansion. This was as true of the relatively advanced economies of Czechoslovakia and Poland as of the less advanced ones of Bulgaria and Yugoslavia (in 1946). It was only as a result of the marked failures of such programs in the more backward states of Central Europe that the Soviets decided in 1947–48 to encourage a slower industrial development in such places as Bulgaria and Yugoslavia — this was one of the reasons for the Tito-Cominform tension, since Tito was quite anxious to industrialize rapidly — and a closer cooperation of these states with the more advanced areas in the bloc. Industrialization, however, has been pushed very forcefully in Poland, where the natural wealth of the Silesian basin makes it an ideal site for the creation of a second Ruhr. Steel production and coal output, which had tripled by 1955, have vastly and steadily increased. Since 1956–57, the East European economies have been advancing, with Soviet assistance and under Soviet direction. The Council for Mutual Economic Aid (CMEA) was reactivated and provided with administrative secretariats. A comprehensive plan was worked out in 1958, covering the sixteen years to 1975, and a program for specialization of the several countries was put forward. Even at the risk of further dependence on the Soviet Union, this plan opened up new directions for rapid economic development. (38e)

The problems of increasing industrial production are even more complicated in the case of Communist China. Starting from a very low level of industrialization, the first goal was to reach, by 1957, the 1927 level of Soviet production. Since then, Chinese progress, while rapid, has been hampered by several false starts, including the disastrous attempt to increase steel production in small units. Between 1952 and 1959, steel output increased about tenfold, electric power almost sixfold, coal fivefold, and cement fourfold. Manufactured consumer goods grew at a less dramatic but still substantial rate: for instance, cotton-yard production increased two to two and a half times. In short, during its first decade or so, the Communist regime in China was quite successful in increasing industrial production. (415; 54b)

As far as the Fascist and National Socialist systems are concerned, the record is somewhat less easy to analyze. For one thing, in Germany foreign trade, essential to the well-being of this overpopulated country, rapidly declined. In 1933 exports still exceeded imports by almost 700 million marks, but by 1935 the surplus had shrunk to 100 million marks, and this trend continued. The situation was to some extent the natural consequence of the National Socialist government's policy of autarky, for it meant that the country's economic resources, limited as they were, had to be organized in such a way as to render the country independent of foreign supplies. Since the ulterior goal was readiness for war, this policy was carried out whatever the intrinsic viability of the activities was when measured by standards derived from the world market. Mining operations for low-grade ore were extended, and oil borings carried through. The synthetic production of such materials as rubber and fibers was vigorously pursued. As a result, a good deal of additional work was provided for the Germans, who were now producing these goods instead of importing them from abroad. Of course, self-sufficiency was never fully achieved, but it did increase considerably. Hitler once admitted Germany's limitations: "We know that the geographical situation of Germany, a country poor in raw materials, does not permit of autarky. It must be emphasized again and again that the government is anything but hostile towards exports." (79) Nonetheless, the policy was pushed as hard as circumstances would allow in order to make Germany ready for war, when imports might be cut off. *Wehrwirtschaft,* or an economy for defense, was the euphemistic expression employed to describe this military economy, which was based on the subordination of commercial motives to national military needs. In light of this objective, it is extraordinary how little Germany was prepared for the world war into which Hitler's policies eventually plunged the country. The only explanation is that the regime, in view of Hitler's conception of a lightning war, did not expect it to last very long or, even less, to turn into a *world* war.

As an illustration of what this search for war materials, combined with the policy of self-sufficiency, meant, one might cite the Goering Works — plants intended to exploit low-grade iron ores found in central Germany that were not economical in the usual sense. These works were part of the rapidly increasing business activity of the party and its agencies. Publishing, printing, and real estate had, of course, been important party activities even in the days of the Weimar Republic, but to these were added in the thirties a considerable number of other fields. Among these, the Goering Works, or more fully the *Reichswerke, A.G. für Erzbergbau Und Eisenhütten, Hermann Göring,* with a capital of 75 million marks, was the most important. From its original mining and steelmaking, it soon branched out in many other directions. It has been called a gangster organization, designed to steal from as many other businesses as possible, especially in such conquered and occupied territories as Austria and Czechoslovakia. (263e) Originally the capital for this enterprise was gathered by Goering, who used every means at the disposal of a totalitarian dictator, especially intimidation. Since the venture had no capitalist appeal and hence could not command credit, Goering intimidated bankers and industrialists into contributing their share (155 million marks out of 400 million in 1939). This brings us to one of the key aspects of the National Socialist economy.

The substitution of fear for confidence fundamentally alters the nature of an economy. It ceases to be "capitalist." *Credit* derives from the Latin word *credo* or "I believe"; since here we find substituted "I fear," such a system might well be called a *timet* system. (290a) Such a system did, in fact, constitute the basis of government finance under the Nazis. Not only industrial enterprise, but the whole field of public borrowing came to depend upon the intimidation of the public. The consequent vast increase in Germany's public debt, eventually reaching nearly 500 billion marks (100 billion dollars), was the consequence. It raised, of course, a serious question of how to go on. One ingenious professor, presumably with tongue in cheek, suggested just before the war that this was Hitler's great invention in the field of public finance, offering an opportunity for every German to help the Führer achieve the goals that his genius sought to realize. (352) The question of ultimate limits to such a system of forced borrowing he answered by saying that at some point there must be a "creative sacrifice." This sacrifice would consist of every loyal German's accepting the cancellation of the Reich's indebtedness, so as to free the Führer's hands for further ventures. It was a neat, sycophantic way of describing state bankruptcy, but it turned out that the sacrifice was quite uncreative and resulted from the collapse of the Hitler regime. While the system lasted, though, it gave the government a good deal of capital it might not otherwise have been able to secure. In a sense, the fiscal operation of a totalitarian economy may thus be compared to that of a constitutional system at war, when large-scale financing of the government is carried out on the basis of patriotic appeals, backed by a good deal of pressure from various sources.

Under this *timet* system there was, obviously, no natural limit to an increase in the government's indebtedness, and the result was a rapidly mounting debt. It rose on an ascending scale as shown by the following figures (in rounded billion marks): 1932, 11; 1933, 12; 1936, 15; 1938, 20; 1939, 30. (340) It was the application of the *timet* system to foreign-trade negotiations that really constituted the essence of Hjalmar Schacht's dealings with the smaller countries, especially the Balkans. Here, too, threats were employed to extract goods and loans in connection with their delivery, which could not have been secured on the basis of free bargaining. (263d) The threats were primarily in the field of foreign trade itself, such as stopping all imports from a particular country, but at times they went a good deal further. "The aim of Germany's trade policy thus became exceedingly simple: to buy from a country as much as you can . . . but without paying." (263m) Thus Germany became more and more of a debtor nation under a clearing system that concentrated all control over foreign-trade balances in the hands of the government. (250)

Franz Neumann made this point as part of his detailed analysis of the National Socialist economy. (263) His central concern was to show that this economy was neither socialist nor state capitalist. To be sure, the law gave the government unlimited power; it could do almost anything and could expropriate anybody, but this law, he thought, in fact hid the reality, and the economy remained "capitalist." He minimized the role of planning and depicted the economy as compounded of two parts: the "monopolistic economy" and the "command economy." The monopolistic economy he interpreted as characterized by a great increase in cartels and monopolies which, aided and abetted by the government and the party, maximized profits. "The structure of [this part of] the German economy is one of a fully monopolized and cartellized economy," in which the small businessman and the worker are at the mercy of the big tycoons. (218) The second part, the command economy, is that section where the interfering and regimenting "state" is at work. Yet he felt that neither direct economic activities of the party and state, in the nationalized sector, nor the control of prices, of investments and profits, of foreign trade, and of labor constituted state capitalism, "in spite of the fundamental changes that are the inevitable consequence of regimentation." Leaving aside the largely semantic question of whether to call the National Socialist economy "state capitalism," it is evident from Neumann's facts, as well as from much evidence that has come to light since (115; 218), that the regime definitely held the central control and direction of the entire economy through the bureaucratic co-ordination of its formerly independent corporate entities, including typically most other associations and group activities. (263n) That key figures in the control set-up were party members as well as businessmen clinches the argument. The key posts in many directorates of banks and industrial combines were also occupied by men who at the same time were powerful figures in the Nazi hierarchy, just as they are in the Communist regimes. If we disregard the Hegelian and Marxist concern with *the* state, what remains is the central direction and control of the entire economy.

European countries have traditionally let certain sectors of the economy be operated by the government. Democratic Switzerland no less than autocratic Prussia have run their railroads and telephone and telegraph services as government monopolies. This is the monarchical mercantilist tradition developed first of all in France, where it continues strong to this day. The policy of letting the government participate in the economy, especially where natural monopolies present the problem of effective control in the public interest, has been greatly expanded since the war. In Britain, France, and elsewhere, banking, mining, and other basic economic activities have been placed under government control. These economies are, therefore, neither capitalist nor socialist in any strict sense, though they are obviously less socialist than the Soviet Union. The term "mixed economy" has been suggested for them. The Fascist regimes, in a sense, also operated such mixed economies. But under such regimes no part of the economy is free from government interference. Central direction and control is concentrated in the hands of the party and its ruler-dictator, and no popularly elected parliament or other representative body exists to interpose its views between the government and the economy. The government is consequently not subject to extended criticism and the rival proposals of alternating party majorities. This does not by any means preclude the influence of businessmen who are members of the party and its ruling groups; quite the contrary. In the case of the Hitler regime, such businessmen were able to manipulate the corporate system, with its cartels and trusts, as well as the control of prices, investments, profits, and foreign trade, to their personal advantage on a large scale. The careers of men like Frick, who was brought to trial at Nuremberg, show how extensive were the possibilities for personal enrichment by these practices. (162b) Such personal careers, however, are incidental to the over-all pattern; they correspond to the careers of skilled managers in the Soviet Union — men like Saburov or Malyshev or the fallen-from-grace Voznesensky. The pattern is one of central control and direction; it came to full fruition in Hitler Germany only during the war, when Albert Speer was invested with dictatorial powers of direction.

The focus of this central direction and control went through three different stages. There was the stage of work-creation programs, the stage of preparation for war under the Four-Year Plan, and the attempt at total mobilization during the war. At each of these stages, various decisions were taken which constituted intervention in the operations of a free market economy and deflected economic development into the channels desired by the totalitarian rulers. It is true that some nontotalitarian countries have, within the context of constitutional democracy, attempted similar central direction — subject to extended public criticism and, therefore, to party competition and rivalry leading to substantial alterations and even abandonment — but this does not alter the fact that interference by central control, combined with the other typical features discussed, is characteristic of totalitarian dictatorship and would not be possible in a freer economy. Such central control operates differently (but not necessarily better) when accompanied by ideological and one-party leadership, by secret-police terror, and by government monopoly of mass communications and weapons. For the inherent potentialities of corruption that such a system entails by its large-scale bureaucratization are greatly enhanced by these totalitarian features. The detailed record now available shows that this corruption was in fact at work in both Fascist systems. Therefore, such data as the increase in undistributed profits, consequent share values, and dividends (on the basis of statistical averages) show that they were what has been rather imaginatively dubbed "vampire" economies. Bogged down in a morass of special favors, which are the very opposite of the workings of the price mechanism of the competitive market economy (290b), they were centrally planned and directed to the pursuit of aggressive and expansive war.

The situation in Fascist Italy under the corporate system is revealing. The essential effect of this system was to put all of Italian industry into one big pool, to make the government assume responsibility for a minimum profit and to grant it in return the power to direct all investment and hence the future development of industry. (310c) That such an arrangement, based as it is upon guaranteed profits, does not constitute a competitive market economy is evident. That there existed differential rewards is not decisive, for they also prevail in Communist countries.

In conclusion, it is readily conceded that the differences between the fascist type of industrial arrangement and the communist one are many and obvious. In one case, the totalitarian system is superimposed on an established industrial structure; in the other, the industrial structure is built almost from scratch. In the fascist economies, the ownership of the means of production is formally left intact and the same "tycoons" continue to preside at board meetings (with the exception of government-sponsored enterprises such as the Goering Works); in the communist economies, industry is state-owned and the managers are state-appointed officials (or, as in some earlier cases, former owners are temporarily kept as state managers). But these do not appear to be really fundamental differences. One needs to go below the surface and ask: who controls the industrial development, who sets its quotas and allocates resources, who determines the ultimate objectives of industrial production, who regulates awards, who controls the personnel, who establishes political standards of loyalty for all those involved?

The answers to these questions suggest that the modern totalitarian regimes are basically alike in recognizing the vitality of the industrial process and in considering it the key to political success, domestic or external. As a result they have made the "battle for production" a central theme of their action programs, and to achieve it they have subordinated the industrial machine to the requirements of the regime. Such questions as who holds formal title to property, how "profits," that is to say, rewards, are determined, and whether former owners and decision makers continue to hold positions, provided they conform to the regime's commands, are of relatively minor significance. What is decisive is the overpowering reality of totalitarian central control by the dictator and his party.

19

LABOR: BOND OR FREE?

The centrally directed economy, and the bureaucratic coordination of all associations and corporate entities that possess a degree of autonomy and self-government under a constitutional democracy, engulf the organizations of labor. This fact is, in a sense, the most disillusioning aspect of communism from the viewpoint of the laboring man. Labor has been told and is still being told that socialism as envisaged in Marxism, that is to say, socialism based upon the dictatorship of the proletariat, means the liberation of labor from capitalist oppression and exploitation. What labor finds, however, is that in reality the all-powerful party through its government, which acts on behalf of the proletariat and presumably embodies its "dictatorship," deprives the organizations of labor, the unions, of their former independent status and transforms them into adjuncts of the governmental bureaucracy. The same thing happens under fascism; here too the "socialist" dictatorship is prepared to coordinate the unions and to synchronize their actions with the policies of the government.

Over the last hundred years, trade unions became important organizations in those countries in which industrialism and capitalism developed. As successors to the guilds of medieval craftsmen, they were built upon the common workmanship and the common interest of workers in a particular "trade." The many highly specialized unions of the American Federation of Labor are typical of this early unionism. Later, as industries grew and plants became larger and larger, there also developed more inclusive unions, less concerned with workmanship and more with the common interests of all the workers in a particular industry, of which the Congress of

Industrial Organizations is typical. The merger of the AFL and the CIO is based upon the recognition that all workers, no matter how organized, have certain common interests and tasks. (104h)

In the earlier period and down to the end of the nineteenth century, employers resented and opposed the free labor unions, and in some countries they do to this day. It has, however, become increasingly clear to management in all advanced countries that labor is not only theoretically entitled to form its own free associations if it chooses to do so — that, in a constitutional democracy, labor has the right to be organized — but that it is actually of great advantage to management in industry to have unions to deal with. Modern labor relations are based upon the freely negotiated contractual relationship between "capital" and "labor," which collective bargaining has brought into being. The idea of a company union, organized and dominated by the employer and management, has been superseded by the free union because the paternalistic conception of the former proved inadequate to the task of representing the worker as a full-fledged citizen in a democratic society.

Among the most important, and for a long time the most hotly contested, weapons of the organized worker was his right to strike, collectively to refuse to continue working until a bargain had been arrived at between his representatives, typically the officers of his union or unions, and the employer. This right to strike, while not found in the constitutions of eighteenth-century vintage, has made its way into more recent constitutional documents, for instance, a number of the American states, France, Italy, and the Federal Republic of Germany. It is also contained in the Universal Declaration of Human Rights issued by the United Nations. However, the assent of the Soviet Union and the satellites could be secured only because this declaration lacks all enforcement machinery; no such right is recognized in the USSR. On the other hand, the Soviet Union's constitution leads off its tenth chapter, dealing with fundamental rights and duties, by article 118 guaranteeing the right to work, adding that this right is "ensured by the socialist organization of the national economy" and that the growth of productive forces, the elimination of economic crises, and the abolition of unemployment — presumably consequences of this socialist organization — contribute to such guarantee. In short, the right is not secured by juridical means, by sanctions and procedures for enforcing them, but by social forces.

Strange as it may seem from an ideological viewpoint, the USSR, the country in which the worker is supposed to be in effective control of the government, rejects the right to strike, along with the idea of free and independent unions. The argument advanced for this policy is basically very simple. Why, it is asked, should one group of workers be able to force its demand upon the rest of the workers, when all of them together control the means of production? The argument would be unanswerable if the workers' control were effective, from a democratic standpoint, instead of being embodied in the monolithic power of the Communist Party, which monopolizes the repesentation of the whole proletariat, including even the farm workers. As a matter of fact, this problem of workers' participation in the control of industry first presented itself in the Soviet Union in simple syndicalist form. Soviets were formed in each plant, and the management of the plant was entrusted to these councils. But the efforts at building a comprehensive structure from the ground up soon ran into snags. The position of the unions and the form of their effective participation proved, in the twenties, to be the real touchstone of Soviet organization.

As early as 1920, at the Tenth Party Congress, strong opposition developed among some trade unionists against the centralizing, statist tendencies of the newly established dictatorship of the proletariat. Led by Shliapnikov and Alexandra Kollontai, the so-called Workers' Opposition came out strongly for a syndicalist utopia in which economic enterprises were to be run by workers organized into trade unions. (312e) At the other extreme, they were opposed by the "statists," led by Trotsky and Bukharin, who urged immediate absorption of the trade unions by the state, on the ground that no conflict was possible between a state of the workers and the workers themselves. Lenin, after briskly attacking the Workers' Opposition for engaging in anarchistic, syndicalist, and non-Marxist agitation, responded with the transmission-belt theory, according to which the trade unions were to act as intermediaries between the dictatorship of the proletariat and the working masses: "Trade Unions are the reservoirs of state power, a school of Communism, a school of management. In this sphere the specific and main thing is not administration, but 'contacts' between the central state administration, national economy and the broad masses of the toilers." (205g) Such a definition obviously changed entirely the nature of the trade union from an institution of workers into an agency of the party and its government. The history of the Soviet trade unions from this moment on is one of steady decline in independence and of their transformation into a bureaucratic institution for dealing with labor problems.

For a while, during the NEP period, the unions remained active on behalf of the working masses, but on the eve of the Sixteenth Party Congress the trade-union leadership was accused of Menshevism and purged. The congress proclaimed the no-conflict theory previously postulated by Trotsky, and rapid development of industry was declared to be the workers' primary interest. The trade unions were told to help the party increase labor productivity, and the process of trade-union submission to the political requirements of the regime was, broadly speaking, put in final form. At the same time, the newly launched policy of industrialization resulted in a rapid expansion in the number of industrial workers, giving rise to numerous problems of administration, organization, welfare, and so on. From 14.5 million industrial workers in 1930, the total grew by 1940 to 30.4 million and by 1948 to 33.4 million. (372) This trend has continued. Statistics since 1948 do not separate the industrial labor force from the white-collar workers. Including these under the heading of "nonagricultural labor," the figures are as follows: 1930 — 18.1 million, 1940 — 40.8 million, 1950 — 43 million, 1959 — 56.2 million. (17a) It became the function of the trade unions to give these masses an organizational framework and leadership. (312f)

In the words of a Soviet student of constitutional law, "The Soviet trade unions are not a formal party organization but, in fact, they are carrying out the directives of the party. All leading organs of the trade unions consist primarily of communists who execute the party line in the entire work of the trade unions." (68) This frank comment, written in 1940, is orthodox doctrine to this day. The constitution provides that citizens "have the right to unite in public organizations" (art. 126), but this right is really a duty; for it is explained that it serves the purpose of developing "the organizational initiative and political activity of the masses."

This conception is elaborated in the party program of 1961 as follows: "The Trade Unions acquire particular importance as schools of administration and economic management, as schools of communism. The Party shall help the trade unions to take a growing share." There then follows a list of the unions' tasks: to increase communist consciousness, to work for technical progress, higher productivity, fulfillment and overfulfillment of state plans and assignments, to improve the skill of workers and their working and living conditions, to protect the material interests and rights of the workers, to ensure that housing and cultural development plans are fulfilled and that other social services (health, social insurance) are improved, to control consumption funds and the work done in the factories. (355b; 89t) Clearly, the activities of the unions are farflung, multifarious, and important; yet they do not alter, but rather confirm, the fact that the Soviet trade unions are agencies of the party.

Their organization, like that of the party, is hierarchical and centralized. Real power lies not with the nominally all-powerful congress, but with a much smaller body, the presidium of the All-Union Central Council of Trade Unions. All unions are in the end subordinate to this body and subject to its instructions. The tasks of the Soviet trade unions, apart from that of raising productivity and struggling relentlessly "for complete elimination of the rotten practice of equal wages" (189b), include the administration of the state program of social insurance, sanatoria, and workers' rest homes, supervision of food served at work and of factory housing conditions, control of the level of political consciousness, participation in planning, and limited grievance intervention on behalf of the workers. Thus, with the exception of the last item, the broad pattern of trade-union functions indicates clearly the extent to which the union has become absorbed into the workings of the totalitarian system.

Worker-management grievances are adjudicated by Norms and Conflicts Commissions (RKK). The majority of such cases arise either because of alleged management injustices or as a result of varying interpretations of existing labor regulations. According to one authority:

To the extent that the existing procedures provide an outlet for the ventilation and adjustment of certain types of grievances, they serve the Party leadership well. The much-publicized cases in which workers' complaints lead to corrective action have important symbolic significance. They help to renew faith in the regime's sense of equity, and they appear to validate the paternal concern of the Soviet rulers for the condition of the masses. Even though the grievance machinery is restricted in scope, such relief as it affords commands popular support and makes a positive contribution to the strength and productive efficiency of the regime. (89n)

Since 1947 the trade unions have been empowered to negotiate collective agreements with management, but here again the right is rather unreal. Such agreements must follow the standard form prescribed by the governmental authorities, while the broad pattern of wages and salaries is centrally determined and decreed. The so-called collective agreements, therefore, tend to become little more than a repetition of the existing prescriptions for the given industrial branch, to which is added a specific statement, incorporated in the agreement, as to the quotas and production goals to be achieved by the workers and management. The agreement becomes a reminder to the workers of what is expected of them rather than a protection of their interests. Soviet workers are not allowed to forget the fact that the Code of Labor Legislation states explicitly that "when a worker fails to fulfill by his own fault the established norm, his wages are paid according to the quantity and quality of his actual output without a guarantee to him of any minimum wages whatsoever" (art. 57). Unlike his capitalist counterpart, according to Soviet legislation "an employer is not obliged to support the worker." (189c)

The Soviet worker evidently toils under severe restrictions imposed upon him by the state. For many years, his eight-hour work day explicitly made no allowance for time off for meals — hence the actual time spent at work is longer — and he worked six days a week. There has been considerable improvement since 1956. Wages and pensions have risen, and the work week has been reduced, now approaching the forty-hour week. But work discipline is harsh in Communist countries. According to Soviet legislation, a worker is subject to severe penalties for late arrival at work. During the war and after, tardiness of even twenty minutes could result in imprisonment. This was modified after Stalin died. Another severe limitation on a Soviet worker's freedom is the legal authority of the government to determine his place of work. The Ministry of Labor

Reserves, set up in 1947, was given the right to assign workers to priority industries. Workers could be frozen in the jobs and denied the right to quit. Noncompliance could result in prosecution by the state. Since December 1938, Soviet workers have been obliged to carry with them special labor books that include, apart from their personal data, a brief statement of their background, employment record, transfers, and the reasons for them. No one can be hired without such a book. Managers, furthermore, retain the labor books during the workers' employment, and a worker who quits without authorization is thus deprived of this vital document. In more vital industries the worker is also obliged to hand over his passport — a document that every Soviet citizen must have for internal travel and identification. He has, however, the right to give two weeks' notice, but too many job changes are risky. Many social-security benefits are tied to a single enterprise.

There also exists a system of labor conscription. A special government body may assign workers to an enterprise with a manpower problem. Workers must sign long-term contracts and may be transferred long distances, especially to those northern and eastern regions for which labor camps at one time supplied the needed workers.

While at work, the workers are constantly exhorted by their party organizations and by the trade unions to engage in "socialist competition" among themselves, and collectively with the workers of other factories, trusts, or institutions. Special rewards are given to those who excel in overfulfilling their norms, the so-called shock workers; since the thirties the successful shock workers have been known as Stakhanovites, after Stakhanov, a coalminer. The Stakhanovites receive special medals and badges, as well as financial rewards. They are entitled to certain privileges, such as free railroad travel, while in some cases their children are entitled to free education. It was estimated that in 1948 some 87 percent of the labor force in the USSR was engaged in "socialist competition." (461) Labor-class solidarity under such circumstances is difficult to maintain. Presumably, one of the reasons for Khrushchev's concern for enlisting popular participation and enthusiasm was to be found in this need for identification and the corresponding sense of solidarity with the regime — it was a matter of the productivity of labor.

No account of Soviet labor would be complete without at least a brief reference to the State Labor Reserves. They give training, under a draft system, to youths over fourteen who are not continuing their studies. After completion of such training, they are assigned by the government to specific occupations where they are needed most. Evaders are prosecuted. The system, apart from its important distinction between those who continue higher education, either through scholarship or, until 1956, by paying the fees, and those who do not, gives the government a cheap and steady supply of manpower to be used for urgently needed projects. Furthermore, the system serves to break the youth away from their rustic environment and to transform them into an urban proletariat.

In all this the Soviet trade unions tend to play a role similar to that of the government under radical laissez faire — the role, that is, of a policeman stepping in only in the case of extreme abuse but not positively striving to help the cause of the working man. The trade unions admittedly render some important services to the labor masses, particularly in terms of health and leisure facilities and in helping out on the lowest levels of labor disputes, although the total regimentation of leisure time is irritating and, in some ways for the average man, perhaps the most obnoxious aspect of totalitarianism. Summing up the role of the trade unions, it is clear that their function is to serve the economic objectives of the system and the political requirements of the regime. To repeat, they are not agencies of Soviet labor, but bureaucratic institutions of the Soviet government and the Communist Party for labor matters.

Beyond this general subjugation of labor in the Soviet totalitarian system, there existed for many years the outright slavery of the labor camps. It is perhaps the most paradoxical feature of a political system erected in the name of Karl Marx that these labor camps should have existed and in an attenuated form still do. For had it not been the most bitter reproach of Karl Marx to the capitalist system that under its so-called "iron law of wages" there was kept in existence a large pool of the unemployed, the "reserve army of industry," who, because they were eager for jobs, kept the wage level down near the minimum of existence? The labor camps that at one time contained millions of people were the communist totalitarian equivalent of the reserve army of industry. They were composed of all kinds of people whom the regime for one reason or another did not like, including so-called slackers — men and women who did not slave hard enough for the low wages that the regime paid to many of its workers, though some favored classes of workers were quite well paid. The labor camps provided workers for projects which were run so uneconomically that even the minimum wages of the Soviet Union did not provide an economic basis for their operation.

Conditions in these labor camps were so appalling that their existence became a concern of the United Nations. An *ad hoc* committee, constituted by UNESCO and the International Labor Organization, was set up in 1952 and, after hearings and presentations by such interested organizations as the Mid-European Study Center, published a report condemning the system. (11a) While the system originated in the Soviet Union, where, in conjunction with a crime wave in the mid-twenties and the later collectivization, an ever larger group of people was incarcerated by the regime, it gradually spread over the entire span of the Soviet bloc. All the satellites, Poland, Czechoslovakia, Hungary, Bulgaria, Rumania, Albania, and East Germany came to employ the system; it is found in Yugoslavia and China, too. In Russia it was in full swing by 1928, when the peasant resistance to forced collectivization in connection with the First Five-Year Plan produced millions of "criminals." The secret "State Plan for the Development of the National Economy of the USSR in 1941" shows that a substantial portion of Soviet output was produced by slave labor.

What was the size and importance of this slave labor in the Soviet economy, and what can be credited to it? In 1941 slave labor produced 5,325,000 metric tons of coal; 34,730,000 cubic meters of commercial timber and firewood, or 11.9 percent of Soviet production; 14.49 percent of all furniture; 22.58 percent of railroad ties; 40.5 percent of chrome ore; and so on. (11b) Road building, rail construction, and mining in remote regions, like Siberia, have been carried through by this slave labor. The estimates of the number of persons involved in this gigantic "industrial reserve army" varies between 8 and 14 million. To these must be added the satellite labor camps, but no reliable estimates have been made. (11c; 63) If we accept a figure of 10 million for the USSR alone as a broad estimate for the Stalinist period, we must conclude that about 5 percent of the Soviet population was thus "employed," a figure that just about corresponds to Marx's industrial reserve army. It is in the light of these facts that the Soviet claim for "labor peace" and their proud boast that no unemployment exists in the Soviet Union must be seen and evaluated. The contrast between an unemployed man in the West, eking out a meager existence on the basis of his unemployment-insurance payments, and an inmate of a Soviet labor camp, systematically starved and brutalized, shows the full measure of difference between democracy and totalitarianism. This difference may be vicariously experienced by any reader of Solzhenitsyn's remarkable *One Day in the Life of Ivan Denisovich*. (333) However, lest he feel too superior, a Westerner ought to compare this account with some realistic appraisals of prisons in the West or chain gangs in the southern United States.

The Fascist dictatorships did not go the whole length of this development before the war, but the Nazi system of slave labor evolved during the war was essentially the same kind of totalitarian reserve army. And all these dictatorships arrived at the subjugation of free trade unions to the party and government. The only difference was in ideological motivation. The Fascists, of course, did not claim that the elimination of the class struggle was the result of its consummation, as is the case in the Soviet Union; rather, they insisted that it be suppressed. The class-struggle doctrine of orthodox Marxism was, in fact, one of the key points of the Fascist attack. The bitterly denounced division of the nation into classes was alleged to be the result of Marxist-Socialist-Communist agitation; hence, after the liquidation of these disturbers of the social peace, a new organization of industrial and labor relations would reunite the nation. The Fascist solution was essentially part of the corporative organization; the National Socialist solution was the Labor Front. In each, the conflict of interest between labor and management-capital was "resolved" by making the assumption that the plant, factory, or industry was a "community" and then to apply the pattern of community organization typical for the regime's own kind of totalitarianism. In Italy this was a matter of subjecting both management and labor to the controlling direction of the "state," while in Germany the employer was made the führer of his workers.

The National Socialist policy of establishing a labor front, which would transform the contractual relations of labor and management into communal relations, cannot be said to have been a success. Yet it completely destroyed the freedom of the unions. (263g; 439) It must be seen in conjunction with related policies of declaring the plant a community in the so-called Charter of Labor of January 20, 1934, (263h) of organizing leisure time in "strength through joy" activities, and of compulsory work assignments. The Labor Front was a party "formation," which included virtually every gainfully employed person, management as well as employees, 25 million in all. It was led by Dr. Ley, one of the early leaders of the Nazi Party. At the outset, it took over the entire trade-union structure, including all of its property. The utter failure of the unions to fight back has been attributed to their bureaucratization under the Weimar Republic, which transformed their leadership into an unenterprising officialdom. Whether they actually could have accomplished much may be doubted. In the Soviet Union, as we have seen, the attempt to maintain some measure of independence, even under Communist leadership, proved unsuccessful. (263i) The same may be said of the small units or cells the National Socialists had organized originally to infiltrate the unions. They too would not maintain the independence of the unions. Instead, the Labor Front assumed the task of indoctrinating labor in National Socialist ideology. These plant communities were grouped according to industries into national communities (*Reichsbetriebsgemeinschaften*), each of which was subject to an office of the National Labor Front. Since the *Führerprinzip* was applied throughout, it is clear that in a sense every worker in every plant in Hitler's Reich was a cog in the vast bureaucratic hierarchy. The union dues the Labor Front continued to collect were in fact taxes, considering that the Front did not represent the workers but the party bureaucracy. (263j)

It might be well to say a word more, therefore, about the "plant community" of the Charter of Labor. It states the concept as follows: "In the plant, the enterpriser as leader and the employees and workers as followers work together for the accomplishment of the objectives of the plant and for the common good of the nation and the state." In the light of this general concept, it further provided that "the leader of the plant decides all matters concerning the plant, as regulated by statute," and that the leader "shall look after the welfare of the followers, while the latter shall place full confidence in him." The paternalistic notion that the employer is responsible for the welfare of his workers was traditional in Germany. (55) It used to be based on the fact that as owner of the plant he must look after those who worked in it, much as a houseowner is responsible for those who enter his house. It had been somewhat shaken by the development of the Works Councils (in the Weimar Republic), which the courts considered ground for asserting that the responsibility was now a joint one. They were a feeble beginning of democracy in industry — the councils now set up under the Codetermination Law in the Federal Republic constitute a further extension of it — and hence the National Socialists immediately transformed them in accordance with their totalitarian leadership notions. Renamed Confidence Councils (*Vertrauensräte*), members were nominated by the manager and the leader of the party cell in the factory and approved by acclamation of the followers.

One cannot but agree with the conclusion that the Nazi innovations in the labor field, as we have sketched them here, were "devices for the manipulation of the working class." (263k) The system was rounded out by two other features, already mentioned: leisure-time activities and the compulsory assignment to a particular workplace. The latter began under the Four-Year Plan in 1938 and became more onerous, as the country faced war and defeat. The contractual relationship as the basis of work became a mockery under these assignments: when a worker was assigned to a plant, he was assumed to have entered into a contract, subject of course to the general labor law. Workers became tied to their place of work, for they were forbidden to leave without permission from the government's Labor Exchange. Firing was likewise made subject to government veto. In short, the freedom of both employer and employee to choose was almost completely destroyed; as in the USSR, the workers constituted a vast reserve army to be assigned at pleasure to the managers of plants operating within the context of the government's plans and directions. Since the government also assumed the right to fix both minimum and maximum wages at the outset of the war, and to regulate all other conditions of work, it is evident that to speak of this economy as "capitalist" in the sense of a free, competitive market economy is untenable: the labor market was neither free nor competitive. It is therefore not surprising that the efforts of the Hitler regime to increase productivity and self-sufficiency failed. While labor productivity rose steadily in the United States between 1933 and 1939, no such development took place in Germany. Instead of increasing productivity, the businessmen exploited labor ruthlessly with the aid and encouragement of the Hitler regime.

To draw a veil over this sordid drama, the Nazi Party developed the "strength through joy" program of organized leisure time. It was actually patterned on the Italian Dopolavoro program, but carried to greater length and surrounded with a great halo of innovation. It is perhaps too much to say that leisure time was regimented, because workers were free to participate or not to some extent, but it certainly was a palliative to sugarcoat the loss of the genuine rights that German labor had possessed as a result of the efforts of its free unions over many decades. Claiming that labor too was a community, a Nazi official put it thus: "to win strength for daily work was therefore the final goal which the new creation sought to achieve." Thus the Italian leisure organization "After Work" became the National Socialist community, "Strength through Joy." (2631)

In Italy, the workers were organized as one of the "pillars" of the corporative organization. Indeed, the organization evolved out of the peculiar Fascist "syndicates," unions that were actually developed in competition with the free unions and gained ascendancy, under the skillful leadership of Edmondo Rossoni, after the Fascists had seized power. The original radical notion, derived from older syndicalist thought, that the union would take over the plants by absorbing management, was in typical Fascist fashion superseded by the idea that "corporations" composed of both employers and employees would accept direction and control of the state. The thought underlying the Fascist corporative set-up was in fact to some extent akin to older conservative and Catholic thought; but whereas the papal encyclical *Rerum Novarum* (1891) had put forward the idea of a corporative structure along medieval lines, that is to say, decentralized and localized in authority, the Fascist conception was "hierarchical" and all authority was derived from the head of the corporate state, the minister of corporations, Benito Mussolini. It was the Italian version of "coordination" under which all associations became Fascist. (310) As one student put it many years ago: "The dictatorship is the necessary rack and screw of the Corporate system." (95h; 220d) The corporative system was initiated by the Charter of Labor of April 21, 1927, which the Grand Council of Fascism adopted as a party measure (it was then a party organ). It was, of course, soon transformed into a governmental policy by statutory enactment and judicial decision. Under it, Italian workers lost all the rights and privileges which their unions had fought for and won. A paternalistic governmental control and direction was substituted for it, closely resembling the Soviet Union's trade-union program, except that in Italy (and in Germany) the nation served as the ideological excuse instead of the proletariat. As a consequence, in Italy the state rather than the party was predominant. Throughout the charter and in its subsequent implementation the government was supreme. The key passages assert that "since the private organization of production is a function of national concern, the organizer of the enterprise is responsible to the State for the direction of production . . . The employed . . . is an active collaborator in the economic enterprise, the direction of which belongs to the employer, who bears the responsibility for it." (95i) Measures of social welfare, such as health protection, scholarships for children, and insurance against disability, illness, and old age, as well as governmental control of minimum wages, holidays, and vocational education, ought not to deceive anyone about the basic political change: both workers and management lost their autonomy, but, in view of labor's weak position, this loss of freedom was for them much more serious; it made this "charter" a solemn mockery. Proclaiming the "freedom of the syndicates," the charter asserted that "only the legally recognized syndicate, subjected to the control of the State, has the right to represent legally all the employers and employed." (95j) It comes almost as an anticlimax when one learns that "strikes are criminal offenses." Only some of the workers participated in this sham organization at first; but under Fascist pressure, it ran as high as 87 percent in industry. (95k) Leaving aside the employers, one can readily see that the unions had ceased to be representative and militant organs of the workers and had become instruments for the disciplining of labor, run by thousands of Fascist officials completely subservient to the government.

It is within this context that Dopolavoro must be seen. It amounted in fact to transforming the rich free associations of the

Italian people, in all the various spheres of cultural and social life, into bureaucratically controlled appendages of the government. Music and art, literary and social leisure activities, including mandolin societies and the like, became Fascist by being absorbed into the huge network of Dopolavoro. In his wonderfully sardonic portrayal of all this humbug, Salvemini, after reporting that exactly 1,155,365 excursions, musical performances, sports exercises, and so on had been taking place under Dopolavoro in 1934, concludes: "The Fascists have not yet come to the point of publishing statistics on the number of kisses exchanged under the auspices of Dopolavoro, but these will soon be counted, and the staggering total will be attributed to the genius of Mussolini." (310)

In conclusion, it seems very clear that under totalitarian dictatorship, in spite of its "popular" participation, labor has lost its freedom and independence, that its organizations have become bureaucratic agencies of the government, and that not only in his working hours, but in his leisure time as well, the worker has become a cog in the totalitarian centrally directed economy. To complete the paradox of his "workers' paradise," any worker who fails to live up to the standards set by the regime is in danger of being made a slave in one of the many labor camps of the regime. Thus the industrial reserve army of capitalism that aroused Marx's indignation has been transformed into an army of "men in bond."

20

AGRICULTURE: ORGANIZING
THE PEASANTRY

Agricultural production has been as central a concern of the totalitarians as industrial production. But the problems to be faced and the policies adopted have been quite different between the regimes and within them. The Communists, first in the USSR, afterwards in Germany, and throughout Eastern Europe as well as in China, started with an appeal based on treating the peasants as brothers of the workers; the Fascists and National Socialists did the same. Yet for the Communists this was a concession based upon a sharp differentiation between the poor peasants, who were part of the toiling masses, and the more well-to-do ones, who were soon denounced as kulaks and lumped together with capitalists. But the Fascists, and even more the Nazis, idealized the peasantry under such slogans as "blood and soil." The concrete situation with which different totalitarian regimes were confronted also played a role: in the Soviet Union more than 80 percent of the population were peasants in 1917, while in other countries at the time of the totalitarian takeover, the percentage was lower (except in China of course). In Italy the peasants were around 60 percent of the population, and in Germany perhaps 30 percent. The situation in the satellite countries — Poland, Hungary, Rumania — resembled that in Italy, while in Czechoslovakia the peasantry constituted about 55 percent. In China, finally, the population was so very largely of the peasant type that the Communist leadership there actually found it necessary to alter the ideology of communism somewhat to take account of the situation, at least in the revolutionary stage. (320b)

The policies pursued by the totalitarian regimes in the field of agriculture cannot be understood unless one appreciates fully the role of the peasantry in the countries concerned. The related issue of the need for "land reform" must also be considered at the start. Only after these two topics have been dealt with can agricultural operations of the totalitarian regimes be adequately analyzed by comparative evaluation. Before we turn to the peasantry, the problem of land reform needs to be briefly sketched. Throughout the world, the problem of large-scale landed estates, in many instances the result of preceding feudal conditions of land ownership (85), has become a focal point of attack for widely demanded reforms. Throughout Asia, "landlordism" has become a battle cry of the embittered peasant masses, who have been kept in conditions of abject poverty. The same may be said of considerable areas of Europe, especially in the east and south. Land reform, meaning essentially the distribution of great estates among independent farmers each receiving a parcel sufficient for effective operation (varying from 20 to 100 acres, depending on conditions of climate, soil, and marketing) and thus obtaining the necessary "means of production," should have been the policy of those regimes aspiring to democratic rule. Unfortunately, time and again, landed proprietors have employed their vested wealth and entrenched social position to thwart the reform efforts of progressive democratic elements. Thereby they prepared the ground for totalitarian movements, both communist and fascist. The communists adopted the land-reform slogan — distribution of land to the peasants — as their most potent weapon in building effective mass support, while the fascists, both in Italy and Germany, not to speak of Rumania, Hungary, and the rest, though in fact allied with the big landholders, talked much of their interest in the peasantry and its rights. Everywhere it is the same story: a land-hungry peasantry, deeply disappointed at the failure of presumably democratic regimes to provide them with the means for making a living, turn to the totalitarians in the hope of a solution and eventually find themselves trapped and transformed into pawns of the totalitarian party and government. For the latter control the means of production and more especially the land, either through outright proprietorship or indirectly by means of an elaborate pattern of bureaucratic techniques.

The peasants, then, demand land reform. What actually is this peasantry? As a human type, the peasant is preindustrialist and precapitalist. Americans are apt to see him in comic-opera perspective, clad in quaint costumes, singing old folk songs and dancing folk dances. This image is not wholly in error; throughout Europe and Asia the peasantry has been the guardian of older, more earthy traditions, habits, and beliefs. But, politically speaking, the most significant feature of the peasant is his attitude toward the land and toward the methods of production he employs in tilling it. Typically the peasant is not market-oriented, but tradition-oriented. The focal point of his outlook is not what brings the best results in terms of market requirements, but what does so in terms of ancestral practices. Frequently the peasant is decidedly fixed, indeed immobile, in his attitude toward the land. Unlike the American or Australian farmer, or even the Danish or Swiss farmer, the peasant thinks of his land not as "capital" of a certain value, but rather as a heritage handed down by his forebears and to be handed on to future generations.

This rootedness, this attachment to the land as a timeless possession, makes the peasant a misfit in modern industrial society, rejected and despised by its protagonists, idolized by romantic adversaries of industrial society. (158; 336) Political parties have had difficulties in assimilating him — the rightist ones because of their tie-up with big landowners, the leftist ones because of their hostility to property, the liberal and middle-of-the-road ones because of their friendliness to industrial capitalism. As a result, the peasant has been the stepchild of democratic parliamentary politics. From time to time, he has formed his own party; peasant parties had come to play a significant role, particularly in the Slavic countries now overrun by the USSR, such as Poland. But these were, of course, minority parties, and since they were led by responsible agrarian leaders they were no match for the demagoguery of the totalitarian movements — both the Bolsheviks and the Fascists made the peasant a major focus of their mass propaganda and continue to do so.* Indeed, Mao has made the role of the peasant the main point of his

---

* Strange as it may seem, peasant parties carry on even after emigrating and have formed an International Union, which publishes a monthly bulletin very representative of the democratic peasants' viewpoint. They speak of themselves, in contrast to the Red International of the workers, as the Green International.

adaptation of Marxist-Leninist orthodoxy to the Chinese situation. (320c) In Yugoslavia, there has been a growing recognition of peasant farm property, and the new constitution recognizes it as a form of private ownership compatible with socialism. Collectivization of agriculture is handled administratively. And in Poland, the re-establishment of a measure of autonomy by Gomulka was soon followed by the dissolution of collective farms and the restoration of peasant proprietorship. The Russian Communists, by contrast, have continued to maintain collective agriculture, even though many changes have been made over the years.

At the start, the Bolsheviks appealed to the peasants as well as to the workers, and in the early years of the regime, the soviets were workers' *and* peasants' councils. All this soon proved a hollow sham. The peasants, who had been happy to distribute the land of the big estate owners among themselves, were decidedly hostile to the Soviet government's coercive policy of regimenting food deliveries. After the failure of an initial effort at conciliation — the New Economic Policy of Lenin (1922–1928) — Stalin turned against the peasantry (89u) and under the First Five-Year Plan undertook the wholesale liquidation of this class. The process was ideologically rationalized by dividing the peasantry into rich and poor peasants and by claiming that the fight was only directed against the former. Actually, they were only the first line of attack and, in developing the collectivist forms of agriculture, the independent peasant was largely eliminated from the Soviet scene (233); the same process is at present being repeated in the European satellites.

The collectivization in the Soviet Union was largely a forcible one. The peasants were pressed into collective farms by open coercion, and flying squads of party activists, Komsomol and secret-police detachments, and even army units roamed through the countryside to subdue the recalcitrant ones. The kulaks, or richer peasants, were rounded up and deported in great numbers to outlying districts of the USSR, where they were settled on barren land and forced to farm collectively. Some were sent directly into labor camps, and the history of the forced-labor camps really begins in this period. Resistance and oppression were particularly severe in the Ukraine, where the soil is rich and the peasants had the greatest vested interest in their landholdings. The regime utilized large-scale deportation here, in an effort to coerce the peasants to accept collective farming; the notorious Ukrainian famine of the early thirties was at least in part the result. Literally hundreds of thousands died of starvation, and the general decline in food production affected the entire Soviet Union. Starving peasants, long queues, beggars — these were common on the Soviet scene at that time. The violence went so far that Stalin was persuaded to apply remedial measures; by his "Dizzy with Success" speech he put a halt to the rapidly deteriorating situation. The broad pattern of collective agriculture had been established, however, and the next few years saw the gradual elimination of the remaining farmers. By 1934, 84.5 percent of agriculture had been collectivized; by 1939, the figure was 93.5 percent. (324; 325c)

World War II and the collapse of Soviet power in the Ukraine and Byelorussia resulted in the destruction of the collective-farm system in the most important agricultural areas. At the same time, the exigencies of the war effort forced the party to ignore some serious abuses of the collective system which were developing in other areas of the USSR. Private garden plots (which collective farmers are allowed to retain on a very small scale) tended to be enlarged by stealth and the livestock of the collective farms was frequently and illegally divided by the peasants. In addition, rumors were circulating that the party was planning to abandon the collective system altogether and to restore land to the peasants. The party, however, had no such intention. As early as 1943 a decree was issued outlining the measures to be followed in the reconstruction of the collective-farm system in the newly reoccupied areas. (183a) As the Germans retreated, the returning Soviet administration immediately set itself the task of recapturing any land taken over by the peasants. After the conclusion of the hostilities, an all-out campaign was launched to invigorate collectivized agriculture, and in a very much publicized decree of 1946, "On Measures to Liquidate the Violations of the Regulations of Agricultural Artels in Collective Farms" (183b), the party charted the struggle for discipline, intensified production, and full collectivization.

The prewar pattern of agricultural organization was thus reestablished. It consisted of some 250,000 collective farms (the kolkhozes), where the workers allegedly owned the land in common, were paid by labor-days (by amount of work they actually performed), and shared the profits and losses of the collective farm, depending on the harvest; there was a smaller number of state-owned farms (the sovkhozes), where the farmers were paid normal wages irrespective of the harvest; and there were some 8,000 machine-tractor stations (MTS), which served the various farms with their machinery, tractors, and technical assistance on a contractual basis. The party leadership, however, was still plagued by the fact that the large number of collective farms made central political direction difficult and resulted in tremendous administrative inefficiency and overlapping. Accordingly, in the early fifties a policy of farm amalgamation was launched, and in four years the number of collective farms was reduced to some 95,000 superfarms, serviced by about 9,000 MTS. Since that time, the MTS, for many years the spearheads of Communism on the collective farms, have been abolished and their equipment "sold" to the farms. With the party much stronger on the farms, the conflicts between farms and MTS increasingly bothersome, and collective farms increased in size — all general consequences of Khrushchev's policies — this change was indicated. But it has in turn caused new problems, especially as far as repair services are concerned. (89v)

In spite of all these efforts, Soviet agriculture has lagged far behind industrial development. This fact has become a source of major worry to Soviet leaders who cannot fail to note that, while industrial production had doubled since 1940, agricultural output is only 10 percent higher at most. The situation appears even more catastrophic when Soviet agricultural statistics for 1954 are compared to 1928, the last precollectivization year. Cattle is 15 percent down, cows 27 percent, while the population has grown from some 150 million to 215 million. Agricultural production standards were and are also extremely low when compared to Western norms; for example, average milk yield per cow in 1954 in the USSR was 1,100 litres as compared to 2,865 in West Germany and 2,531 as early as 1937 in Sweden. (245) Similarly, corn yield by bushel per acre was 17.8 in the USSR; in the United States, 37.1. (430b) Furthermore, in the period 1955–1959 the comparative crop yields for the USA and the USSR in centners (hundred pounds) per hectare were: grain — USSR 9.7, USA 21; potatoes — USSR 91, USA 194. (17b) Many other statistics could be cited, but these are sufficient to illustrate the gravity of the situation, particularly if one also considers the rapid growth of the urban population in the USSR. No wonder that the party and its leadership remain concerned.

Under the aegis of Khrushchev, a vast project for cultivating underdeveloped or entirely virgin lands was launched. (89w) It was made necessary not only by the considerations sketched above, but also by the fact that agriculture in the USSR is concentrated in regions subject to great weather hazards. The need to spread the risks had become apparent to the Central Committee. Kazakhstan in particular and Central Asia in general became the foci for this new push for which the energies of the youth were to be mobilized. Thousands of young Komsomolites left the cities, some willingly, others pressured into volunteering, to work on the virgin soil. They were to live on newly set-up state farms, a development suggesting a further extension of the factory-production system into agriculture. (441n) The project for various reasons fell short of expectations. Indeed, Kazakhstan has become a major headache for the regime. Even so, "the gamble on the new lands appears to have paid off," according to one authority. (89w)

The scope of this new program was huge. It envisaged a tremendous "young man, go *west*" movement, which within a few years might have resulted in a republic like Kazakhstan becoming a predominantly Slavic-populated region. Such a development would have had important political repercussions in breaking down the resistance of these regions to centrally directed innovations. In the years 1954–1956, the Soviet regime hoped to bring under cultivation some 28–30 million acres of virgin land, some 19 million of which were in Kazakhstan alone. The area under cultivation in Kazakhstan would then have increased from about 10 million to 28.5. By 1960, the program called for over 100 million acres. (17b) This project naturally has created a great need for outside settlers, who can come only from the overpopulated regions and urban centers in Russia and the Ukraine.

The virgin-lands policy was only a part, though a dramatic one, of Khrushchev's new approach to the problems of agricultural production. Himself a farmboy, he brought to these problems a measure of realism that many of the highly urbanized Communists lacked. His policies evolved rapidly, and almost every year brought new changes. (459a; 442g, h) It is beyond the present task to review this development in any detail. However, certain major features deserve brief presentation. The changes were, of course, tied in with the over-all evolution of the USSR, and more particularly with the revitalization of the party. Whereas under Stalin the party was weak in the rural areas of the Soviet Union, with decidedly less than a majority even of the leadership on the farms committed to the party, now the vast majority of farm managers and other high officials are party members, and the local party leaders are held responsible for production on the farms. At the same time, the consolidation of farms has gone forward in two directions, through the joining together of a number of collective farms and through the extension of the state farms. Indeed, in the virgin lands almost all farms are of this latter type. In the opinion of experts, the difference between the two types is gradually disappearing. Originally, the collective farms were supposed to be the collective property of the kolkhozniks, who shared in the produce on the basis of work-day units. These units were credited to each collective-farm member on the basis of his work, with tractor and other machine operators, managers, and the like, receiving a multiple credit. Considering that these shares were only what was left over after the government and various other claimants had been satisfied, the share on the weaker farms was often way below that of unskilled workers in factories and on state farms; the result was a flight from the farms. Even the grant of garden plots, a few animals, and other bits of "private" property rarely helped much; at the same time, it invited kolkhozniks to skip the collective work in favor of their personal plots, which in some years accounted for almost 40 percent of their real income. This remarkable diversion of energy to private activities resulted in the fact, reported for 1959, that almost 40 percent of all meat and milk in the Soviet Union came from the garden plots, as well as 60 percent of the eggs, 45 percent of the potatoes, and approximately 35 percent of the green vegetables. (370a) In view of this situation, it is not surprising that the Soviet leadership has sought to regulate it by various restrictions; none has proved too successful. Even so, the abolition of private plots has not thus far been envisaged, although the increase in the number of state farms (from 8.7 percent to 32 percent in some key products) on which workers are paid wages as in a factory may eventually lead to it. These state farms are really vast; by 1960 the average sown area of such farms was 22,000 acres, as against 6,800 acres for the collective farms. This figure indicates the trend toward gigantism, which has given rise to the suggestion that rural Soviet citizens are living in a sort of "neo-serfdom," where the former landed proprietor is replaced by the central bureaucracy and its local helpmates.

There have been great changes in the central bureaucracy as well. The Ministry of Agriculture, a huge apparatus under Stalin, has been reduced to a research and extension body, while other entities, notably Gosplan and the All-Union Economic Council have become responsible for planning, and the All-Union Farm Machinery Association (successor to the MTS set-up, though no longer the "owner" of farm machinery) responsible for the supply of new farm machinery, spare parts, fuel, and fertilizer. These organizations function within the context of an administration that is concerned with the production and procurement (sale) of all agricultural products (89y) and is closely tied in with party leadership. In the course of this evolution, the production and procurement of agricultural produce has become very sharply separated from the industrial sector, so that at present the two are treated almost as two distinct economies. At the same time, this administration has been freed from some of the complications that the former organization produced. Yet party guidance is firmly maintained through committees up and down the line, and "party and Komsomol members are expected to take a leading role in the life of the collective and state farms." That this expectation is not always fulfilled, Khrushchev himself repeatedly recognized. But with the great majority of collective-farm chairmen and state-farm directors being party members, party guidance cannot fail to be decisive. As a result, the secret police plays a greatly reduced role in Soviet farm life, while prosecutors and courts, including the comrades' courts, are more in evidence. Yet, despite the party's hard work, agriculture "continues to present the Soviet leadership with its most serious problems." (89z) Continuous denunciations of the "backward" collective farmers highlight the fact that the peasant is the "evil genius" of communist as of fascist totalitarian dictatorship. All the details add up to the conclusion that collectivized agriculture, because of the very nature of the farmer's work, does not produce the results that a self-reliant and independent farm life will produce. Even so, the results are not wholly negative. As a recent report noted: "Agricultural production in the USSR has been characterized during the last decade by noticeable, but spotty, progress." (459b) There is, however, little likelihood that production levels will become equal to those in the United States or other Western nations. Unlike Poland, the USSR seems disinclined to accept the proposition that a "family farm system is not only much more efficient than the Soviet System, it is much more dynamic." (459b) Instead, the solution is sought, as has been shown, in expanding the large agricultural enterprise, the state farm.

There is no apparent intention on the part of the Soviet regime to abandon its commitment to a policy of collectivization, and the Soviet pattern has become the model for satellite development, albeit a somewhat more moderate one. The excesses and brutality of the early thirties have not been repeated by the satellite regimes, where subtler methods of coercion, such as excessive taxation, discrimination, and occasional show trials, have been adopted. As a result, progress in collectivizing has been slow. According to one study of the Polish economy, "the share of socialized agriculture in the total areas in agricultural use . . . increased from about 8 percent in 1947, nearly all in state farms, to about 20 percent in 1953, of which about 12.8 percent was in state farms and the remainder in producer cooperative farms." (3) By 1955 the percentage had grown to only 27. The figures for the other satellites were higher, although still below the comparable Soviet rate of collectivization by the end of 1955: 45 percent of the arable land was collectivized in Czechoslovakia, 35 percent in Rumania, 33 percent in Hungary and East Germany. The most "advanced" was Bulgaria: by May 1956 some 75 percent of the arable land was collectivized. Still the Soviet pattern and regulations are followed closely and have been made the basis for satellite agricultural policies, except in Poland where, as mentioned above, the Gomulka regime re-established peasant proprietorship.

In China, by contrast, the peasantry has undergone a fate very similar to that in the USSR under Stalin. Great pressure has been put on the peasants to enter into the agricultural producers' cooperatives, with a duplication of the Soviet practices of coercion, economic dislocation, and suffering. (376) When in the mid-fifties the cooperatives broke down, partly as a result of the displacement of agricultural labor that was intensified by the "great leap forward" in 1956–57, Mao plunged forward on this front also, suggesting first the combining of cooperatives into larger units and finally into "communes." There were 26,425 communes by September 30, 1958, replacing roughly twenty times that number of cooperatives and ranging in size from 1,413 households to 11,841; their number has since been further reduced. (54c; 346b) Their organization is military, indeed Spartan, with common mess halls, a militia, and a hierarchical structure by which communes divide into production brigades and these in turn divide into teams. There are said to be about 500,000 brigades. The core purpose of the communes was and is the break-up of the family and its household; children are raised in common nurseries and kindergartens so that three quarters of the women are freed for "productive" labor, that is to say, absorbed into the work force. By this means the manpower shortages that the mass industrialization and water-conservation movements had created might be met. This communalization was proclaimed as constituting socialism and the decisive step toward the realization of communism. While earlier enthusiastic estimates have been revised, and the program of radical collectivization of all property toned down, communalization has greatly enhanced the party's role by putting most peasants and workers into party-controlled units. "The commune system is the best possible means for solidifying and strengthening the power of the Communist Party in China," a qualified observer wrote in 1960. (346c) On the other hand, a later commentator suggests that "the evolution of the rural communes has been a process of continuous retreat from communist policies." (54d) The fact that communalization has become associated with disastrous crop failures has persuaded the leadership (as in the Soviet Union) that full scope must be given to personal initiative, according to the principle "to each according to his work" (1962 editorial in *Jen-min Jih-pao* [People's Daily]). Thus, the commune system as originally conceived has become a hollow shell, hiding a return to the pattern of cooperatives. This return seems to be fairly permanent and parallels the development in the Soviet Union. It is therefore not too much to say that, as an economic measure, communalization is a failure because it causes a decline in agricultural production. Whether it has also been a failure as a political measure and a social reform seems more doubtful. The communes continue as an organizational device to facilitate party control; they also provide a continuing challenge to family concerns. (237b)

The Fascists and National Socialists repeated the demagoguery of the Bolsheviks on a grander scale, as far as the peasants were concerned. They too, of course, proclaimed themselves workers' parties, but among the workers the peasants were considered to hold a special place. There is a sound psychological and sociological reason for this: the peasants have, through their attachment to the land, a peculiar affinity to nationalism. To be sure, theirs is a defensive nationalism, and when the dictatorship launches forth into foreign wars, the peasantry becomes restive and abandons the regime (470) — though there may be occasional exceptions like the Ethiopian war that the Italian peasants are said to have supported. This was also the case at the time of the French Revolution. It was the peasantry that turned from the radicalism of the revolutionaries to Napoleon and deserted him when he set out to conquer Europe. But after all is said and done, it still remains a crucial factor in the fascist movements of our time that the peasantry, hostile to both the internationalism and the industrialism of the socialists, inclines toward supporting fascist movements because they claim to oppose industrialism (anticapitalist) and internationalism (nationalist). The peasantry feels strongly about its possession of the land and about the defense of the homeland, the fatherland. It has been claimed by peasant leaders in Italy that the peasantry did not really support fascism. In a deeper sense this is true, for the aggressive imperialism and big-business monopolism with which Italian Fascism developed was deeply antagonistic to peasant interests and peasant views. But in the early stages, the peasants provided substantial support to the Fascists. Mussolini always claimed that the peasants were his staunchest supporters. (235b) In the case of Hitler, we can even prove the proposition statistically. The largest part of Hitler's electoral support came from the peasantry in the early days. Curiously enough, the very regions in which the democratic movement had been strongest among the peasants, Holstein and Baden, were the ones that turned toward Hitler, whereas in the staunchly conservative and Catholic regions of upper Bavaria the peasantry remained hostile. (140; 443) A similar phenomenon can be observed in Italy in the contrast between Tuscany and southern Italy, which is now being repeated in the struggle between Communism and

Christian Democracy. (310e) This peasant support is frequently overlooked in analyses that stress the "middle class" support of fascism, which, while undoubtedly a fact, would not have provided the necessary votes for Hitler's building of an electoral following of nearly 40 percent.

But if the peasants were wholly deceived by the Bolsheviks and by their support decreed their own death warrant, they were nearly as much disillusioned by the Nationalist Socialist regime. To be sure, the regime protested its love for the peasants throughout. It developed a special facet in its official ideology, the "blood and soil" line. Under this banner the racial purity of the peasants was linked to their attachment to the land (*Boden*) as proof of their high value in the folk community. National festivals were held, with a sumptuous display of costumes and folk dances, and at the great party rallies, or *Parteitage,* the peasants were conspicuous participants. But behind this facade of make-believe, the reality of Nazi agrarian policy turned out to be decidedly contrary to the peasants' interest, and not only in terms of international adventures. It has been rightly observed that agriculture was more strictly regimented than any other field of economic activity. The party organization invaded the villages and bestowed leadership upon the most loyal party members rather than upon the most respected tillers of the soil. Since farming is a very exacting business, the best farmers resented the extent to which the Nazis placed a premium upon political activity. The Nazi frontal attack upon the churches (see Chapter 23) added fuel to the fire. In the end, peasant support for the regime almost completely disappeared.

It may be well to sketch briefly the agrarian policy of the Hitler regime. At the center we find the organization of the Reich Food Estate (Reichnährstand). This term, derived from older romantic and feudal views about the revival of a medieval corporate order, did in fact designate a complete bureaucratization of the agrarian sector of the economy. The formerly autonomous "chambers of agriculture" were transformed into dependent arms of the government and its ministry of agriculture and of the party and its corresponding organs. Walter Darré, the architect of this Reich Food Estate and its effective leader under Hitler, professed the official peasant ideology of blood and soil. But, in fact, he attempted to convert all agricultural producers into National Socialists who

would help to win the "battle for food." His policy toward the
peasantry had three major features: the control of prices, the control of inheritance, and the control of planting. In all of them, the
technique employed was that of bureaucratic coercion and terrorist
police and party work rather than economic incentives. As far as
prices were concerned, both direct and indirect fixing were practiced, making farm operations dependent on government fiat rather
than on the free market. Since the peasant had never really accepted
the free market, this change seemed at first a gain for the peasantry,
but since the price fixing soon proved to be motivated by the military and industrial needs of the regime, rather than the interests of
the farmer, it resulted in noncooperation and eventually even sabotage. Its potentialities for large-scale corruption discredited the regime.

More extraordinary than the price fixing, though perhaps economically less significant, was the forcible entailing of farm property.
Cast in terms of protecting the peasant against losing his farm since
bankruptcies had, as in the United States during the Great Depres-
sion, caused widespread agrarian unrest, this legislation had an
initial appeal. (307) But it soon turned out to be another link in the
chain by which the peasantry was subordinated to the party and the
government. The laws provided that a farmer could not sell or pass
on his farm without securing the assent of the local government
and party officials. He could also lose his farm if the local party boss
was not satisfied with the way he was operating it. In short, proprie-
tary rights were made dependent upon bureaucratic discretion. An
incidental result was that farmers could no longer get credit; the
government stepped into the breach and provided credit facilities,
thereby welding another link in the chain. Finally, the government
could take over the farm, if in the judgment of the local Nazi farm
leader the property was not being administered "in conformity with
demands which must be made on farming in the interest of the
feeding of the people." The Nazis developed legislation concerning
the planting of certain crops, often in disregard of local climatic
and soil conditions, thereby also arrogating to themselves this crucial function of farm management. Now some of these policies will
be recognized as fairly common in democratic countries, including
the United States, but the decisive difference is, as always, one of
method. In democratic countries, such policies result from extended

debates in representative assemblies in which all relevant interests are fully represented; they are subject to continuous revision, and they typically rely upon such economic incentives as subsidies to accomplish results. The agricultural policies of the Nazi regime were, on the other hand, decreed by government and party bureaucrats in accordance with the leader's over-all policy decisions. While the outward forms of peasant proprietorship remained, at least within the narrow limits left by the legislation we have just described, the actual substance of an independent peasantry completely disappeared. But the peasants were not liquidated, as in the Soviet Union, with the very significant result that, after the defeat of the Nazis, the peasantry could re-emerge as a significant factor in the German social structure. As a result the Communist rulers of East Germany have had to undertake the task of liquidation, as they have in the other satellites. The process of collectivization has gone steadily forward; collective farms have come into existence and are becoming the predominant form of agricultural enterprise, as in the Soviet Union. But the very fact that they had to be instituted shows that the Nazi policy had not destroyed the peasantry.

In Italy the process was not carried as far as in Hitler Germany. Italian Fascists failed to tackle the task of land reform. Since Italy was a country of large agricultural estates (*latifundia*), its true need was land reform on a considerable scale, such as is now being undertaken at last. The Fascists, though well aware of the problem, substituted a program of reclamation, such as that in the Pontine marshes, which the previous democratic regime had initiated. The total effect upon the position of the Italian peasantry was minimal, but it lent itself to dramatic proclamations on the part of Mussolini. (310e)

In conclusion, it is fairly clear that the agricultural sector of the totalitarian economy presents peculiar difficulties to the rulers of these regimes. The nature of agricultural production is such that it is unsuited to large-scale organization and control; but, at the same time, its product, food, is vital, for even totalitarians have to eat. The drive for additional land presents itself as a way out of the difficulties involved in making the available land more productive. This drive, epitomized in the German "living space" (*Lebensraum*) ideology, reinforces the totalitarians' propensity to foreign conquest.

Considering the disastrous consequences of such expansion, as far as the support of the peasantry is concerned, the peasantry may well in fact have been the Achilles' heel of the Fascist regimes. Whether the lag in agricultural production by which the Soviet Union is afflicted will serve to play a similar role there — leading either to the collapse or to the radical modification of totalitarianism — remains to be seen. In any case, the natural requirements of agricultural production, namely, many small-scale independent proprietors working the soil on their own responsibility, seem to present a major obstacle to totalitarian rule. It is no accident that, as Jefferson among others insisted, such a population of farmers is the best foundation for a free and democratic society. Recent trends in the Soviet Union and elsewhere, notably Yugoslavia, suggest that Communist regimes are aware of the problem. A noncollective system of agriculture would constitute a very serious infringement of the collective directed economy. Maybe methods can be evolved, such as those being tried in Poland and Yugoslavia, for directing agricultural producers without depriving them of a measure of personal ownership of their farms. National Socialist precedents are not without significance here. When one considers other recent indications that a search is on for modifying comprehensive central planning, he cannot exclude the chance that collective farming may be attenuated in an effort to win the "battle for bread and butter."

VI

Islands of Separateness

IV

21

THE GENERAL PROBLEM
OF RESISTANCE

In spite of the effort of the totalitarians to destroy all separate existences, there remain in all these dictatorships some groups that manage to offer some resistance to totalitarian rule. The family, the churches, the universities and other centers of technical knowledge, the writers and artists — each in response to the rationale of their being — must, if they are to survive, resist the total demands of the totalitarians. They are islands, islands of separateness, in the totalitarian sea. As we have seen, the totalitarian regimes seek to divide and rule in the most radical and extreme way: each human being should, for best effect, have to face the monolith of totalitarian rule as an isolated "atom." By being thus atomized, the people with its many natural subdivisions becomes the "mass," and the citizen is transformed into the mass man. This mass man, this isolated and anxiety-ridden shadow, is the complete antithesis to the "common man" of the working free society. (107c) It is, therefore, rather misleading to speak of the subjects of such regimes as "citizens." They are rather denizens or even serfs of the ruling party, and only the members of that party as participants in governing the society can rightfully be said to be citizens, at least according to Aristotle's carefully developed notion of citizenship.

But men resist this totalitarian effort — not only those within the particular structures of family, church, and technical establishment, but all kinds of individuals. If one studies, for example, the social composition of the July 20, 1944, uprising in Germany, one finds that persons of all walks of life were involved. Soviet opposition to

Stalin also was widely distributed among the population. (99; 302d; 295c) The same is true of the French resistance and the Polish resistance from 1939 to 1945, the latter taking the dramatic form of a veritable political organization of the underground. (247; 168)

In exploring the human motivations which lead to resistance, one finds that they are as varied as human personalities are. Moral indignation and thwarted ambition, religious scruples and personal revenge, patriotic fervor and class antagonism, these and many other contrasting impulses, ideas, and convictions have entered into the complex skein of resistance movements and acts. We say "acts" because it is important to realize that a great deal of resistance consists of isolated individual acts of protest. The old German lady demonstratively shopping at Jewish stores on boycott day, the Polish peasant helping to derail a train, the French shopkeeper going out into the street in the dark of night and writing on an empty wall, "À bas Vichy!" — these and many other similar token acts constitute what one might call symbolic resistance. As one studies the Gestapo records, it becomes evident that there was a great deal more of this kind of thing going on than has become known to the outside world; it presumably is going on in totalitarian regimes now.

Under totalitarianism, however, such resistance, whether passive or active, encounters difficulties, which are generally underestimated in countries where a measure of passive resistance and even nonviolent coercion, as in strikes, is accepted because the recognized rights of the citizen enable him to adopt a resisting posture under the protection of law and constitution. (50) Conscientious objectors have been allowed to resist draft laws, and indeed such resistance has in turn been legalized, as have been strikes and other forms of passive resistance. Totalitarian regimes are characterized by a ruthless suppression of all such behavior, and resistance, even mere symbolic acts, have involved all the risks of criminal behavior. By contrast, there exist the subtle temptations that a Polish writer has brilliantly analyzed. (251a)

The problem of resistance is basic to the modern world. Albert Camus has offered the most sophisticated analysis in terms of the "man revolted," meaning thereby anyone who is revolted by the injustice and violence of a system of coercive order, who revolts against it, and who eventually finds himself revolted by the violence committed by the new system. (48) He argues that the reason for such revolt is that any moral judgment which fails to take reality into account becomes immoral and murderous. His is basically a plea against every kind of fanaticism and for that moderation, the *bonne mesure,* which enables a person to see himself in perspective. And he concludes: "Finally, when the revolution, in the name of power and history, becomes this deadly and unmeasured mechanism, a new revolt becomes sacred, in the name of measure and life." (48a) Much in line with the view that the island of separateness is the ultimate escape, he argues that such a revolt, such a resistance, is based upon the village and the professional group.

Throughout Soviet history, the record clearly shows, there have been symbolic acts of resistance. In addition, actual plots and conspiracies to overthrow the Bolshevik regime — quite a few, doubtless, fabricated by the secret police for the sake of eliminating inconvenient elements (37j), but others probably genuine — accompanied the rise of the totalitarian dictatorship. (66b) The course of early Soviet history actually could be traced in terms of the plots, conspiracies, and efforts to overthrow the regime. There is incontrovertible evidence that, for many years after the revolution, sporadic outbreaks against the Communist regime continued to occur. Individual acts of resistance took the form of industrial sabotage, efforts to foil state delivery quotas, defection to the outside world, and others. (161g) Former Soviet citizens have often testified that their parents made great efforts to indoctrinate their children against Soviet propaganda. Similarly, the press in the satellite regimes often refers to acts of individual resistance among students or clergymen. (78a)

It is evident that none of this activity seriously threatens the power of a totalitarian regime. But there have also been cases of larger groups of persons engaging in concerted acts of sabotage. We find, especially among the farming and working population, extended use of the slowdown as a weapon employed to combat the collectivization program, which the peasants in Russia, and lately in Central Europe, violently opposed. There have been numerous cases of Communist officials' being assassinated, local party buildings burned, collective farmers assaulted by noncollectivized peasants.

Stalin himself testified to the violence of the collectivization period in the USSR in his conversations with the Western leaders during World War II. Even more serious in nature were the efforts by the various non-Russian nationalities of the USSR to assert their national distinctiveness through separatism and eventual statehood. To this day, one can read in the Soviet press virulent denunciations of "bourgeois-nationalists" in the national republics, and periodic purges of such resisters are a common feature of the Soviet scene. (37k; 161h) But after all is said and done, the most this sort of activity does is to maintain the self-respect of those participating because of the shared common danger.

It must be remembered, however, that the nationalist type of resistance is not entirely resistance to totalitarian dictatorship. Instead it is rooted in the sense of national freedom and patriotism that was also the central motif in the resistance movements against the German conquerors during World War II in France and elsewhere, as it was a mainspring in the Soviet zone of Germany. Such resistance, especially when supported vigorously from the outside, as was the French movement after 1942, has a psychological basis quite different from the hopeless resistance to totalitarianism with which we are here primarily concerned. (247) But the distinction is not a sharp one, as shown by the story of the uprising of the German workers of June 17, 1953. Starting from a labor demonstration against excessive work demands, the uprising spread like wildfire throughout the Soviet zone of Germany, since it was misinterpreted as in keeping with the New Course of the Soviet Union. It was not directed against the foreign occupying power, although the deep resentment aroused by Soviet policies no doubt played its role. Rather it was mounted to overthrow the East German Communist regime and to reorganize the zone along more democratic lines. (29) Even more dramatic was the 1956 uprising in Hungary and the corresponding events in Poland. This is not the place to detail the story, but certain key features deserve mention. The Hungarian revolt has been termed an "unexpected revolution" by a distinguished analyst, who undertakes to show that what seemed a sudden event was in fact the result of a number of residual disruptive forces, which the rapidity of the Stalinist imposition of Communism had suppressed but not eliminated. But these forces could not have come into play if there had not been a split in the top leader-ship. As a consequence, this writer concludes that "only another succession crisis, in conjunction with acute economic difficulties, is likely to create conditions favorable to open mass protests." (173a)

The Hungarian revolt seemed to suggest to some writers that there existed a real possibility for the forcible overthrow of a totali-tarian regime. They argued that only the outside intervention of the Soviet Union prevented it from occurring in Hungary. But was the Soviet Union really an "outsider"? Was not the totalitarian regime in Hungary a working part of the Soviet bloc of which the Soviet leadership is the key control? Should not the uprising be placed within the context of a process of re-establishing a measure of "polycentrism," of autonomous centers of national Communism, that is to say, national totalitarian regimes? It has been rightly observed that, in his efforts to resolve this problem of a commu-nism suited to Hungary, efforts that Gomulka was at the same time successfully developing in Poland, Nagy "was transformed from a Communist whose practical perspectives were essentially domestic and on broad issues subordinated to general Soviet require-ments, into a national Communist willing to put the purposes of Hungarian Communism above the imperatives of Soviet policy." (38f) Yet the revolt of the masses got out of hand, turned against communism itself, and was dissipated as a mere movement of dra-matic protest; as such it was unplanned and without strategy for so difficult a task, like the German revolt of 1953. (241; 93)

There are, of course, those more elaborate undertakings, known as resistance movements, in which extended preparations are made by large numbers of persons with the purpose of overthrowing and destroying the totalitarian dictatorship and replacing it by some freer system. Such movements are more likely to occur at the begin-ning or at the end of a totalitarian dictatorship. The extended civil war in Russia, after the Bolsheviks seized power, is perhaps the most sizable effort of this kind. It must be noted, however, that the democratic forces in Russia found themselves, in the course of the civil war, between the hammer and the anvil. On the one side, there was the Bolshevik dictatorship, with the flaming and bloodthirsty rhetoric of Trotsky; on the other, the reactionaries Denikin, Wran-gel, and Kolchak. These representatives of the old order succeeded in retaining control over large portions of the former tsarist army and were able to launch a large-scale fight against the Bolshevik government, established in Petrograd. Not until 1920, after two years of continued battles, did the Bolsheviks succeed in establishing effective control over the former tsarist empire, and they were still faced with the problem of national separatism in the Caucasus. (276) However, one of the most unfortunate results of tsarism was the weakness of organized resistance to Bolshevism once it did establish itself in power. The instances mentioned earlier were the last gasps of the old system, but its final heritage was a new autocracy.

Large-scale resistance to totalitarian power has been much more in evidence when the totalitarian system is challenged from without by a force powerful enough to encourage organized resistance from within. The uprising of July 20, 1944, occurred at a time when the doom of the Nazi regime was a foregone conclusion for all but the most fanatical followers of Hitler. Nonetheless, it was a remarkable undertaking in which there really culminated a protracted series of efforts to remove the Hitler regime by force. In spite of the failure of several earlier attempts, the main leaders of the movement carried on. As already mentioned, they came from all classes of the population except the peasantry. Workers and clergymen, businessmen and army officers, government officials, professors, and students formed part of the far-flung conspiracy, which almost succeeded. By a mere chance, Hitler was not seriously hurt, and the Nazis drowned the effort in blood. More than two thousand men and women were executed, often after brutal tortures and public humiliation. (100; 399; 295; 76d) But although this most extended effort at violent resistance against a native totalitarian ruler failed, it nevertheless served an important moral purpose after the collapse of the regime. This spiritual end, however, must be weighed against the frightful loss of valuable democratic leadership. No really significant movement of this kind crystallized in Italy until the Allied armies had conquered a substantial part of the Italian soil. The partisans who were organized to assist the Allied armies did put up an heroic struggle at the end, but it was a fight waged in close cooperation with these armies. (308)

The comparable effort of General Vlasov never achieved the

scope of the July 20 uprising. The Vlasov defection from Stalin in the early stages of the Nazi-Soviet war, as well as local efforts to aid the Germans in their military activities, could count on the greatest mass support in the period of German successes on the battlefield. Had it not been for the stupidity of the Nazi leadership, a most effective movement against the Communist regime might have been stimulated. (99b) Greater in scope and more spontaneous in its development was the Polish resistance, considered the most effective in Europe, which culminated in the Warsaw uprising of 1944. This popular movement, although it was launched immediately after the Nazi-Soviet partition of Poland in 1939, at first was designed to provide the skeleton institutions of a Polish state in readiness for the Allied victory. However, as German atrocities mounted, more and more it took the form of an "underground state," waging organized warfare against the occupiers. The Civil Directorate of Resistance organized a vast network of underground publications, schools, and universities, even police and courts. This High Command of the Home Army directed, by 1944, the operations of a field army of some 300,000 men engaged in guerrilla activities, as well as urban squads designed to carry out sabotage, diversionary activities, and executions of particularly oppressive Nazi officials. In August 1944, when the Soviet troops were approaching Warsaw, the Polish Home Army units in Warsaw — numbering some 30,000 men — seized the city after several days of bloody streetfighting against the retreating Wehrmacht and SS. However, for political reasons, the Red Army halted its advance, leaving the rebellious city to its own resources. After 63 days of lonely house-to-house resistance, the city finally fell and was razed to the ground on Hitler's orders. (168b; 185b; 29) In view of this background and the long antecedent history of Polish resistance to foreign domination, it is not surprising that strong anti-Communist resistance has existed in Poland, ever since Moscow took over. This was finally admitted by the regime itself, when it stated in 1956 that "enemies of the people" had killed some 30,000 of its supporters between 1945 and 1956, prior to the Poznan uprising in June 1956. The Poznan demonstration, much like the East German one, became a genuine attack on the regime, though presumably it was not planned in advance. The skillful coup d'état by Gomulka, securing a measure of independence from Moscow and the withdrawal of Soviet military forces, was by contrast very carefully planned and executed with superb adroitness and sang-froid. (38g)

It can be seen that generally the Nazi dictatorship stimulated much more violent resistance than the Soviet, not only at home but also in captive areas. This fact is only partially due to the greater sophistication of the police methods of the MVD and the ability of the Communists, because of their ideological position, to recruit local cadres of support. The Nazi program, particularly in the occupied countries, was a thoroughly negative one. The entire population soon became aware that they were doomed to a position of perpetual subjugation, inferiority, and, in some cases, total extinction. This policy the Nazis proclaimed openly, and their subsequent measures bore out the proclamations. The populations, with their schools closed, career opportunities liquidated, and the national economy ruined and exploited, had no choice but to resist. And resist they did en masse, stimulated by open atrocities. The Soviets, on the other hand, most carefully mask their atrocities (the secret executions at Katyn being only one example), loudly proclaim their friendship for "the people," and allow the population certain positive goals to strive for, such as industrialization with all its subsequent career opportunities and hopes. The political opposition is thus caught on the horns of a bitter dilemma: to resist might mean to harm the national economy, by driving the Soviets into more violent measures. The nation's youth, even if opposed to the regime, still cannot fail to notice the positive advantages of cooperation, especially on a nonpolitical plane. Nonresistance soon finds a most convenient rationalization.

Resistance to Soviet tyranny has thus been most effective when a common basis for such resistance was evident. The most violent expressions of it accordingly occurred on a national basis, when the local communities became convinced that they were being destroyed by Soviet settlers, by Russians flocking into new cities. Similarly in the captive nations, open resistance, sabotage, and guerrilla activity decreased once the period of open Soviet plundering stopped, around 1946–47, and more refined methods of economic and political "integration" were developed. At the same time, the populations could not fail to note the large-scale efforts to build factories, the rebuilding of such cities as Warsaw (which the Poles considered a national shrine), the often fantastic projects for a glorious future, to be achieved by the most stupendous labors. All of this, however, is a potent weapon in the Communist arsenal for the weakening of political resistance.

It can be seen from these experiences that the chances of success in overthrowing a totalitarian regime are slim indeed. Many outsiders have been unjust in demanding, and unwise in expecting, the growth of resistance movements in the more developed totalitarian systems. It is extremely difficult to mount an effective opposition to a totalitarian dictatorship precisely because it is totalitarian. No organizations are allowed unless they bear the stamp of official approval and are effectively coordinated with the ruling party. Nor do the means exist by which an enterprising person might gather others for effective cooperation. The regime's total control of all the means of mass communication, as well as post, telephone, and telegraph; its complete monopoly of all weapons (except insofar as the military can manage to establish some measure of independence; finally, its all-engulfing secret-police surveillance, which utilizes every available contraption of modern technology, such as hidden recording devices, as well as the older methods of agents-provocateurs and the like — these and related features of totalitarianism make any attempt to organize large numbers of people for effective opposition well-nigh hopeless. People have criticized a man like Goerdeler for his foolishness in preparing lists of people and formulating written programs for action both before and after the overthrow of the regime. This sort of criticism is not without good foundation, but the critics fail to show how they would organize any large number of people without even these rudimentary devices for effective communication. What the critics, in other words, are really saying is that no resistance movement has any reasonable prospect of success, and that therefore anyone undertaking it is lacking in judgment. The only answer is that which one of the German resisters gave his wife six days before the attempt to kill Hitler: "The most terrible thing is to know that it cannot succeed and that, in spite of that, it must be done for our country and for our children." (197c) If this is true, and we believe it is, that no effort at resistance is likely to succeed, then no outsider has a right to adopt an attitude of righteous indignation at the failure of the people living under a totalitarian dictatorship to offer such resistance. It is one of the central rules of all sound ethics, a rule stressed by such a rigorous moralist as Kant, that no one is obliged to undertake actions that are beyond what he can do (*ultra posse nemo obligatur*). At this point, the will to become a martyr for a cause begins, and to do this is always "beyond the call of duty." (26)

There is little disposition in free America to dispute the *right* of resistance to totalitarian tyranny, even though resistance to established government is hardly regarded with tolerance when directed against the American government. With Lincoln, Americans are inclined to say that there is no appeal from ballots to bullets — but against totalitarian violence, resistance seems to them not only allowable, but morally required. It is often forgotten that the problem of a right of resistance has been a serious concern of political thinkers for hundreds of years and that the weight of religious doctrine has been against it, though some exceptions have been allowed. (211; 313) On the whole, passive resistance is about all that both Protestant and Catholic moral teachings will permit. For the rest, the sufferings that the abuse of governmental powers inflicts are to be endured as a scourge by which God chastises a sinful mankind. However, the insistence of the churches that the people, even though obeying totalitarian regimes, must not accept totalitarian values places the churches in fact in opposition to these regimes. In the light of this situation, it is not surprising that so much of the impetus toward building an effective resistance has originated in religious circles. It has usually been the result of a profound internal struggle, a veritable "revolution in the conscience." This struggle has been the most intense where the actual killing of a totalitarian leader was being envisaged. (25; 197c) When this side of the problem is given proper attention, it seems quite preposterous that people living in freedom and security should demand that the subjects of totalitarian rule rise and overthrow their rulers. All the outsider can do is to assist the subject population as far as possible in bearing its burden. Such aid has been limited indeed.

In short, it can be said that even within the grip of a total demand for identification with a totalitarian regime, some persons and even groups of persons manage to maintain themselves aloof, to live in accordance with their personal convictions, and perhaps to organize some minor opposition to the regime. They are often inspired by hopes that the regime might be forcibly overthrown, farfetched as such hopes have proved in the past. Yet such islands of separateness are not only eloquent testimonials to the strength of human character and to the unquenchable thirst for freedom; they are also helpful in preserving some human beings for a better day.

22

THE FAMILY

The basic and the most persistent of human groups is the family. Political thought has always recognized it, even in the days before the individual person was accepted as the foundation of the political order. Hence it is not surprising that the family should constitute an island of separateness that appears in all totalitarian regimes. All these regimes have been inclined to combat the family. In China, where the family was traditionally venerated as the sacred bond, "familism" and "filialism" have been targets of the regime's brainwashing terror. The destruction of this devotion of son to father, and the substitution for it of a devotion to party and regime, are mainstays of the totalitarian approach. It has even been suggested that "the desperate urge to sweep away decaying yet still powerful filial emotions and institutions" produces the totalitarian approach to man. (217f)

There was originally a striking contrast in the approach of the communist and the fascist ideologies to the family, but this difference has been replaced by approaches that closely parallel each other, characterized by an acceptance, even a promotion, of the family. Yet the image is basically altered: no longer the preserver of tradition and the seedbed of personality and character, the family is seen primarily as the procreator of children who will strengthen the regime, as essentially an instrument for enhancing the power of the totalitarian dictatorship; family policy becomes an element of population policy. It is fitted into the over-all planning of the regime's social and economic efforts. At the outset, however, this was not the view of the Bolsheviks. On the contrary, they tended to deprecate the family, interpreting it as an institution linked to private property and typically bourgeois in nature. This dogmatic view had its roots in the preoccupation with the strictly economic phases of social structure and dynamics, though it was perhaps reinforced by the Bohemian style of living of many of the ideologues of Marxist persuasion. Just as Marxism had a blind spot when it came to assessing the bureaucratic prospects resulting from the socialization of the means of production, so also it did not perceive the importance of stable personal relations within such a bureaucratic structure. Hence, at first, the Communists made not only divorce and abortion easy, but they encouraged sexual promiscuity on a large scale. (379c) The disruptive potentiality of such policies, clearly perceived by Lenin who denounced it, became increasingly apparent during the twenties, with the result that, after extended "discussion" in the early thirties, the trend was sharply reversed. In 1933 homosexuality was made a criminal offense, and decrees against abortion followed in 1936. Severe restrictions on the grounds for divorce were imposed in 1944, and since then Soviet publications have been at great pains to emphasize the importance to the regime of the family unit.

The role of the family is especially great in the development in the child of Soviet patriotism . . . Parents who are patriots develop in their children love for their native language, for the profound beauty of the national folklore and songs, and for the native country and scenery . . . Love of country begins to blend in his [the child's] consciousness with love for the socialist people and State regime and for the Bolshevik Party and its leaders. (407)

The Soviet people, the Communist Party and government concern themselves with strengthening the family, with the proper rearing of the younger generation. (419e)

In 1955 the Soviet press launched an extended discussion of the nature of "socialist morality," which again made manifest both the victorianism of Soviet morals and the importance that the regime attaches to the institution of the family. (238c) Citing numerous cases of broken families, the press reiterated the duty of party members to act as watchdogs for family unity and maintenance of socialist morality. This may mean removing a child from the family when its influence is considered undesirable. A child may be placed in a state institution, if a mother fails to raise the child properly; she is then deprived of the rights of motherhood. Boarding schools for children from broken homes are now on the increase. (All this, however, is a far cry from the extremes to which the Chinese Communists have gone.) Such a policy is decidedly more in keeping with totalitarian needs, especially once the regime has become fairly confident that the family is no longer the center of hostility. The provisions of the law of 1955 once again legalizing abortion can also be understood, if seen in this light: the regime has been assured that natural increase in population is high enough; it is now encouraging family life; and at the same time it wishes to eliminate secret, and often fatal, illegal abortions. (419f) What is more, "the pattern of family life has changed in directions congruent with the needs and demands of the regime . . . The regime is no longer fighting the family . . . because in a large measure the Soviet family has been captured, and captured from within, by the regime." (161i)

The Fascists sought from the very beginning to strengthen the family. The argument was usually cast in terms of the role of women. More especially Hitler, in keeping with his blood-and-soil ideology, announced with his customary coarseness that women belonged in the kitchen and should devote themselves to the raising of children. Mussolini voiced similar opinions, and both movements faithfully repeated the slogans. In *Mein Kampf* Hitler wrote: "The object of woman's education must be immovably directed to the making of future mothers." At the same time, the Fascists and Nazis wanted women to take a keen interest in their politics, to be totally committed to the ideology. Hence they would also proclaim: "Intellectual women? No! But those whose interests in life do not reach beyond the limits of the household are not fit to become the forebears of the kind of new generations which the Reich needs." (351)

In keeping with these ideological proclamations, Fascists and National Socialists offered various kinds of assistance: loans to young couples seeking to get married, prizes for mothers with many children, and aid during pregnancy, especially for women who were working. In the late thirties, civil servants in Fascist Italy were required to be married, and all bachelors in government employ were discriminated against and heavily taxed. A hot debate raged over whether to expel bachelors from the party altogether. Mussolini was very fond of arguing that Italians had to reproduce more rapidly in order to become "great" and "found an empire." The very same type of assistance is now being offered in the Soviet Union and in the satellite regimes.

The Soviet government gives special allowances to mothers of illegitimate children or, if the mother so desires, provides special state institutions to care for them. Mothers of large families receive, apart from Medals of Motherhood for six or seven children and Medals of Maternal Glory for more than seven, substantial income awards. Birth allowances range from 250 to 2,500 rubles (from the third to the eleventh child), with monthly allowances from 40 to 150 rubles. (189d) The government also gives special consideration to working mothers, providing them with leaves of absence with pay usually for about 112 days, nurseries at the factories, and so on. In the satellite regimes, similar policies prevail; in Hungary, the government has even decreed a special tax on bachelors, as did the Italian Fascists before them.

All these forms of assistance are concentrated upon hastening and reinforcing the procreative function of family life. Beyond this, the totalitarian dictatorship by its very nature is obliged to pursue policies hostile to family life and family cohesion. Its desire for total absorption of the man or woman in the totalitarian mass movement propels it into efforts to counteract, indeed to break down, the closed circle of the family.

As was noted at the beginning of this chapter, the family has always been recognized as the most elementary of social groups, and by many political thinkers the family has been considered the essential underpinning of all organized political systems. Aristotle in particular stressed this view, in combating Plato's radical proposals for organizing a political elite on the basis of a community of wives and property and on communal education of the young. (4; 278) Indeed, in the course of the centuries it became one of the commonplaces of political thought, and writers of the most divergent schools, Thomas Aquinas and Marsilius, Bodin and Althusius, Harrington and Montesquieu, Kant and Hegel, all agreed on the basic function of the family as the foundation of the political order. In spite of this almost universal agreement among political philosophers, there was relatively little discussion of just what were the characteristics of this basic institution, and the term "family" has stood for a great variety of social groupings, from the many-numbered patriarchal family to the small contemporary union of man and wife, rearing one or two children and united in romantic love for each other. Only fairly recently have anthropology and sociology devoted detailed scientific attention to the complex variety of structural models and the problems resulting from them.*

Family policy has everywhere become the concern of legislative bodies, and important enactments have been the result in, for example, Sweden and Switzerland. (259; 176) These developments are due to the fact that it is increasingly recognized that the intimate group must be strengthened and protected as a counterbalance to the alienation and isolation of man resulting from the increasing size of organization, both political and economic, in the contemporary world. Totalitarians, by contrast, although causing alienation in extreme form for all but the insiders, have in various ways sought to break up the cohesion of the intimate family grouping. We have described the way in which the mass organization of youth and the propagandist development of the school have been employed for this purpose. Besides, the encouragement of women to work in industry, the continuous appeal for men to attend meetings and to participate in collective enterprises, the whole governmental effort to organize leisure activities and to facilitate divorce and abortion — all these various undertakings have tended to weaken the family by depriving it of its functions. The following Supreme Court decision in Poland is but one of many characteristic of this particular stage in the development of totalitarian society: "[The Supreme Court has considered] the District Court wrong in holding that the petitioner's claim that serious political differences had separated him from his wife could not be a ground for divorce . . . A marriage must be based on ideological unity which cannot prosper if there are conflicting views on basic political and social problems, especially if one partner represents a progressive, the other however a reactionary creed." (283) In breaking up the family

---

* Without detailed reference, the work of the following may be mentioned: Briffault, Burgess, Calhoun, Frazer, Groves, Malinowski, Mead, Morgan, Ogburn, Thurnwald, Westermarck, Zimmermann. A survey of American writings is given by Ernest R. and Gladys H. Groves, *The Contemporary American Family* (Philadelphia, 1947), especially ch. 2; the kinship problem is treated within a systematic context by Talcott Parsons, *The Social System* (Glencoe, 1951), ch. 5.

group, totalitarian dictatorship has merely completed a cycle that started under industrial capitalism, when the factory began to take men out of their homes for the greater part of the day and, by paying them wholly inadequate wages, further encouraged the factory work of women and children. These consequences of industrial capitalism have been extended, by the methods described above, to the middle classes, who had maintained a rigid family system during the earlier phases of this development.

But in spite of policies hostile to family cohesion, the family has proved a haven for the persecuted and has served to counteract the tendency of our time to isolate and eventually to collectivize the individual. Consequently, the totalitarian movements, and more particularly their secret-police systems, have tried to break into the charmed circle of the family. Indeed, members of families have been encouraged to testify against other members, and this betrayal of the most intimate relationships has been praised as "patriotism" and loyalty to the totalitarian leadership. It is not an accident that one of the official heroes of the Soviet youth movement is one Pavlik Morozov, who earned his place in the galaxy of Soviet heroes by denouncing his parents to the NKVD. It appears that his father, a farmer, was opposed to collectivization, and young Pavlik reported this fact to the local secret-police officials. The father was duly "unmasked" and liquidated as an enemy of the people. Pavlik was subsequently murdered by his fellow villagers, who were enraged at this display of Soviet loyalty. His "martyrdom" earned him a lasting place in the manuals of the Pioneers and the Komsomolites. (437) Former Soviet citizens testify that, at the height of the terror in the thirties, it was dangerous to discuss political matters even in the family circle, for the young were constantly exhorted by the party not to hesitate to denounce their closest relatives. And while such views may easily be exaggerations induced by the all-pervading atmosphere of fear, they do serve to reveal the type of atmosphere that a totalitarian regime tries to generate even within the family circle itself.

It would, however, be a great mistake to see the family under totalitarianism in the perspective of these special cases. They are, in a sense, as untypical as the Stakhanovs and the Hennekes and are exceptions to the rule. The annals of resistance movements are replete with stories of the aid offered by the family to the man or woman who seeks to fight the regime. But these are merely the dramatic expression of a much more general phenomenon, namely, that the anxiety-ridden subject of a totalitarian dictatorship, in his isolation and alienation from all ordinary community living, seeks refuge in the intimate relations of family life. It is, of course, difficult to document this generalization adequately, for the anony-mous life of every man is not recorded for the social scientist to inspect. However, where we do catch glimpses of this situation, it confirms the general impression. (295b; 25; 197a) How long it will last is a more difficult question. In the view of some, "it is not with the traditional family as it earlier existed that the regime has com-promised, and which it has restored to its former standing as a pil-lar on which the state rests. On the contrary, only the changes in the family that came about over the years, and the fact that in many ways the old family and its value system were transformed and no longer threatened the regime, made the compromise . . . possible." (161j) But whether the new family may not likewise become in many cases an island of separateness is a question left open by these comments, and there exist some indications that this is so. Investiga-tors of the development of the postwar German family have been able to show, on the basis of extended interview material, that family cohesion was strengthened by the Nazi effort to weaken it, and that quite a few families made a conscious effort to broaden family ties. (315; 392) Both tendencies were further intensified dur-ing the postwar debacle, when the total collapse and break-up of country and social structure left the family as almost the only dependable "community group."

The same was true of the earlier Soviet days. The family, accord-ing to the testimony of many former Soviet citizens, became the sole refuge where anti-Communist sentiments were freely voiced and where religious rites were maintained. Many Soviet émigrés recall that their parents attempted to counter the official propa-ganda to which the children were exposed in the schools and in the youth organizations. Some remember sharing their parents' indigna-tion at the purge policies of Stalin. One, for instance, reported that "in 1937 in connection with the execution of Tukhachevsky and the military conspiracy, I stopped believing in the Soviet regime . . . These people had great merit . . . My father told me often about Yakir. He served in his division during the civil war. And what he told me about him was always good. He became indignant when all this happened, and I was indignant with him." (37i) The transmission of parental feelings against the Soviet regime was particularly marked in the agricultural areas, where the official influence of the party had been the slowest in making itself felt and where collectivization had left the deepest wounds. In time, however, family attitudes themselves underwent a change. It became apparent that the Soviet regime would not collapse, and more and more parents, out of consideration for their children's future, became inclined not to impede their children's adjustment to the new system. This theme is repeated quite frequently by refugees from the Soviet Union and Communist China. Furthermore, the process of urbanization and industrialization tended to weaken family bonds and to deepen the abyss between the prerevolutionary and the postrevolutionary generations. Of course, such things as arrests or executions always tend to bind the family together, but generally speaking the family has gradually weakened in its resistance to the regime. Indeed, some émigrés openly admit that they became alienated from their parents because it seemed that the parents had counterrevolutionary views. Anti-Soviet sentiments thus served sometimes to undermine parental influence, giving the party full control of young minds. By now, most Soviet parents are themselves of the postrevolutionary generation, and the family tends to be integrated into the system. This is less true, of course, in the satellite areas where, as in the early days of the USSR, the family still remains a bastion to be stormed and subdued. (118; 117)

It is perhaps not without interest that even in East Germany the same general trends can be observed. The situation is complicated by the extent to which family bonds extend westward into the Federal Republic. Again, the regime seeks to reorganize and at the same time to strengthen the family. (81) Again, the family finds itself battered by the demands of the regime upon all its members, but more particularly upon the youth whom it has organized extensively and seeks to influence through the propaganda carried on inside the schools and out. But again, we also find the family providing the essential "castle," the haven of refuge not only for those who are persecuted and those who resist, but also for large numbers of isolated men and women who have retreated into this group's intimacy as an escape from totalitarian demands.

In conclusion, it might be said that the family, because of its basic and universal nature, because of the intimacy and human warmth of its bonds, has been a true oasis in the desert of totalitarian atomization. It has not only resisted this atomization, but the totalitarians have found themselves obliged to make substantial concessions to family stability, primarily in order to buttress their search for the ever larger reservoirs of human manpower needed for the totalitarian enterprise. In doing so they have undertaken to reshape the family in terms of their own system, to deprive it of its autonomy, and to make it serve the regime as an initiator of effective indoctrination.

23

THE CHURCHES

"Religion is the opium of the people!" This famous slogan of the Communist-Marxist movement conveys a good part of the essence of the totalitarian approach — its hostility to all organized religion. The Communists especially were inclined to see the churches as willing helpmates of the established capitalist order, and to see the faith they encourage as merely "superstition" nurtured for the purpose of misleading the common man and of preventing him, by belief in a nonexistent God and by fear of a nonexistent afterlife, from taking a rational view of government, history, and the economy. The Fascists and National Socialists, committed in this as in so many other matters to ideological opposition to the Communists, denounced this doctrine of Marxism and, as a result, were mistaken by quite a few observers to be defenders of the church and of the Christian religion. In candid programmatic declarations, however, both Mussolini and Hitler made it very clear that they were equally hostile — clear, that is, to anyone who still knew and understood the meaning of the Christian faith and of the church, namely that it exists for the purpose of its practice on this earth. This must be said in spite of the fact that high-ranking dignitaries in both Catholic and Protestant churches, in both Italy and Germany, failed to perceive this basic conflict and sought to strike compromises built upon an acceptance of Fascist and National Socialist ideology. (418a)

It is true, however, that the Fascist and Nazi movements at the outset pursued policies that seemed to be radically at variance with the well-known "godless" movement of the Bolsheviks, who openly attacked and eventually undertook a large-scale liquidation of the ecclesiastical organization of the Russian Orthodox Church. (181a) In their policies, the Bolsheviks were guided by the Marxist position on the subject of religion and by the violent policy declarations of Lenin. To quote but two such statements:

> Religion is a kind of spiritual vodka in which the slaves of capital drown their human shape and their claims to any decent human life. (205h)

> All oppressing classes of every description need two social functions to safeguard their domination: the function of a hangman and the function of a priest. The hangman is to quell the protest and the rebellion of the oppressed; the priest is to paint before them a perspective of mitigated sufferings and sacrifices under the same class rule . . . Thereby he reconciles them to class domination, weans them away from revolutionary actions, undermines their revolutionary spirit, destroys their revolutionary determination. (203b)

So instructed, the Bolshevik regime launched an intensive antireligious campaign in the twenties, which lasted, with some relaxations and oscillations, until the end of the Great Purge in 1936–1938. The most violent periods involved the years 1922–23, 1929–30, and 1937–38. The first attack was designed to decapitate the Russian Orthodox clergy and involved the temporary arrest of the Patriarch and the deportation of the acting patriarchs. At the same time, "spontaneous" local actions on the part of zealous Communists were encouraged, resulting in the pillaging and closing of the churches. Local religious communities were "encouraged" to vote for decisions to close their churches and to transform them into museums or halls of culture. In 1925 the League of Militant Atheists was set up to give this campaign more effective expression. This was followed by an intensification in the antireligious campaigns carried on in the schools. Violence became quite open during the Yezhovshchina, and large numbers of the clergy were indicted for "antirevolutionary wrecking." The Russian Orthodox clergy was intimidated and subdued, and the church no longer represented an effective impediment to totalitarian rule.

The Fascists and Nazis claimed to fight this policy, which had aroused the indignation of the Western world, by erecting a totalitarian dictatorship strong enough to withstand the Bolshevik onslaught. But in conjunction with this claim, they propounded views that made religion purely a function of political needs. They insisted upon a "political faith," which must be the cardinal point of reference. (369) Hitler put this quite clearly and unequivocally in *Mein Kampf*:

For myself and for all true National Socialists there exists only one doctrine: nation and fatherland. What we have to fight for is to make secure the existence and the expansion of our race and of our nation, to rear its children and to keep pure the blood, the freedom and the independence of the fatherland, so that our nation may get ripe for the mission which the creator of this universe has assigned it. *Every thought and every idea, every doctrine and all knowledge have to serve this purpose.* (148b)

Mussolini was no less explicit in expounding such a "secular religion." In his *Doctrine of Fascism*, we read:

Fascism is a religious conception in which man is seen in his immediate relationship with a superior law and with an objective will that transcends the particular individual and raises him to conscious membership of a spiritual society . . . The man of Fascism is an individual who is nation and fatherland, which is a moral law binding together individuals and the generations into a tradition and a mission . . . the nation is created by the state which gives the people, conscious of its own moral unity, a will and therefore an effective existence . . . knows no limit to its development and realizes itself in testing its own limitlessness . . . Fascism, in short, is not only the giver of laws and the founder of institutions, but the educator and promoter of spiritual life. (268c)

But these views do not preclude accepting religion, or even the churches, as useful helpmates in the struggle for power that is politics. Both Hitler and Mussolini admitted, and the latter indeed stressed, the value of religion within this context: "In the Fascist State religion is looked upon as one of the deepest manifestations of the spirit; it is therefore not only respected, but defended and protected," Mussolini wrote, and he added that Fascism did not vainly seek to expel religion from the minds of men, as Bolshevism had tried to do. But what if the church, what if the religion the church "embodies," demands something different from the Fascist state? The fight of Fascism with the church over the education of youth is typical here, and it is because of this potential clash between the two that the totalitarian dictatorship considers the problem a serious one. The church is another island of separateness that cannot be allowed to remain separate and apart, that must be subjugated and coordinated.

From the other side of the dilemma, the Soviet Union found itself in the position of acknowledging the role of religion and the value of ecclesiastical organization, provided it could be made the handmaiden of the totalitarian dictatorship; so eventually the two ideologies, seemingly worlds apart at the outset, met upon a common ground that is in keeping with the inner rationale, the dynamism, of the totalitarian society. But this rationale is confronted in the sphere of religion, as in that of the family, with "limits," resulting from the very nature of the total claim which religion makes upon the man who confesses it. Hence the story of religious opposition, suffering, and resistance to the inroads made by totalitarian political demands. One writer put it very well: "Had Hitler really known the Christian church, there would have had to exist a deathly enmity from the first day on." (42a) As it was, Hitler, like Mussolini, pretended to be defending the church against Marxism and to be protecting it against its corruption through participation in politics. He even claimed to be creating the "conditions for a truly deep, inner religiosity." (239; 42b) What is to be thought of this concern of Hitler's can be seen from one of his reported conversations: "What do you think, will the masses ever become Christian again? Never! . . . but the priests . . . will betray their God to us . . . and replace the cross by the swastika. They will celebrate the pure blood of our nation instead of the blood of their previous redeemer." (288) We find the very same views expounded in his *Secret Talks,* where we find such statements as "the party does well to keep its distance from the church," "I do not care for articles of faith," and "I do not permit priests to concern themselves with secular matters." (152c; 150f) He criticized S. H. Chamberlain for believing in Christianity as a spiritual world, and Mussolini for having made compromises with the Catholic Church. "By himself he is a free spirit," he said of Mussolini, meaning that the two agreed that Christianity was a "dying branch." He remarked that he would "march into the Vatican and carry out the whole bunch." (152d) It is necessary to face these brutally frank sentiments of the true Hitler in order to grasp the purely tactical meaning of expressions like the one cited, which are meant to suggest that Fascism considers religion an important factor in national life. In *Mein Kampf* he had written that "the movement sees in both churches [the Protestant and the Catholic] equally valuable supports for the continued existence of our people." Hitler planned to tackle the problem of the churches after the war as "the last great problem" and to transform them into organizations for celebrating the racial "faith" in which he believed. (152e; 150h)

In the light of all the evidence, one might well ask whether the frank and frontal attack of the Bolsheviks was not the lesser evil. Neither in the Soviet Union in the twenties nor more recently in the satellites has there been the same amount of danger about churches, being caught in the meshes of totalitarian religious corruption, although recent tendencies in the Russian Orthodox Church are disturbing. But they are probably the consequences of the Soviets' adopting a line of approach more nearly akin to that of the Fascists: allowing the churches to operate on a very restricted basis and forcing them to abstain from all concern with secular issues in exchange for supporting the regime. The Soviet regime has thus been able to capitalize on the traditional submissiveness of the Russian Orthodox Church to state authority, dating back to the tsarist period. The Russian Orthodox clergy had spinelessly supported tsarism and, after the period of persecutions, had little stamina left for opposing the Soviet regime.

The turn in the church-state, or rather church-party, relations in the USSR came during the war, when the regime liberalized its religious policy and the church gave its blessings to the Great Fatherland War against the German invader. It was at that time that Stalin characterized himself, in an interview with a sympathetic American priest, as "an advocate of freedom of conscience and freedom of worship" and even suggested the possibility of co-operation with the pope "in the struggle against coercion and persecution of the Catholic Church." (338) Although this cooperation never materialized, the treatment of the Russian Orthodox Church never returned to its prewar severity, and the church became in some ways, at least politically, an appendage of the party. Before the 1953 elections to the Supreme Soviet, the Moscow Patriarchate stated that nowhere in the world was the church as free as in the USSR, and gave its blessings to those who cast their votes for the

Communist bloc of candidates. The clergy has also been extensively utilized for propaganda purposes in connection with the various peace campaigns sponsored by the Soviet regime, and the patriarchs have been active in sponsoring these petitions abroad.

The Russian Orthodox Church has justified its cooperation with the Soviet regime, which some church members may possibly dislike, in terms of God's will and "giving unto Caesar what is Caesar's." Opposition to Soviet antireligious policies, however, still persists. In the twenties there were many cases of underground religious movements, of brave clergymen of all creeds, including Catholics, Protestants, and Jews (181c), preaching the word of God at the risk of their lives, religious congregations meeting secretly, and youth groups organizing to maintain the faith among the young. Even secret theological study groups operated in order to fill the gaps created by the arrests and deportations of the clergy. (464c; 181b; 132) The war, resulting in the opening of the churches under the German occupation and in the liberalization of the Soviet policy toward the churches, also served to reawaken religious activity. Even several theological seminaries were opened, with old, prerevolutionary, theological scholars permitted to teach in them. Despite the fact that the life of a priest in the USSR is one of the greatest uncertainty, including always the possibility of arrest, the number of applicants exceeded the capacity of these schools, suggesting that even after several decades of Soviet rule there were young people willing to risk serving God. At first, however, the regime was inclined to feel that religion would soon disappear once the church had been taken over and the young denied religious instruction in the state schools. That this did not happen is evidenced by efforts of the regime's propagandists to rationalize the persistence of religious feeling among some circles of the population. As one leading student of these matters put it: "Whatever the strength of religious feelings in a hundred years' time, there can be little doubt that the Holy Scriptures of the great religions will still be read and studied and at least to some extent venerated." (181d) The Soviets themselves have another explanation. The presence of "religious survivals" is due to the fact that "the consciousness of the people . . . usually lags behind the changes in the life of society . . . This applies particularly to religion, a form of social consciousness which lags behind the base more than all other elements of the superstructure and possesses a greater degree of independence. Another cause of the tenacity of religious survivals is the influence of capitalist encirclement." (323)

Old religious ways have been particularly strong in resisting Soviet atheism in the Moslem areas of the USSR, which include some thirty million Moslems. The Soviet regime has been engaged repeatedly in violent campaigns to break up the influence of the mullahs by closing the places of worship and subjecting the clergy to persecution. In the Crimea, for instance, long a center of Moslem tradition, not a single mosque was open by 1941. Yet, immediately after the German occupation, some fifty mosques were spontaneously set up by the former congregations. (464d) Later, Soviet propagandists linked Islam with colonialism and imperialism, and stated that "Islam reflects the social yoke and the views of the exploiters." (471; 181e) At the same time, the regime has sought to win sympathy and support from Moslems outside the Soviet Union. Concessions have been made in an effort to transform the USSR's Moslem leadership into helpmates of Soviet foreign policy, and their role in anticolonialist and peace movements has been encouraged.

In 1954 the antireligious campaign was stepped up. The Central Committee issued a decree, exhorting its members and the Komsomol to engage in more active antireligious propaganda and to combat the "last remains" of religion. But the committee's decree, "On Errors in Conducting Scientific-Atheistic Propaganda Among the Public," was not designed to stimulate a new period of open repression. Rather, it was to guide party members in their atheistic indoctrination without disturbing the relationship of party and church, since the church had become useful. Commentaries on this decree, therefore, stressed the fact that such propaganda must be careful not to degenerate into violence, which in effect might be more harmful to the party. *Partiinaya zhizn,* the organ of the Central Committee, emphasized that the method was now one of education and not of coercion. (434f)

And the regime could well afford such moderation. The previous coercion had destroyed any will to resist among the higher clergy, who now usefully serve the state. The process of urbanization has broken up the established village routine, which also involved religious ritual. The new urban centers, with their new modes of life, leave little room for religion, and Soviet efforts aim to keep it so. Thus, while some religious feeling may continue, religion in the USSR no longer finds an institutional expression that could challenge the supremacy and the monopoly of the party, even in the nonmaterial aspects of life. (161k)

In the Communist satellites, antireligious activity seems to have learned a great deal from Soviet experience. Thus in communities where either religious feeling or the church was not strong, suppression was rapidly applied. In countries like Poland, where the church has had a long history of national struggle, more cautious measures have been adopted. Despite the arrests of some hundreds of priests, religious activity by the Roman Catholic Church continues on a large scale, new churches have been built, and old ones rebuilt. A Catholic university still operates in Lublin. But at the same time, the regime is steadily working to subvert the independence of the church. A collaborationist group, known as "patriot priests," was organized, ostensibly to defend Poland against German aggression. The Primate of Poland, Cardinal Wyszynski, known as an outspoken opponent of Communism, was forcibly removed to a monastery. In 1952 and 1953 the first arrests occurred among the bishops, and some were charged in public trials with being American spies. The government, on its own authority, appointed the patriot priests to fill their sees. The process of subjugation, although still not as far advanced as in Yugoslavia or Hungary (where the cardinals were sentenced to prison), is thus following the Soviet model, although it encounters much more resistance from both the clergy and the population. (329; 78b) Following a temporary accommodation after Gomulka's return to power in 1956, the regime has steadily moved back to its policy of weakening religion and the church.

These efforts of the churches in the captive nations resemble what the churches, or rather groups within the Protestant and Catholic churches, attempted under the Nazis (and to a very limited degree under Mussolini). The story is an involved one. During the early days of the movement and immediately after its seizure of power, there was very substantial support for it from the Protestant clergy. Its links with pre-Weimar Germany and its antisocialist and anti-Catholic outlook had made many of them look with favor upon a movement that claimed to fight these forces and to seek the re-establishment of a conservative, Christian order of things. Their traditional authoritarianism and nationalist patriotism inclined them to overlook the un-Christian views and actions of the movement, and as a matter of fact a substantial number of Protestant clergymen remained National Socialists to the bitter end.

But there did arise a most vigorous opposition within Protestant ranks. The fight was kindled in part by an issue that struck at the very heart of Hitler's ideology: the racial issue. No Christian who understood the teachings of the church, and more especially no clergyman, could possibly accept the view that a member in good standing must be excluded from the church because he, or his father or grandmother, had been a Jew. Men like Pastor Niemöller, himself originally a National Socialist, rebelled at this flagrant violation of Christian teachings.

Perhaps even more important, though, was the issue of ecclesiastical self-government. The party's interference in the churches' affairs aroused their immediate opposition. Among Protestants this opposition was further intensified by the movement of the "German Christians," which culminated in a scandalous speech by one Krause in the Sportpalast on September 26, 1933. (42c) The German Christians were essentially National Socialists who favored a creed which was only nominally Christian, but in fact a replica of the National Socialist ideology: fight against Marxism, Jews, cosmopolitanism, and freemasons, and for the purification of the race. The Protestant clergy had to wage their fight against these perverters of the Christian faith. Since the German Christians had the advantage of the political support of state and party, this resistance was most difficult and dangerous, but it was carried on relentlessly and at great personal sacrifice. When the German Christians gained control of the church and elected the Reich Bishop, the opposing clergy, high and low, formed in March 1934 the Confessional Church (Bekennende Kirche), * which held its first synod in Barmen-Wuppertal, May 29–31. This synod arrived at a pointedly oppositional agreement: "In opposition to the attempts to unify the German Evangelical Church by means of false doctrine, by the use of force, and of insincere practices, the Confessional Synod declares: the Unity of the Evangelical Churches in Germany can only come into being

---

* The literal translation would be "Confessing Church," and it may be the more correct one since the views of the church's members had nothing to do with the confessional.

from the Word of God in faith through the Holy Ghost." They further maintained that the introduction of alien principles threatened the unity of Protestant Christians and that only those who remained true to the Gospel and the creed of the church (in contrast to the German Christians) represented the legitimate church. Denouncing the German Christians, they continued: "We reject the false doctrine that the Church might and must acknowledge as sources . . . besides the one word of God . . . other truths as God's revelation . . . We reject the false doctrine that there are realms of life in which we belong not to Jesus Christ, but to other masters . . . We reject the false doctrine that the state should or could go beyond its special task and become the sole and total order of human life."

This was clearly a declaration of war against the very essence of the totalitarian dictatorship, and the Council of Brethren (Bruderrat), which was formed to carry forward the fight, constituted a true resistance to the regime. Besides Niemöller, Bishop Meiser of Bavaria and Bishop Wurm of Württemberg, as well as Karl Koch, who had headed the Gospel and Church group of opponents of the Nazi trends, were leaders of this movement. We cannot trace in detail here the complex story of this opposition. Though not successful in restraining the regime's acts, it nonetheless lasted from the beginning to the end of the dictatorship, with various advances and retreats on both sides, but maintaining intact the essential Christian teachings. It was responsible for the fact that a large majority of the Protestant clergy became unsympathetic if not hostile to the regime, that, of the 18,000 Protestant pastors, approximately 10,000 spoke out in 1935 against the regime's Church Law, and that 11,000 again rejected the regime's attempt to settle the conflict in January 1939. Approximately 6,000 Confessional Brethren confronted the 2,000 German Christians among the clergy, and these men were subjected to vigorous persecution by the regime and considerable numbers perished in concentration camps. It would seem that only a minority of the Protestant pastors supported the regime actively, with nearly a third being in opposition. If proof were needed beyond the figures made available since the war, it is contained in a Gestapo report of February 15, 1938. "The Confessional Front embraces by far the largest majority of Protestant theologians and likewise the majority of believing church members." (42d) No other organization, unless it were the Catholic Church, was able to mount a comparable opposition, to resist a totalitarian system for twelve full years. It was a true "island of separateness," resting upon the strength of Christian convictions among Protestants, stirring them into new life and genuine dedication. (145; 131; 77; 163)

But what about the Catholic Church? We find resistance here too, but of a somewhat different order. Considering the leading role of the Center Party in the Weimar Republic, and the great vigor of Catholic lay activity behind it, the Catholic clergy before Hitler's seizure of power maintained not only a standoffish but an openly hostile attitude toward the Nazi movement, going so far as to declare in 1932 that a good Catholic could not be a member of the party. United through its episcopate in a way inconceivable for Protestants, the Catholic Church stood firm against the movement until it actually became the government. Thereafter, unfortunately, they sought to accommodate themselves, in the manner of the church in Italy, hoping for a while to be able to secure an effective modification of the movement's totalitarian goals. The Center Party, after protracted study, decided to vote for the Enabling Act, giving Hitler unlimited power (March 1933). At the same time, rightist elements in the church promoted a concordat. (418b) It was concluded between the Reich and the church on July 20, 1933. However, the experience was similar to that of the church in Italy; the provisions of the concordat, guaranteeing the church its essential autonomy, were honored mostly in the breach; for example, in education, school, university, and adult, the church could only with the greatest difficulty retain some of the controls the concordat had envisaged. Similarly, the Catholic press and associations were put under severe pressure, and the bishops protested in a pastoral letter (1934).

As the regime became more fully totalitarian, the clashes increased until, in January 1935, the Nazis launched a full-scale attack against the church, seeking to destroy the Catholic press, Catholic education, Catholic associations, and even the influence of the priests over the faithful. They succeeded with press, education, and associations, but the congregations tried to stand firm. (371) The press was abolished or "censored"; education was driven from the schools, while confessional schools were virtually eliminated; and the associations were "coordinated," like all others. The pretenses used by the Nazis in explaining these attacks were, first, currency violations by ecclesiastical bodies and, second, sexual and other crimes by priests, monks, and lay brethren. The small amount of genuine evil which these accusations involved was, in typical totalitarian propaganda style, blown up to assume the significance of an essential characteristic. (197b) They served to discredit the church to some extent, until a substantial group of ecclesiastical dignitaries, under the leadership of Clemens August Count von Galen, Bishop of Münster, and Konrad Count von Preysing, Bishop of Berlin, insisted on taking a stand. Galen liked to spice his sermons of defiance with such remarks as "they can take my head, but not my convictions." There were also Bishop Sproll of Rottenburg and Bishop Bornewasser of Trier, as well as the redoubtable Cardinal Archbishop of Munich, Michael von Faulhaber. They did, however, continue to insist upon the church's hostility to political rebellion and tyrannicide and created very grave conflicts of conscience by these equivocations. (209c)

But when speaking of these high dignitaries, we must not forget the vast number of more humble ecclesiastics, priests, monks, and nuns, who actually suffered more violent persecution because the Nazi government never quite dared to take vigorous action against the high dignitaries of the church, although it is highly probable that they would have done so after a victory in the war. Both *Hitler's Secret Conversations* and *The Goebbels Diaries* refer several times to this prospect. (150h; 125c) In any case, the regime did not show much forbearance with regard to the rest of the clergy; by the end of 1939 approximately 5,700 priests had been arrested, and nearly half were in concentration camps at that time. (229; 262a) This is about a fifth of the entire Catholic clergy. In short, the struggle was quite an open one, and the Catholic Church, like the Protestant, mounted a vigorous campaign of resistance. Churchmen, high and low, spoke out against the outrages of Nazi doctrine and action. They had their own "Catholic Niemöller," Jesuit Father Mayer who, though protected by Cardinal Faulhaber, was arrested in 1937. When this happened, the cardinal ordered protests to be read from every pulpit in the diocese.

However, the nature of the Catholic struggle was different from the Protestant, for it rested upon the church's hierarchical authority. Therefore it took clear and decisive form only after Pope Pius XI issued his encyclical *Mit Brennender Sorge,* which was read from every Catholic pulpit on March 21, 1937. In it the pope said:

> With deep anxiety and increasing dismay, we have for some time past beheld the sufferings of the Church and the steadily growing oppression of those men and women who have remained true to her . . . He who takes the race, or the people, or the state, or the form of government, or the bearers of the power of the state, or other fundamental elements of human society, which in the temporal order of things have an essential and honorary place, out of the system of their earthly valuation and makes of them the ultimate norm of all, even of religious values, and deifies them with idolatrous worship, perverts and falsifies the order of things created and commanded by God.

The pope said also that the church's efforts at accommodation had been made in the hope of preserving the essential basis of work for the Christian church, but that it had become clear that the true intention of Hitler was to destroy Christianity, as indeed it was. It has been suggested that the Catholic shift was in part motivated by the vigorous opposition that the Confessional Church was making; perhaps so. But there was enough provocation given by the Nazis themselves in their mounting attacks on the church to produce a reversal of the policy of accommodation. The Catholic clergy had been divided from the beginning, as had the Protestant, and it was in fact a matter of the opposing minority's gaining papal support that turned the tide in favor of outright opposition. (119; 342a; 76) In this respect, the Catholic Church had a distinct advantage, counterbalancing its slower start: once the authorities of the church had taken a stand, the unity of action of most Catholic clergymen was pretty well assured. These well-documented facts about the reality of Catholic resistance have been obscured recently by the argument over whether the pope should have denounced Hitler's extermination policy, raised by the remarkable play *The Deputy.* The controversy has brought forward the entire range of issues involved in resistance to totalitarianism as presented here.

Catholic authorities were faced with a most curious contrast when Austria and Poland were taken over by Hitler. In the former case, an abject subjection on the part of Cardinal Innitzer and the Catholic clergy had to be counteracted by the Holy See in order to bring the Austrian into line with the German episcopate, many of whom were outraged by the action of their Austrian colleagues. In Poland, on the other hand, the persecution of the church, as of the people, was so violent that after a report by Cardinal Hlond, in December 1939, the new pope, Pius XII, became even more firmly committed to a radical anti-Nazi position than his predecessor; in the sequel it also became an anti-Fascist position. In Poland particularly, the Nazis gave full vent to their anti-Christian feelings and subjected the Catholic Church to a policy of unmitigated terror. At first, the most intense violence was restricted to those parts of the clergy which were in the western part of Poland, arbitrarily incorporated into Germany itself. Since these territories were to be considered German in character, the presence of Polish Catholic clergy was highly inconvenient. Accordingly, mass arrests occurred in 1939, and the clergy was exposed to a policy of persecution until the end of the war. This policy soon spread to the other occupied parts of Poland, and mass deportations of the clergy to concentration camps took place. All in all, the Nazis arrested and placed in concentration camps 3,643 priests, 341 monks, 389 novices, and 1,117 nuns. Of these, 2,517, including 4 bishops, succumbed to their tortures or were executed. (297)

As a matter of fact, after Hitler had plunged Germany into war, the Catholic hierarchy, like the Confessional Church, was confronted with a difficult problem. They did not wish to be unpatriotic by seeming hostile to the fatherland; yet the intensification of totalitarian trends under the impact of war necessitated a sharper rejection of Hitler and his movement. Among the most moving documents portraying this conflict are the sermons of Bishop Galen after the bombardment and destruction of Münster. Virtually from amidst the rubble, the staunch anti-Nazi denounced the tyranny of the Gestapo. In one of his sermons he said: "The right to life, to inviolability and to liberty are an indispensable part of every moral social order . . . Any state which oversteps these limits imposed by God and which permits or causes the punishment of innocent men undermines its own authority and the respect for its dignity." And he compared the church to the anvil that must resist and will survive the hammer striking it. The same line was taken by the Bavarian bishops, who in 1941 issued a pastoral that said: "We

German bishops protest against each and every violation of personal freedom . . . we are concerned not only with religious and Church rights . . . but also the God-given rights of men" — ancient Catholic doctrine, but often forgotten in more recent times. (342b; 332; 249; 350) It all culminated in a protest by the entire episcopate, meeting at Fulda on March 22, 1942, which was immediately suppressed by the Nazis but distributed widely:

> For years a war has raged in our Fatherland against Christianity and Church . . . We emphasize that we stand up not only for religious and clerical rights . . . but likewise for the human rights bestowed by God on mankind . . . We demand legal evidence for all sentences and the release of all fellow citizens who have been deprived of their liberty without such evidence . . . The Nazis wish to destroy Christianity, if possible . . . Before the soldiers whose Christian faith gives them the strength for heroic battles and sacrifices return home . . . we call upon you . . . to support our efforts . . . Decisively and firmly we refuse the suggestion that we should prove our patriotic faith through faithlessness toward Christ and His Church. We remain eternally true to our Fatherland just because and at any price we remain faithful to our Saviour and our Church. God bless our country and our holy Church. God grant an honest, happy, lasting peace to the Church and to the Fatherland. (430c; 216b)

This in turn was followed by a pastoral of August 29, 1943, which recited at length the violations of Christian doctrine by the actions of the totalitarian dictatorship and more especially the killing of "unproductive" persons. It had been initiated on orders from Hitler and had aroused not only the ire but the most vigorous action of protest by bishops, especially Galen. The same protest was made two weeks later in a pastoral entitled, "The Ten Commandments as Living Law of All Nations." (262b)

While the Catholic Church in Italy did not assist Fascism's rise to power, she later entered into rather close and unfortunate relations with the regime. Many lay Catholics, of course, became Fascists, and a number of the higher clergy, notably Cardinal Schuster of Milan, became outspoken in their advocacy of Fascism. The high point of these relations was reached with the conclusion of the Lateran treaty in 1929. This treaty seemed favorable to the church on paper; it carried with it the church's endorsement of the regime.

Soon afterwards difficulties arose in connection with the education of youth (see Chapter 12), but at the outbreak of the Ethiopian war, priests enthusiastically welcomed the war as "carrying Christian civilization" to a barbaric people (Schuster). New difficulties then arose in connection with racialism, and Pope Pius XI spoke out sharply against such radicalism. He even considered repudiating the treaty, but died before he took this step. Nonetheless, throughout the war, the clergy supported the regime, although a significant minority developed a resistance movement which played a key role in the liberation and provided many of the Catholic lay leaders of postwar Italy. The Italian church's relation may therefore properly be described as an ambivalent one, with the hierarchy retaining the right to criticize and even to condemn the regime, which sharply differentiates its position from that of the Russian church, with its abject dependence on and subjection to the Bolshevik government. (120g)

In conclusion, we can say that the Christian churches have shown themselves to be a real bulwark against the claim to total power of the totalitarian dictatorship, perhaps more real than any others. Whether Protestant or Catholic, the genuine Christian cannot accept totalitarianism. For Christianity claims the whole man and the last word with regard to man's values and man's destiny. This claim the totalitarians cannot accept. They may temporarily seek to compromise, but if they accepted this claim they would cease to be totalitarians. This is what has happened in Spain. In its gradual retreat from totalitarianism to a personal and military dictatorship, Franco's regime has had the steady support of the Catholic clergy. Its highly conservative inclination has, at the same time, made it resist all popular, democratic tendencies.

It would be pure speculation to try to delineate the parallel problem in countries like China. To date there is no indication that the Confucians or Buddhists have been able to mount a defense comparable to that of Western Christians. But this may not mean that these peoples are prepared to accept a "secular religion" of the totalitarian kind forever. Perhaps the family will prove itself the comparable bulwark of human dignity, though the evidence so far is rather discouraging. (300b; 117) By contrast, the islands of separateness represented by the Christian churches, as guardians of the individual conscience and its religious freedom, are likely to outlast even a long-term totalitarian dictatorship. The extent to which they still exist in genuine form in the Soviet Union is rather uncertain. But, in the catacombs of an unknown religious underground, the spirit of Christian men may be reborn.

24

THE UNIVERSITIES
AND THE TECHNICIANS

The attitude of the totalitarians toward science and hence toward the universities is an ambivalent one because, on the one hand, their ideology is supposed to rest upon scientific foundations, while, on the other, the antidogmatic attitude of all true science fits ill into the totalitarian scheme of things. Their escape takes the form of a crude utilitarian view of science as merely a means to an end. This ambivalence permits the existence of another "island of separateness," especially in those fields of learning which are somewhat remote from the totalitarian ideology. Yet even these tended to be invaded by the totalitarian dogmatism, as shown by Stalin's efforts in the field of language and literature (see Chapter 12) and the Nazis' denunciation of Einstein's theory of relativity.

Science and the universities play a very special role in Western culture and society. If we take science in the broad (and proper) sense of any field of learning distinguished by a method or methods upon which a group of scholars are agreed as the most suitable for treating a particular subject, whether it be life, government, or human anatomy (110h), then the very autonomy of such groups of scholars clashes with the totalitarian conception, as it does indeed with all authoritarian conceptions of government. The extent of power wielded affects the seriousness of the clash, however, and it is bound to be the most serious in a totalitarian society. Yet Western culture has developed many of its distinctive traits, and more especially its technology, as a consequence of its dedication to learning in the distinctive sense of modern science. Indeed, human culture all over the globe is being not only profoundly affected, but revolutionized as a result of the impact of modern technology. And as we have tried to show, totalitarian dictatorship is itself the "logical" outcome of some of these technological trends. This is not true in the sense of modern technology's having "caused" totalitarianism, but in the sense of having made it possible. Without it, several of its distinctive traits, more especially propaganda, the terror, and central planning, would be quite impossible; the dictatorships set up by Lenin, Mussolini, and Hitler would merely have been autocracies of the older despotic or tyrannical variety (for which they were and are mistaken by many, both friend and foe, as was shown in Chapters 1 and 2). The undeniable fact that totalitarian dictatorship rests upon modern science and technology produces an inner contradiction with many implications. It means that totalitarian dictatorship, in interfering with science, saws off the branch it is sitting on, especially as long as it competes in the world at large with free societies, in which the progress of science is unimpeded.

It is fairly clear from the record that totalitarian societies were and are parasitic, as far as science is concerned. They avail themselves, that is, of its fruits without contributing fully toward the maintenance of the plant that produces them. This parasitism takes two forms. On the one hand, there is the exploitation of past scientific and technological work. Both Mussolini and Hitler lived by the attainments of the societies which they at the same time sought to liquidate. The universities and the teaching staffs, their libraries and laboratories, were taken over and put to work within the context of the regime, like so many other existing things (especially the economy, embodying past technological advance). They continued to function, with certain slowdowns and breakdowns, in their accustomed manner, continued to provide education, to produce new knowledge and so on, even though the regime did not feed them but starved them, from a spiritual viewpoint. On the other hand, there is also the parasitism that exploits the progress and the inventions of free societies. There is no intrinsic parasitism involved in the free exchange of scientific knowledge; quite the contrary. But when this exchange becomes largely a one-way traffic, the parasitic nature of the recipient is made evident. The contributions of Soviet science to the general progress of science are limited. (253c) All the violent proclamations of the Bolsheviks and their claque celebrating the "triumphs" of Soviet science cannot hide the fact that the USSR has continually fed upon scientific progress in the free countries. The most dramatic expression of this fact are the efforts of the Soviets to secure the essential data in atomic and hydrogen physics by the most elaborate kind of espionage. This statement remains true even though the achievements of the Soviets in certain fields have been extremely impressive and, with the launching of the sputniks, have achieved world-wide recognition. Very large investments have been made in particular areas of science that serve the regime, and therefore shifts of policy, such as Khrushchev's emphasis on agricultural production, may have striking results in fields that have hitherto been parasitic. Still, the overall result is spotty. The way in which science in all its reaches declines under totalitarian impact can be seen in particularly striking fashion in the successive depletions under the Nazis and the Communists in East Germany, as described in one detailed study. (257a)

In order to be able to engage in this kind of parasitic activity, the totalitarian dictatorship must nonetheless have the cooperation of "bourgeois" scholars who are willing to continue their work. Indeed, this continuation of scholarly work aroused the dismay and indignation of the outsiders and victims of these regimes, who felt that the guardians of truth and scholarship ought to rise in wrathful resistance against the totalitarian dictatorship (382; 136), or should at least depart and refuse to lend a helping hand in keeping the totalitarian regime going. There is much to be said for this viewpoint, at least in general moral terms. The fact is, however, that scientists and scholars, by the very nature of their task and training, are the least likely men to mount an effective resistance to a totalitarian regime. There have been, to be sure, quite a few cases of noble, if somewhat ineffectual, efforts on the part of scholars, but these were exceptions and they occurred rather late in the evolution of the totalitarian system, at a time when resistance was no longer effective. One of the main reasons is that the very antidogmatism of science causes scholars to be puzzled and perplexed in the face of so startling a development as a modern dictatorship. There are, of course, numerous scholars who are driven away by the totalitarian masters, but their position is that of victims of the regimes, not fighters in the cause of academic freedom. Still, scientists and scholars in the USSR while under constant pressure play an important, though quiet, part in defending academic freedom, the freedom to study and the freedom to teach, within the limited sphere of the possible. In the past few years there have been a number of remarkable statements by leading academicians and scientists — quite daring in the Soviet context. These people have criticized certain aspects of the school reforms as endangering cultural progress, have demanded less interference with the strictly scholarly pursuits of scientists, have called for more flexibility in the instruction of advanced students. There have been lively controversies over such new developments as cybernetics, whereas in earlier years an authoritative political pronouncement would have stifled scientific controversy. Quite a few have learned how to utilize skillfully the totalitarian ambivalence toward science, if not humanistic scholarship.

Hitler's views on science and the universities are a curious reflection of this totalitarian ambivalence. He mingled the harsh contempt of the man of action for the man of thought, with a ready dependence on science to support him in his pseudo-scientific biologically inspired views. In this connection, he repeatedly spoke of the "humility" which science instills in man as it shows him the limits of his knowledge, and he even betrayed an awareness of the nondogmatic, tentative character of science. He showed himself ready to voice some of the popular slogans of scientific progress in the manner of Haeckel, and at one point even exclaimed that the truth will win out in the end. (152f; 150i) But this "truth" that is going to win out in the end does not, in Hitler's more usual view, transcend reality (148c; 164); rather it is a tool that is to be employed by the practical man of action for the purpose of realizing "the iron laws of nature," which he contrasted with the "ideas of some crazy ideologues." Rarely has a man written his own epitaph in more persuasive form. And Hitler's confusion on the point is due to his basic failure to fathom, or even to grasp superficially, the conditions for the growth of modern science.

True scientific and scholarly activity is, of course, of great long-range benefit to any political order, including a totalitarian dictatorship. In a sense, therefore, the preservation of this island of separateness could even be justified by the central leadership. We find occasional observations of this sort, not only in the Soviet Union but also in Hitler Germany. In such grudging recognition of the role of the independent scholar, the totalitarian ambivalence regarding science and scholarship finds its reluctant expression. (253d)

The inner contradictions of Soviet thinking on the subject of science are more complex than those in other totalitarian approaches. We have already had occasion to deal with dialectical materialism (Chapter 7) and with Stalin's notions on linguistics (Chapter 12), as well as the Lysenko theories involving the inheritance of acquired characteristics. Since Marx's and Engels' pretensions to scientific insight are much more insistent (and also better founded) than those of Mussolini and Hitler, the Soviet approach to science and the universities has been one of slow evolution. A considerable number of leading Russian scholars fled, of course, being evidently part of the bourgeoisie, while others lent their aid in providing the essential underpinning of Communist ideology. The most striking instance is Pavlov, whose experiments on the influence of environment tended to support the radical environmentalism of the reigning ideology; he remained to transform the universities into cooperating instruments of the regime.

A leading scholar in the mid-fifties built his analysis of the scientist in the Soviet Union on the identification of five primary premises in the fields of scientific endeavor. (253e) These are materialism, antiformalism and antisymbolism, verification through practical results, the partisanship of science, and the modification of scientific dogma only through action of the political leadership. His able discussion of these several premises and their kinship with certain Western trends culminates in two propositions that display the inherent ambivalence of Soviet doctrine: first, there does not appear to be any significant difference between a decision in regard to scientific orthodoxy and a decision on foreign policy or domestic politics; and second, during the last years of his lifetime, Stalin himself was often quoted as reasserting the theme that science cannot advance except through open, free, and creative discussions. (253f) The apparent contradiction of these two views as stated remains unresolved. "The Bolsheviks do not, and perhaps cannot, fully realize the instrumental nature of scientific knowledge, since they try to make science the anchor of their total belief system." It is equally true, however, that the Bolsheviks do not, and perhaps cannot, fully realize the nature of scientific truth, since they make truth a function of the political order. And yet they need to know the truths of advancing science and scholarship as much as their rivals. It may, therefore, be questioned whether policy decisions in these fields are still as rigidly party-controlled as they once were.

It seems that the regime has moved away from earlier attempts to make such decisions and allows various controversies to rage within the scientific community, provided they do not go too far; at the same time, it supports tendencies and developments which seem promising in view of the requirements of the regime, without repressing its antagonists. In this connection, it needs to be remembered that there are differences among fields. Even Stalin did not interfere in physics or mathematics, and the party is naturally more sensitive to history, law, and philosophy than to the natural sciences.

The increase of cultural contacts in recent years between the USSR and the West has served Soviet purposes by facilitating technological and scientific borrowing, but it has created problems as well. For in overcoming the isolation of Soviet scientists and introducing them once again to the international community of their colleagues, it has become more difficult to control the direction of their work and to inhibit deviant lines of thought and research. Soviet scientists who are exposed to the standards and concerns of reputable foreign colleagues are, one might guess, buttressed in their own work and convictions, and grow more resistant to political pressures that contradict the major tendencies of international science.

For this reason, one of the recurrent themes in Soviet writing on scientific research is the emphasis both on ideological orthodoxy and on the importance of the quest for knowledge, including open and even controversial discussion. The obvious contradiction between the two postulates, given the totalitarian setting, usually results in the stifling of free thought to the detriment of scientific advance. That the Soviets are not unaware of the dangers of this situation is suggested by the following plea in *Literaturnaya gazeta:*

Why is it sometimes so difficult to organize one or another discussion? Why are certain of our scientific disputes more like personal quarrels and altercations than like serious and principled discussions of the essence of great scientific problems? Why is it that with us valuable works, if they are opposed to the views of the leading "school," are not always noticed? What can explain the mistakes made in a number of cases in awarding prizes in science? . . . It seems to us that one of the reasons for all this is the canonization of certain scientific trends. (426a)

The party theoretical journal, *Kommunist,* re-echoes this by claiming that "a struggle of opinions, professional controversies, and discussions are more and more becoming the norm in our scientific and scholarly groups," and adds, "this is undoubtedly to the good." Yet, in the very same article, *Kommunist* states explicitly that "discussion of any scientific problem should be based above all on the Leninist principle of the party nature of science and scholarship, and participants in a discussion must approach the solution of all disputes from a position of Marxist-Leninist methodology, the only scientific basis for cognition of the objective world. Fruitful discussion can be based only on the Marxist outlook." (422c) A related problem appears to face the medical profession in its endeavor to maintain integrity. The Hippocratic Oath, mainstay of professional medical ethics outside of totalitarian reach, was abolished by the Bolsheviks because it "symbolized bourgeois medicine," that is to say, the independence of strict objectivity. But the Soviet doctor "is proud of the fact that he actively participates in the building of socialism." (94) Yet the inherent claim of the expert's true knowledge is strong enough to make many doctors, in spite of their being mere government employees, retreat into an island of separateness, "to tone down as much as possible some of the harsher and more repulsive aspects of the regime." (339d) It is obvious that, insofar as such medical professionals succeed, they are really helping the regime by mitigating the consequences of the inherent contradiction.

The case of the physician is actually a special instance of the situation of the technician and expert in general. His specialty separates him by the special claims of expert knowledge he possesses. Thus the requirements of management have led to an entire set of practices quite contradictory to the official rules on all levels of the directed economy. As the most thorough of the studies of this phenomenon points out, Soviet managers strive to attain their goals as formulated by the regime, but, in their efforts to achieve these goals, objective needs set them apart from the regime's preoccupations. (18b) Perhaps even more impressive is the case of the military. Here the "technical" requirements of victory on the battlefield would seem to be decisive and would persuade even a totalitarian regime to accept an "island of separateness." But such is not the case (see Chapter 27). Yet the disregard of technical and professional truths, notably in the case of the German military, has had disastrous consequences (123b), and the inner contradiction can lead to jeopardizing the very existence of the regime, as in Germany.

The result of this inner contradiction has been that universities and other institutions of higher learning have been greatly expanded under totalitarian dictatorship, while they have at the same time been "politicized," that is to say, subjected to a variety of political controls and fitted into the over-all planning of the regime. It is easy to misinterpret these developments, especially when their true nature is obscured by a "progressive" Western terminology. The most striking instance of this sort of danger was perhaps the work of Sidney and Beatrice Webb (379d; 60), but many others have committed similar errors. Basically, the policies of the communist and fascist dictatorships in the field of higher education are remarkably alike and consist of the following measures. The universities are deprived of their autonomy and subjected to rigid bureaucratic controls. More particularly, the rectors (presidents) and deans are made appointees of a special government agency, and the teaching staff is made removable at pleasure. At the same time, programs of ideological indoctrination are instituted in which the "true science" of certain laws is expounded to faculty and students alike. In all institutions of higher learning, party and youth-group cells are instituted, which control, and terrorize, not only their fellow students but also the faculty. Ideological and party qualifications are given increasing weight in the selection of students as well as faculty.

In addition to these politicizing aspects of totalitarian university life, there is the stress on technological specialization in response to the needs of the regime's over-all planning. It has been called "polytechnization" in the Soviet Union, and it means that there is an insistence upon narrow specialization of the student, and the steady increase in specialized schools of one sort or another. In addition, and this is peculiar to the USSR and its satellites, there is an enormous expansion of higher technical training. Admittedly, the Soviet Union started from a small base, and its rapid industrialization has greatly increased its need for technical cadres. Still the figures are imposing, as shown in the accompanying table. (72b; 363c)

Soviet Higher Educational Establishments

Year	Number of institutions	Thousands of students	1960–61 multiple
1914–15	105	127.4	19
1927–28	148	168.5	14
1935–36	718	563.5	–
1940–41	817	811.7	2.95
1950–51	880	1,247.4	1.92
1955–56	765	1,867.0	1.28
1958–59	766	2,178.9	1.10
1962–63	738	2,944.0	–

It will be noted, however, that while universities quadrupled in number, other institutions of higher learning and the student body increased about tenfold. In keeping with this general trend, we see that the five-year plan for the Soviet Zone of Occupation in Germany specified an increase from 19 to 26 universities and institutions of higher learning and an increase of students from 27,700 (in 1951) to 55,000. (257b) But, in all cases, this increase is accompanied by the insistence on *training,* with fixed curricula, an extended academic year, and narrow specialization, as we have said, combined with a great deal of political indoctrination.

In what sense can institutions of higher learning and more especially their faculty and students remain islands of separateness? It would seem on the face of it as if they were completely integrated into the regime and hence incapable of any "separateness." The answer must be found in the nature of scientific and scholarly work. The preservation of some of the spirit of free inquiry is something both more precious and more elusive than any kind of political resistance, though the latter may spring from it. Many protests from individuals and groups occurred under the Fascist dictatorships, and presumably more can be found in the Soviet Union and the satellites if the records were thrown open. There is no point in reciting the individual acts, such as harboring a Jewish colleague, fighting the Nazi student group over a boycott, attending religious services of a minister belonging to the Confessional Church, and so on. In themselves they are unimportant, but in the aggregate they add up to a manifestation on behalf of independence and separateness; they imply a rejection of the total claim. Perhaps more important are such acts as the participation of a number of professors at the University of Freiburg, including Gerhard Ritter, Constantin von Dietze, Walter Eucken, and Erik Wolf, in the uprising of July 20, or the student-led underground at the University of Munich, which resulted in the execution of Hans and Sophie Scholl as well as Professor Huber, or the leadership provided by Professor Chabod to the partisans in the Val D'Aosta, or the courageous fight carried on by Professor Carlo Antoni and his friends in Rome. (310d; 302c; 76c; 216c)

But the real issue is of a different kind. As we have already said, it results from the very nature of scientific work. It primarily affects the teacher, but it also involves the student, and the artist and writer in the bargain. One can dramatize the issue in terms of the apocryphal remark of Galileo's: "And yet she moves!" (112h; 311) For the man who knows, according to this anecdote, cannot be made by the decision of a political authority to forget and unlearn what he knows. Yet this is precisely what is implied by the fifth principle of the Soviet approach to science, namely, that all basic principles are to be decided upon by the key totalitarian leadership or the dictator. We know today that there remained in the German and Italian universities considerable numbers of scholars, teachers, and students, who quietly continued their work along genuine scientific lines, who accepted Einstein and not his Nazi detractors, who taught Christian principles, even if they had to do so in esoteric terms, who realized that Hitler was a psychopath, even if they were prevented from saying so. This kind of experience does not perhaps add to the moral stature of German professors (whether professors of other nationalities do much better, the record to date would lead one to doubt), but it shows that the scholar can retreat into the inner sanctum of the intimate group and the private communication that permits him to preserve an island of separateness in the totalitarian sea. In other words, the totalitarian, like other authoritarians before him, finds it impossible to penetrate the invisible walls that surround the haven of scholastic enterprise, even though he can reduce the number of men and women belonging to it. Such objectivity has, therefore, occasioned great anger on the part of the Communists.

A regular "struggle against objectivism" characterizes all totalitarian dictatorships, but especially the USSR. Besides the well-known phrases on this score uttered by Fascists in the past, we have this kind of statement from contemporary Communism:

The struggle against the reactionary bourgeois ideology prevalent in the universities . . . is essentially identical with the struggle against objectivism . . . Objectivism serves directly the ideological war-preparation of American imperialism . . . With the help of objectivism the American imperialists and their German minions seek to break down the moral resistance of the German people and more especially its intelligentsia . . . Bourgeois objectivism is not compatible with true science and objectivity. It denies the fact of continuous progress in nature and society; for this development takes place through the ineluctable struggle of the New, which is coming, against the Old, which is dying . . . because such objectivism places the Old and the New as equally deserving of attention upon the same footing. Thus objectivism wishes to produce the appearance of nonpartisanship . . . In fact, objectivism is thus the most devious, the most insincere form of partisanship for the Old, the Outlived, that is to say, it is the ideology of the Reaction. We must unmask it . . . and fight it and take the side of the New, the Progressive . . . We must take the part of the laboring class, which is the most progressive class of mankind, and the part of that science which expresses labor's interests and which is therefore the most progressive science — Marxism-Leninism. (416)

Passages such as these make it quite clear why the totalitarian cannot be accepted by the scholar and scientist.

The situation is in this respect especially extreme in Communist China, owing to the practice of thought control (see Chapter 15). Scholars by the thousands have been terrorized into confessions of guilt in the pursuit of objective science. The pitiful confession of Professor Chin Yüeh-lin contains a striking illustration of the destruction of the inner sanctum from which resistance to the total "truth" of the totalitarians might spring. Thus he confessed that he "disseminated the purely technical viewpoint in logic . . . the formalistic viewpoint . . . to think highly of Wang Hao, who even now is serving the interests of American imperialism by being connected with an American university." (117h)

Such a confession, while perhaps extreme, makes it clear why the scholar and the scientist cannot stay away completely from the totalitarian system without cutting himself off from his work. Many scholars, therefore, pay lip service to the ideological trappings. The introductions and the conclusions of their books become symbolic rituals by which the scholars make their act of obeisance to the regime, while continuing their search for the truth in the substance of their texts. The success of such attempts depends on the degree of personal courage, diplomatic evasion, and the esoteric nature of the research involved. It is no accident that recent years have seen a remarkable revival in satellite academic circles of interest in ancient and medieval history, literature, and the mathematical sciences. That some Soviet scientists escape into obscure subjects is illustrated by the following dissertations allegedly submitted to the Moscow Institute of Economics of the Academy of Sciences: "Investigation of the Size of Spots on the Lady Bug," "Inquiry into the Length of Fish Gills." (480) Every relaxation in government control reveals the extent to which academicians attempt to maintain the separateness between their own values and those required by the regime. For instance, after Khrushchev's attack on Soviet architecture, a violent debate arose in Warsaw, and many non-Communist architects came out with sharp criticisms of the Soviet-style ornamental architecture which the regime had imposed on Warsaw reconstruction between 1949 and 1954. Referring to that period as "the hermetically sealed one," the architects insisted that more attention be paid to recent Italian and South American styles and repudiated the arbitrary standards of taste imposed upon them. That such pressures develop in free societies as well cannot be denied by anyone who has lived through the McCarthy era in the United States. But they are passing phenomena that cannot penetrate the "castle" that is the modern university. It is these castles the totalitarians seek to conquer. Stalin once said: "We are confronted by a fortress. The name of this fortress is science with its innumerable branches. We must conquer this fortress. Youth must take this fortress, if it wishes to build the new life, if it wishes to replace the old guard." Khrushchev made a new attack upon it in terms of the popular slogan about "school and life," insisting that everyone seeking higher professional training must go out into factory and field to get acquainted with the realities of a worker's life. It has become policy in the Soviet Union since 1958. There is, of course, a kernel of truth and general validity in this position, which has served as the educational philosophy of some institutions of higher learning in the United States as well as other countries.* At the same time, the very occurrence of such an appeal in the Soviet Union seems a mute testimony to the existence of islands of separateness in the institutions of learning.

The fortress, then, that Stalin talked about appears to be unconquerable. Why? Because it is no fortress at all. Science is a method of human beings who are engaged in the search for truth, and that truth is a hard mistress who expects to be wooed in accordance with her nature. As the totalitarians marshal youth to conquer truth, they are likely to find those youth who are capable of the pursuit, who have the imagination, sensitiveness, and sharpness of mind to discover new truths, becoming new recruits for a value that transcends the totalitarian enterprise. As they enter the island where the quiet of study and inquiry reigns, they become separated from the loud battle cries of the totalitarian regime.

* The Werkstudenten (working students) movement in Weimar Germany was built upon a cognate notion; it embodied the conscious effort of doing what many American students do as a matter of course and as a result of economic need.

25

LITERATURE AND THE ARTS
by Gail W. Lapidus

During the past decade, the continuing tension that exists in the relationship between totalitarian regimes and their writers and artists has been dramatically highlighted. The hesitant stirrings that followed Stalin's death and marked the beginning of a cultural thaw developed, in Poland and Hungary, into movements of social and political protest. In China, the brief campaign during 1957 to "let a hundred flowers bloom, let a hundred schools contend" was quickly terminated by the regime when "poisonous weeds" blossomed instead. Even today in the Soviet Union the uneasy truce prevailing between the government and the writers conceals a continuing struggle over cultural policy that has important political implications.

The attitude of the totalitarians toward literature and the arts is, like their attitude toward science, an ambivalent one. Art is viewed in utilitarian rather than aesthetic terms and is considered to be an instrument in shaping the new society. Writers, in Stalin's words, are "engineers of the human soul." But engineering is not necessarily art. An excessive disregard for aesthetic qualities resulted in a general cultural deterioration, and the arts drove away the very souls they were intended to educate. This stagnation has on several occasions itself become a cause of concern to the authorities and explains the intermittent efforts of these regimes to sponsor, in however limited and grudging a fashion, a liberalization of cultural policy that continually threatens to burst its bounds.

In the early years of the Soviet regime, the social purpose of art was rather broadly interpreted, and diverse tendencies flourished in an atmosphere of relative freedom. So long as writers refrained from directly attacking the regime, they were permitted to indulge in endless debate about the function of art in the new society. Beginning in 1928, however, with the elimination of both the Left and the Right oppositions within the party and the launching of the five-year plan, the arts too were mobilized for socialist construction. In 1932, with the creation of the Union of Soviet Writers, all other literary organizations were abolished and the writers were brought under the direct control of the party. The cultural atmosphere prevailing at the time is revealed in a moving letter by the distinguished novelist Zamyatin, written to Stalin himself to appeal for permission to leave the Soviet Union:

I know that I have a most inconvenient habit of speaking what I consider to be the truth, rather than saying what may be expedient at the moment. Specifically, I have never concealed my attitude toward literary servility, cringing, and chameleon changes of color. I have felt, and I feel today, that this degrades both the writer and the revolution . . . The death of my tragedy *Attila* was a genuine tragedy for me. It made entirely clear to me the futility of any effort at changing my situation . . . Everything was done to close to me all avenues for further work. I became an object of fear to my erstwhile friends, publishers, and theaters. My books were banned from the libraries. My play . . . was withdrawn from the repertory . . . Any publishing organization that attempted to publish my works was immediately placed under fire . . . The last door to the reading public was closed . . . The writer's death sentence was pronounced and published. (2a)

Not only were the artists organized and their creative efforts subjected to increasing control and censorship, but an attempt was made to shape the actual content of literary and artistic productions. In 1934 socialist realism was proclaimed the official form of Soviet art. What distinguishes socialist realism from traditional forms of realism is its effort to portray reality "in its revolutionary development" so as to educate the working classes in the spirit of socialism. The artist's vision will overlook the imperfections of the present and will capture and emphasize only those aspects of reality that will be enshrined in the future. Socialist-realist art is permeated with purpose and filled with optimism. It glorifies the achievements of Soviet society and encourages its advance toward communism by portraying the successful conclusion of a great enterprise, the heroism of the builders of socialism, or the metamorphosis of an individual or group under the beneficent influence of the party. As Khrushchev himself explained: "Literature and art are part of the whole people's struggle for Communism . . . The highest social destiny of art and literature is to mobilize the people to the struggle for new advances in the building of communism." (174b) Modernist tendencies are rejected altogether as examples of "bourgeois formalism" and "art for art's sake," serving no progressive social purpose and reflecting an alien individualism.

Socialist realism, however, is more than a theory of art. It is also a theory of the role of the artist in society, which explains and justifies his submission to political control. If it is the function of the artist to enlist the masses in the struggle for communism, it is the party that is the final judge of what will promote or hinder the building of communism at any particular moment. Thus Khrushchev continues: "For the artist who truly wants to serve his people the question does not arise of whether he is free or not in his creative work. For him, the question of which approach to the phenomena of reality to choose is clear. He need not conform or force himself; the true representation of life from the point of view of the Communist *partiinost* is a necessity of his soul. He holds firmly to these positions, and affirms and defends them in his work." (174b) The new artistic method, when applied in the atmosphere of the purges of the mid-thirties, had a disastrous effect upon Soviet culture. Leading writers, such as Babel and Pilnyak, were exiled or disappeared. Others, out of conviction or fear, subordinated their work to the demands of the regime. A few remained aloof, turning like Pasternak to translations, or to children's tales, while continuing to write with little hope of publication.

The relaxation of ideological controls during the war years led to a brief cultural renaissance. Writers took advantage of the political situation to deal with new, nonideological themes in a new way. The sufferings and the stoic heroism of ordinary people replaced the superhuman achievements of Communist heroes. The portrayal of simple human emotions in a lyrical style intruded into a literature that had verged on journalism. As the end of the war approached, literature expressed the widespread sense of weariness and hope for relaxation in these poignant lines:

And after victory we will make a halt,
Drink a cup, and rest to our heart's content. (344)

The regime responded to these tendencies with a new wave of repression attacking passivity and retreat from political concerns as anti-Soviet and calling once again for an optimistic and ideologically inspired literature, which would aid the state in rearing a new generation of fighters for communism. Offending publications were suspended, and offending writers, such as Akhmatova and Zoshchenko, were consigned to oblivion.

A new period of cultural stagnation followed. The public itself lost interest in contemporary Soviet literature and turned to the nineteenth-century classics, while theater attendance steadily declined to the point where even the authorities became concerned enough to hint that certain changes might be desirable. Stalin's death in 1953 accelerated both the demands of the artists for a degree of liberalization and the willingness of the regime to sponsor it as a part of a larger effort to encourage more initiative and creativity in Soviet life.

Ehrenburg's novel *The Thaw*, which gave its name to this period, expressed the widespread feeling of change and the mood of expectancy. Moreover, the book contained a sharp attack on the literary policies of the postwar years in its portrayal of two figures who are artists. One of them, Volodya Pukhov, is an "official artist" who has won success and fame by adapting his work to the demands of the regime. The other, Saburov, has remained true to his inner inspiration and lives a lonely, poverty-stricken life. In response to Saburov's defense of his independence, Volodya concedes that nowadays Raphael himself would be excluded from the artists' union, but he insists that, since lying, dodging, and maneuvering are common practices, it is foolish not to indulge in them oneself. In the end, however, moved by the sincerity and depth of Saburov's works, Volodya admits that he envies him.

Ehrenburg was not alone in his call for greater freedom. The poet Tvardovsky, in a long poem called "Horizon Beyond Horizon," complained about the state of Soviet literature, which had become so indigestible that one felt like screaming. Another author Pomerantsev, called for an end to artificiality and stereotypes in literature, criticized the discrepancy between reality in life and reality as it was portrayed in the arts, and demanded that sincerity, rather than *partiinost,* serve as the criterion of literary value. Other works by other artists called for greater freedom to experiment with form and to express individual emotions. The representatives of the more orthodox school of art responded with attacks on the liberals for their nihilism and for their effort to divorce literature from life, while the party attempted to keep the demands for liberalization within bounds without resorting to the practices of the past.

It was Khrushchev's denunciation of Stalin in 1956 which set loose the still pent-up demands of the writers for greater freedom and gave dramatic encouragement to the liberals. The de-Staliniza-tion campaign enabled them to link their own demands to the policies of the regime. They could argue that socialist realism and the heavy-handed system of controls that accompanied it were not inherently "socialist," but rather aberrations that resulted from the "cult of personality." Some efforts were made to glorify the twen-ties as the golden age of Soviet culture and to call for a return to the relative freedom of that period.

Along with increasingly widespread demands for cultural liberal-ization, there was an outburst of literary works of social and polit-ical criticism. A revulsion against the atmosphere of falsehood and the "varnishing of reality" that had prevailed under Stalin was expressed in the emphasis upon the need for truth and honesty in both literature and life. Typical of the idealism that this demand expressed was the poem "Zima Station" by the young Yevgeny Yevtushenko. It begins with the poet's review of his own life and his regret that noble impulses were translated into prudent actions rather than noble deeds. He returns to his childhood home to find an answer to his problem, rejecting ready-made solutions in favor of a personal quest. After a series of confrontations reflecting dis-quiet with the events of the past years and the distortions which the ideal of communism has undergone, the poet takes leave of the town and imagines its last words to him:

> Search, search. Roam the whole wide world.
> Yes, truth is good; happiness is better,
> But without truth there can be no happiness.*

* Yevtushenko, "Stantsiya Zima," *Oktyabr,* no. 10 (1956), pp. 26–47.

A similar return to humanistic values and a revulsion against moral relativism marked other literary works of this period. The solitary individual who remained true to his own identity replaced the "positive hero" of socialist realism. Criticism extended to the bureaucracy itself, which was portrayed as indifferent to the needs of the people, self-seeking and petty-bourgeois in its motivations, stifling real creativity and initiative in deadening routine. Dudintsev's novel *Not by Bread Alone* was a typical example of this genre in its attack on the privileges of the bureaucratic class, its corruptness and egotism and vulgarity summed up in the person of Drozdov.

This literary outburst posed a serious dilemma for the regime. On the one hand, the thaw was not necessarily contrary to its interests. To a certain extent, criticism of the Stalin era aided the party in its effort to dissociate itself from the past and mobilized opinion behind the campaign for de-Stalinization. Moreover, the criticisms of the bureaucracy paralleled the party's own campaign against bureaucratization and the stifling of initiative. As Khrushchev once confessed in speaking of Dudintsev's novel, Mikoyan had recommended that he read it with the remark that the author sounded like Khrushchev himself. However, the danger lay in the constant tendency of the liberalization to overstep the bounds that the regime sought to preserve. Criticism of isolated shortcomings would be welcomed, but any tendency to generalize them into criticisms of the system itself, even in the name of revolutionary ideals, had to be cut short. The party could not allow any other group to arrogate to itself the mantle of true Leninism.

The line between desirable and undesirable criticism was a difficult one to maintain, for conflict was basically a struggle over the *extent* of de-Stalinization. The liberals were eager to go much further than the party would allow in questioning the foundations of Stalinism, and they therefore threatened both the legitimacy of the party's leadership and its function of social control. Not all of the literary ferment was political in orientation. Along with the demand for greater freedom for cultural activity, there was a desire for liberation from politics altogether, and for the opportunity to experiment with artistic themes and forms that were unrelated to social and ideological goals. But even this was a threat, for if aesthetic rather than political criteria were crucial in evaluating art, the party would lose its directing role.

Finally, the growing coherence and organization of the writers frightened the party. The new and outspoken literature won wide popularity for its authors, while public discussions and poetry readings gave them a direct contact with public opinion outside the official channels. Also, as contacts increased among members of the cultural intelligentsia, its solidarity grew and it was able to present a more united front in the face of criticism. Isolation and atomization disappeared and resistance became bolder. Thus, in response to Khrushchev's indignant reaction to a December 1962 exhibition of modern and abstract art, two petitions reached the Central Committee, with a long and distinguished list of signatures embracing not only writers and artists but academicians and scientists. Both letters defended the exhibition, one going so far as to state:

Such an exhibition has become possible only after the 20th and 22nd Party Congresses. Our appraisals of this or that work shown at the exhibition may differ. But if we all address this letter to you now, it is because we want to say in all sincerity that, unless different artistic tendencies have an opportunity to exist, art is doomed to extinction. We see how your words at the exhibition are being interpreted by artists of the only schools which flourished under Stalin, permitting no one else to work, or even to live. We are deeply convinced that this was not your intention. (2b)

However, this was indeed the party's intention, and beginning with Khrushchev's attack on the exhibition there has been a concerted drive to restore a certain ideological purity to the arts and to reinforce party controls by selecting scapegoats and putting pressure on the less outspoken writers to moderate the demands of their colleagues. The present uneasy truce that exists in the arts is testimony to the continuing ability of the party to absorb pressures from outside and turn them to its own purposes. The writers and artists thus remain as an island of separateness, reluctant to subordinate their work completely to the demands made by the party, yet unable to offer any real resistance.

Writers and artists form an island of separateness in other totalitarian regimes as well as in the Soviet Union, although the specific forms of their existence and the character of the conflict are shaped by differing national situations, cultural traditions, and the stage of development of the totalitarian system itself.

The National Socialist and Fascist regimes never attempted a comprehensive control over cultural life. Both these systems were too short-lived to accomplish more than the first steps of social transformation, and they were too preoccupied with pressing political and economic problems to concern themselves excessively with the state of the arts. Their cultural policies therefore resemble those of the Soviet regime in its early years, when a certain amount of freedom prevailed provided there was no overt criticism of the regime. Many of the more outspoken writers and artists emigrated in order to continue their activities undisturbed, but even within the country opposition to the regimes could make itself felt through a variety of subterfuges, which provoked a contest of wits between the official censors and the critics.

In China as in the Soviet Union there has been a tug of war between the writers and the regime, marked by alternating cycles of repression and relaxation. The Chinese Communist regime has not been immune to the problems that beset other totalitarian systems in their relations with the literati. Chinese intellectuals were profoundly influenced by the whole tradition of nineteenth-century Russian writers who assigned themselves the task of social criticism. Even those writers most committed to the success of the revolution in China carried their critical attitudes over into their relations with the Communist Party. They attempted to preserve for literary activity a degree of independence from party control and rejected the method of socialist realism imported by the Chinese party from the Soviet Union. Their attitudes clearly conflicted with the efforts of the Chinese Communist Party to arrogate to itself alone the function of exposing any defects in the new society.

The launching of the "hundred flowers" campaign in 1956 was an attempt to stimulate new creative efforts by the whole intelligentsia and to enlist their enthusiasm in social construction. As in the Soviet Union and the Eastern European satellites, however, liberalization tended to overflow what the party considered its proper bounds. Writers attacked socialist realism as an "imported" method that resulted in a confusion of literature with politics. They not only rejected party control over culture, but turned to attacks on the party itself. Criticism of bureaucratism and privilege were the expression of the struggle between the artist and his party-minded, frequently uninspired supervisors. The depth of dissatisfaction that this brief relaxation revealed within the creative intelligentsia and the movements of protest that threatened to get out of hand led to a rapid reimposition of control, but the underlying tensions remain.

Similar tensions existed in the relationship of regime and artist in Eastern Europe, intensified because Stalinism did not last long enough to destroy the values and social ties of the prewar intelligentsia and to create a new class of literati thoroughly imbued with Communist values. De-Stalinization in Poland and Hungary in particular thus had a profound impact, and literary criticism developed into outright political resistance. A more detailed study of these two situations reveals both the potentialities and the limits of literary protest.

In the early postwar years, the consolidation of control over Eastern Europe by the various Communist regimes compelled the writers and artists to make a difficult choice. By no means ignorant of the position of their colleagues in the Soviet Union, they were nonetheless encouraged to believe that developments in the People's Democracies would follow a more democratic course. The party encouraged them to believe that only a socialist society could fully liberate their creative talents and make culture accessible to the masses. As one prominent Polish writer explained the decision of a colleague to join the party: "He was, at least, a popular writer whose readers were recruited from the masses. His highly praised prewar novel had sold scarcely a few thousand copies; now he and every author could count on reaching a tremendous public. He was no longer isolated; he told himself he was needed not by a few snobs in a coffee-house, but by this new workers' youth he spoke to in his travels over the country." (251b) The party made few demands upon the writers at first, provided they refrained from openly criticizing either the regime or its Soviet ally. At the same time, it was generous with its patronage of the arts. But this policy did not last. Suppression all too quickly followed upon toleration as the People's Democracies were transformed along Stalinist lines into replicas of the Soviet totalitarian regime. The response of the writers was various. Some were drawn into increasing cooperation and involvement with the regime at the expense of their art. Others remained aloof, writing "for the desk drawer," circulating an occasional manuscript secretly, or participating in informal discussions with like-minded colleagues. A large segment of the intelligentsia thus resisted the efforts of the regime at total social atomization and preserved a distinct identity and social ties. The death of Stalin and the resulting thaw enabled this cultural "underground" to emerge into public view.

The themes of the literature of the thaw in Poland and Hungary closely resembled those dwelt upon by Soviet artists, although the European artists were if anything even more outspoken in attacking the betrayal of humanist and progressive values under Stalin. Criticisms of stifling bureaucratic controls over the arts were widespread, as were attacks on the whole method of socialist realism. What had at first been demands for more freedom for party intellectuals and artists increasingly became rallying cries for nonparty intellectuals and artists who had never accepted the premises of party control over the arts and who now overtly reasserted their traditional belief in absolute freedom for all creative work. Stagnation, it was argued, was the inevitable result of linking art to any power system and compelling it to approve and to justify instead of remaining independent and critical.

Even more dangerous to party control than criticism was the actual organization of the intelligentsia. Certain journals and periodicals, and the cultural circles and clubs that spread throughout Poland and Hungary during this period, became centers of independent literary, social, and ultimately political initiative, which accelerated the disintegration of party controls and which provided a common meeting ground for those who wished to bring about real social and political changes.

The events of 1956 and the years after demonstrated, however, the limits of resistance. Any fundamental changes in the political system of either country, even had the resistance been more unified in seeking such changes than it actually was, was precluded by the fact that the satellites were not fully independent states but offshoots of the Soviet system. Certain domestic reforms and changes could be won, but any dramatic change involved a confrontation with the Soviet Union. Moreover, whatever temporary and limited success could be achieved were due to the disorientation and wavering of the party leadership itself. Once the initial effects of de-Stalinization had worn off and the party had once again consolidated its control and unified its policies, the opposition was reduced to relative impotence. Today an uneasy truce prevails, one which allows a greater degree of freedom for experimentation in culture than exists in the Soviet Union but which nevertheless precludes any real threat to the political power of the satellite regimes. The writers and artists continue to form an island of separateness, but only an extraordinary combination of unlikely circumstances could enable them to launch another movement of actual resistance.

The position of the writers and artists within the various totalitarian systems raises the problem of the extent and limits of resistance possible within a totalitarian system. The conflict between these groups and the regimes results from the fact that the totalitarian system makes demands that the literati are unable to accept fully if they are to preserve their artistic integrity; they in turn demand a degree of freedom for artistic endeavor, which is a threat to the regime's total control of social activity. The ability of the writers and artists to achieve even a limited degree of freedom has depended upon political circumstances that they can manipulate but not ultimately control. The incomplete development of a totalitarian regime, the exigencies of war or crisis, the campaign for de-Stalinization, all have provided them with opportunities to extend their sphere of freedom. Outbursts of literary protest have been possible because of party indecision or party sponsorship. Although all these episodes reveal the extent to which the writers and artists constitute an island of separateness, resisting total assimilation to the totalitarian system, they also reveal the limits to any effective political resistance.

VII

*Totalitarian Expansionism
and the Future*

26

THE MILITARY ESTABLISHMENT

The degree to which a totalitarian movement succeeds in politicizing the army is indicative also of the extent to which the society
itself has become totalitarian. Indeed, not the least striking distinction between modern totalitarian regimes and traditional dictatorships is the different ways in which they treat the armed forces. In
the case of the latter, the army usually provides the actual power
basis for such regimes and to a great extent retains its autonomy of
action. Most of the traditional dictators of our age, such as Pilsud-
ski, Kemal Pasha, or even Franco, not only based their power on
the army, but actually came to power from the army and through
the use of the army. Naturally, under such circumstances, the army
tended to remain in a sacrosanct position, jealously watching its
many prerogatives and privileges, and retaining a distinct political
identity of its own. As developments in some of the non-European
states, notably Turkey and Pakistan, suggest, that type of regime
may have a distinct future wherever a totalitarian movement lacks
adequate backing. Military dictatorships have in the past been typically concerned with maintaining the status quo. The new regimes
are characterized by a progressive and modernizing outlook. (378;
22)
   In a totalitarian system, the military is subject to the total claim
of the movement and party. The totalitarian movement is the
source of the dictator's power, despite occasional expedient compromises with other groups, particularly in the early stages of its development. As soon as power is seized, efforts are made to neutralize and then to integrate the armed forces into the totalitarian
fabric. Indeed, in terms of the mature type of totalitarian system,

the ultimate goal is to make the armed forces into a mere branch of the totalitarian party. The army would be then a sort of totalitarian militia, supporting the external policies of the regime in much the same way that the totalitarian secret police buttresses the regime's domestic policies.

Political necessity, however, creates its own imperatives. When Hitler seized power in 1933, the political situation was such that any immediate effort to limit the influence of the Reichswehr would have been disastrous for the NSDAP. The totalitarian dictator realized that he held power thanks, to some extent, to the tolerance and benevolent neutrality of the armed forces, and he was not yet in a position to do away with them. (349a) Another factor of paramount importance in temporarily maintaining the integrity of the Reichswehr was the internal struggle for power between Hitler and Goering, on the one side, and the more radical, revolutionary elements led by Röhm and his storm troopers, on the other. Röhm's program of integrating the army into the SA so as to create eventually a party pretorian guard played into Hitler's hands, but it also aided the continued maintenance of Reichswehr independence. It played into Hitler's hands because it induced the army to back him in the final showdown. Precisely because Hitler needed this backing, he was unable to act vigorously against the army in the fashion in which he acted against the other Weimar institutions. The attack on the army had to wait.

The army was thus able to resist, passively at least, the process of totalitarian subjugation. Nazi foreign-policy goals, furthermore, postulated the need for strong armed forces, to be built up as rapidly as possible. This again made it inexpedient for the Hitler regime, even after solidly entrenching itself in power, to attack the army. Such an effort would have produced obvious dislocation and confusion and would have most likely impaired the fighting capacity of the new Wehrmacht. The officer corps, on the other hand, while often not masking its suspicions of the domestic political objectives of the regime, could not fail to note that at long last it was getting all the sinews of war it needed. The marriage of convenience was thus bearing fruit.

In fact, as the Nazi controls were gradually strengthened, it became fashionable to remark that so-and-so has "emigrated into the Army," clearly implying that there at least one was relatively free from totalitarian control and could pursue, to a degree, one's career on a purely professional basis. Such a situation, however, was anomalous and could not last within the framework of a totalitarian revolution. Even before the outbreak of the war in 1939, a number of leading German generals, such as Blomberg, Beck, and Fritsch, were removed from command and replaced by more spineless officers. At the same time, young Nazi stalwarts were being increasingly introduced into the lower command echelons. This process naturally became more marked as the war casualties took their toll, while the later reversals and defeats resulted in the appointment of Hitler partisans to the top command posts.

This process of penetration of the army with politically devoted elements was not the only method used by the Nazis to neutralize and integrate the armed forces. The fact is that, despite all these efforts, Hitler and his lieutenants were never fully certain of the loyalty of the officer corps, and the events of July 1944 bore out the correctness of their suspicions. For this reason, even while strengthening the Wehrmacht, the German political leadership set busily about developing a parallel military structure, which was to be the pretorian guard of the National Socialist movement and a countervailing force to the professional army. The SS, accordingly, became a second army, independent of the OKW (High Command), and at its peak could boast of over 800,000 elite troops, organized in some 40 divisions.

The unsuccessful uprising of July 20, 1944, further enhanced the position of the SS, and Himmler was given the task of commanding all the reserve armies on the home front. At the same time, a thorough and bloody purge took a heavy toll of the Army High Command, a large part of which was implicated. (386; 123c; 46f; 302) A particular effort was made to humiliate the condemned officers, and some of them were hanged in the nude on meat hooks. In an effort to institutionalize direct party controls in the armed forces, Martin Bormann, the party secretary, was given command of a network of political officers of the commissar type, known as NSFO (Nationalsozialistische Führungs-Offiziere, or leadership officers). Their task was to make certain of the political loyalty of the military. The party secretary, and not the military, was also charged with the task of creating the Volkssturm, a sort of home guard of old men and youngsters, for the purpose of a last-ditch stand. This process of complete politization of the army, however, came too late, for within ten months the German military machine itself fell apart.

In Italy, as in Germany, the totalitarians after seizing power had to cope with an established army and a professional officer corps. Here, throughout the Fascist era, the army remained a haven for royalist sentiments and a source of latent, and finally active, opposition to Mussolini. Indeed, the fall of the dictator in the summer of 1943 was engineered by the combined resources of the royal court and the military high command. Mussolini, after being dismissed as Capo del Governo by King Victor Emmanuel, was arrested on the steps of the Quirinale palace and transported away in a military ambulance. These technical arrangements of the coup were symbolic of the military forces that Fascism had shrunk from destroying.

At the time of the march on Rome, the Italian army was the only force capable of defending the liberal and democratic order against the rising power of the Fascists. Mussolini, therefore, was extremely careful not to offend the armed forces, and at every occasion he emphasized both his hostility to pacifism (exemplified by his military service and wounds) and the Fascist admiration for the "Army of Victory." Even after the seizure of power and the reorganization of the original squadristi (the armed guards of the Fascist Party) into the Milizia Volontaria per la Sicurezza Nazionale (MVSN), the army leaders were assured that the MVSN was merely an auxiliary arm of the party and would not threaten the army's monopoly of the uniform and the sword. "The officers of the militia are the chiefs of the revolution; the officers of the army are the architects of the military machine which won the war. Mussolini does not intend to use the army as a political arm," said an early Fascist statement. (92)

As in the case of Germany, the foreign ambitions of the regime made necessary a strong army with a high professional morale. For this reason the Fascist regime felt it inexpedient to engage in a headlong clash with the military circles that were needed for the expansion of the armed forces and that appeared to be content with the Fascist program of rapid armament. A pragmatic modus vivendi seems to have developed and, although since the military reorganization of 1926 the Duce had been in command of the armed forces with the chief of staff directly responsible to him, no direct process of politicizing the military was launched. In fact, during the rapid expansion of the army during the thirties, although MVSN was not integrated into the regular units as shock troops, its units were during the Ethiopian war placed under the command of army officers. During World War II efforts were made to promote young Fascists to leading posts, but to the very end senior officers of a royalist orientation generally remained part of the professional cadres. The fact that the top staffs were not members of the Fascist Party made possible the secret negotiations between the Allied and Italian high commands in 1943, prior to the official surrender of Italy. For a brief spell afterwards, Mussolini, upon his spectacular release from captivity by Skorzeny's German paratroopers, attempted to build up, on the basis of the former MVSN, his own Republican Fascist Army under the command of one of the few higher officers who remained true to Fascism, Marshal Graziani. These efforts, however, were merely the last gasps of Fascism.

Italian Fascist experience with the armed forces, as well as the ambivalent attitude of the Fascist movement toward the monarchy, raises once more the important question of whether Italy may legitimately be included as an example of a totalitarian system. On the one hand, it is important to point out that the Fascist movement in Italy never fully succeeded in mastering and politicizing the military. On the other hand, party and military agents influenced military policy, promotions, and the like, as brought out in the Bastrocchi trial. There prevailed a genuine dualism between army and MVSN until the outbreak of World War II, the army being much smaller than the MVSN with its 700,000 men. After the outbreak of the war, the position of the party rapidly deteriorated. No such organization as the Waffen-SS was developed in Italy, but then Italy only "joined" the war and became increasingly dependent upon Germany in the course of it. Yet, until 1939, the party and its militia effectively held the army in check, and no such coup as the one in Argentina which overthrew Peron's dictatorship would have been possible. (120h) When the impact of outside blows and military defeats made it clear that Fascism was leading Italy to ruin, the military, with the collusion of the monarchy, was able to shake off the controls superimposed upon it by the Fascist leadership and to take effective action of the type that their colleagues in Germany were not able to initiate successfully.

The situation in Russia was quite different from that in Germany or Italy after the totalitarian seizure of power. The tsarist army disintegrated completely under the stresses of war and domestic sedition. The Bolshevik revolution was achieved with scattered, unequipped, and ill-trained Red Guards and the Kronstadt sailors. The great masses of the soldiers merely drifted home, casting away their weapons. The army of the *ancien régime* was no more. But this, initially at least, did not trouble the Bolsheviks. For many years the army had been in their eyes the symbol of imperial oppression, and Marxist theory emphasized frequently that this coercive tool must be destroyed, together with the state it buttressed. Lenin, for instance, declared: "A standing army is an army that is divorced from the people and trained to shoot down the people . . . A standing army is not in the least necessary to protect the country from an attack of the enemy; a people's militia is sufficient." (205i)

As in the German case, however, political imperatives intervened. The Civil War, efforts to invade the Baltic states, and the Russo-Polish war could not be fought with nonprofessionals under modern conditions of weaponry. A revolutionary army had therefore to be created to defend the revolution against counterrevolutionary coups and to spread the red banner to adjoining areas. This revolutionary army had to have leaders, and the only available officers were former tsarist commanders. The Bolsheviks had no choice but to accept them and give them the command of the newly created Red Army of Workers and Peasants. Trotsky, the organizer of the Red Army, rationalized it thus: "As industry needs engineers, as farming needs qualified agronomists, so military specialists are indispensable to defense." (357) Some 48,000 former tsarist officers were accordingly given command posts in the revolutionary army.

The regime, however, was fearful of a Bonapartist coup and was determined to prevent it. One of the first steps taken in connection with the admission of former officers into the ranks of the new army was to decree that political commissars would supervise the operations of the military commanders. The commissars were given power to countermand orders and even to arrest the commanders whenever it was deemed necessary. Their function was defined as follows: "The military commissars are the guardians of the close and inviolable inner bond between the Red Army and the workers' and peasants' regime as a whole. Only irreproachable revolutionaries, staunch champions of the proletariat and the village poor, should be appointed to the posts of military commissars, to whom is handed over the fate of the Army." (373) Following the conclusion of hostilities, the new Soviet regime at first decided not to set up a centralized military organization, but rather to rely on a decentralized territorial militia army. This plan, however, soon proved to be inefficient and by the mid-thirties energetic efforts were being made to develop a centralized, hierarchically commanded army. By then most of the tsarist officers had been weeded out, and a Soviet-trained officers' corps had replaced them. (387) Still, Stalin continued to suspect the army command, and in 1936–1938 most of the higher-ranking Soviet officers were eliminated in a series of lightning and fierce purges. The situation was thus radically different from both the German and the Italian cases.

During the same time the regime was making certain that the officer corps was composed of loyal elements, an institutional framework of controls was being constructed to ensure that loyalty. In its Stalinist form, which with minor modifications continues to the present, it combined a tripartite network of political officers, party cells, and secret-police agents. (40a) The political officers, who were no longer known as commissars but as Zampolits (abbreviation for Deputy Commanders for Political Affairs), existed in every unit, starting with the company, and were responsible to their own superiors for the political loyalty of their men as well as the officers. At the apex of the political officers' network stood the Main Political Administration of the Soviet Armed Forces (GPUVS), which was also a section of the Central Committee of the Communist Party. The Zampolits wielded considerable power and were particularly important through their periodic assessments of the state of political consciousness of the officers and men. In order to stimulate that consciousness, they organized constant political activities and conducted regular indoctrination study courses. Since then the party, in keeping with the general trend, has continued to play a significant role. To be sure, in the first few years after Stalin's death, there was a marked tendency for the military to achieve a measure of independence. This came to an end when Marshal Zhukov was purged under accusation of having encouraged such a trend, as well as seeking personal glorification, while failing to give the party adequate recognition for its contribution to the victorious war. (449a) In fact, Zhukov and his associates had manifested a high degree of independence in revising the old Stalinist doctrines. Khrushchev accepted compromises, as long as he needed the army's neutrality in the succession struggle. Once he had achieved predominance, he made short shrift of the military. (89aa; 209d; 240f) Party primacy was re-established; the memory of Lenin's position was conjured up; the political officers were up-graded; and a measure of interchange between the political and military officers was organized. At the same time, party units were reinforced by an intensive drive for party members among soldiers and sailors. Their criticism of higher-ups was encouraged, and the party remained pre-eminent. Thus the party cells organize the activities of the party members serving in the armed forces and are the nerve centers for propaganda and agitation among the troops. What was said of Stalin's day is even more true now, because of the more vital role of the party in Soviet life. "The party organizations of the armed forces are an organic part of the Bolshevik Party . . . They enlightened the Red Army men, cemented their ranks, implanted strictest discipline among them, rallied them around the Bolshevik Party and educated them in the spirit of selfless devotion to the motherland and the cause of Communism." (424a) In keeping with such views, party members are charged with organizing small study circles to read party literature. They sponsor special movies for the troops and devote their leisure time to the indoctrination of the non-Communist military personnel. The party organizations thus provide the necessary support to the official functions of the political apparatus in the army. (424b) The Main Political Administration has continued to wield its massive controls down to the battalion level, with Zampolits in charge.

In the event that these controls fail to ensure a positive and enthusiastic approval for the Soviet regime, the secret police may step in. Secret-police officers operate in all units, starting with the regiment, and are charged with the general task of security. They are to make certain that no "disloyal" elements penetrate the Soviet armed forces. However, the role of the secret police has considerably declined. The testimony of former Soviet officers, according to which the secret police carried on extended activities, especially during the war, may no longer be valid. (40b) Still, the KGB representatives are there, and their counterintelligence work is extensive. Not very much is known in detail. The secret-police special sections, while subject to their commanders, are responsible to and report directly to their own command in Moscow.

Communist China did not face the problem of the military in the same way that the Soviet Union did. Since the Communist movement grew slowly in the twenties and thirties as a military formation, the Chinese military establishment has from the beginning been an integral part of the system. Presumably the problem is not so much one of control as it is one of effective professionalization. Little is known about progress in this direction, but during the Korean War the Chinese gave an impressive demonstration of their fighting ability with conventional weapons. A similar situation has existed in Cuba. Here, too, the original thrust came from the very elements that had been fighting under Castro, and no independent military cadres are troubling the regime. With the inspirational leader as the top fighting man, crowned with all the glory of military success, the characteristic conflict with civilians has been absent. In both regimes, the totalitarian claim was in part born of military necessity and military operation. This may help to explain the radicalism of their revolutionary violence.

In the Soviet Union, too, the politization of the army is nearly complete. In October 1962, it was reported that almost 90 percent of all Soviet officers were party members or Komsomolites, and for the entire military establishment the figure was 82 percent. (441s) It is therefore evident that any expectation of separate action by the military in these totalitarian regimes is highly unrealistic. There is no doubt a "military viewpoint" urged in party and government arguments over policy issues, but the leader's view is practically certain to prevail. It is he who controls the essential levers and he who may "press the button" that would unleash nuclear war. Hence the armed forces are an integral part of the totalitarian system, poised for attack in support of the regime's policy of world-revolutionary expansionism, entrenched for the defense of an armed camp. National sentiment and traditional patriotism serve to reinforce this commitment of the military to the established regime. (116) This state of affairs does not exclude the possibility of the military's playing a considerable role in cooperation with dissident elements in the party. The military constitutes an important interest group in the Soviet system, and it may not be ignored. The removal of Khrushchev has caused a good deal of discussion concerning the share the military had in his fall. As has been noted, there was some rather sharp criticism of his defense and weapon policies, which aroused the ire of some branches of the military, especially the conventional forces. Even so, it is impossible at this writing to assess the influence that the military might have had on the dramatic events of October 1964. Whatever it was, the basic fact of the integration of the military into the Soviet regime was never put into jeopardy. Under modern conditions of a government's monopoly of effective weapons, the military's commitment to the regime provides not only a powerful instrument for foreign policy, but also a firm protection for the regime's survival.

Of the totalitarian systems subjected to analysis in this chapter, it is the Communists' handling of the army which comes closest to the model image of the complete integration of the military into the totalitarian movement. Such a process is not without obstacles, and former Soviet military personnel testify to the constant strains and tensions these controls themselves generate. It is very doubtful, however, that the existing impediments to political indoctrination and integration are in themselves sufficient to produce anything like a major crisis in the totalitarian control of the armed forces, as long as the system is not itself subjected to a major challenge from the outside. Only then could latent dissatisfaction and hostility develop into a positive reaction against totalitarian control. But even under such circumstances, if Fascist and Soviet experience during World War II has any meaning, the likelihood of a successful military coup is doubtful. (99a; 386b) This, in itself, constitutes a significant difference between totalitarianism and the older traditional dictatorships.

27

THE FOREIGN POLICY OF EXPANSION

"Workers of the world, unite!" is the summary slogan of the *Communist Manifesto*. It is the call to world revolution to which the Soviet Union has at least ideologically steadfastly adhered. "Today Germany, tomorrow the world!" was the battlecry of the Nazi Party, as Hitler set out for aggression and war. These virulent world-revolutionary appeals are an innate part of totalitarian dictatorship. They correspond to the "passion for unanimity" which these regimes display in their dealings with the people already under their control, and also indicate their inherent propensity for disturbing the peace. There can be little doubt that, without an outward projection against a real or imaginary enemy, these regimes could not marshal the fanatical devotion the system requires for survival. Such a projection may be actualized, as in the Soviet Union, China, Germany, and Italy, or it may be potential or even vicarious, as in the satellites. Nor is this merely a matter of size; for Cuba, though small, is radically expansionist, and so is Ghana. (442c) Wherever the world-revolutionary call is heard, the political community is in a permanent state of emergency and causes other countries to be similarly alerted. How to cope with the constant emergency created by the totalitarians has therefore become one of the most serious problems for constitutional and democratic regimes. These governments are further handicapped by the priority of domestic over foreign policy. (106) Curiously enough, the Communists have actually proclaimed this priority as a principle of their own foreign policy. (209e) But in view of their world-revolutionary goals, the claim is patently hypocritical. Hitler and Mussolini were more candid in this respect; they both expounded the older doctrine of "reason of state" (108) and its corollary, the principle of the "primacy of foreign policy." Again and again the cry is heard that some kind of accommodation must be found, some over-all agreement be reached, through a summit conference or through traditional diplomacy. Advocates of these projects never seem to realize that nothing worse could happen to a totalitarian system than such general pacification, since it would deprive it of its enemies. To appeal for peace while at the same time doing everything to prevent it from "breaking out" is a key feature of the relations of a totalitarian dictatorship with the rest of the world.

This problem has been aggravated by the inability of democratic states to adjust themselves to the fact that the totalitarians completely reject the traditional patterns of diplomatic behavior in the international arena. Such behaviorial patterns, institutionalized by custom and the usage of many years, are embodied in a certain ritual and certain consequent niceties. In a sense, therefore, diplomatic protocol — guiding the general conduct of international affairs and conferences — serves to limit the area of diplomatic warfare to accepted fields of battle, and the actual conduct of the warfare to mutually accepted weapons. The totalitarians accept all these to the extent that such rules and conventions do not limit their freedom of action; the moment they do, they reject them unhesitatingly.

The totalitarian dictator thus proclaims total freedom of action for the achievement of his total goals. The startled world, accustomed, during the last one hundred years at least, to traditional diplomatic manners, thought it extremely bad taste for Ribbentrop, when presenting his credentials as Hitler's Ambassador to the Court of St. James, to greet the astonished English monarch with a resounding "Heil Hitler!" The world probably forgot, however, that a similar act of scornful rejection of established international manners had already occurred more than fifteen years earlier, when the first Soviet delegation arrived at Brest-Litovsk to negotiate with the stiff and formal German delegates. As soon as the Soviet delegation had detrained and exchanged official greetings with the German representatives, Radek, who accompanied the Soviet delegation, broke loose and began to distribute revolutionary tracts among the curious German military onlookers gathered at the station.

The democratic states are thus confronted with a pattern of behavior completely at variance with their own. The totalitarian operations are designed always in terms of their goals, and restrictions are only reluctantly accepted. The diplomatic notes of such regimes, for instance, are usually couched in language that a few decades ago would have constituted a *casus belli* for any self-respecting nation.* Abuse, tendentious lies, and vituperation are all part of the normal contents of a note from a totalitarian dictator, be it from Nazi Germany a few years ago or from Communist China today. To a student of modern totalitarianism this should come as no surprise. For such notes, mirroring in part the totalitarian vision of the world, are not really meant to further understanding between nations, as the citizens of a democratic state would desire. They are tools that are aimed either at forging domestic opinion or at shattering the morale of the opponent. This attitude has become so embedded in totalitarian practice that now even notes designed to influence wavering foreign opinion, as for instance the 1954 Soviet notes to France on the European Defense Community or Khrushchev's Vienna memorandum for President Kennedy on Germany, cannot abstain from inserting a few vituperative remarks about capitalist or imperialist aspirations.

Similarly, in international conferences, the totalitarians have succeeded frequently in substituting competition in vituperation, in which they have a definite edge, for a more formal type of negotiation. At the same time, much to the amazement of more conventional statesmen, negotiators of the totalitarian dictator, particularly Communist ones, utilize such meetings for open appeals to the populations of their opponents, urging them to rise and revolt. It was truly two baffled men who, in the persons of Ambassador Kuehlmann and General Hoffman, reported to Berlin in January 1918 on the first negotiations with the Soviet delegates. What perplexed them, presumably, was that the Brest-Litovsk conference had become the first international gathering where a green table was used as a soap box for agitation. It was there that Trotsky declared on his and his colleagues' behalf that "we do not belong to the diplomatic school. We should rather be considered as soldiers of the revolution." (397) This kind of conduct has by now become

* One need only to recall the famous Ems Dispatch and the Franco-Prussian War of 1870 as an example.

established practice. Soviet leaders use foreign conferences, as well as domestic occasions, to couple denunciations of the leaders of the West with ringing appeals to the "brotherly" English and American peoples.

A striking demonstration of the agitational character of totalitarian diplomacy was provided by the Khrushchev-Bulganin visit to India and Burma in November and December 1955. Western diplomats were appalled by the brutal tone and mendacious character of the speeches delivered by the Soviet leaders to throngs of cheering Indians and Burmese. Completely disregarding the possibility that their remarks might embarrass their hosts, Khrushchev and Bulganin used every opportunity to vilify the West, accusing it of a variety of imagined crimes ranging from helping Hitler attack Russia to planning to subvert the newly won freedom of the Asian peoples (most of which had been granted by the West). What surprised Western observers had failed to learn is that totalitarian leaders refuse to consider state visits in the light of traditional Western diplomacy, which harks back to ancient customs of royal courtesies and polite exchanges of hospitality. To them, such an occasion is an opportunity to make open propaganda against the enemy. It has been something of a surprise to many that the same kind of distortion and misrepresentation has also been characteristic of communication between the Soviet Union and Communist China. It had previously occurred in the relations between the USSR and Yugoslavia, and it had, of course, been typical of the language exchanged between the Communists and the Fascists. These intertotalitarian exchanges demonstrate the "naturalness" of such discourse and its logical relation to the totalitarian mentality.

Naturally, then, normal exchange of diplomatic representatives is considered by the totalitarian dictator to be part of the total struggle. His diplomats, while insisting on the customary diplomatic privileges, do not hesitate to serve as organizers of fifth columns or underground cells and espionage networks. At the same time, efforts are made to deny even the customary privileges to democratic diplomats in the totalitarian zones of influence; instead they cause continuous trouble, ranging from severe travel restrictions to such wanton acts as the imprisonment of the American consul Lester Ward in Mukden or the murder of the Polish consul general Matusinski in Kiev in 1939. This, to a totalitarian dictator, is merely a question of tactics, and it may help to illustrate the fundamental operational differences between democratic and totalitarian relations with the world. Still, the totalitarians regard international law as an important tool in foreign policy; in fact, Soviet diplomats are both skillful and rigid in their exploitation of legal advantage, and international law has become a field of intense, if one-sided, scholarly activity in the Soviet Union. (174; 401a) The ideological cast of its outlook may be gleaned from a standard definition given by a leading Soviet jurist: "International law can be defined as the aggregate of rules governing relations between states in the process of their conflict and cooperation, designed to safeguard their peaceful *coexistence,* expressing the will of the *ruling classes* of these states and defended in the case of need by coercion applied by states individually or collectively" (italics added). The instrumental nature of international law as a tool in the international class war is clearly brought out. (410a; 221a)

A review of the intricacies of totalitarian foreign policy in its detailed development is beyond the scope of our analysis. (38; 224; 106; 14; 97) But it is of great importance to study the general problems presented by this world-revolutionary premise of the totalitarian dictator. Before we consider the similarities between the different systems, one basic difference between fascist and communist dictatorships must be pointed out. It is found in the field of ideology (see Chapter 7). Fascists of all shades glorify war. The glorification of war by Mussolini, as he preached the resurrection of "the grandeur that was Rome," is well known. The theme was elaborated upon by Hitler. War was the necessary school for men, Hitler insisted, and only through the trials of the warrior could the manly virtues be developed and maintained. His views were echoed in speeches and writings of Nazi subleaders again and again. "Every German who by his blood belongs to the great community of the German people is first a soldier, a fighter for his nation," Victor Lutze, chief of the SA, told a group of foreign diplomats and press representatives on January 24, 1936. In an official publication on the training of German youth for military service by Hellmut Stellrecht, published in 1935, we read that "it is absurd to make a man a soldier for two years only, and after he is grown up. The preparation for military service ought to begin in the earliest possible years of youth, and should be continued and extended until the

culminating point of training is reached by service in the army."
Similarly, the Italian Balilla had stated: "Therefore, everyone of you
must consider himself a soldier, a soldier even when he is not
wearing the green-gray uniform, a soldier also when he is at work
. . . a soldier bound to the rest of the army." (95a)

In lieu of many other such passages, Mussolini may be cited for
the key proposition, later reiterated again and again by him as well
as others: "Fascism . . . believes neither in the possibility nor the
utility of perpetual peace . . . War alone brings up to its highest
tension all human energy and puts the stamp of nobility upon the
peoples who have the courage to meet it. All other trials are substi-
tutes, which never really put men into the position where they have
to make the great decision — the alternative of life and death."
(95b) This glorification of war and the warrior, which rests on the
ideological stress laid on a collective command over the total dedication of the individual, stands at the center of the fascist view of
man. (123d; 127b; 266e) It contrasts sharply with the communist
emphasis on the worker. For the communist, war is primarily the
war of classes rather than of nations. But this class war, which
culminates in revolution, is not considered in itself a good. Indeed,
the eventual world order of communism is said to be a peaceful
order, although communism rejects the possibility of genuine peace
between communism and capitalism. This rejection is the result of
what the Soviets consider a realistic view of imperialist and capitalist warmongers and their plots against the "socialist fatherland."
Their readiness to prepare for war is due to the bellicose view of
man as a class-bound being, motivated by economic interest; but
somehow all this bellicosity will, they claim, end when the world
revolution has been consummated. War is a necessary means to the
end the Communist strives for; it is not an end in itself. The
conflict between Moscow and Peking is in part cast in terms of an
argument over the interpretation of these positions. Obviously,
neither Marx nor Lenin addressed himself to the problem of
whether international war, especially when involving nuclear
weapons of total destruction, should be waged as part of the class
struggle. Mao has said that even 900 million casualties would not be
too great a price to pay for transforming the world into a communist one, to which the Soviets replied that this was criminal adven-

turism and asked whether this view would be shared by the millions thus to be sacrificed. (240g) Still, Mao does not glorify war for its own sake, as did the Fascists.

That is why the Communist leaders are able to profess simultaneously, and probably with some degree of sincerity, their contradictory beliefs in the possibility of coexistence of communist and capitalist worlds and in the inevitability of conflict between the two, ending in the total extinction of the capitalist world. Soviet leaders have frequently gone on record as believing in peaceful coexistence, and many quotations to this effect could be cited. This was also true of Stalin, who told an American interviewer in 1947: "Yes, of course. This [coexistence] is not only possible, it is reasonable and fully realizable. At the most tense times during the war differences in form of government did not prevent our two countries from uniting and conquering our enemy. To an even greater degree it is possible to retain these relations in peace time." (427) This view was implied in a reaffirmation in a declaration of a congress of Communist parties in 1960, which said: "Peaceful coexistence does not mean a reconciliation of socialist and bourgeois ideologies. On the contrary, it assumes intensification of the struggle of the working class and of all Communist parties for the triumph of socialist ideas." (328a; 172b; 221b)

This position follows quite logically from what we have previously said concerning the Communists' conviction in the ultimate victory of their cause. It is precisely because they assume, on allegedly *scientific* grounds, that capitalism is doomed that they are willing to coexist with it. For peaceful coexistence to them is by no means a static situation. In the communist conception of reality, such coexistence does not stop the unfolding of history, which the Communists feel they must further, and the fall of capitalism still remains the object of feverish activity despite the absence of a major armed conflict. Indeed, war is a means, but only one of many; other means frequently as effective are social and economic decay, anticolonial eruptions, and racial strife. Only when they fail may war be necessary. Thus Molotov was not contradicting Stalin when he declared that "the feverish efforts of imperialists, under whom the ground is giving way, will not save capitalism from its approaching doom. We are living in an age in which all roads lead to Communism." (441f) The same view has been expressed many times by Khrushchev, who re-emphasized such expansionism in connection with his efforts at revitalizing the party and its ideology.

Does any practical importance attach to this difference in outlook on war between the Fascists and the Communists? To the democratic statesman, confronted with the Soviet Union today, the difference is primarily this: it makes the Soviet Union a more dangerous enemy in the long run. While it was foolish to doubt the warlike propensities of Hitler and to assume that they could be appeased, it is probably unwise to assume that the USSR will seize the first chance that is offered by superiority in nuclear weapons to attack the United States. (116) The Soviets, as they gain strength, may become bolder in challenging the American position in contested areas; they are likely to remain circumspect about a general war. One does not have to accept at face value the protestations of those who claim that the leaders of the Soviet Union are so confident about the eventual victory of Marxism that they will not see any reason for starting wars. Stalin, at one point, is said to have told an English visitor who queried him on this point that every so often a kick well administered might help a lot. But such kicks, such limited wars, are means toward achieving the over-all end of world revolution; they are not something to be gloried in for their own sake.*

Although the struggle for world conquest that is the totalitarians' natural bent has certain affinities with the imperialism of a preceding age, the two must not be misunderstood as identical. Mussolini, to be sure, wrote that "imperialism is the eternal immutable law of life." To him, the would-be warrior, imperialism was "at bottom, nothing other than the need, the desire, and the will to expansion which every individual and every live and vital people possess." He added that "imperialism is not, as is usually thought, necessarily aristocratic and military. It may be democratic, pacific, economic, spiritual." (95c) But such a broad conception of imperialism blurs the significant features. Hannah Arendt rightly observes that "imperialism is not empire building and expansion is not conquest." (5d)

---

* The only Marxist writer of note who leaned toward glorifying violence for its own sake was Georges Sorel who, in his *Reflexions sur la violence*, stressed the value of bloody combat for the development of the morale of the proletariat. Mussolini acknowledged his indebtedness to Sorel. See the illuminating preface to the English edition by E. A. Shils (Glencoe, 1950).

They are all related, but should be clearly distinguished. And the conquest of the world for a totalitarian movement is something else again. While the older imperialism was an outgrowth of the industrial economy, the will to conquer the world that animates the totalitarian systems is intimately linked with their ideological preoccupations. It is the outward thrust of that passion for unanimity which brooks no disagreement with what the movement proclaims as "the truth."

As a consequence, the totalitarian attack is a continuing one. It takes the form of organizing subversive activities within communities abroad, based upon the ideology of the movement. The Italian Fascists and the German Nazis tried in countries like the United States to mobilize those elements which by background and tradition "belonged" in their camp. At one time, immediately preceding the United States's entry into World War II, all the programs in the Italian language broadcast in Boston were in the hands of Fascist agents. (411) The Nazi Bund sought to provide effective support for Hitler's party line, especially among German-Americans. (23) Similar activities were carried on wherever there were German minorities that could be organized for this purpose. A particularly dramatic instance was the large-scale subversion undertaken by the Sudeten German organizations of National Socialist bent, which eventually comprised a large percentage of the German-speaking population of Czechoslovakia. (35) Hitler acknowledged this development in the spring of 1938 and made it the basis of an annexationist appeal. In his speech before the Reichstag on February 20, 1938, he spoke of ten million "Germans" who lived in Austria and Czechoslovakia and announced that the protection of their personal, political, and convictional freedom was a national interest of the German Reich. Similar thoughts recur throughout his speeches and writings. (150; 151; 191) Eventually the policy was generalized to include all sympathizers with Hitler's notions, regardless of nationality. But the resultant policy of organizing fifth columns, led by quislings, was less successful than is commonly assumed, as careful research has revealed. (165)

These efforts, while dangerous enough, were more easily dealt with than the world-wide movement of Communist parties, because of the limited appeal that the supremacy of a particular "folk" has for the rest of the world. In some countries, the Communist Party has been outlawed, but there is no country in the world in which there does not exist such a party, and in some of them it is large enough to affect the nation's political decisions whenever a major disagreement develops. The substantial majority for the European Defense Community that existed in France outside Communist ranks was routed by the Communists when they made common cause with its opponents from other quarters. (398) This is only perhaps the most striking instance of the "enemy within" effectively determining a country's foreign policy by parliamentary means. Similar results are continually achieved in France and Italy, though rarely in other countries where the party is not strong enough. In these places, the Communist Party devotes its efforts to infiltrating the government services, the educational institutions, and more particularly the trade unions. This latter effort can be very serious, if the unions concerned happen to operate vital key industries which might cripple an effective defense effort. Even in the United States, where Communism is notoriously weak, some unions have been under Communist domination. (61; 323; 26; 80)

Communist subversion has often been able to penetrate the higher levels of governmental and professional work, as a number of trials in Britain, Germany, France and the United States have shown. But it has not achieved significant proportions. It is precisely this ability of the Communists to recruit local supporters that makes them so much more effective and dangerous than the Nazis. Communist control over the captive nations in Eastern Europe, much more stable than under the Nazi occupation, owes a great deal not only to the actual Soviet military occupation, which was instrumental in seizing power, but also to the ability to raise local cadres, which then could penetrate easily any attempts to develop an anti-Communist underground. Under these circumstances repressive measures are far more effective. (39b)

This "strategy of terror," which has been made even more unsettling by the development of nuclear weapons that presumably could be placed in strategic centers by a relatively small group of saboteurs without too much difficulty or even danger of detection, has not so far been met by any significant countermoves by those opposed to the totalitarian dictatorships. The timid efforts to broadcast cheering bits of information into the totalitarian lands, while probably of some limited value, can in no way be compared in effect with totalitarian subversion. Consequently, extension of Soviet control over one territory after another has been proceeding since 1945 almost with the annual regularity of the seasons. After the first big grab of that first year, netting Poland, Rumania, Hungary, and Yugoslavia, there have been the additions of Czechoslovakia, East Germany, China, North Korea, North Vietnam, several African nations, and Cuba, with Iraq and Laos infiltrated and gravely endangered. (175) Comparable efforts in Greece, Iran, and Indonesia have been stopped for the time being, but it seems to be only a matter of time before the next victim is "bagged."

As the Soviet sphere expands, there have of course developed a number of stresses and strains, as well as deviant regimes of Communist totalitarianism. The most dramatic case is that of Communist China, of course, to which we shall return. There is also the case of Yugoslavia. She was temporarily alienated from the Soviet bloc, but the breach has been lessened, if not healed, by Khrushchevian diplomacy. It is well to remember that, first, Yugoslavia never left the Soviet bloc, but was expelled much against her hopes; and second, that Yugoslavia was probably the most communized satellite in Eastern Europe by the time of the break in 1948. The loss of Yugloslavia stemmed from a surprising miscalculation of Stalin and, allegedly, Zhdanov. The Soviet leaders assumed that, because of the high revolutionary fervor and strength of the Yugoslav Communist Party and its ambitious political and economic goals, the very thought of separation from the Soviet bloc would make the party reject Tito's leadership and replace him with more amenable successors. The expulsion of Tito from the Cominform, however, did not produce his fall from power. The reason for this may be found in precisely what was assumed to be the ground for so confidently expecting his fall: the Yugoslav Communist Party was sufficiently strong and sufficiently rooted not to need outside assistance by 1948. Despite the expulsion of its leader, it could maintain its cohesion and still hold its power. (361) Efforts at healing the breach, which looked promising in 1956, were only partially successful. Tito has continued his policy of playing West and East against each other. At one time there was even talk of "Titoism" in China. The error of this expectation has since been revealed. China, far from modifying the Soviet Communist position in a Western direction by toning down its totalitarian radicalism and expansionism, has on the contrary gone beyond Bolshevism in its revolutionary fervor and anti-Westernism. It is taking the line of "left deviation" rather than "right deviation," to use the Soviet mode of talking. The difference is crucial in international relations and policy, in that the position of Mao makes it much more difficult for Western diplomacy to exploit this deviation. To be sure, De Gaulle believes he can do so, but it is doubtful whether he understands the ideological force of totalitarian expansionism. Although the Soviet Union has not yet repeated the mistake of expelling Communist China from the bloc, there are indications that this may happen. (38g) In any case, the differences between the Soviet Union and China have become a significant factor in world politics. (129; 238e; 397.1)

The relations between the totalitarian dictator and the world, then, are those of constant struggle, varying only in pace and intensity. The world-revolutionary aspirations of the communist movement have become intertwined with the ancient Russian imperial propensities, based upon historical reminiscences and geographical inducements, the so-called necessities of geopolitics. (220) This novel combination results in providing the Soviet imperial expansion with an ideological underpinning far more potent than the older Panslavist and Third Reich ideologies. This must be kept clearly in mind, especially since a number of well-known writers have claimed the opposite. It has been argued that "Nazism and Bolshevism owe more to Pan-Germanism and Panslavism (respectively) than to any other ideology or political movement," and that "this is the most evident in foreign policies, where the strategies of Nazi Germany and Soviet Russia have followed so closely the well-known programs of conquest outlined by the pan-movements." (5e; 179) The USSR certainly does not owe *more* to Panslavism than to Communism, even if one agrees that their policy followed the Panslavist "program of conquest." Neither China nor Germany played the role in Panslavism which they adopt in Soviet policy and ideology. Yet in Russia there developed a significant shift toward nationalism after 1934, and there were some curious points of kinship between the thoughts of the Panslavist Danilevsky and those of Stalin. They both saw the struggle between the Slavic world and the West as inevitable, wanted Russia to turn to Asia for support, and were profoundly convinced that the prolonged war with the

West would end in Russian victory. But these thoughts were framed, in Stalin's mind, in the rigid dialectical formulas of ortho- dox Marxism-Leninism and completely lacked the romantic note that is such a curious feature of Panslavism. (236)

There is more of a direct relation between the Nazi position and Pan-Germanism, since Hitler explicitly acknowledges in *Mein Kampf* his indebtedness to von Schönerer, the Austrian leader of the Pan-German movement. (148a) To claim it as the primary ingredient of Nazi ideology, however, is surely not feasible. While Hitler's writings and speeches often use Pan-German slogans, the key to Nazi ideology is the race myth. The recently discovered "second book" of Hitler, which is primarily concerned with foreign and international affairs, does not, according to its learned editor, alter anything very significant in the understanding of his foreign policy, except to confirm its racist and general expansionist line. (151) His race doctrine is, in spite of some anti-Semitism in the ranks of the Pan-German League, a far cry from the old-fashioned imperialism of that league, which never had any substantial popular support. Pan-Germanism lacked the emotional depth of Panslavism, as it lacked historical roots. It possessed a shrill quality and a demagogic superficiality, which contrasts unfavorably with the ro- mantic dreams of a Danilevsky or a Dostoevsky. (384)

In conclusion we might say that the dictator's aspiration to world rule is inseparable from the ideology of the movement and from the party which provides the framework for the dictator's operation in this as in other fields. It is, conversely, quite evident that the possi- bility for peaceful coexistence of the nations peopling this world presupposes the disappearance of the totalitarian dictatorships. Since, according to their own loudly proclaimed professions, their systems must be made world-wide, those who reject the system have no alternative but to strive for its destruction. Any relaxation of the vigilance required to face such ideological imperialists as the totalitarians is likely to result in a disaster such as the Second World War, or worse. This point was well illustrated by the Cuban crisis of October 1962; its full political and legal significance is still ob- scure. (221c) It would seem that the American president acted at the very last moment.

But Hitler is gone, and so is Stalin and his nationalist propensi- ties. His place was taken by Khrushchev, who revived the world-revolutionary line in the name of Lenin. He coupled this line with the line of peaceful coexistence, as we have seen. He never wearied of predicting the downfall of capitalism while insisting upon its occurring gradually and peacefully. In doing so, he spoke for a rapidly developing Soviet Union, which occupies a position of reasonably secure power and plenty and which, like the United States, would fashion its foreign policy to aid and assist its friends and sympathizers, but would do so short of war. Communist China is challenging this concept. Although also developing rapidly, China is far from a position of security in either power or plenty. Nor is she part of the European world; her teeming millions share the resentment of Western imperialism and white supremacy, which has been destroying the old empires and bringing into being a very different world. (272) The question remains: who shall rule this world? It is the key question of totalitarian foreign policy.

28

THE STAGES OF DEVELOPMENT
AND THE FUTURE

In much of the foregoing discussion, there have been some implicit notions about the stages or phases of totalitarian development. From time to time, explicit statements have been made. At the very outset, we suggested that totalitarian dictatorship does not come into existence by a "seizure of power," as is assumed in so much of the literature regarding the subject. What is seized is the control of the existing government, customarily referred to as the state, and a dictatorship is set up in order to realize the totalitarian ideology of the party that has "seized the power." But the total transformation of the existing society that this ideology calls for quickly runs into numerous and formidable obstacles. The series of critical situations thus created give rise to the swift enlargement of power and the totalitarian radicalization of the means of control; in the course of this process, the totalitarian dictatorship comes into being.

In view of the gradual emergence of the totalitarian features of these dictatorships, it is evident that these systems have not been the result of intentional action. (146) True, the total character of the ideology led to a dim appreciation of the difficulties, and to a corresponding ideological acceptance of force and violence. The acceptance of violence also carried with it the acceptance of fraud, and more especially propagandistic fraud on a large scale, as a more special form of violence, namely, that done to mind and sentiment. But force, fraud, and violence have always been features of organized governments, and they do not constitute in themselves the distinctive totalitarian operation. This operation we have defined in terms of a syndrome of interrelated traits or features, the emergence of which signalizes the consummation of the totalitarian evolution. It is easy to identify these features, once they have come into full play: Italy, Germany, Russia — they all had emerged by about 1936 as totalitarian dictatorships; China and a considerable number of satellites have followed suit in the years since the Second World War. All exhibit the six traits we have identified as characteristic: a total ideology, a single mass party led by a dictator, a terroristic secret police, a monopoly of mass communication, a monopoly of weapons, and a centrally planned economy. Often they also carry on an expansionist foreign policy.

The collapse of two of these totalitarian dictatorships occurred as a result of war and foreign invasion. If we study these wars, we find that they were the natural consequence of the ideologies of these particular dictatorships. Demonstrably, the ideologies themselves, with their glorification of violence, were at least in part responsible for the grave errors in judgment that launched the leaderships into their belligerency. Other difficulties contributed to the defeat; some of these are once again definitely traceable to ideological and other defects of these regimes. More particularly, the concentration of all power in a single man's hands, when combined with the absence of any sort of continuing critical evaluation of governmental operations, greatly enhanced the probability of erroneous judgments with fateful consequences.

But the end of these particular regimes, linked as they were to specific features of their ideology, must not mislead one into readily assuming the early demise of totalitarianism. One need not go so far as to envision a world which will be divided among three warring sets of totalitarians in order to appreciate the possibly lasting qualities of totalitarian dictatorship. More particularly, the inroads of totalitarianism into the Orient, where despotic forms of government have been the rule for thousands of years, ought to give one pause and prevent any too optimistic estimate of the totalitarians' lack of capacity for survival. We noted at the outset that autocratic regimes have often lasted for centuries, even when their oppressive practices became ever more pronounced. Therefore the mere maturing of totalitarian autocracies into regularized patterns of organized coercion need not spell their destruction; quite the contrary. Since the end of totalitarian dictatorship is purely a matter of speculation, to which we shall return at the end of this discussion, let us start with its beginning.

As we just noted and indicated at various points in our study, the totalitarian dictatorship emerges some time after the seizure of power by the leaders of the movement that had developed in support of the ideology. The typical sequence is therefore that of ideology, movement, party, government. The point of time when the totalitarian government emerges may be reasonably fixed and delimited. It is that point at which the leadership sees itself obliged to employ open and legally unadorned violence for maintaining itself, particularly against internal opposition due to ideological dissensions arising from within the movement's own ranks. In the Soviet Union, this point is marked by Stalin's liquidation of his erstwhile colleagues in the USSR's leadership and more particularly by his epochal struggle with Trotsky. In Nazi Germany, Hitler's bloody suppression of Röhm and his followers represents this totalitarian breakthrough. In Mussolini's Italy, the Matteotti murder and its sequel are one turning point, the attack on Abyssinia another. In China, the totalitarian government seems to have emerged full-fledged because a kind of totalitarian government had been in existence for a considerable time prior to the Communists' establishment of control over all of China, namely, in those provinces they had controlled and developed in their war against the Japanese. But even here the true totalitarian maturation may be fixed at the point where there occurred the purge of competitors to Mao Tse-tung's absolute dictatorial control.

The development in the Eastern European satellites of the USSR follows a definite pattern, too, culminating in the totalitarian breakthrough some time after the seizure of control by the Communists. However, in these regimes it may be claimed that the establishment of a totalitarian dictatorship was definitely willed at the outset. We do not know for sure, and there are indications that at least the local leadership had some illusions to the contrary, expressed in notions about the more democratic form that the Communist regimes would take in Poland, Czechoslovakia, and Hungary. But it is likely that the Soviet leaders had definite plans for the structuring of the society conceived in their own image, to become "people's democracies" in their parlance, "totalitarian dictatorships" in ours. This inference is supported at least in part by the remarkable parallelism in the development of all these regimes. On the other hand, highly authoritative voices from within the Soviet Union have taken a line which makes it conceivable that the Soviet leadership itself was uncertain and only "crossed the Rubicon" toward the totalitarian breakthrough in the light of actual situational needs. Thus we read, in an article by E. S. Varga, "The social order of these states differs from all states known to us so far. It is something completely new in the history of mankind." (428) A. Leontiev even went so far as to claim that neither Marx nor Lenin foresaw or could foresee such a form of state, the reason being that these regimes were organized in response to a specific and novel historical situation. (438b) But whether intentional or not, here too the totalitarian features came into existence not immediately upon the seizure of power, but some time afterward and regularly in connection with the purging of dissident elements, presumably men who had questioned the need for setting up a regime in the image of the Soviet Union. (37j)

In a study of some years ago (234; 322), it was shown that the totalitarian dictatorship in the satellites developed in accordance with a definite pattern. The spark that set off the totalitarian breakthrough was the defection of Tito from the Cominform. It highlighted, as in corresponding situations in older totalitarian systems, the dangers inherent in the survival of potential centers of dissent within the Soviet-controlled Communist movement. It brought on the total dominance of the several societies by Russian-directed Communist parties, except of course in Yugoslavia, where it enabled the anti-USSR group of the Communist Party to establish totalitarian predominance. (78c; 112i)

If one inquires how this breakthrough was conditioned, one finds two antecedent stages in these regimes. During the first, the totalitarian movement achieved a key position within an as yet nontotalitarian political environment. It therefore entered into coalitions with other parties to form a government. It was maintained that this represented a novel and unique form of democracy, unlike the USSR, and that its political task was to liquidate the old ruling class and to seize control of the major instruments of power: the resistance movements, trade unions and other associations, the armed forces, land reform and socialization, and the key ministries such as Interior, Justice, Communications, and Education, which would yield control of the police and courts as well as mass communication media and propaganda. It is evident that this pattern corresponds to the features characteristic of a totalitarian dictatorship as we have analyzed it. Hence it is hardly surprising that, in the second stage, the government is definitely molded in the image of the totalitarian dictatorship. The pretense that these regimes were novel and unique was dropped, and their kinship with the USSR as a model for building the communist society was frankly proclaimed, as well as their dependence upon Soviet political and military support readily acknowledged. During this phase, opposition was destroyed and dissenters were purged from the party coalitions. Opposition leaders fled or were liquidated, while their parties were either reduced to impotence or dissolved. While this was going on, the Soviet Union itself gradually shifted from moderation and tolerance toward tight control and intransigence, preparing the ground for actual total control at the point of the breakthrough.

This phase came to an end with Stalin's death. Since then, national autonomy has been gaining in all the satellites, especially after the return of Gomulka, the resumption of friendly relations with Tito, and the growing conflict with Communist China — itself an expression of this phase. It has brought "polycentrism" into being. It is an established fact, and it is likely to increase rather than decline. It seems that totalitarian states, because of their ideological basis, "find it, as a rule, more difficult to coexist with each other than old-fashioned big powers." (193a) Such polycentrism is a response, at least in part, to the emotions of cultural, regional, and national identity through which forces are at work that transcend Marxism. This polycentrism is fraught with tensions and difficulties, because of the lack of an "operative theory of communist international relations." (193b) But in spite of all the diversity, there is a good deal of parallel evolution in the Soviet Union and the satellites, as they seek to operate their regimes without physical terror. These ongoing efforts have encountered very serious economic difficulties, since rising expectations have not been fulfilled and the intellectuals' rebelliousness has increased. (172c)

The reason for sketching these developments in the satellites is that they throw some light on the evolution of totalitarian dictatorship in the major countries. For without drawing sharp lines, we find the coalition with nontotalitarian parties in Italy and Germany, the compromise with remaining bourgeois and rich peasants' groups in Russia, as well as Hitler's and Mussolini's "deals" with big business and the churches, and similar compromises. These were accompanied by an insistent emphasis on the democratic features of the new regime. If it has been stressed in discussions of the satellites that their "road to socialism" was easier than the Soviet Union's had been, there is an element of truth in such an assertion; the lack of a "model" had indeed been a striking feature of the development of totalitarian dictatorship in the Soviet Union, as we mentioned at the outset. The lack of such a model cannot be claimed with quite the same justification in the case of the Fascists and National Socialists; for while they doctrinally rejected the Soviet Union altogether, there is a good deal of evidence that they followed its example in a number of respects concerning vital features of the totalitarian system. When they instituted the secret police and the monopoly of propaganda, the corresponding transformation of education, the organizing of youth, and central planning, and when they developed the technique of a rigidly hierarchical party apparatus, the Fascists followed essentially Soviet models. To what extent this was a matter of conscious imitation does not seem very important, since these features are inherent in the dynamics of a totalitarian movement. It may, however, be well to trace this "phasing" through some of its distinctive component fields, more especially ideology, party, and secret police. This sketch provides a summary of what has been discussed in greater detail earlier.

We saw when discussing ideology that the radical change which a totalitarian ideology demands necessarily occasions adjustments and adaptations to reality and its situational needs when an attempt is made to "realize" such an ideology. The totalitarian revolutionaries are, in this respect, not in a different situation from other revolutionaries before them. In the French revolution especially, the violent controversies over the ideological "meaning" of the revolution led to the terror. But since the ideology lacked that pseudo-scientific ingredient which has enabled the Communist and Fascist totalitarians to insist on the "mercilessness of the dialectics" (Stalin) and on "ice-cold reasoning" (Hitler), a totalitarian ideology did not develop. Whether its exponents are convinced or merely pretending, the totalitarian ideology requires that it be maintained even while it is being adapted to changing situations. It is at this point, when the inner contradictions of the totalitarian ideology become evident, that the totalitarian breakthrough occurs. For since there is no longer any possibility of maintaining the ideology on logical grounds, total violence must be deployed in order to do so. The mounting fierceness of the conflict between the Soviet Union and Communist China, in which tongue-lashing vituperation accompanies armed conflict at the border, appears to be a projection of this inherent "dialectic."

In the development of the party, which is closely related to this ideological evolution, an analogous process takes place. In the original movement, when the party fights for success against a hostile environment, all the leader's authority, or a very large part of it, springs from the genuine comradeship that unites the effective participants. After the seizure of power, this relationship continues to operate, but — owing to the new situation confronting the leadership with the vast tasks of a government that aspires to accomplish a total change and reconstruction of society — it becomes rapidly bureaucratized. Not only the government but the party is transformed into an increasingly formalized hierarchy. As is always the case, the apparat acquires its own weight and operates according to the inherent laws of large-scale bureaucracy. At the point of the totalitarian breakthrough, purges of former comrades reveal that it is no longer a matter of "belonging" to a movement, but one of submitting to autocratic decisions that determine a person's right to belong to the party.

Hand in hand with this development goes that of the secret police. In order to become the instrument of total terror that the police system is in a matured totalitarian system, it must acquire the requisite knowledge of its human material, the potential victims of its terroristic activity. Centers of possible opposition have to be identified, techniques of espionage and counterespionage have to be developed, courts and similar judicial procedures of a nontotalitarian past have to be subjected to effective control. Experience and observation show that the time required for these tasks varies. In the Soviet Union, the tsarist secret police provided a ready starting point, and hence the Soviets got under way in this field with the

Cheka very quickly. The entrenched liberal tradition in Italy allowed the Fascists to organize the secret police effectively only in 1926, and it took another two years before it really took hold of the situation. The National Socialists, although anxious to clamp down at once, did not perfect their secret-police system until well after the blood purge of 1934, when Himmler first emerged as the key figure in the manipulation of this essential totalitarian tool.

It is at the point at which the totalitarian breakthrough occurs that the total planning of the economy imposes itself. For it is then that the social life of the society has become so largely disorganized that nothing short of central direction will do. In a sense, this total planning is the sign of the culmination of the process. In Soviet Russia, it is the year 1928, in Nazi Germany 1936, while in Italy it comes with the instituting of the corporative set-up in 1934 (it had been grandiloquently announced in 1930), though perhaps the Ethiopian war was even more decisive. It is not important in this connection to what the planning effort amounts; it will vary in inverse proportion to the economic autonomy of the country. The crucial point is that this total planning imposes itself as the inescapable consequence of the totalitarian evolution in the economic field. It is therefore not surprising that plans should have sprouted all over the satellite regions, and that even Communist China should have produced a plan, announced in 1952 and starting in 1953, even though many of the essentials of planning are absent in that vast and unorganized country. Even the statistical basis for planning in China appears to be in a rather primitive stage. (396b) Even so, planning has been undertaken on an ambitious scale, with uncertain results. The schism that has developed between the Soviet Union and Communist China is in part concerned with the resulting problems. More especially, the communes as a possible answer to the agricultural problem were, as we have seen, at one time embraced as the "great leap forward," but have since been virtually abandoned. Khrushchev had presumably tried to dissuade the Chinese leaders, but only with the result that they became more aggressive, presenting as one Soviet source put it their "totally unsound and harmful policy . . . as an objective law." (442e) As the conflict widened, the language became abusive in ideological terms, each nation calling the other a "betrayer of the revolution," a "stooge of capitalism," a "traitor to imperialism," and the like. There can be little doubt that this open break will profoundly affect the future of totalitarianism and of the world that has to live with it.

What can be said about the projection of totalitarian dictatorships into the future? We exclude here the problems raised by the possibility of a world-wide conflict between totalitarian and nontotalitarian regimes; such a war, while possible, is too speculative in its military and political implications to allow reasonable reflections. But the internal evolution of the totalitarian dictatorships, given a species of peaceful coexistence, allows for some projection on the basis of past experience.

One possibility should be excluded, except in the satellites: the likelihood of an overthrow of these regimes by revolutionary action from within. Our entire analysis of totalitarianism suggests that it is improbable that such a "revolution" will be undertaken, let alone succeed. (112j) The records of the resistance in the several totalitarian regimes that have collapsed reinforce this conclusion. When the characteristic techniques of a terroristic police and of mass propaganda are added to the monopoly of weapons that all modern governments enjoy, the prospect of such a revolutionary overthrow becomes practically nil. This may be true, though one doubts that, "even if opposition were less savagely repressed, the people of the totalitarian countries, no matter how badly off or how dissatisfied they are, would not want to engage in any large-scale struggle — they seem to feel that disorder, chaos, and destruction would make them even worse off." (112k) The doubt is suggested by the events of June 17, 1953, in East Germany and those of the fall of 1956 in Hungary. But the dismal failure of these upheavals unfortunately confirms the conclusion that revolution is not likely to succeed even if it is begun.

What then is going to be the course of totalitarian development? If one extrapolates from the past course of evolution, it seems most likely that the totalitarian dictatorships will oscillate between an extreme of totalitarian violence and an opposite extreme of an actual breakdown. The first extreme is illustrated by the Stalin regime in its later phase and by Hitler's after 1942; the second by Hitler's in 1945, Mussolini's in 1944, and Hungary in 1956. But these oscillations are not merely cyclical; they are part of a steady evolution in totalitarian rule which can be described as a maturing process. The

notion that this evolution means that totalitarian regimes will become more and more total * is not tenable; rather the various forces
at work to industrialize and urbanize totalitarian societies, both
intended and automatic, oblige the rulers to work out suitable
adaptations in their methods of rule. These efforts have at times
persuaded well-informed observers to expect the emergence of a
constitutional order (see Chapter 10). But the process is more complex. It may well be true that the requirements of bureaucratic
organization will assert themselves and lead to a less violent form
of autocratic regime. (253g) But a number of other factors, some of
them countervailing in impact, are at work, such as the personality
of the dictator, the success of the regime in mastering its foreign
and domestic problems, and major technological breakthroughs. In
this connection, it is argued that the technological needs of an
advancing industrial civilization will play a decisive role. There is
the possibility here of an inherent conflict between industrialization
and totalitarian dictatorship, through the rise of a class of managers
and technicians. These, when allied with the military, might wish
to abandon the ideology and the party and thus bring the totalitarian dictatorship to an end. This development is conceivable, but
not very likely. It may be doubted that such managers and technicians have any imaginable conception of the ground upon which
the legitimacy and hence the authority of their continuing power
might be built. (403)

One feature of the probable future course that can be predicted
with some confidence is related to totalitarian foreign policy. In the
past, when tensions and partial breakdowns in autocratic systems
increased, the employment of violence likewise increased in order to
solve these tensions. As part of this general pattern, autocratic organizations have tended to turn to violent aggression as a way of
solving their difficulties. In totalitarian regimes, it appears that ideology plays a greater role in this respect. In the case of the Hitler
regime, one of the initial decisions after the seizure of power was to
gear the national economy to a large-scale war preparation. Internal
developments, as well as actual strength, were largely ignored by
the dictator. In the case of the Soviet Union, there is no doubt that
the Soviet leaders have tended to emphasize international relaxation
at times of internal difficulties. This was as true in the days of the

* That was our view as expressed in the first edition, p. 300.

Popular Front as it was in the era of "the spirit of Geneva." At the same time, however, the ideological doctrine of class war can be utilized to develop aggressive belligerency in subject populations throughout the world. The Soviet regime, by maintaining a sham sense of identity with these populations, can abet their revolutionary efforts and exploit them politically. The situation has, however, been greatly complicated and in a sense weakened by the conflict with Communist China.

The degree of direct Soviet involvement in such "revolutions" varies; in some areas, as in Europe, such upheavals were in fact created by Soviet armies; in others, as in Asia, the Communists have merely exploited and channeled a stormy situation. When United States military strength blocked further Soviet advance in Europe, Stalin, in response to this, intensified the totalitarianization of the satellite nations and encouraged the Chinese Communists in their revolutionary activity. Since then the Chinese have "taken over" at least a part of this role. They are continuing, on the earlier Soviet pattern, to encourage revolutionary movements in Asia and elsewhere and to give them ideological and institutional backing. The Soviet Union will continue to exploit any relaxation to undermine the military barriers built up against it in Europe and to mobilize some of the sympathy existing for the USSR in European intellectual circles. (8) There is also no doubt that areas of conflict and unrest in the Middle East will provide the Soviet Union with ample opportunities for political maneuvers to set in motion a revolutionary chain of events, but such activities will recurrently be restrained in the Soviet "national interest," that is, such economic advantages as credits and imports. All of this will be carried on without direct clash with the still preponderant military might of the United States, while at home energetic efforts will be pursued to solve agricultural and related problems, if the Soviet Union's view prevails against Communist China's.

It therefore appears, as we have observed, that the Fascist regimes, drawn into a policy of war on the traditional pattern by the ideological blindness of their leaders, committed themselves in advance to an open conflict, the outcome of which was more than doubtful. Except for a very few areas, such as Austria, their opportunities for creating revolutionary upheavals to exploit were limited. The Communists, launching a broad economic and social revolution at home, can combine these domestic measures with foreign expansion, short of war. It is rather unlikely that they would launch a major and open campaign of aggression because of internal difficulties. They accept such difficulties as part of the revolutionary process. Their refined, yet often brutal, system of controls dooms any effective resistance in advance (see Chapter 22). The possibility of open war may increase, however, as the Communists gain in military preponderance. A chilling indication of such a development occurred after the sputnik success; voices in the Communist camp became more strident and ventured open challenges.

Whether it is possible, in terms of a developmental construct, to forecast the probable course of totalitarian evolution seems doubtful. We prefer the simple extrapolation of recent trends and the estimate of broader potentials in terms of long-range observation of autocratic regimes throughout history. (112 1) Considered in such terms, the prospect of totalitarian dictatorship seems unclear. Leaving aside the possibility of liquidation by war, there might conceivably be internal transformation. "It is possible," as one highly qualified observer says, "that the 'wave' of totalitarianism has reached its high water mark. And it may well be that in the not too distant future it will start rolling back." (112m) It may be. But if one such totalitarianism disappeared, others may appear to take its place, owing to the endemic conditions that have given rise to them. Totalitarian dictatorship, a novel form of autocracy, more inimical to human dignity than autocracies in the past, appears to be a highly dynamic form of government, which is still in the process of evolving. Whether it will, in the long run, prove to be a viable form of social and political organization remains to be seen. Nonetheless, large portions of mankind may have to pass through its crucible before becoming ready, if they survive the ordeal, for more complex and civilized forms of political organization. "Socialist legality" may have an important role to play in this process. For an increasing recognition of law and legal restraints, by limiting autocracy, may provide a middle ground between the extremes of violence and anarchy, which past experience has shown to circumscribe the range of totalitarian change.

Some Bibliographical Notes

Bibliographical References

Index of Authors Cited

Index

SOME BIBLIOGRAPHICAL NOTES

Any study of totalitarianism should involve, in great measure, original research. Fortunately, recent years have seen intensive efforts to tap the available research data, and the books in English cited below represent some, but not all, of the more serious efforts to shed light on the problems with which our book has been concerned. However, a great deal of original research still remains to be done, and a student of totalitarianism would find it extremely rewarding to explore some of the available original sources. To mention but a few: the proceedings and documentary evidence of the Nuremberg trials represent a rich fount of information on the Nazi system. Easily available and thoroughly indexed, they are a "must" for anyone undertaking to examine the Nazi system. Similarly, such materials as *Hitler's Secret Conversations* or *The Goebbels Diaries* shed a great deal of light on the thinking of the most important Nazi figures. *Völkischer Beobachter, Der Stürmer,* or *Das Schwarze Korps,* and other Nazi publications (each major institution had its own) are almost indispensable to this type of research. Similarly in the case of the USSR, the Soviet press, both national and local, is extremely helpful to research on current and past problems. Thus *Partiinaya zhizn,* the party journal, reflects many of the current problems faced by the leadership; *Kommunist* gives the ideological flavor; *Voprosy ekonomiki* discusses economic matters; *Vedomosti verkhovnogo soveta SSSR* gives texts of official decrees, etc.; not to mention *Pravda* and *Izvestiya* for day-to-day coverage. The list of available publications runs into many tens. Party congresses and conferences, compiled in lengthy stenographic reports, are invaluable for research not only on the party but on the state and economy. One could stretch such lists ad infinitum, but the above should suffice as a preliminary guide for a student undertaking serious study of the totalitarian problem.

Such research and analysis will, of course, benefit from available studies of totalitarianism, and the number of such studies in English is rapidly multiplying. Remarkably few of them, however, have attempted to undertake a broad synthesis of the problem in terms of the admittedly distinct experience of the Fascist-Nazi and the Communist experiments.

An able effort to do so was made some years ago by S. Neumann in his *Permanent Revolution* (1942), a book still deserving of close scrutiny by a student of totalitarianism. In it Neumann undertakes to detect the unifying element of such varying systems as the Nazi and the Soviet and finds it in the permanent revolution. A more recent undertaking is that of the collective volume on *Totalitarianism* (1954; recently reissued in paperback), edited by C. J. Friedrich, consisting of a series of papers presented at a conference of the American Academy of Arts and Sciences in March 1953. The authors include H. Arendt, R. Bauer, C. J. Friedrich, A. Inkeles, G. Kennan, H. D. Lasswell, and other authorities, and a specific effort is made to consider the totalitarian problem in its entirety. Insofar as more general theoretical works on the rise of totalitarianism are concerned, one must mention H. Arendt's challenging and stimulating volume, *The Origins of Totalitarianism* (1951), as well as J. Talmon's very scholarly, although controversial, *Totalitarian Democracy* (1952). Both try to find the meaning of totalitarianism in terms of certain intellectual traditions of the Western experience.

There are more books available on specific totalitarian systems, both from the institutional-operational and the theoretical standpoint. M. Fainsod's treatment, in his *How Russia Is Ruled* (1953), of party controls in Soviet institutions is the outstanding study of Soviet totalitarianism in action; its revised edition (1963) has been an invaluable guide through the mazes of post-Stalin Soviet politics. Helpful also for the same guidance are the volumes by W. Leonhard, *The Kremlin since Stalin* (1962), and B. Meissner, *Russland unter Chrushchow* (1960). I have also found useful J. N. Hazard, *The Soviet System of Government* (1964), and the collections of studies edited by P. E. Mosely (*The Soviet Union, 1922–1962,* 1963) and by A. Brumberg (*Russia under Khrushchev,* 1962). B. Moore's *Soviet Politics — The Dilemma of Power* (1950) is a well-documented and thoughtful analysis of the relation between theory and practice in the development of the Soviet system. His later *Terror and Progress — USSR* (1954) is a model of reflective consideration of projected trends of political development. W. Kulski's *The Soviet Regime* (1954), an encyclopedic collection of basic data, casts light on almost every facet of life under that system. J. Towster's *Political Power in the USSR* (1948) has useful material on the institutional development of the USSR, while Z. K. Brzezinski's *Permanent Purge — Politics in Soviet Totalitarianism* (1956) analyzes the political process in totalitarianism as manifested in the party purges, with particular emphasis on the experiences under Stalin. Insofar as the historical aspects of the USSR are concerned, one might suggest E. H. Carr's monumental, even though somewhat doctrinaire, volumes on *The Bolshevik Revolution* (1951–

1954); R. Pipes's *The Formation of the Soviet Union* (1954, 1964), dealing particularly with Soviet absorption of the Central Asian and Caucasian regions, as well as N. S. Timasheff's *The Great Retreat* (1946), written under the impact of wartime compromises in Soviet policies. In terms of biographical studies which cover the working of totalitarian dictatorship, one may well refer to L. Fischer's and S. T. Possony's 1964 studies of Lenin. For Stalin, I. Deutscher's and B. Souvarine's volumes, both entitled *Stalin* (1949 and 1939 respectively), as well as B. D. Wolfe's (see below), are still useful. Students of Soviet affairs can also take advantage of a number of scholarly journals, devoted almost exclusively to the study of communism. Leading among them are *Problems of Communism, The Slavic Review, The Russian Review,* as well as *Current Digest of the Soviet Press,* an excellent source for Soviet material.

Comparatively thorough treatment of the Nazi system is to be found in F. Neumann's *Behemoth* (1942) and in E. Fraenkel's *The Dual State — A Contribution to the Theory of Dictatorship* (1941); the latter focuses on the persistence of a complex legal order in spite of the arbitrary action emanating from the totalitarian leadership. A UNESCO study, edited by M. Baumont, *The Third Reich* (1955), is the most recent attempt to discuss the nature and institutions of the Nazi system, but on the whole it suffers from inadequate documentary research and fails to utilize, among other things, sociological tools of analysis. For the early phase, the volumes (in German) by Bracher and Bracher-Sauer-Schulz provide a searching interpretation, based upon thorough documentation (see bibl.). Mention might also be made of W. Shirer's overrated *The Rise and Fall of the Third Reich* (1960). Important for the international aspects is *Hitler's Europe,* edited by A. and V. Toynbee (1954). Biographical studies, which are in fact historical surveys of the regime focused on the person of the dictator, are useful for a better understanding of the Nazi system: outstanding among them are A. Bullock's *Hitler — A Study of Tyranny* (1952), to which must now be added the as yet untranslated participant-observer interpretation by H. B. Gisevius (1963). Insofar as Italy is concerned, there is a great need for further work to supplement the earlier studies. However, Salvatorelli's standard history (1952, in Italian) is a good guide.

One should mention in addition works dealing with some other dictatorial and totalitarian regimes, such as the Chinese, the satellite, or the Argentinian before 1955. Literature on them is increasing both in volume and quality. Besides the earlier studies by B. Schwartz (1951) and R. L. Walker (1955), we now have the illuminating books by J. Lifton, J. W. Lewis, and P. S. Tang (see bibl.). H. Blanksten, in his

Peron's Argentina (1953), gives an early assessment of the then-budding Argentinian totalitarianism. F. Borkenau's *European Communism* (1953) deals more broadly with communist totalitarian movements in Europe, as does M. Einaudi in his *Communism in Western Europe* (1951). Similar studies are available, or are being prepared, on other regimes. An excellent comparative study is Z. K. Bzrezinski's *The Soviet Bloc* (1960), with broad-ranging bibliographical references. His *Ideology and Power in Soviet Politics* (1962) serves to bring the interested reader up to date on the views of my former coauthor.

Problems of theory, in terms of specific totalitarian regimes, also come in for their due share of consideration. Naturally, there is no substitute for the original works: the Marxist classics of Marx, Engels, and Lenin. Certainly Stalin and Trotsky are relevant also. Equally important is the work of Mao Tse-tung, now available in four volumes (translated), to which a fifth has been added recently. Similarly, Hitler's *Mein Kampf*, Rosenberg's *Der Mythos dez Zwanzigsten Jahrhunderts* (1930), as well as Mussolini's more limited contributions, call for careful study. There is a great abundance of interpretative works, based on the above, which deal with a number of facets of the respective ideologies. Among the more recent studies, one may point to A. Meyer's *Marxism — The Unity of Theory and Practice* (1954), as well as his *Leninism* (1957), L. Haimson's *The Russian Marxists and the Origins of Bolshevism* (1955), and J. Plamenatz's *German Marxism and Russian Communism* (1954). B. D. Wolfe's *Three Who Made a Revolution* (1948) is a biographical classic on the earlier days of Lenin, Trotsky, and Stalin, and recounts the ideological clashes of the prerevolutionary era. *The Appeals of Communism* (1954), by G. Almond, is an important attempt to relate the role of ideology to the personal viewpoint and experience of party members in several selected countries. Somewhat of that type, but dealing more specifically with Central Europe and written in a literary style of high order, is C. Milosz's *The Captive Mind* (1953), perhaps the best treatment available on the intellectual under communism. The problem of continuity and discontinuity finds exhaustive treatment in the collective volumes *Continuity and Change in Russian and Soviet Thought* (1955), edited by E. J. Simmons, and *The Transformation of Russian Society* (1960), edited by C. E. Black. Needless to add, the above list is highly selective and mentions merely some of the more recent works.

National Socialist ideology, probably because of the inherently primitive nature of its system of thought, has attracted fewer thinkers to a critical exposition of its meaning. An early attempt to understand the essence of Nazism was made by H. Rauschning in his *The Revolution of Nihilism* (1939). R. A. Brady developed a general exposition of Nazism in *The Spirit and Structure of German Fascism* (1937), from a Marxist standpoint. Plessner's *Die Verspätete Nation* (1935, repr. 1959) links ideological to historical considerations. A thorough comparative evaluation of Fascist ideology has recently been put forward by Ernst Nolte, *Der Faschismus in seiner Epoche* (1963). Fascist ideology is also treated in the general works cited previously, and there is an early piece by A. Rocco, *The Political Doctrine of Fascism,* which is rather expository and formal. No over-all, thorough examination and critique of the theoretical tenets of Fascism is available in English.

As we have noted in our book, terror and propaganda occupy a central place in the totalitarian scheme of social reconstruction. Most of the general works cited above do discuss them, although frequently failing to show the inherent connection between them. In addition, one might cite a few selected books dealing with this particular aspect of totalitarianism. Recently, a considerable discussion has been developing over the question as to whether and to what extent it is still possible to speak of "terror" in the Soviet Union and the satellites. The references to what is said about this problem in the text give the necessary indications. A special issue is presented by practices in Communist China. Among personal recollections of Soviet prisons and camps, the following may be suggested: G. Herling, *A World Apart* (1952); J. Gliksman, *Tell the West* (1948); A. Weissberg, *The Accused* (1951); F. Beck and W. Godin, *Russian Purge and Extraction of Confession* (1951). The first two deal with Soviet camps, the latter two essentially with prisons. Accounts of released German prisoners confirm the pattern of life as presented in these reminiscences. They have been implemented by some remarkable Soviet literary works, such as Dudintsev's and Solzhenitsin's. Some more specific aspects of Soviet terror are treated in the gripping accounts of the Katyn massacre of 4000 Polish officers by J. Mackiewicz in *The Katyn Wood Murders* (1951); Z. Stypulkowski in his *Invitation to Moscow* (1951) tells the story of Soviet brainwashing in preparation for a Moscow show trial; N. Leites and E. Berhaut, in *The Ritual of Liquidation* (1954), analyze fully the confessions of the great trials in the thirties; while D. Dallin's *Soviet Espionage* (1955) gives a thorough treatment of that aspect of Soviet operations. An official study of Soviet forced labor is to be found in the report edited by R. N. Baldwin in 1953, entitled *A New Slavery — Forced Labor: The Communist Betrayal of Human Rights* (1953); while A. Inkeles together with R. A. Bauer assessed the penumbra created for the average man in their highly informative *The Soviet Citizen* (1959). Earlier, Inkeles gave a thorough description of Soviet propaganda in his *Public Opinion in Soviet Russia*

(1950), covering radio, press, and oral indoctrination. The process of remaking the Soviet man, including his training, finds coverage in R. A. Bauer's *The New Man in Soviet Psychology* (1951) and in K. Mehnert's *Soviet Man and His World* (1961).

The German equivalent for the above, apart from the general works cited previously, is considerable. First of all, most of the governments of wartime occupied countries published detailed accounts of the atrocities committed in them. In addition to these, we may recommend E. Kogon's excellent study of the concentration-camp system, somewhat overtitled as *The Theory and Practice of Hell* (1950). For sociological aspects of the same problem, consult *Human Behavior in the Concentration Camp* (1953), written by a Dutch psychiatrist, E. Cohen, on the basis of personal experience in the camps. A general treatment of Nazi terror and atrocities is to be found in the *Scourge of the Swastika* (1954) by Lord Russell. As one of the many accounts of personal experiences, we can recommend the recollections of a Jewish girl who wrote, under the name of Ka-tzetnik 135633 (the number tattooed on her), a stirring indictment entitled *House of Dolls* (1955). Even more moving is Anne Frank's *The Diary of a Young Girl*. Nazi propaganda operations are described in D. Sington and A. Weidenfeld, *The Goebbels Experiment — A Study of the Nazi Propaganda Machine* (1943), while an "inside" look can be had from the Goebbels and Dietrich diaries. A worth-while study on the fifth column is *The German Fifth Column during the Second World War* (1956), by L. de Jong.

The problem of the armed forces under a totalitarian regime is given a historical survey in F. D. White's *The Growth of the Red Army* (1944), while the specific matter of political and police controls is summarized in a series of accounts by Soviet officers in Z. K. Brzezinski's *Political Controls in the Soviet Army* (1954). Ideology and strategy are discussed fully in D. Garthoff's *Soviet Military Doctrine* (1954) and his later *Soviet Strategy in the Nuclear Age* (1958). The relationship of the German army to Nazi totalitarianism is given detailed treatment in J. Wheeler-Bennett's *The Nemesis of Power* (1953) and in T. Taylor's *Sword and Swastika* (1952), both of which add much, though neither is without bias, to the wartime treatment by H. E. Fried, *The Guilt of the German Army* (1942); a broader historical perspective on the problem can be found in G. Craig's *The Politics of the Prussian Army* (1955).

For economic aspects of the totalitarian problem, the older studies by H. Schwartz, *Russia's Soviet Economy* (2nd ed., 1954), N. Jasny, *The Socialized Agriculture of the USSR* (1949), and H. Dinerstein, *Communism and the Russian Peasant* (1955), have been implemented and

to some extent superseded by A. Nove's *The Soviet Economy: An Introduction* (1961) and A. Bergson's *The Real National Income of Soviet
Russia since 1928* (1961). Many special studies cited in the notes have
thrown light on particular aspects. For the National Socialist economy,
we lack thorough studies by economists, though F. Neumann is illuminating. See also G. Reimann, *The Vampire Economy* (1939), M.
Sweezy, *The Structure of the Nazi Economy* (1941), as well as the more
general works.

The problems of resistance have been illumined by works concerned
with the German and Hungarian uprisings, as well as a growing body
of biographical material. Recently, the question of the Catholic Church
and more especially the Vatican's conduct in face of totalitarian regimes
have been highlighted by R. Hochhuth's play *The Deputy* (1963) and
significantly augmented by two thoroughly documented scholarly studies,
one by W. Kolarz on *Religion in the Soviet Union* (1961), the other by
G. Lewy, *The Roman Catholic Church and the Third Reich* (1964).

There have appeared quite a few highly useful collections of papers,
including those edited by Brumberg and Moseley (see above) and W.
Laqueur and L. Labedz, *Polycentrism* (1962). A good many of the
studies included in our references, especially on foreign policy and ideology, could be added to what has been said in these general comments.
In addition, we might suggest that a student of totalitarianism would
benefit by consulting the growing literature on this subject appearing
lately in foreign languages, particularly in French and German and to
a lesser extent in Italian. For instance, among the French studies, we may
point to J. Monnerot's *Sociologie du communisme* (1949), now translated into English, which is an extremely interesting analysis of the
ideological aspects of the problem, although drawing a somewhat forced
analogy between communism as a secular religion and Mohammedanism (see our chapters on ideology). H. Chambre's *Le Marxisme en
Union Sovietique — Ideologie et institutions, leur évolution de 1917 à
nos jours* (1955) is an attempt to consider theory with reference to
practice and points to the instrumental character of Soviet ideology.
C. Bettelheim's detailed *Les Problèmes théoretiques et pratiques de la
planification sovietique* (1951) gives an uncritical review of Soviet planning. R. Aron's *L'Opium des intellectuels* (1955) is a provocative indictment of the intellectuals' response to communism, while J. Lacroix
in his *Marxisme, existentialisme, personnalisme* (1950) discusses criti-
cally the new Soviet man. M. Merleau-Ponty addresses himself specifically to the problem of the purge trials in his *Humanisme et terreur*
(1947). There is also considerable literature in French on fascist totalitarianism. A remarkable study of Nazi leader psychology is F. Bayle,

Psychologie et ethique du National-Socialisme — Etude anthropologique des dirigeants SS (1953). On the whole, available French works tend to emphasize the theoretical and ideological aspects of Fascist and National Socialist totalitarianism, but much of it is rather on the doctrinal side and not in line with more recent thought on totalitarianism. We might mention J. Bainville, *Les Dictatures* (1935), D. Guérin, *Fascisme et grand capital* (6th ed., 1945), A. Rossi, *La Naissance du fascisme* (1938), M. Prélot, *L'Empire fasciste* (1936), and F. L. Ferrari, *Le Regime fasciste italien* (1928). Besides these, two works of a rather unusual cast deserve the attention of the student of totalitarian dictatorship: A. Fabre-Luce, *Histoire de la révolution européenne* (1954), and L. Rougier, *Les Mystiques économiques — Comment on passe des démocraties libérales aux états totalitaires* (1949).

Students wishing to consult German studies beyond those already mentioned will do well to acquaint themselves with the *Zeitschrift für Zeitgeschichte,* published by the Institut für Zeitgeschichte in Munich since 1953 and containing many significant monographs. The same institute has also been publishing special studies. Other pertinent studies in German, as well as in Italian and Russian, can be found in the bibliographical references that follow, and there is no need to recite them here.

BIBLIOGRAPHICAL REFERENCES

These references are arranged alphabetically by authors with the particular reference to the pages grouped by letters in parentheses. The asterisk (*) introduces subsequent references to the entry.

1. Abel, Theodore, *Why Hitler Came into Power*, New York, 1938.
2. Alexandrova, Vera, *A History of Soviet Literature*, New York, 1963. *(a) pp. 108–109. * (b) p. 412.
3. Alton, T. P., *Polish Postwar Economy*, New York, 1955, p. 198.
4. Aristotle, *Politics*, bk. I.
5. Arendt, Hannah, *The Origins of Totalitarianism*, New York, 1951. *(a) *passim*. *(b) *passim*. *(c) esp. pp. 387ff, concerning the role of the secret police; also p. 76 in Friedrich (ref. 112). *(d) p. 130. * (e) p. 400.
6. Arendt, Hannah, *On Revolution*, New York, 1963.
7. Arendt, Hannah, *Eichmann in Jerusalem: A Report on the Banality of Evil*, New York, 1963.
8. Aron, Raymond, *L'Opium des intellectuels*, Paris, 1955. *(a) pp. 315ff. The author argues this case with persuasive insistence for the French Left, whose ideology, or myths, he compares with that of the Right, asking finally whether the age of ideologies is coming to an end. *(b) pt. 1, pp. 15–114, where the *mythes* of the French Left are subjected to a searching critique.
9. Aron, Raymond, *Paix et guerre entre les nations*, Paris, 1962.
10. Aspaturian, V. V. See ref. 224a.
11. Baldwin, Roger N., ed., *A New Slavery — Forced Labor: The Communist Betrayal of Human Rights*, New York, 1953. *(a) *op. cit.* *(b) p. 53. *(c) p. 60.
12. Bauer, Raymond A., *The New Man in Soviet Psychology*, Cambridge, Mass., 1952. See also ref. 130.
13. Beck, Ludwig, *Gegen den Krieg*. A memorandum submitted to Hitler (see also ref. 123).
14. Beloff, Max, *The Foreign Policy of Soviet Russia, 1929–1941*, New York, 1947.
15. Bereday, Brinkmann, et al., *The Changing Soviet School*, Boston, 1960. *(a) *passim*. *(b) pp. 240–270.
16. Bergson, Abram, *The Real National Income of Soviet Russia since 1928*, Cambridge, Mass., 1961. *(a) esp. interesting is ch. 14, "USSR versus USA." *(b) ch. 15.
17. Bergson, Abram, and Simon Kuznets, eds., *Economic Trends in the Soviet Union*, Cambridge, Mass., 1963. *(a) p. 77 (W. Eason). *(b) ch.

390   *Bibliographical References*

5 (D. G. Johnson), esp. at 209–210 where the statistical complications are detailed.

18. Berliner, Joseph S., *Factory and Manager in the USSR*, Cambridge, Mass., 1957. *(a) pp. 312ff. *(b) *passim*, but esp. ch. 18. *(c) chs. 10–12.

19. Berman, Harold J., *Justice in the USSR — An Interpretation of the Soviet Law*, Cambridge, 1950; 2nd ed. 1963. *(a) details the full complexity of totalitarian law; see also ref. 374 (b) p. 56. *(c) p. 327. *(d) pp. 238–247. *(e) p. 377. [p. refs. to 1st ed.]

20. Bettelheim, Bruno, *Dynamics of Prejudice*. New York, 1950.

21. Bienstock, Gregory, S. M. Schwartz, and A. Yugow, *Management in Russian Industry and Agriculture*, London, 1947.

22. Binder, Leonard, *The Ideological Revolution in the Middle East*, New York, 1964. He rates Communist as a "by no means widely popular tendency." pp. 154ff.

23. Bischoff, Ralph F., *Nazi Conquest through German Culture*, Cambridge, Mass., 1942.

24. Bottai, G., *Vent' anni e un giorno*, Rome, 1949, esp. p. 96. See also ref. 120f.

25. Bonhoeffer, Dietrich, *Letters and Papers from Prison*, ed. E. Bethge, trans. R. H. Fuller, London, 1954. See also Ritter (ref. 295b).

26. Borch, Herbert von, *Obrigkeit und Widerstand*, Tübingen, 1954.

27. Borgese, G. A., *Goliath, The March of Fascism*, New York, 1937, pp. 271–344. For a bitter criticism of this tendency, see Ludwig, (ref. 219), p. 231.

28. Borkenau, F., *European Communism*, London, 1953. *(a) *passim*, for a detailed treatment of this period. *(b) p. 288.

29. Bor-Komorowski, General T., *The Secret Army*, London, 1951.

30. Bracher, Karl Dietrich, *Die Aufloesung der Weimarer Republik*, Stuttgart, 1955; 2nd ed. 1957. *(a) ch. 4, esp. pp. 100ff. *(b) pp. 118f. *(c) p. 120.

31. Bracher, Karl Dietrich, and Wolfgang Sauer and Gerhard Schulz, *Die Nationalsozialistische Machtergreifung — Studien zur Errichtung des totalitaeren Machtsystems in Deutschland, 1933–34*, Cologne, 1960. *(a) pp. 4–5, where Bracher accepts our view. See also comments by Schulz, pp. 371ff. *(b) pp. 476ff, esp. 496ff, gives a detailed account, superseding earlier ones (author, Schulz). *(c) *ibid.* *(d) pp. 897ff (Sauer). *(e) ch. 3, secs. 1 and 2, pp. 516ff (Schulz). *(f) pt. 2, ch. 5, sec. 5; pt. 3, ch. 2, sec. 1; pp. 748–749 for the quotation in text. *(g) pp. 748, 750.

32. Brady, R. A., *The Spirit and Structure of Fascism*, New York, 1937.

33. Brant, Stephen, *Der Aufstand, Vorgeschichte, Geschichte und Deutung des 17 Juni 1953*, Stuttgart, 1954.

34. Brecht, Bertold, *Furcht und Elend des III Reiches*, New York, 1945, for a pointed indictment. Unfortunately, the author, as a Communist, fails to draw the obvious parallel with the USSR and the activities of men like Vyshinsky.

35. Brown, Macalister, "Expulsion of German Minorities from Eastern Europe: The Decision at Potsdam and its Background," unpubl. diss., Harvard University, 1952.

36. Brumberg, Abraham, ed., *Russia under Khrushchev: An Anthology,* New York, 1962. *(a) pp. 207ff (Grossmann). *(b) pp. 200ff (Nove), where remedial efforts are described.

37. Brzezinski, Zbigniew K., *The Permanent Purge: Politics in Soviet Totalitarianism,* Cambridge, Mass., 1956. *(a) ch. 9, for a thorough discussion of this conflict. *(b) *ibid.* *(c) *ibid.* *(d) *ibid.* *(e) chs. 4, 5, 6, 7. *(f) *op. cit.,* for a general theoretical treatment, as well as specific Soviet data; see also ref. 120f. *(g) p. 133. (h) ch. 4 for more detail; see also ref. 419b. *(i) p. 216, for quotation cited. *(j) chs. 1, 2, 7. *(k) chs. 5, 8, and app. 2.

38. Brzezinski, Z. K., *The Soviet Bloc — Unity and Conflict,* Cambridge, Mass., 1960. *(a) p. 384. *(b) pp. 92–97. *(c) pp. 284-6. *(d) pp. 124ff, 285–286. *(e) pp. 248ff. *(f) pp. 63–64, 182ff. *(g) ch. 15.

39. Brzezinski, Z. K., *Ideology and Power in Soviet Politics,* New York, 1962. *(a) esp. pp. 97ff. *(b) ch. 5, esp. p. 140.

40. Brzezinski, Z. K., ed., *Political Controls in the Soviet Army,* New York, 1954. *(a) for a detailed treatment. *(b) p. 54 (I. Dmitriev).

41. Bry, Carl Christian, *Verkappte Religionen,* Locham-Munich, 1963 (1st ed., Gotha, 1924).

42. Buchheim, H., *Glaubenskrise im Dritten Reich,* Stuttgart, 1953. *(a) p. 83. *(b) pp. 81–83, for discriminating commentary; see also ref. 239. *(c) pp. 124ff, for this event and its antecedents. *(d) p. 78, for Richtlinien, as summed up. *(e) pp. 13–17, for penetrating comments; see also ref. 148c.

43. Buchheim, H., "Die Organisatorische Entwicklung der Politischen Polizei in Deutschland in den Jahren, 1933-34," *Gutachten des Instituts für Zeitgeschichte,* 1958.

44. Buchheim, H., *Totalitäre Herrschaft — Wesen und Merkmale,* Munich, 1962. *(a) pp. 14, 24.

45. Buhler, N., and S. Zukowski, *Discrimination in Education in the People's Democracies,* New York, 1944, quotation from *Lidove Noviny,* April 27, 1951. This study is a useful handbook on the iniquitous practices followed by the satellite regimes.

46. Bullock, Alan, *Hitler — A Study in Tyranny,* London, 1952. *(a) *passim.* *(b) p. 367; also p. 349. *(c) ch. 9, esp. pp. 469ff. *(d) ch. 18, p. 328, for citation of minutes of Council of Ministers, Sept. 4, 1938. *(e) p. 328. *(f) pp. 680–689. *(g) p. 371ff.

47. Burns, Findley, Jr., "The Roman Catholic Church in Germany and National Socialism," unpubl. seminar report, Harvard University, 1951. *(a) see also ref. 203b. *(b) quotation cited.

48. Camus, Albert, *L'Homme Révolté,* Paris, 1951. *(a) p. 376. (trans. ours).

49. Carr, E. H., *The Bolshevik Revolution, 1917–1923,* 4 vols., New York, 1951–1954. *(a) vol. 4, "The Interregnum." *(b) vol. 4.

50. Case, Clarence Marsh, *Non-Violent Coercion,* New York, 1923.
51. Castellan, Georges, *Le Rearmament clandestin du Reich 1930–35, vue par le Bureau de l'Etat-Major Français,* Paris, 1954.
52. Catlin, G. E. G., *Systematic Politics,* Toronto, 1962.
53. Chalupa, V., *Rise and Development of a Totalitarian State,* Leiden, 1958.
54. Cheng, Chu-yuan, *Communist China's Economy 1949–1962 — Structural Changes and Crisis,* Seton Hall, 1963. *(a) ch. 8; quote on p. 139. *(b) esp. ch. 7. *(c) pp. 37ff. *(d) p. 50; the author offers a useful comparative table showing the retreat to a system of cooperatives (work groups).
55. *Civil Code* (BGB; German), para. 616–618.
56. Clay, Lucius D., *Decision in Germany,* New York, 1950, pp. 358–392. See also ref. 405a.
57. Coulton, Rushborn, ed., *Feudalism in History,* Princeton, 1956.
58. Counts, G. S., and N. Lodge, *I Want To Be Like Stalin,* New York, 1947, translation of a Soviet propaganda textbook on civil training. See also *Il libro della IV classe elementare,* which shows how the Fascists used even the grammar section for propaganda purposes.
59. Crankshaw, Edward, *The New Cold War — Moscow v. Peking,* Penguin Books, 1963.
60. Crowther, J. C., *Industry and Education in Soviet Russia,* London, 1932.
61. Curran, Joseph, *President's Report on the State of the Union,* Sixth National Convention of the National Maritime Union (CIO), Sept. 22, 1947, p. 108, for a case study. See also ref. 323.
62. Czech-Jochberg, E., *Hitler — Eine deutsche Bewegung,* Oldenburg, 1930.
63. Dallin, David J., and Boris I. Nicolaevsky, *Forced Labor in Soviet Russia,* New Haven, 1947, esp. ch. 6. See also ref. 11c.
64. Dallin, David J., *Soviet Foreign Policy after Stalin,* New York, 1961.
65. Danev, A. M., *Narodnoe obrazovanie: Osnovie postanovlenia, prikazy i instruktsii,* Moscow, 1948, p. 123, quoted in Kulski (ref. 189a), pp. 491–492.
66. Daniels, Robert Vincent, *The Conscience of the Revolution: Communist Opposition in Soviet Russia,* Cambridge, Mass., 1960. *(a) *passim.* *(b) esp. chs. 11, 12.
67. Deakin, F. W., *The Brutal Friendship,* London, 1962.
68. Denisov, A. I., *Sovetskoe gosudarstvennoe pravo,* Moscow, 1940, p. 60.
69. De Jong, Louis, *The German Fifth Column in the Second World War,* trans. from the Dutch by C. M. Geyl, Chicago, 1956.
70. Delzell, Charles, *Mussolini's Enemies,* Princeton, 1961.
71. Deutscher, Isaac, *The Prophet Armed,* New York, 1954, p. 158.
72. De Witt, Nicholas, *Soviet Professional Manpower: Its Education, Training and Supply,* Washington, D.C., 1955. *(a) pp. 58–61. (b) chs. 4, 5.
73. Dietrich, Otto, *Zwölf Jahre mit Hitler,* Munich, 1955 (Engl. ed., *Hitler,* Chicago, 1955). (a) *op. cit.* (b) p. 154. (c) trans. ours.
74. Djilas, Milovan, *The New Class,* New York, 1957. *(a) pp. 37–70.

*(b) p. 73. *(c) ch. 2. He builds his argument on the proposition that the bureaucracy constitutes the new class (cf. the so-called "socialist ownership," p. 47).

75. Draper, Theodore, *Castro's Revolution — Myths and Realities,* New York, 1962.

76. Dulles, Allen Welsh, *Germany's Underground,* New York, 1947. (a) p. 136 and elsewhere; see also ref. 302a. (b) see also ref. 302b. (c) pp. 119ff; also ref. 309d. *(d) pp. 175–195.

77. Duncan-Jones, A. S., *The Struggle for Religious Freedom in Germany,* London, 1938; see also ref. 145.

78. Dziewanowski, M. K., *The Communist Party of Poland,* Cambridge, Mass., 1939. *(a) ch. 14. *(b) ch. 13, esp. pp. 249ff. *(c) chs. 10, 11.

79. *Economic Conditions in Germany: A Report for the Department of Overseas Trade,* Washington, D.C., 1936, p. 2.

80. Einaudi, Mario, *Communism in Western Europe,* New York, 1951.

81. Eisenstadt, S. N., *The Political Systems of Empires,* London, 1963. *(a) pp. 15ff, 364f. *(b) pp. 14ff and entire section.

82. Elkins, Stanley M., *Slavery — A Problem in American Institutional and Intellectual Life,* Chicago, 1959.

83. Elliott, William Y., *The Pragmatic Revolt in Politics,* New York, 1928, ch. 4. See also ref. 334.

84. *Encyclopedia Italiana,* Mussolini's essay, quoted by Finer (ref. 95), p. 175, presumably in Finer's translation. (a) *op. cit.* (b) see also Oakeshott (ref. 268).

85. *Encyclopedia of the Social Sciences,* VI, 203ff, article on Feudalism.

86. *Entsiklopedicheskii slovar,* I (Moscow, 1953), 355, figs. for 1936–1951.

87. *Entwurf des Familiengesetzbuches der Deutschen Demokratischen Republik,* Bonn, 1955.

88. Erlich, Alexander, *The Soviet Industrialization Debate, 1924–1928,* Cambridge, Mass., 1960. *(a) see esp. ch. 9. *(b) pt. 1, esp. pp. 24ff. *(c) *passim;* unfortunately, this able analysis does not deal with the organizational and political aspects as such.

89. Fainsod, Merle, *How Russia Is Ruled,* Cambridge, Mass., 1953. *(a) p. 166. *(b) ch. 6, for detailed treatment. *(c) p. 175 (rev. ed.) *(d) p. 529; also *Kommunisticheskoe vospitanie v Sovetskoi shkole,* Moscow, 1950, pp. 313ff. *(e) ch. 9, for a more detailed treatment, in terms of historical outline and organizational pattern. *(f) *passim.* *(g) ch. 13, for a thorough discussion of the Soviet secret police. *(h) pp. 384–387. *(i) p. 152. *(j) pp. 152–180, for a detailed treatment of the growth of party bureaucracy. *(k) p. 329. *(l) p. 341. *(m) p. 436. [The references that follow are to the rev. ed. of this work, 1963.] *(n) p. 522. *(o) p. 175. *(p) p. 450. *(q) p. 452. *(r) pp. 511–512. *(s) pp. 511–513. *(t) pp. 518ff. *(u) pp. 527ff, for details. *(v) pp. 550ff. *(w) pp. 545ff, for a sane assessment. *(x) pp. 555ff. *(y) p. 567 offers a chart to show the full complexity of this structure. *(z) p. 569; on pp. 569–576 Fainsod gives what appears to be a well-balanced assessment of the

tensions in Soviet agriculture. *(aa) pp. 483ff. *(bb) pp. 394ff. *(cc) pp. 403ff.

90. Fainsod, Merle, *Smolensk under Soviet Rule,* Cambridge, Mass., 1958. *(a) ch. 20. *(b) ch. 11 and *passim.* *(c) pp. 67ff, for a detailed account. *(d) pp. 103–105.

91. Fanelli, G. A., *Idee e polemiche per la scuola fascista,* Rome, 1941. See also ref. 95e.

92. Fasoni, I., *Esercito e Milizia, con pensieri di S. E. Mussolini e di S. A. R. il Duce d'Aosta,* Mantua, 1923, p. 14.

93. Fejtö, F., *Behind the Rape of Hungary,* New York, 1957.

94. Field, Mark G., *Doctor and Patient in Soviet Russia,* Cambridge, Mass., 1957, for a good description of the system (quotation is on pp. 174–175).

95. Finer, Herman, *Mussolini's Italy,* New York, 1935. *(a) p. 185. *(b) pp. 175–176. *(c) pp. 180–181. *(d) pp. 471–472. *(e) pp. 475ff. A good recent Italian study on this subject has not been published, but there are interesting sidelights on it in Salvatorelli (ref. 309); among Fascist writings, we note Fanelli (91) and Malfi (225), as well as the study of Gentile, edited by Vettori (367). *(f) esp. pt. 3, for adequate stress on the passion for unanimity. *(g) pp. 321ff. *(h) p. 499, where he says, "the observer of this system cannot escape the impression that the term 'Corpororative' has been used, if not invented, to rouse a sense of wonder in the people, to keep them guessing, to provoke inquiry and to contrive, out of the sheer mystification of an unusual word, at once to hide the compulsion on which the dictatorship finally depends and to suggest that a miraculous work of universal benevolence is in the course of performance." This impression or conclusion of the direct observer was strikingly documented by Salvemini (ref. 310). *(i) pp. 503–504; arts. 7 and 9 of the charter. *(j) art. 3. *(k) p. 506, n. 1.

96. Fischer, Fritz, *Griff nach der Weltherrschaft,* Dusseldorf, 1962.

97. Fischer, Louis, *The Soviets in World Affairs,* 2nd ed., Princeton, 1951; Vintage Books, 1960. See also ref. 106.

98. Fischer, Louis, *The Life of Lenin,* New York, 1964.

98.1 Fischer, Ruth, *Stalin and German Communism,* Cambridge, Mass., 1948.

99. Fischer, George, *Soviet Opposition to Stalin: A Case Study in World War II,* Cambridge, Mass., 1952. *(a) see also Wheeler-Bennett (ref. 385). *(b) for a detailed study.

100. FitzGibbon, Constantine, *20 July,* New York, 1956. See also ref. 302b.

100.1 Flechtheim, O. K., *Die Kommunistische Partei Deutschlands in der Weimarer Republik,* Offenbach, 1948.

101. Forsthoff, Ernst, *Der Totale Staat,* Hamburg, 1934. *(a) p. 17; see also pp. 24 and 38ff, where a nation is defined.

102. Fraenkel, Ernst, *The Dual State — A Contribution to the Theory of Dictatorship,* New York, 1941. *(a) *passim.* *(b) *passim.* *(c) these problems have been made the focal point of this penetrating study of the Hitler regime, though the distinction of a legal and a prerogative state is not identical with that of government and party. The title is

unfortunate, however, since neither the old bureaucracy nor the Nazi Party was, properly speaking, a "state." But the dualism was unquestionably there. *(d) *passim.*

103. Frank, Elke, "The Wilhelmstrasse During the Third Reich: Changes in Organizational Structure and Personal Policies," unpubl. diss., Harvard University, 1963. *(a) The author shows on the basis of extensive archical research how very minor purges were effected in connection with policy shifts. *(b) gives fascinating detail regarding this process. *(c) *passim* shows the cross currents of factional rivalries.

104. Friedrich, Carl J., *Constitutional Government and Democracy,* Boston, 1950. *(a) ch. 9, "The Constitution as a Political Force." *(b) p. 419; Lasswell's definition (ref. 195, p. 169) is inapplicable to the totalitarian party altogether, since it stresses the formulating of issues and elections. Weber's definition is found in *Wirtschaft und Gesellschaft* (380), p. 167. *(c) pp. 548ff, for greater detail and the literature cited there. *(d) pp. 564ff. *(e) ch. 2, a development of Weber's conception; see also ref. 380b. *(f) pp. 652ff; see also ref. 137. *(g) ch. 23, for further discussion of the problems and experiences of democratic planning. *(h) ch. 22, esp. the literature cited there. *(i) chs. 2, 19. *(j) esp. chs. 7–9. *(k) ch. 24. *(l) ch. 7.

105. Friedrich, C. J., *The Philosophy of Law in Historical Perspective,* Chicago, 1950; 2nd ed. 1963. *(a) ch. 8. *(b) ch. 4. *(c) ch. 22. *(d) pp. 176ff and app. 2.

106. Friedrich, C. J., *Foreign Policy in the Making,* New York, 1938, for an early assessment; see also Beloff (ref. 14) and Fischer (ref. 97).

107. Friedrich, C. J., *The New Image of the Common Man,* Boston, 1951. *(a) ch. 3. All attempts to define propaganda in terms of the content of the communications or the psychological effect tend to obscure these crucial political features. Ch. 3 explores the implications of these insights for democratic theory. *(b) ch. 3, for this problem in its broadest aspects. *(c) esp. the prologue.

108. Friedrich, C. J., *Constitutional Reason of State,* Providence, 1957. *(a) see ch. 2.

109. Friedrich, C. J., *Puerto Rico — Middle Road to Freedom,* New York, 1959.

110. Friedrich, C. J., *Man and His Government,* New York, 1963. *(a) ch. 9. *(b) ch. 18. *(c) ch. 28. *(d) ch. 4. *(e) ch. 5 offers a general theory of utopias. *(f) at pp. 95ff. I have given a general analysis of the political myth and its functions, and pointed out the particular importance of the founder myth. *(g) ch. 14, for the basic problem. *(h) ch. 1, esp. pp. 6ff. *(i) ch. 10, esp. pp. 188ff, outlines such a typology. *(j) ch. 30, for further detail and refs. *(k) ch. 13. *(l) n. 1, pp. 24–27. *(m) ch. 12; see also ref. 431 (*Nomos,* vol. 1).

111. Friedrich, C. J., *Transcendent Justice — The Religious Dimension of Constitutionalism,* Durham, 1964. *(a) *passim.*

112. Friedrich, C. J., ed., *Totalitarianism,* Cambridge, Mass., 1954. *(a)

H. Arendt, p. 76. *(b) P. Kecskemeti, pp. 345–360, for interesting, if somewhat contrasting, discussion. *(c) J. Gliksman, pp. 60–74. *(d) pp. 274–275; see also ref. 412d. *(e) H. D. Lasswell, p. 367. *(f) J. P. Nettl, pp. 296–307; see also ref. 260. *(g) H. J. Muller, pp. 232–244, primarily concerned with the Lysenko case. *(h) G. de Santillana, pp. 224–262. *(i) A. Gyorgy, pp. 381ff, does not share this view. *(j) P. Kecskemeti, pp. 345–360, where the decline of the revolution as a form of political action has been argued persuasively on purely observational grounds. The reason for revolution's becoming "an extinct political form" appears to be the weapons monopoly. *(k) p. 359. *(l) H. D. Lasswell, pp. 360–372, deems probable the emergence of a world of one or more "garrison states." In the course of his analysis he qualifies his former concept of the garrison state and introduces that of a garrison police state that is, in effect, a totalitarian dictatorship. The only alternative he allows is that of a world federation of constitutional democracies; the continuation of something like the present situation he does not include among his alternatives. *(m) P. Kecskemeti, p. 360.

113. Friedrich, C. J., and associates, *The Soviet Zone of Germany,* printed as a manuscript by the Human Relations Area Files, Yale University, 1956.

114. Fritz, Kurt von. See ref. 405 (*Antike und Abendland*).

115. Galbraith, J. K., *U.S. Bombing Survey,* Washington, D.C., 1946.

116. Garthoff, Raymond, *Soviet Strategy in the Nuclear Age,* New York, 1958.

117. Geiger, H. K., *The Urban Slavic Family and the Soviet System,* unpubl. diss., Harvard University, 1954.

118. Gentile, Giovanni, *Genesi e strutturi della societá,* Florence, 1936.

119. *German Foreign Policy, Documents on,* Series D, vol. 1, 1949, esp. pp. 940ff.

120. Germino, Dante, *The Italian Fascist Party in Power — A Study in Totalitarian Rule,* 1959. *(a) p. 136. *(b) p. 128; the view is found in his thesis, p. 57, but not in his book. *(c) chs. 1 and 2, for detailed analysis based entirely on Italian materials. The Opera Nazionale Fascists was subdivided according to the several age groups into the sons and daughters of the wolf (Figli and Figlie della Lupa), the Balilla and Piccole Italiane, the Avanguardisti and Giovane Italiane (14–18), the Giovani Fascisti and Fasciste (18–21); besides there were the Gruppi Universitari Fascisti (18–28). *(d) trans. from *Regime fascista* (see 446b). *(e) pp. 110–117. *(f) esp. pp. 56ff, regarding the "Changes of the Guard." *(g) see also D. A. Binchy, *Church and State in Fascist Italy,* London, 1941, and A. C. Jemolo, *Chiesa e stato in Italia negli ultimi cento anni,* Turin, 1954. *(h) we are indebted to Germino for this evaluation of the Italian situation. See also E. Canevari, *La Guerra Italiana,* Rome, 1949, and Q. Armellini, *La Crisi dell' esercito,* Rome, 1946.

121. Gilbert, Felix, *Adolf Hitler,* New York, 1950.

122. Gilbert, G. M., *The Psychology of Dictatorship, Based on Examination of the Leaders of Nazi Germany,* New York, 1950. *(a) pp. 300ff. *(b)

Gilbert suggests this point on p. 301, when he expresses the opinion that the war would have been avoided. Nolte (ref. 266) overstates this position, by declaring that the subleaders were found to be "better men than most people in the rest of the world had assumed" (p. 484).

123. Gisevius, H. B., *Adolf Hitler*, Munich, 1963. *(a) ch. 6, esp. pp. 424ff. *(b) *passim* and ch. 8. *(c) pp. 517ff. *(d) *passim*.

124. Gliksman, Jerzy G., *Tell the West*, New York, 1948. See also ref. 144.

125. *The Goebbels Diaries*, trans. and ed. Louis Lochner, London, 1948. *(a) p. 519. *(b) *passim*. *(c) see ref. 150h.

126. Glum, Friedrich, *Philosophen im Spiegel und Zerrspiegel — Deutschlands Weg in den Nationalsozialismus*, Munich, 1954. For Fichte, see pp. 79–103; for Hegel, pp. 104–133.

127. Granzow, Brigitte, *A Mirror of Nazism: British Opinion and the Emergence of Hitler, 1929–1933*, London, 1964. *(a) intro. by Bernard Crick. *(b) *passim* and p. 231.

128. Greene, William C., "Platonism and its Critics," *Harvard Studies in Classical Philology*, vol. 61, Cambridge, Mass., 1953. See also ref. 284.

129. Griffith, William E., *The Sino-Soviet Rift*, Cambridge, Mass., 1964.

130. Grundel, E. G., *Die Sendung der jungen Generation*, Munich, 1932, esp. pp. 327ff. The literature on these several kinds of "new man" is considerable. For critical perspective, see Bauer (ref. 12); also Leites (ref. 201), esp. chs. 4–9.

131. Gurian, Waldemar, *Hitler and the Christians*, New York, 1936. See also ref. 145.

132. Gustavson, Arfved, *Die Katakombenkirche*, Stuttgart, 1964.

133. Hallgarten, George W. F., *Why Dictators? The Causes and Forms of Tyrannical Rule since 600 B.C.* New York, 1954. This study, in contrast to ours, explores what totalitarian dictatorship has in common with former "tyrannies."

133.1. Harnack, Adolf von, *History of Dogma*, trans. from the 3rd German ed., 1961 (Dover), vol. 2.

134. Harper, Samuel N., *Civic Training in Soviet Russia*, Chicago, 1929.

135. Harris, Seymour E., *Economic Planning*, New York, 1949, ch. 2; Harris does not give attention to the authoritarian quality of this "plan," since he generally fails to differentiate between democratic and autocratic planning.

136. Hartshorne, Edward Y., *The German Universities and National Socialism*, Cambridge, Mass., 1937.

137. Hayek, Friedrich A., *The Road to Serfdom*, Chicago, 1944.

138. Hazard, John N., *The Soviet System of Government*, Chicago, 3rd ed. 1964.

139. Heberle, Rudolf, *From Democracy to Nazism*, Baton Rouge, 1945.

140. Heberle, Rudolf, *Landbevölkerung und Nationalsozialismus*, Stuttgart, 1963.

141. Heimann, Eduard, *Vernunftglauben und Religion in der modernen Gesellschaft*, Tübingen, 1955, p. 160; apart from this point, Heimann's

brilliant analysis of Marxist "theocracy" largely fits our presentation here. See also Schwartz (ref. 320).

142. Henderson, Sir Nevile, *The Failure of a Mission*, New York, 1940. *(a) p. 282. *(b) pp. 258–301.

143. Hensley, Francis H., *Hitler's Strategy*, Cambridge, Eng., 1951, pp. 238–239.

144. Herling, G., *A World Apart*, trans. Joseph Marek, New York, 1951.

145. Hermelink, Heinrich, *Kirche im Kampf: Dokumente des Widerstands und des Aufbaus . . . 1933–1945*, Tübingen, 1950, p. 499. The literature has become fairly extensive, e.g., Gurian (ref. 131), Duncan-Jones (77), Micklem (249); for documents, Jannasch (163). Our interpretation was materially aided by a study made in our Harvard seminar by Parker D. Wyman in 1952, "The Protestant Churches of Germany and National Socialism" (unpubl.).

145.1. Hersch, Jeanne, *Idéologies et réalité*, Paris, 1956.

146. Heuss, Theodor, *Hitlers Weg — Eine historische-politische Studie über den Nationalsozialismus*, Stuttgart, 1932.

147. Hippel, Fritz von, *Die Perversion von Rechtsordnungen*, Tübingen, 1955.

148. Hitler, Adolf, *Mein Kampf*, Munich, 1925–1927. *(a) pp. 109ff. *(b) p. 234; in Hitler's text, the whole first passage is italicized, but in our view it is the second that deserves special emphasis. Trans. is ours. *(c) pp. 293, 316, 418, and the penetrating comments by Buchheim (42), pp. 13–17, who shows that Hitler drew a sharp contrast between "Programmatiker" and "Politiker," between the theorist and the politician, and that in the end the politician wins out because only he can "from the realm of the eternally-true and the ideal take that which is humanly possible and let it take form." Here the pragmatic utilitarian conception of truth is particularly striking; cf. Jaspers (ref. 164). *(d) pp. 428ff.

149. Hitler, Adolf, *My Battle*, trans. E. T. S. Dugdale, Boston, 1933. *(a) p. 24. *(b) p. 25. *(c) pp. 75–81.

150. *Hitler's Secret Conversations, 1941–1944*, ed. H. R. Trevor-Roper, New York, 1953. *(a) *passim*. *(b) *passim*. *(c) pp. 341–342. *(d) pp. 389–390; see also ref. 152b. *(e) pp. 117–118; see also ref. 152c. *(f) pp. 74–75, 448–451. *(g) pp. 447–448. Hitler's comments in *Tischgespräche* (152), pp. 370–375, show that he considered the concordat "eigentlich hinfällig" (actually invalid) and intended to proceed against the church after the war; see also pp. 355–357. *(h) pp. 69–71; see also ref. 152f. There also appeared a German edition, not as complete as the English (see next ref.). *(i) pp. 83–87.

151. *Hitlers Zweites Buch — Ein Dokument aus dem Jahr 1928*, intro. and notes by G. L. Weinberg, Stuttgart, 1961.

152. Hitler, Adolf, *Tischgespräche*, ed. H. Picker, Bonn, 1951. *(a) chs. 4–7. *(b) p. 128; see also ref. 150d. *(c) pp. 339ff; see also ref. 150c. *(d) p. 349. *(e) pp. 370–375. *(f) "Science is nothing but a ladder which one climbs. With each rung one sees a bit further" (p. 340); "In the

subconscious everyone has a sense of limits of human power" (p. 341); "One understands that man has the ability to understand these laws [the laws of nature]. Then one must become humble" (p. 352); see also pp. 344–345 and ref. 150f.

153. Hitler, Adolf, *Le Testament politique de Hitler — Notes recueillies par Martin Bormann,* ed. F. Genoud, Paris, 1959. *(a) p. 88. See also a reiteration of his racist ideology, pp. 78ff, ending with the statement, "L'abces juif, nous l'avons crevé comme les autres."

154. Hitler, Adolf, *Speeches, April 1922–August 1939,* trans. and ed. Norman H. Baynes, Oxford, 1942.

155. Hochhuth, Rolf, *Der Stellvertreter* (The Deputy), Reinbek bei Hamburg, 1963. *(a) intro. *(b) see also the interesting collection of comments, published under the title *Summa Injuria,* Reinbek bei Hamburg, 1963.

156. Hodgman, Donald R., *Soviet Industrial Production, 1928–1951,* Cambridge, Mass., 1954.

157. Holzman, Franklin D., *Soviet Taxation: The Fiscal and Monetary Problems of a Planned Economy,* Cambridge, Mass., 1955.

158. Homans, George C., *English Villagers of the Thirteenth Century,* Cambridge, Mass., 1941, for a recent and detailed analysis of the peasantry in the middle ages. How unrelated these idealized images are to the actual reality has often been pointed out.

159. *Il Consiglio di Stato nel quinquennio 1936–1940. Relazione al Duce del Fascismo Capo del Governo,* 2 vols., Rome, 1942, for the major decisions of the Consiglio di Stato during Fascism's most totalitarian period. The Consiglio di Stato not only continued under the Italian Republic, but its personnel remained virtually identical with that under the Fascists.

160. Inkeles, Alex, *Public Opinion in Soviet Russia,* Cambridge, Mass., 1950, 1958. *(a) for a thorough analysis of the institutions and operations of Soviet propaganda and agitation. *(b) p. 275. *(c) p. 248. *(d) p. 333.

161. Inkeles, Alex, and Raymond A. Bauer, *The Soviet Citizen — Daily Life in a Totalitarian Society,* Cambridge, Mass., 1959. *(a) ch. 19. *(b) pp. 185–186; see also ref. 339. *(c) pp. 179, 187. *(d) ch. 6 provides a very good, general survey of this field. *(e) pp. 136ff. *(f) pp. 132ff. *(g) chs. 11 and 14, where the phenomena of hostility and political cleavage are discussed. *(h) ch. 15. *(i) chs. 8–9, for a general assessment of family policy; hostility is discussed in ch. 11. *(j) p. 230. *(k) pp. 280–281 claim that "religion has much less hold on the population." *(m) pt. 3, esp. ch. 10.

162. International Military Tribunal. *(a) see testimony of Speer. *(b) Hans Frick trial data: I, 24, 27, 72, 298–301; XXII, 544–547, etc.

163. Jannasch, W., *Deutsche Kirchendokuments: Die Haltung der Bekennenden Kirche im Dritten Reich,* Zurich, 1946; see also ref. 145.

164. Jaspers, Karl, *Die Wahrheit,* Bonn, 1953; see also ref. 148c.

165. Jong, Louis de. See ref. 69.

166. Jollos-Mazzuchetti, Lavinia, ed., *Die Andere Achse, Italienische Reistenza und geistiges Deutschland*, Hamburg, 1964.

167. Katkoff, V., *The Soviet Economy, 1940–1960*, Baltimore, 1961. *(a) 1958 figures, p. 154.

168. Karski, J., *The Story of a Secret State*, Boston, 1943. *(a) *passim*. *(b) ch. 11; also contains quoted statement about Polish resistance.

169. Kautsky, John H., *The Political Thought of Karl Kautsky — A Theory of Democratic, Anti-Communist Marxism*, unpubl. diss., Harvard University, 1951.

170. Kautsky, Karl, *Parlamentarisum und Demokratie*, Stuttgart, 3rd ed. 1920. *Das Erfurter Programm*, Stuttgart, 9th ed. 1908.

171. Kennan, George F., *Russia and the West under Lenin and Stalin*, Boston, 1961.

172. Kennan, George F., *On Dealing with the Communist World*, New York, 1964. *(a) ch. 3. *(b) ch. 1 contains a roseate view of the potentialities of coexistence. *(c) *passim*.

173. Kecskemeti, Paul, *The Unexpected Revolution — Social Forces in the Hungarian Uprising*, Stanford, 1961. *(a) *passim;* quotation on p. 151.

174. Khrushchev, Nikita, Secret Speech to the Twentieth Congress, 1956, in *The Anti-Stalin Campaign and International Communism*, ed. Russian Institute, Columbia University, New York, 1956, pp. 1–90. (b) "For a Close Link Between Literature and Art and the Life of the People," *Kommunist*, no. 12, 1957.

175. Kirkpatrick, Jeane J., ed., *The Strategy of Deception: A Study in World-Wide Communist Tactics*, New York, 1963. Esp. valuable are the intro. and chs. by Walker and Duchacek.

176. König, Rene, *Materialien zur Soziologie der Familie*, Bern, 1946, esp. pp. 165–179. See also ref. 259.

177. Koestler, Arthur, *Darkness at Noon*, New York, 1951. See also ref. 178.

178. Kogon, Eugene, *Der SS — Stat — Das System der Deutschen Konzentrationslager*, Berlin, 1946. (Abbr. Engl. ed., *The Theory and Practice of Hell: The German Concentration Camps and the System Behind Them*, London 1950.) See also Rousset (ref. 304). Important also are the various novelistic accounts contained in the works of writers such as Koestler, Silone, Sengers. Their portrayal was confirmed by what was found in the camps after the war and what was brought forward in the trials of criminals, both war and other.

179. Kohn, Hans, *Panslavism — Its History and Ideology*, Bloomington, 1953.

180. Kohn, Hans, *Revolutions and Dictatorshps*, Cambridge, Mass., 1939, pp. 200–210.

181. Kolarz, Walter, *Religion in the Soviet Union*, New York, 1961. *(a) This carefully documented study bears out our general position; see also ref. 132. *(b) pp. 93ff. *(c) chs. 6–9, 10; space does not permit summarizing these complex relations. *(d) p. 480; see entire ch. on the future of religion. *(e) ch. 13.

182. Kolnay, Aurel, *The War Against the West*, New York, 1938.

183. *KPSS v rezolyutsiyakh i resheniyakh syezdov, konferentsii i plenumov Tsk* (resolutions and decrees of the Central Committee) vol. 3, Moscow, 1954. *(a) pp. 437–474. *(b) 495–501.

184. *Kommunisticheskoe vospitanie v sovetskoi shkole*, Moscow, 1950, pp. 313ff. See also ref. 89d.

185. Korbonski, S., *W. Imieniu Rzeczypospolitej*, Paris, 1954. *(a) for a complete account by one of its political chiefs, the head of the Directorate of Civil Resistance. *(b) *op. cit.*

186. Kozhneznikov, F. I., *Mezhdunarodnoe pravo* (International Law), for the Academy of Sciences of the USSR, 1957. *(a) p. 7, for the definition.

187. Kramer, G. G., in *The Third Reich* (UNESCO), New York, 1955, ch. 18.

188. Krausnick, Helmut, "Vorgeschichte und Beginn des militaerischen Widerstandes" in *Die Vollmacht des Gewissens*, Tübingen, 1956.

189. Kulski, Wladyslaw W., *The Soviet Regime*, Syracuse, 1954. *(a) Danev quote, pp. 491–492. *(b) p. 513. *(c) quote from *Voprosy trudovovo prava*, p. 414. *(d) p. 319. The official rate of exchange was then four rubles to a dollar. The purchasing power, however, ranges somewhere between ten to forty rubles to a dollar.

190. Labedz, Leopold, ed., *Revisionism — Essays on the History of Marxist Ideas*, New York, 1962. *(a) offers very stimulating essays on the evolution of revisionism from Bernstein to the "New Left." *(b) chs. 16, 17.

191. Laffan, Robert G. D., *The Crisis over Czechoslovakia*, London, 1938, for the progress of negotiations; see also ref. 151.

192. Lange, M. G., *Totalitäre Erziehung*, Frankfurt, 1954. *(a) p. 30. *(b) pp. 39ff, where this law is discussed.

193. Laqueur, Walter, and Leopold Labedz, eds., *Polycentrism*, New York, 1962. *(a) p. 5 (Laqueur). *(b) p. 19 (Croan).

194. Laski, Harold, *Reflections on the Revolutions of Our Time*, New York, 1943.

195. Lasswell, Harold D., and Abraham Kaplan, *Power and Society*, New Haven, 1950. *(a) para. 3.1, 6.1, 6.3. For the meaning of myth and symbol, see our text, ch. 7, where the views of Parsons and Lasswell are further discussed. *(b) p. 103. *(c) p. 159; see also ref. 104b.

196. Lasswell, Harold, and Dorothy Blumenstock, *World Revolutionary Propaganda*, New York, 1939. *(a) chs. 7, 8. *(b) ch. 1.

197. Leber, Annedore, *Das Gewissen steht auf — Lebensbilder aus deutschen Widerstand, 1933–1945*, Berlin, 1954. *(a) see ref. 169b. *(b) see ref. 295b. It is worth observing how many of the leaders of the political resistance were basically motivated by religious convictions; this striking fact is convincingly documented here. *(c) p. 126.

198. Lederer, Emil, *The State of the Masses*, New York, 1940. *(a) esp. chs. 4 and 5, where the delusion of a classless society in the Marxist sense is shown to be the basis for totalitarianism.

199. Leibholz, Gerhard, *Der Strukturwandel der Modernen Demokratie*, 1952.

He agrees with us that totalitarian dictatorship is the most significant political phenomenon of the twentieth century.

200. Leites, Nathan C., and E. Bernaut, *Ritual of Liquidation: The Case of the Moscow Trials.* Glencoe, 1954, for a thorough study.
201. Leites, Nathan C., *A Study of Bolshevism,* Glencoe, 1953. *(a) p. 24. "The party aims at a radical transformation of the world." The study is based upon such a concept of ideology, or rather that aspect of it which Leites calls its "operational code." *(b) chs. 4–9; see also ref. 130.
202. Lemkin, Raphaël, *Axis Rule in Occupied Europe,* New York, 1944, pp. 15ff.
203. Lenin, V. I. *Sochineniya* (Works), Moscow, 3rd ed. 1935. *(a) XXIV, 293. *(b) XVIII, 296. *(c) XVIII, 443–444. *(d) IV, 468. *(e) 4th ed., XII, 143.
204. Lenin, V. I., *Revolutionary Army and Revolutionary Government—1905,* New York, 1943, III, 313.
205. Lenin, V. I., *Selected Works,* 12 vols., New York, 1943. *(a) "State and Revolution," VII, 24. *(b) "Revolutionary Army and Revolutionary Government," III, 313. *(c) "War and Peace," VII, 297. *(d) "Proletarian Revolution and Renegade Kautsky," VII, 123. *(e) "What Is To Be Done?" II, 152. *(f) speech to the Seventh Congress, 1918, VIII, 318. *(g) IX, 70. *(h) "Socialism and Religion," XI, 658. *(i) "To the Rural Poor," II, 281.
206. Lenin, V. I., *Uber den Parteiaufbau,* Berlin, 1958. This interesting collection of speeches and papers by Lenin was first published in Russian.
207. Lenin, V. I., *Russische Korrespondenz,* 3 vols., no date. *(a) II, 638, 982.
208. *Leninsko-Stalinskii Komsomol—Vernyi pomoshchnik i boevoi rezerv Kommunisticheskoi Partii,* Moscow, 1952, for a Soviet account.
209. Leonhard, Wolfgang, *The Kremlin since Stalin,* New York, 1962 (Ger. ed., 1959). *(a) pp. 506–507. *(b) pp. 246ff. *(c) pp. 279ff, 295ff. *(d) pp. 363ff. *(e) pp. 12ff. *(f) pp. 504ff. He here puts it in terms of modernization rather than liberalization. *(g) pp. 506ff. He suggests that there are five "pillars" of the regime, with the party predominant.
210. Lepeshkin, A. I., "The Notion of the Constitution: Role and Significance of the Constitution of the USSR for the Political Life of Society," unpubl. paper contributed to the *Freudenstadt Round Table of IPSA,* September 1962.
211. Lerner, D., *The Nazi Elite,* Stanford, 1951.
212. Leto, Guido, Memoirs. *OVRA. Fascismo—Antifascismo,* Bologna, 2nd ed., 1952.
213. Leto, Guido, *OVRA. Fascismo—Antifascismo,* 2nd ed., Bologna, 1952, for an apologetic descriptive account of the operations of OVRA, published since the war by one of its officials.
214. Lewis, John D., and Oscar Jaszi, *Against the Tyrant: The Tradition and Theory of Tyrannicide,* Glencoe, 1957.
215. Lewis, John W., *Leadership in Communist China,* Ithaca, 1963. *(aa)

passim, esp. pp. 270ff. This author, by writing in terms of Chinese ideological formulations, tends to minimize Mao's dictatorship, while maximizing his role as an infallible "pope." *(a) ch. 8, esp. pp. 247ff. *(b) pp. 32f, 226f, 244f, 273. *(c) ch. 1, esp. pp. 31ff. *(d) pp. 31ff, 99f, 101ff; quote on p. 32. *(e) pp. 70ff; see also ref. 228c. *(f) *passim.* *(g) ch. 8. *(h) pp. 32–33 *(i) pp. 67–68. *(j) pp. 249ff; quote on p. 252.

216. Lewy, Günter, *The Catholic Church and Nazi Germany,* New York, 1962. *(a) *passim* and ch. 1. *(b) ch. 8. *(c) ch. 11; see also ref. 371.

217. Lifton, Jay, *Thought Reform and the Psychology of Totalism: A Study of Brainwashing in China,* New York, 1961. *(a) *passim.* *(b) pp. 27, 128. *(c) p. 423. *(d) pp. 425–427. *(e) p. 246. *(f) p. 471. *(g) pp. 359–387. *(h) This confession of a former Harvard professor is reprinted in full on pp. 473ff; quote on p. 474.

218. Lochner, Louis P., *Tycoons and Tyrant,* Aurora, 1954, for a contrasting view.

219. Ludwig, Emil, *Mussolini,* Berlin, 1932. See also ref. 27.

220. McKinder, Halford J., *Democratic Ideals and Reality,* New York, 1919. This geopolitical kind of approach to Russia is highlighted by its famous hypothesis about the heartland of the Eurasian plain and its world-historical destiny.

221. McWhinney, Edward, *Peaceful Coexistence and Soviet-Western International Law,* Leiden, 1964. *(a) pts. 1, 4. *(b) pt. 2, pp. 30–48. *(c) pt. 5.

222. Machiavelli, Niccolò, *Il Principe.*

223. Machiewicz, J., *The Katyn Wood Murders,* London, 1951.

224. Macridis, R. C., ed., *Foreign Policy in World Politics,* Englewood Cliffs, 2nd ed. 1962. *(a) V. V. Asputurian, "Soviet Foreign Policy." See also the same author's interesting contribution to J. L. H. Keep and L. Brisby, eds., *Contemporary History in the Soviet Mirror,* New York, 1964.

225. Malfi, Erasmo, *Scuola e G.I.L.,* Rome, 1939. *(a) see ref. 319. *(b) According to him, the school is a political institution, and school and youth organizations together form the unitary instrument of Fascist education.

226. Mair, Lucy, *Primitive Government,* London, 1962.

227. Mannheim, Karl, *Ideology and Utopia: An Introduction to the Sociology of Knowledge,* Oxford, 1936, 1950. *(a) *passim.*

228. Mao Tse-tung, *Selected Works of Mao Tse-tung,* 4 vols., London and New York, 1954–56; 5th vol., 1961. Also: *On People's Democratic Dictatorship,* 1949, 7th ed. 1959. *(a) 1961 vol.; see also ref. 215, ch. 1. *(b) vol. 1, quoted at greater length in ref. 215, pp. 21–22. *(c) vol. 4 (1956), pp. 111ff.

229. Martin, Hugh, *Christian Counter-Attack: Europe's Churches against Nazism,* London, 1944, p. 25. This figure may be compared with the figure 1,493 given for a single concentration camp, Dachau, for March 15, 1945, and covering 25 nations, among which the Germans supplied

261, Poles 791, French 122, Czechs 73, Austrians 64, and so on. See Neuhäusler (ref. 147), p. 349. Neuhäusler also gives (pp. 336–348) a long list of clergy in the Dachau concentration camp in 1943, based on a report of an inmate, which was smuggled out. Altogether, Neuhäusler's account is the most detailed story of individual and group efforts of Catholics to resist the nazification of the church.

230. Marx, Karl, *Das Kapital,* Hamburg, 1867, I, 23–24.
231. Marx, Karl, and Friedrich Engels, *Die Deutsche Ideologie,* Berlin, 1953, pp. 35–36 and *passim.*
232. Maunz, T., *Gestalt und Recht der Polizei,* Hamburg, 1943, pp. 51–52.
233. Maynard, John, *The Russian Peasant,* London, 1943. The brutal violence of the process is not given adequate attention in this book.
234. Medalie, Richard J., "The Stages of Totalitarian Development in Eastern Europe," *Public Policy,* vol. 7, Cambridge, Mass., 1956. Earlier Seton-Watson attempted to generalize upon the more conventional subject of the "seizure of power"; see his *East European Revolution* (ref. 322). We benefited greatly from Medalie's discussion of these phenomena.
235. Megaro, Gaudens, *Mussolini in the Making,* New York, 1938. *(a) *passim.* *(b) pp. 21ff.
236. Mehnert, Klaus, *Weltrevolution durch Weltgeschichte; die Geschichts-lehre des Stalinismus,* Stuttgart, 1953; *Stalin versus Marx; the Stalinist Historical Doctrine,* London, 1952), gives a more balanced analysis of this "nationalist" trend and the way in which Stalin developed it out of the ideological transformations required by the exigencies of the Soviet Union. Mehnert links the trend to such phenomena as Stalin's post-mortem purge of M. N. Pokrovsky, the historian, and of N. Ya. Marr, the linguist. In these changes Mehnert surmises to have been embodied a new messianic conception of Russia's role as the "savior" of mankind; and he cites Stalin's toast of May 24, 1945, as one of the striking bits of evidence in support of his general contention. At the same time, he stresses, as we do, that this kind of Marx-derived messian-ism must not be confused with the older mystic and Panslavist versions, in spite of the kinship between them.
237. Mehnert, Klaus, *Peking und Moskau,* Stuttgart, 1963. *(a) generally stresses the autocratic tradition. *(b) pp. 186–188; calls Mao the greatest peasant leader of modern times. *(c) develops the conflict in terms of national character.
238. Mehnert, Klaus, *Soviet Man in His World,* New York, 1962 (Ger. ed., Stuttgart, 1958). *(a) p. 35. *(b) pp. 34–35. *(c) ch. 4, interesting for personal detail. *(d) pp. 261ff; states, on the basis of many personal contacts, that "fear is the constant companion" of men in the Soviet Union. *(e) pp. 262ff.
239. Meier-Benneckenstein, Paul, ed., *Dokumente der Deutschen Politik,* Berlin, 1935, I, 39.
240. Meissner, Boris, *Russland unter Chrushchow,* Munich, 1960. *(a) ch. 1, where the debate in the Central Committee in 1956 is detailed. *(b) chs.

27–29. *(c) ch. 32. *(d) ch. 15. *(e) ch. 32. *(f) ch. 9. *(g) pp. 260ff.

241. Méray, Tibor, *Thirteen Days that Shook the Kremlin: Imre Nagy and the Hungarian Revolution,* New York, 1959.

242. Merriam, Charles E., *The Making of Citizens,* Chicago, 1931; the leading volume of a series that dealt in separate monographs with Switzerland, Great Britain, France, Italy, and others. These studies are of somewhat uneven value, but they are all built upon the assumption underlying Merriam's entire enterprise, that the "making of Fascists" and the "making of citizens" is essentially the same kind of undertaking. Actually the difference is as great as that between liberating and enslaving a man.

243. Merriam, Charles E., *Political Power, Its Composition and Maintenance,* New York, 1934, pp. 104–105, for a similar list; Merriam here discusses the importance of ceremonialism in politics.

244. Merton, Robert K., et al., *Reader in Bureaucracy,* Glencoe, 1952. *(a) C. J. Friedrich, "Some Observations on Weber's Analysis of Bureaucracy," pp. 27–33; see also ref. 380. *(b) Frederic S. Burin, "Bureaucracy and National Socialism: A Reconsideration of Weberian Theory," stresses this point; but he builds his analysis partly on the semantically misleading terminology of Karl Mannheim — functional versus substantive rationality — and partly on the notion that the party and SS bureaucracy may be called an "ideological" bureaucracy and yet, he said, not be concerned with substantive rationality. But if the party apparatus is an ideological "bureaucracy," then its distinctive feature is precisely its concern with values or ends — the distinctive feature of substantive reality — rather than with being rational in terms of legally fixed ends. All these terminological difficulties, occasioned by Max Weber's cumbersome conceptual scheme, do not prevent Burin from making a very useful analysis, showing the decomposition of the bureaucracy of the government. *(c) see also ref. 232.

245. Mertsalov, V. S., *Politika krutogo podema i selskoe khozyaistvo SSSR,* Munich, 1955, p. 37.

246. Meyer, Alfred G., *Leninism,* Cambridge, 1957. *(a) pp. 189–191, for interesting comment. See also his *Marxism — The Unity of Theory and Practice,* Cambridge, Mass., 1954.

247. Michel, Henri, *Histoire de la Resistance,* Paris, 1952.

248. Michels, Robert, *Political Parties: A Sociological Study of the Oligarchical Tendencies of Modern Germany,* New York, 1915, 1949. He argues that there is no such thing as a democratic, cooperative party, that all parties are "oligarchic"; he overstates a good point.

249. Micklem, Nathaniel, *National Socialism and the Catholic Church, 1933–1938,* London, 1939. See also ref. 145.

250. Miller, Douglas, *You Can't Do Business with Hitler,* Boston, 1941, p. 73, gives a description of the clearing system: "Exporters in Germany would ship, for example, to Jugoslavia and be credited in dinars by the central bank in Belgrade, with the two banks balancing accounts. Pay-

ment was credited to the exporters in each country in their local currency, and at the turn of the year the balance would be carried forward in favor of one or the other country to apply against next year's transactions."

251. Milosz, Czeslaw, *The Captive Mind*, New York, 1953. *(a) p. 231. *(b) p. 102.

252. Moore, Barrington, Jr., *Soviet Politics — The Dilemma of Power: The Role of Ideas in Social Change*, Cambridge, Mass., 1950, p. 406. *(a) p. 406. *(b) chs. 8 and 12, for a more detailed discussion. *(c) pp. 280–281. The total includes all Soviet workers employed in bureaucratic activities. *(d) p. 163.

253. Moore, Barrington, Jr., *Terror and Progress USSR: Some Sources of Change and Stability in the Soviet Dictatorship*, Cambridge, Mass., 1954. *(a) p. 194. *(b) *passim*. *(c) ch. 5, for a thoughtful, balanced treatment. *(d) p. 129. Moore recognizes this point and shares the belief that "the Soviet scientist still retains a substantial degree of autonomy in spite of all the planning." *(e) ch. 4, esp. pp. 100ff. *(f) pp. 110–111; quotation on p. 112. *(g) *passim;* this view has been for some time espoused by Kennan and others.

254. Moore, Barrington, Jr., *Political Power and Social Theory: Six Studies*, Cambridge, Mass., 1958. *(a) p. 80.

255. Mora, S., and P. Zwierniak, *Sprawiedliwosc Scwiecka*, Rome, 1945. See also ref. 343.

256. Morstein-Marx, F., *Government of the Third Reich*, New York, 1936. *(a) pp. 114ff.

257. Müller, Marianne, and Erwin Egon, *Stürmt die Festung Wissenschaft*, Berlin-Dahlem, 1953. *(a) *op. cit.* *(b) p. 213, quoting an article by Walter Ulbricht in *Neues Deutschland*, July 23, 1950.

258. Mussolini, Benito, *Opera Omnia De*, ed. Eduardo and Julio Susmel, 31 vols., Florence, 1951.

259. Myrdal, Alva, *Nation and Family: The Swedish Experiment in Democratic Family and Population Policy*, New York, 1941.

260. Nettl, Peter, *The Eastern Zone and Soviet Policy in Germany, 1945–50*, London, 1951, pp. 1–35. Ger. ed., *Die Deutsche Sowjetzone bis heute*, Frankfort, 1953.

261. Neufeld, H.-J., Jürgen Huck, and Georg Tessin, "Zur Geschichte der Ordnungskrise, 1939–1945," *Schiften des Bundesarchivs*, vol. 3, 1957.

262. Neuhäusler, J., *Kreuz und Hakenkreuz: Der Kampf des Nationalsozialismus gegen die Katholische Kirche und der Kirchliche Widerstand*, Munich, 1946. The reliability of this source has been questioned by Lewy (ref. 216). But he in turn fails to give adequate attention to the extent of Catholic resistance, in spite of the official attitude which he documents well. *(a) I, 349, 335–348; see also ref. 229. *(b) II, 68ff.

263. Neumann, Franz, *Behemoth*, New York, 1942. *(a) see also Sweezy (ref. 345) and Brady (ref. 32). Neumann's analysis is much the ablest of the three. The "imperialist" interpretation ties in with Thorstein

Veblen's earlier analysis of German and Japanese militarism and imperialism. *(b) Neumann is perhaps the leading writer stressing the charismatic nature of Hitler. *(c) p. 360. *(d) pp. 327ff. *(e) pp. 298ff. *(f) pp. 349–361. *(g) pp. 337–349, 413–428. What is otherwise a well-informed discussion of this problem is marred by his preoccupation with proving that, in spite of the destruction of the free unions, capitalism continues to exist. He admits that capitalism requires "free labor," but undertakes to escape from the clear consequences of this fact by introducing a distinction between three different concepts of "freedom," which are said to correspond to "stages" in capitalist development. The distinctions have a degree of validity, but they do not succeed in supporting his main argument. For a detailed analysis of the Labor Front, see also Cole (ref. 439), utilized by Neumann. The German literature, given by both, should also be consulted. *(h) p. 613, n. 14, for German literature regarding this. *(i) pp. 403–413. Neumann writes with bitterness of this failure, but, communism apart, it is not clear just what he thinks the Social Democratic Party and the unions should have done. *(j) p. 418. Neumann rightly concludes that "the Labor Front has driven the process of bureaucratization to its maximum." *(k) p. 425. *(l) p. 429, for quotation, with inadequate references. *(m) p. 377. *(n) pp. 349ff.

264. Neumann, Franz, *The Democratic and the Authoritarian State*, Glencoe, 1957. *(a) This is unfortunately the basic fault of this posthumous volume by the distinguished student of the Hitler regime.

265. Neumann, Sigmund, *Permanent Revolution*, New York, 1942. *(a) p. 77. *(b) p. 79.

266. Nolte, Ernst, *Der Faschismus in seiner Epoche, Action Française, Italienischer Faschismus, Nationalsozialismus*, Munich, 1963. *(a) This learned author calls Rosenberg's book "das vorgebliche Grundbuch der nationalsozialistischen Weltanschauung" (p. 61). *(b) The sociological background is analyzed in detail on pp. 193–243, 343–356. *(c) pp. 308ff. *(d) see esp. pp. 278ff, 445ff. *(e) pp. 506ff.

267. Nove, Alec, *The Soviet Economy*, London and New York, 1961. *(a) pp. 73–91. *(b) *passim*, for a good general review of the Soviet economy.

268. Oakeshott, Michael, *The Social and Political Doctrines of Contemporary Europe*, Cambridge, Eng., 1939. *(a) pp. 164ff, for a reprint of this. *(b) pp. 164ff, esp. p. 166; trans. of *La Dottrina del Fascismo* (1934). *(c) reprint of article on Fascism (1932).

269. Orlov, A., *The Secret History of Stalin's Crimes*, New York, 1953. See also ref. 343.

270. Pareto, Vilfredo, *The Mind and Society*, trans. A. Bongiorno and A. Livingston, New York, 1935 (trans. of *Trattato di sociologia generale*, Florence, 1923, last ed.), esp. pp. 389–480.

271. Parkinson, C. N., *Parkinson's Law*, London, 1957.

272. Parkinson, C. N., *East and West*, Boston, 1963. The experienced author provides a broad background of the conflict, which he believes

healthy and important to maintain, counting the Soviet Union (Russia) among the Western powers; see esp. ch. 20.

273. Parsons, Talcott, *The Social System,* Glencoe, 1951. *(a) p. 349. *(b) p. 10. *(c) p. 11.

274. Parsons, Talcott, and A. M. Henderson, *Max Weber, The Theory of Social and Economic Organization* (ed. and intro. Parsons), New York, 1947; esp. pp. 329–341. See also ref. 380b.

275. Peralta, Jeronimo M., *Peron y la Revolución Justicialista,* Buenos Aires, 1951, for an "authorized" analysis. Ch. 10 contains the twenty basic tenets of the movement.

276. Pipes, Richard, *The Formation of the Soviet Union: Communism and Nationalism, 1917–1923,* Cambridge, Mass., 1954; rev. ed. 1964.

277. Plamenatz, John P., *German Marxism and Russian Communism,* London, 1954, pp. 8–36; points out that the Communist emphasis on *diamat* is often merely lip service. What communists refer to as dialectical materialism is not that at all, but historical materialism. Genuine dialectics has little to do with it.

278. Plato, *The Republic,* bk. 5.

279. Plato, *The Laws.*

280. Plessner, Hellmuth, *Die Verspätete Nation,* Stuttgart, 1959.

281. *P.N.F., Atti* [Proceedings], 16 vols., Bologna, 1931–1939, III (1934), 312. Includes the *Fogli di ordini* and *Fogli di disposizioni* of the national party secretary.

282. Polanyi, Michael, *Personal Knowledge,* Chicago, 1959. *(a) pp. 290–291.

283. Polish Supreme Court, judgment of a civil division of the PSC of 11–29 Dec. 1951 — Reference No. C 1083/51, Law Publishing Company, Warsaw, 1953, vol. 2.

284. Popper, Karl R., *The Open Society and Its Enemies,* London, 1945, vol. 1, perhaps the most outspoken of the Platonic critics. This aspect of Plato's philosophy is the genuine link with the views of the totalitarians of our time. It has given rise to a heated controversy over whether Plato was or was not a totalitarian. In terms of our criteria, he clearly was not. See also ref. 353.

285. Popper, Karl, *The Poverty of Historicism,* London, 1957.

286. Possony, Stefan T., *Lenin: The Compulsive Revolutionary,* Chicago, 1964. This author, mainly concerned with factional intrigue and political controversy among the various factions, is impatient with "mere" ideas. Very interesting on the score of Lenin's "persuasiveness." See also ref. 98.

287. Raschofer, Hermann, *Die Sudetenfrage, ihre völkerrechtliche Entwicklung vom ersten Weltkrieg bis zur Gegenwart,* Munich, 1953, pp. 144–164.

288. Rauschning, Hermann, *Gespräche mit Hitler,* New York, 1940, p. 51 (Engl. ed., *Hitler Speaks,* 1939). We used our own trans. from the original. We agree with Bullock and Trevor-Roper that Rauschning's account is confirmed by later evidence and is hence an important source.

289. Rauschning, Hermann, *Hitler's Speeches*, New York, 1942.
290. Reimann, Gunther, *The Vampire Economy*, New York, 1939. *(a) for greater detail; the term is our own coinage. *(b) Reimann stressed this aspect.
291. Reitlinger, G., *The SS — Alibi of a Nation*, New York, 1956.
292. *Report of the Case of the Anti-Soviet and Right-Trotskyite Bloc* (*Sudebnyi otchet po delu Anti-Sovetskogo i Pravo-Trotskistkogo Bloka*), Moscow, 1938, p. 697; Andrei Vyshinsky's address.
293. *Report of the Proceedings of the Anti-Soviet Trotskyite Center*, Moscow, 1937, pp. 162–163; Shestov's last plea.
294. *Report of the Proceedings of the Case of the Anti-Soviet Trotskyite Center*, Moscow, 1937, p. 127.
295. Ritter, Gerhard, *Carl Goerdeler und die deutsche Widerstandsbewegung*, Stuttgart, 1954. *(a) see also ref. 302b. *(b) pp. 388–434. Merely as illustrations we mention Carl Goerdeler's brother as his most intimate associate, and the brothers Bonhoeffer (see Dietrich Bonhoeffer's *Letters and Papers from Prison*, ref. 251; the most important letters are to his parents). But perhaps most impressive of all is the account that has been presented from Gestapo records by Annedore Leber (ref. 197), where again and again the crucial support is shown to have come from the family. *(c) for a more detailed background of the key leader, Goerdeler.
296. Ritvo, Herbert, *The New Soviet Society, The New Leader*, New York, 1962. This useful publication contains the last program of the CPSU. *(a) quotation on pp. 10–11. *(b) pp. 9–10 and pt. 2, esp. pp. 109ff. See also the helpful introductory comment.
297. *The Roman Catholic Church in People's Poland*, Warsaw, 1953, p. 105.
298. Rosenberg, Alfred, *Der Mythos des Zwanzigsten Jahrhunderts*, Munich, 1930, p. 2.
299. Rosenthal, Walter, Richard Lange, and Arwed Bomeyer, *Die Justiz in der Sowjetischen Besatzungzone*, 3rd ed., Bonn, 1955. For the concrete evidence of the perversion of judicial administration, see ref. 364, covering, in two parts, the period down to and including 1943.
300. Rostow, W. W., et al., *The Prospects for Communist China*, Cambridge, Mass., 1954. *(a) *passim*. *(b) pp. 116–123; unfortunately, Rostow speaks of the "complex value system" of traditional Chinese society as an "ideology."
301. Rostow, W. W., *The Stages of Economic Growth: A Non-Communist Manifesto*, Cambridge, Eng., 1960.
302. Rothfels, Hans, *The German Opposition to Hitler*, 2nd ed., Chicago, 1948. *(a) esp. pp. 85ff. *(b) this was by no means the only motivation. See also Dulles (ref. 76). There is a growing literature on July 20; among these, the recent study on the key leader, Carl Goerdeler, by Ritter (ref. 295) is outstanding *(c) p. 101 and *passim*. *(d) *passim*.
303. Rounds, Frank, *A Window on Red Square*, Boston, 1953, pp. 46–48.

304. Rousset, David, *The Other Kingdom*, New York, 1947. See also ref. 178.
305. Royal Commission, *Reports on Espionage in Canada, 1946, and Australia, 1955* (Ottawa and Canberra), for excellent source material.
306. Rüstow, Alexander, *Ortsbestimmung der Gegenwart*, 3 vols., Zürich, 1950, 1952, 1957. *(a) I, 74ff. *(b) I, 54–55.
307. Salomon, Ernst von, *Der Fragebogen*, Hamburg, 1951, for a dramatic description of this little-known phase of Germany's revolutionary situation.
308. Salvadori, Massimo, *Storia della resistenza italiana*, Venice, 1955; this avoids the Communist bias of some other interesting studies on the Italian resistance.
309. Salvatorelli, Luigi, and G. Mira, *Storia del Fascismo*, Rome, 1952. *(a) *op. cit.* *(b) p. 745. *(c) see also ref. 319. *(d) for the Italian record.
310. Salvemini, Gaetano, *Under the Axe of Fascism*, New York, 1936. *(a) p. 383. *(b) pp. 385–386. *(c) Salvemini rightly stressed the corrupt features of corporativism, but failed to bring out this inherent rationale of the corporate state. See also L. R. Franck, *Les Etapes de l'économie fasciste italienne*, Paris, 1939, and Carl T. Schmidt, *The Corporate State in Action*, New York, 1939. *(d) *passim;* see also ref. 95h. *(e) pp. 294–295.
311. De Santillana, George, *Galileo Galilei — Dialogue on the Great World Systems*, Chicago, 1953 (learned intro., pp. xi–lviii). See also his essay on "Phases of the Conflict Between Totalitarianism and Science," ref. 112h.
311.1. Sartori, Giovanni, *Democratic Theory*, Detroit, 1962, esp. ch. 7.
312. Schapiro, Leonard, *The Communist Party of the Soviet Union*, London, 1960. *(a) p. 167. *(b) pp. 392ff. *(c) p. 431. *(d) pp. 306–308. *(e) pp. 198ff. *(f) p. 418. *(g) p. 425.
313. Scharffenorth, Greta, *Römer 13 in der Geschichte des Politischen Denkens*, Heidelberg, 1964.
314. Schein, Edgar H., with Inge Schneier and Ithiel de Sola Pool, *Coercive Persuasion: A Sociological Analysis of the Brainwashing of American Civilians by the Chinese Communists*, New York, 1961.
315. Schelsky, Helmut, *Wandlungen der deutschen Familie der Gegenwart*, 2nd ed., Stuttgart, 1954. See also Wurzbacher (ref. 292). The two works were done in conjunction and complement each other, Schelsky, broadly speaking, dealing with the external, Wurzbacher with the internal, relations of the family since 1945. In all, 180 families were studied intensively.
316. Schmitt, Carl, *Staat, Bewegung, Volk — Eine Dreigliederung der Politischen Einheit*, Hamburg, 1933.
317. Schneider, Hans, *Das Ermächtigungsgesetz vom 24 März 1933*, 2nd ed., Bonn, 1961 (1st ed., Munich, 1954).
318. Schneider, Herbert W., *Making the Fascist State*, New York, 1928, p. 228.
319. Schneider, Herbert W., and Shepard Clough, *Making Fascists*, Chicago,

1934, ch. 5; see also Finer (ref. 95), pp. 475ff. There is no good recent study on this subject, but there are interesting sidelights on it in Salvatorelli (ref. 309). Among Fascist writings, we note Fanelli (ref. 91) and Malfi (ref. 225), as well as the study on Gentile (ref. 367).

320. Schwartz, Benjamin, *Chinese Communism and the Rise of Mao,* Cambridge, Mass., 1951. *(a) see also ref. 141. *(b) *passim.* *(c) pp. 191–199.

321. Seabury, Paul, *The Wilhelmstrasse: A Study of German Diplomats under the Nazi Regime,* Berkeley, 1954.

322. Seton-Watson, Hugh, *The East European Revolution,* 2nd ed., New York, 1952; see also ref. 234.

323. Selznick, Philip, *The Organizational Weapon: A Study of Bolshevik Strategy and Tactics,* New York, 1952, pp. 171–214, for a broader analysis. See also ref. 61.

324. *XVII Syezd VKP(b)* (17th party congress), Stenographic Report, Moscow, 1934, p. 15.

325. *XVIII Syezd VKP(b)* (18th party congress), Stenographic Report, Moscow, 1939. *(a) p. 28. *(b) for details, particularly the reports of Molotov and Kaganovich. *(c) p. 19.

326. Shirer, William L., *The Rise and Fall of the Third Reich,* New York, 1960.

327. Shklar, Judith N., *After Utopia — The Decline of Political Faith,* Princeton, 1957.

328. Shulman, Marshal D., *Stalin's Foreign Policy Reappraised,* Cambridge, Mass., 1963. *(a) p. 263, where one reads "the greater flexibility of the peaceful-coexistence policy . . . represented not so much a departure from the policies of the late Stalin era as the fruition of those policies."

329. Shuster, G. N., *Religion Behind the Iron Curtain,* New York, 1955.

330. Silone, Ignazio, *Bread and Wine,* London, 1936. See also ref. 178.

331. Sington, Derrick, and Arthur Weidenfeld, *The Goebbels Experiment — A Study of the Nazi Propaganda Machine,* London, 1942. *(a) esp. chs. 2, 3. *(b) p. 17. It may, however, be argued that the real dualism was that between Goebbels and Dietrich. In the party, Dietrich's position was equivalent to Goebbels'; he was Reichsleiter as press chief of the Reich and, although he was Goebbels' subordinate as secretary of state in the Ministry of Propaganda, he wore another hat as press chief of the government, which gave him direct access to Hitler.

332. Smith, Patrick, ed., *Clemens August von Galen — The Bishop of Münster and the Nazis,* London, 1943; sermons. See also ref. 354b.

333. Solzhenitsyn, Alexander, *One Day in the Life of Ivan Denisovich,* New York, 1963.

334. Sorel, Georges, *Réflexions sur la violence,* 2nd ed., Paris, 1910. Engl. ed., trans. T. E. Hulme and J. Roth, *Reflections on Violence,* Glencoe, 1950. See the interesting intro. by Edward A. Shils in the Engl. ed. Very significant also for his early recognition of the important doctrine of the myth — Elliott (ref. 83), ch. 4.

335. Spirito, Ugo, *Capitalismo e Corporativismo,* Florence, 1936. Reviews: *Critica fascista* and *Lavoro fascisto.*

336. Stalin, J. V., *Anarchism or Socialism* (1907), in Collected Works, Moscow, 1952, I, 294–295.

337. Stalin, J. V., *Problems of Leninism,* 11th ed., Moscow, 1940. *(a) pp. 659–699. *(b) pp. 115–116, "The October Revolution and the Tactics of the Russian Communists," 1924. *(c) pp. 591–597, "Dialectical and Historical Materialism." *(d) p. 451.

338. Stalin, J. V., *Soviet Policy during the Great Patriotic War* (materials and documents), New York, II, 79–80. Interview between Stalin and Rev S. Orlemanski, May 12, 1944.

339. Starlinger, W., *Grenzen der Sovietmacht,* Kitzinger-Main, 1954. *(a) *op. cit.* *(b) for interesting and supporting evidence where the disintegration of the MVD "state" is described. Starlinger is inclined to interpret the system as a "state within the state" in line with Kogon (ref. 178). *(c) *passim.* *(d) gives valuable details on the efforts even in retention camps.

340. Sternberg, Fritz, *From Nazi Sources: Why Hitler Can't Win,* New York, 1939, p. 73.

341. Stolper, Wolfgang F., with Karl W. Roskamp, *The Structure of the East German Economy,* Cambridge, Mass., 1960. *(a) contains an interesting evaluation of dependent planning.

342. Strobel, Ferdinand, ed., *Christliche Bewährung: Dokumente des Widerstands der Katholischen Kirche in Deutschland, 1933–1945,* Altero, 1946. *(a) this, together with Neuhäusler, supersedes the earlier meritorious document collection published in 1940 in London, entitled *The Persecution of the Catholic Church in the Third Reich: Facts and Documents.* *(b) p. 299 for quote; see also Smith (ref. 332), which gives his sermons. Teeling (ref. 350) is important because of its critical view of Catholic failings, by a Catholic. For a recent reassessment, see ref. 216.

343. Stypulowski, Z., *Invitation to Moscow,* London, 1951. See also Orlov ref. 269) and Mora and Zwierniak (ref. 255).

344. Swayze, Harold, *Political Control of Literature in the USSR,* Cambridge, Mass., 1962; quote from the poem "Evening," by Alexei Surkov, p. 35.

345. Sweezy, Maxine Y., *The Structure of the Nazi Economy,* Cambridge, Mass., 1941.

346. Tang, Peter S. H., *Communist China Today,* vol. 1, Washington, D.C., 1957; 2nd ed. 1961. *(a) pp. 87ff. *(b) ch. 10; figs. on p. 462. *(c) p. 484. *(d) pp. 97ff.

347. Tasca, A., *Nascita e avvento del Fascismo,* Rome, 1950. Mussolini's attitude toward democracy was ambivalent. Fascist theory was much more frankly elitist than Nazi ideology.

348. Taylor, Edmond, *The Strategy of Terror,* Boston, 1940. *(a) This wartime analysis overestimates this "terror" and considers it very important; for a more empirical analysis, see ref. 165.

349. Taylor, Telford, *Sword and Swastika,* New York, 1952. *(a) *passim;*

a detailed account which is carefully documented from the Nuremberg trial record. Unfortunately, it does not cover the resistance within the military adequately.

350. Teeling, William, *Crisis for Christianity,* London, 1939; see also ref. 342.
351. Tell, Rolf, *Nazi Guide to Nazism,* Washington, D.C., 1942, for quotation from *Volk im Werden,* 1934. This "guide," compiled during the war, was evidently edited with a view to arousing indignation; yet the contradiction in the Nazi approach to the family becomes apparent in the quotations offered.
352. Thoma, R., *Die Staatsfinanzen in der Volksgemeinwirtschaft,* Tübingen, 1937.
353. Thorson, Thomas L., *Plato, Totalitarian or Democrat?* New York, 1963. This author offers a convenient collection of writings, pro and con, on the theme of Plato's alleged totalitarianism, but the alternative suggested by the title is a false one.
354. Timasheff, N. S., *The Great Retreat: The Growth and Decline of Communism in Russia,* New York, 1946.
355. Triska, Jan F., ed., *Soviet Communism: Programs and Rules,* San Francisco, 1962. *(a) see estimate of editor in his introduction. *(b) pp. 102ff; see also ref. 296.
356. Trotsky, Leon, *Itogi i perspektivy,* Moscow, 1919, p. 42. See also ref. 71.
357. Trotsky, Leon, *Kak vooruzhalas revolutsiya* (How the Revolution Armed Itself), Moscow, 1923–1925, I, 29. Trans. as *The Revolution Betrayed,* by Max Eastman, 1937. *(a) pp. 87–104.
358. Trotsky, Leon, *Nashi politicheskie zadachi,* Geneva, 1904, p. 23. In the same publication, Trotsky decried Lenin's "malicious and morally repulsive suspiciousness."
359. Trotsky, Leon, *Sochineniya,* 21 vols., Moscow, 1924–1927, XIII, 6–14; quoted in Deutscher (ref. 71), p. 450.
360. Tucker, Robert C., *The Soviet Political Mind,* New York, 1963. *(a) *passim.* *(b) p. x, and esp. ch. 2, which offers convincing support for our position. *(c) pp. 3–19.
361. Ulam, Adam, *Titoism and the Cominform,* Cambridge, Mass., 1952, for a penetrating analysis.
362. Ulam, Adam, *The New Face of Soviet Totalitarianism,* Cambridge, 1963.
363. United States Congress, Joint Economic Committee. *(a) 86th Cong., *Comparisons of the United States and Soviet Economies,* Washington, 1959. *(b) 88th Cong., *Annual Economic Indicators for the USSR,* Washington, 1964, p. 77. *(c) 86th Cong., Hearings before the House Subcommittee of the Committee on Appropriations, *Comparison of the United States and USSR Science Education* (National Science Foundation), Washington, 1960.
364. *Unrecht als System — Dokumente über planmässige Rechtsverletzung in der Sowjetzone Deutschlands,* published by the Untersuchungsaus-

schuss Freiheitlicher Juristen, in two parts, covering the period down to and including 1954 (part 1 also in Engl.).

365. Vagts, Alfred, *Hitler's Second Army,* Infantry Journal, Washington, D.C., 1943, ch. 12.

366. Veblen, Thorstein, *Imperial Germany and the Industrial Revolution,* New York, 1915, 1939, 1954. See also ref. 263a.

367. Vettori, Vittorio, ed., *Giovanni Gentile,* Florence, 1954. See also ref. 319.

368. Vögelin, Eric, *The New Science of Politics,* Chicago, 1952.

369. Vögelin, E., *Die Politischen Religionen,* Vienna, 1938.

370. Volin, Lazar, *The Agricultural Picture in the USSR and USA,* U.S. Department of Agriculture, Economic Research Service, Washington, D.C., 1962. *(a) p. 7.

371. Vollmer, Bernhard, *Volksopposition im Polzeistaat — Gestapo- und Regierungsberichte 1934–1936,* Stuttgart, 1956.

372. Voznesensky, N. A., *Voyennaya ekonomika SSSR v period otechestvennoi; voiny,* Moscow, 1947, p. 66. Publ. in Engl. as *The Economy of the USSR during World War Two* (Washington, D.C., 1948).

373. *Vserossiiskii (pyatii) syezd sovetov rabochikh, krestyanskikh, soldatskikh i kazachikh deputatov* (All Russian Congress [Fifth] of Soviets of Workers', Peasants', Soldiers', and Cossacks' Deputies), Stenographic Report, Moscow, July 4–10, 1918, p. 213.

374. Vyshinsky, Andrei Ya., *The Law of the Soviet State,* trans. Hugh W. Babb, New York, 1948 (Engl. trans. of *Sovetskoe gosudarstvennoe pravo,* which really means Soviet State Law). *(a) p. 48. *(b) p. 50.

375. Waite, Robert G. L., *Vanguard of Nazism: The Free Corps Movement in Postwar Germany, 1918–1923,* Cambridge, Mass., 1952.

376. Walker, Richard L., *China under Communism: The First Five Years,* New Haven, 1955, ch. 6.

377. Walther, Otto, *Verwaltung, Lenkung und Planung der Wirtschaft in der Sowjetischen Besatzungszone,* Bonn, 1953.

378. Ward, Robert E., and Dankwart A. Rustow, eds., *Political Modernization in Japan and Turkey,* Princeton, 1964.

379. Webb, Sidney and Beatrice, *Soviet Communism: A New Civilization,* New York, 1935. *(a) *passim.* *(b) ch. 10, pt. 2, pp. 887ff; note esp. p. 921 — these facts are made the basis of a "justification" of the Soviet regime by Laski (ref. 194). *(c) pp. 1054ff. *(d) esp. ch. 10 (c), pp. 887ff. Progress is here defined in terms of "literacy" (p. 894), number of schools (p. 892), or "learning by doing" (p. 898). For the last, Crowther (ref. 60) is cited as authority, and the concept is related to a principle presumably enunciated by Samuel Butler (Thoreau stated it considerably earlier); but there is a vast difference between the reality to which the term refers in the West and the regimented assignment to work places in the USSR and the satellites.

380. Weber, Max, *Wirtshcaft und Gesellschaft,* Tübingen, 1925. *(a) p. 167; see also ref. 104b. *(b) esp. pp. 128–133, 650–678, and the corresponding sections in Parsons (ref. 274), pp. 329–341. See also ref. 381, esp. pp.

196–244, 416–444; also Friedrich's development of Weber's conception (ref. 104, ch. 2), which is further explicated in a chapter in Merton (ref. 244), upon which the analysis is based.

381. Weber, Max, *From Max Weber: Essays in Sociology,* trans., ed., and intro. H. H. Gerth and C. Wright Mills, Oxford, 1946. See also ref. 380b.

382. Weinreich, Max, *Hitler's Professors — The Part of Scholarship in Germany's Crimes Against the Jewish People,* New York, 1946. For a less emphatic treatment, see Hartshorne (ref. 136).

383. Weizsäcker, Ernst von, *Memoirs,* Engl. trans. J. Andrews, London, 1951.

384. Wertheimer, Mildred S., *The Pan-German League, 1890–1914,* New York, 1924, for an older but still largely adequate study.

385. Wheeler-Bennett, John, *The Forgotten Peace,* Brest-Litovsk, 1918 (New York, 1939).

386. Wheeler-Bennett, John, *The Nemesis of Power: The German Army in Politics, 1918–1945,* London, 1953. *(a) pt. 3. *(b) *passim.*

387. White, Dmitri Fedotoff, *The Growth of the Red Army,* Princeton, 1944. *(a) *passim.* *(b) *passim.*

388. Widmayer, R., "The Communist Party and the Soviet Schools, 1917–1937," unpubl. diss., Harvard University, 1952; see also ref. 134.

389. Wittfogel, Karl, *Oriental Despotism,* New Haven, 1957. *(a) argues that the power structures of oriental despotism were "total"; his evidence, while impressive, does not suffice to establish that these autocracies were structurally like the totalitarian dictatorships of our time, or that the political process was the same. *(b) ch. 5, esp. pp. 141ff. *(c) He would identify what he calls hydraulic despotism with modern totalitarianism, but the argument is really about general "totalism," as discussed.

390. Wittke, Carl, *Democracy Is Different,* New York, 1941.

391. Wolfe, Bertram D., *Three Who Made a Revolution,* New York, 1948.

392. Wurzbacher, Gerhard, *Leitbilder des gegenwärtigen deutschen Familienlebens,* Dortmund, 1951. See also ref. 315.

393. Yakovlev, B., *Konsentratsionne Lageri SSSR,* Munich, 1955, for a recent attempt to identify, locate, and describe the Soviet camps.

394. Yaroslavsky, E., *Bolshevik Verification and Purging of the Party Ranks,* Moscow, 1933, p. 13, quoting Lenin addressing the combined session of the All-Russian Central Executive and the Moscow Soviet, April 4, 1919.

395. Yaroslavsky, E., *Kak provodit chistku partii,* Moscow, 1929, for an early discussion.

396. Yin, Helen and Yi-chang, *Economic Statistics of Mainland China (1949–1957),* Cambridge, Mass., 1960. *(a) *passim.* *(b) p. ix, "not to advocate or underwrite their accuracy or reliability which is a separate problem."

397. Yoffe, A. A., *Mirnye peregovory v Brest-Litovske* (official Soviet record), Moscow, 1920, p. 104.

397.1. Zagoria, Donald S., *The Sino-Soviet Conflict, 1959–1961*, Princeton, 1962.

398. Zellentin, Gerda, *Die Kommunisten und die Einigung Europas*, Frankfurt-Main, 1964.

399. Zeller, Eberhard, *Geist der Freiheit*, 2nd ed., Munich, 1954.

PERIODICALS AND ARTICLES

400. *American Historical Review.* *(a) G. L. Weinberg, "Hitler's Image of the United States," 69: 106ff (1964).

401. *American Journal of International Law.* *(a) Edward McWhinney, "Peaceful Co-Existence and Soviet Western International Law," 56:951ff (1962). *(b) John N. Hazard, "Codifying Peaceful Co-Existence," 55:109ff (1961).

402. *American Political Science Review.* *(a) Giovanni Sartori, "Constitutionalism: A Preliminary Discussion," 56:853–864 (1963); argues for the notion that the constitutions of totalitarian dictatorships are a "facade." But is this true? Do they not have a definite function, and are not all constitutions to some extent facade?

403. *American Sociological Review.* *(a) E. V. Walter, "Violence and the Process of Terror," 29:248ff (1964). This author has very usefully systematized the general points of his analysis. However, he errs in excluding psychic and economic forms of violence, thereby obstructing an understanding of Khrushchev's system. *(b) *ibid.* This oscillation, though vital to understanding terror as a process, is not dealt with by Walter. *(c) *ibid.* A useful term for the phenomenon to distinguish such "areas" of terror from a "system of terror." But looked at by themselves, they in turn appear as "systems."

404. *Annals of the Academy of Political Science.* *(a) J. Bennett, "The German Currency Reform," 267:43–54 (January 1950); see also ref. 561. *(b) A. Bergson, J. H. Blackman, and A. Erlich, "Postwar Economic Reconstruction and Development in the USSR," 263:52–72 (May 1949); see also refs. 441, 409b. *(c) R. A. Scalapino, "The Sino-Soviet Conflict in Perspective," 351:1–14 (January 1964).

405. *Antike und Abendland.* Kurt von Fritz, "Totalitarismus und Demokratie im alten Griechenland und Rom," 3:47–74 (1948).

406. *Aviation Age.* "Russia Threatens US Engineering Leadership," February 1955, for all the data in this paragraph.

407. *Bolshevik.* *(a) 17:51 (1948). *(b) V. Kolbanovsky, "Ukrepleniye semyi v sotsialisticheskom obshchestve," 17:53–63 (September 1949).

408. *Buletinul Oficial*, no. 51 (June 9, 1950), decree no. 583.

409. *Bulletin of the Institute for the Study of History and Culture of the USSR.* *(a) 2.1:10 (1955). *(b) 2.3:5 (1955). *(c) 3.2:11 (1956).

410. *Canadian Yearbook of International Law, 1963.* *(a) Edward McWhinney, "Soviet and Western International Law . . . Interbloc Law . . . ," pp. 40–81.

411. *Common Ground.* C. J. Friedrich, "Foreign-Language Radio and the War," 3:65–72 (1942).

412. *Confluence.* *(a) C. J. Friedrich, "Religion and History," 4.1:105–116 (1955). *(b) C. J. Friedrich, "Authority and Loyalty," 3.3:307, 316 (1954). *(c) Friedrich, *ibid.,* and the literature cited there.

413. *Dziennik Ustaw Rzeczypospolitej Polskiej,* 22:188 (1950); see also ref. 429.

414. *I. Fogli di ordini,* 31:244 (Rome, 1935).

415. *Foreign Affairs.* *(a) George F. Kennan, "America and the Russian Future," 29:351–370 (1950–51).

416. *Forum.* Wolfgand Schubardt, "Der Kampf gegen den Objektivismus an den Universitäten und Hochschulen unserer Republik," March 21, 1951, p. 3 (Communist student publication). See also the comment in Müller (ref. 257), pp. 219ff.

417. *The Geographical Review.* D. B. Shimkin, "Economic Regionalization in Soviet Union," 42:611 (October 1952).

418. *Hochland.* E. W. Böckenförde, "Der Deutsche Katholizimus im Jahre 1933," 53:215ff (1961), and 54:217ff (1962). *(a) This author has recently shown, in this remarkable documentary study, how far misunderstanding went. *(b) gives the essential documentation and answers effectively the criticism offered by Buchheim in the same journal, vol. 53, 1961.

419. *Izvestiya.* *(a) July 11, 1955. *(b) August 10, 1930; see also ref. 37h. *(c) May 26, 1955, p. 2, on the setting up of the USSR State Planning Committee to guide long-range planning and the USSR Economic Committee to guide short-range planning. *(d) April 6, 1955. *(e) January 23, 1955. *(f) November 30, 1955, for decree. *(g) August 7, 1955, on the award of the order of the Red Banner of Labor to the Metropolitan of Kolomna. *(h) March 27, 1956.

420. *Journal of the History of Ideas.* Lacey Baldwin Smith, "English Treason Trials and Confessions in the Sixteenth Century," vol. 15 (October 1954).

421. *Journal of Politics.* *(a) Carl J. Friedrich, "Political Leadership and the Problem of Charismatic Power," 23:3ff (1961). *(b) E. P. Zinner, "Revolution in Hungary: Reflections on the Vicissitudes of a Totalitarian System," 21:3–36 (1959).

422. *Kommunist.* *(a) M. Strepukhov, "Powerful Instruments for Mobilizing the Masses to Carry Out Party and Governmental Decisions" (trans.), 6:91–102 (April 1955). *(b) 10:4 (July 1955). *(c) 7:117–128 (May 1955). Compare this with the following statement (trans.) in *Literaturnaya gazeta* (ref. 426b): "'Cautious' people, who consider the appearance and establishment of different trends in one and the same field of knowledge 'dangerous,' generally declare that this, as they say, may lead to the appearance or reanimation of reactionary trends which contradict the Marxist-Leninist outlook."

423. *Komsomolskaya pravda.* *(a) March 24, 1954, p. 2. *(b) March 30, 1954. *(c) 1954 figures, March 20, 1954, p. 1.

424. *Krasnaya zvezda* (official army paper). *(a) October 22, 1946. *(b) October 1, 1950, and May 21, 1953.
425. *Lidove Noviny,* April 27, 1951, quoted by Buhler and Zukowski (ref. 45).
426. *Literaturnaya gazeta.* *(a) January 11, 1955, p. 1. *(b) *ibid.;* see also ref. 422c.
427. *Look.* "Interview with Elliott Roosevelt," February 4, 1947.
428. *Mirovoe khozyaistvo i mirovaya politika.* E. S. Varga, "Demokratiya novogo tipa," 1947, p. 3.
429. *Monitor Polski,* A-45, p. 519. See also ref. 413.
430. *New York Times.* *(a) August 30, 1955, L. Dubrovina, RSFSR Deputy Minister of Education. *(b) July 24, 1955, p. 6E. *(c) June 7, 1942, for quotations of striking passages of the pastoral letter. These are curiously not contained in Neuhäusler's account, though he quotes others from a "gemeinsame Hirtenbrief." *(d) August 25, 1955, p. 4.
431. *Nomos — Yearbook of the American Society for Political and Legal Philosophy.* Vol. 1 (1958) deals with authority, 2 with community, 3 with responsibility, 4 with liberty, 5 with public interest, 6 with justice — they all contain contributions valuable for the theory of totalitarianism by authors who are cited in our bibl.
432. *Nowe Drogi.* *(a) January 1947; the secretary-general of the party, Gomulka, went as far as to claim that there was no need of a dictatorship of the proletariat in Poland, since communism in Poland would arrive through an evolutionary process. *(b) July-August 1948, p. 17, the resolution of the Cominform on the situation in the Communist Party of Yugoslavia.
433. *Nowa Kultura.* S. Sobocki, "Egzamin," 34(282):4–5 (August 21, 1955).
434. *Partinaya zhizn.* *(a) 5:8–13 (March 1955). *(b) 6:30–34 (1955). *(c) March 1955. *(d) 3:60–61 (1955). *(c) 6:1–2 (March 1955). *(f) 15:9–15 (November 1954).
435. *Peking Review.* Yao-pang Hu, "For the Revolutionization of Our Youth! Report on the Chinese Communist Youth League . . ." 28:8–22 (July 10, 1964).
436. *Pergale,* 4:52 (April 1950).
437. *Pionerskaya pravda,* September 12, 1952.
438. *Planove khozyaistvo.* *(a) 2:5–6 (1941). *(6) A. Leontiev, "Ekonomischeskie osnovy novoy demokratii," 4:69 (1947).
439. *Political Science Quarterly,* Taylor Cole, "The Evolution of the German Labor Front," 52:532–558 (1937), and literature cited there; see also ref. 263g.
440. *Politische Vierteljahrsschrift.* *(a) Irving Fetscher, "Faschismus und Nationalsozialismus — Zur Kritik des sovietmarxistischen Faschismusbegriffs," 3:42ff (1962). *(b) Peter C. Ludz, "Offene Fragen in der Totalitarismus — Forschung," 2:319–347 (1961).
441. *Pravda.* *(a) December 29, 1936, p. 2. *(b) October 9, 1952, p. 2. *(c) July 4, 1947. *(d) October 9, 1952, Malenkov, report of the Central

Committee. *(e) April 16, 1953. *(f) November 7, 1947, speech on the thirtieth anniversary of the revolution. *(g) December 18, 1917. *(h) October 9, 1952, p. 6, Nineteenth Party Congress, credentials report; see also ref. 895. *(i) June 22, 1954, article on China and the path of socialist industrialization. *(j) July 17, 1955. *(k) January 21, 1955; for 1954 achievements, the annual report of the Central Statistical Administration (TsSU), "Results of the State Plan for the Development of the National Economy of the USSR in 1954" (trans.) *(l) January 21, 1955. *(m) September 19, 1953. *(n) February 23 and 24, March 6, 1954, for Khrushchev's report, and stories on Komsomolites leaving for the east. *(o) October 27, 1954. *(p) October 10, 1952, p. 5. *(q) April 11, 1956. *(r) *op. cit.* *(s) October 25, 1962. *(t) 1963 figures, January 24, 1964.

442. *Problems of Communism.* *(a) T. H. Rigby, "How Strong Is the Leader?" September 1962, pp. 1–8, argues for Khrushchev's dominance, as Loewenthal does in the same publication, July 1960. We read: "evidence strongly contradicts the view that Khrushchev's power remains severely limited" (p. 1). *(b) Paul Hollander, "Privacy: A Bastion Stormed," November–December 1963. *(c) Boris Goldenberg, "The Cuban Revolution," and Andres Suarez, "Castro between Moscow and Peking," in "Cuba and Castroism," September–October 1963; see also ref. 75. *(d) Harry Gelman, "The Sino-Soviet Conflict: A Survey," March–April 1964. *(e) *ibid.,* p. 7. *(f) Leon Smolinski and Peter Wiles, "The Soviet Planning Pendulum," in "Economic Problems and Prospects," November–December 1963. *(g) S. Bialer, "The Peasant versus the Consumer: A Crisis in Prices," September–October 1962; esp. p. 20: "It can also be stated with certainty that the fantastic achievements planned by 1965 and 1970 remain as visionary as ever." *(h) Allen B. Ballard, Jr., "An End to Collective Farms?," July–August 1961.

443. *Public Opinion Quarterly.* C. J. Friedrich, "The Agricultural Basis of Emotional Mass Nationalism," 1:50–61 (1937), for the Nazi situation.

444. *Quarterly Journal of Economics.* *(a) J. S. Berliner, "The Informal Organization of the Soviet Firm," 46:342–365 (August 1952). *(b) *ibid.*

445. Radio Moscow, September 1954.

446. *Regime fascista.* *(a) March 1, 1930. *(b) November 23, 1938, p. 1, as trans. by Germino (ref. 120d).

447. *Review of Politics.* *(a) Hannah Arendt, "Ideology and Terror: A Novel Form of Government," 15:309ff (1953). The antecedents in earlier discussions of the law of nature are inadequately recognized, since Arendt takes only the normative (scholastic) law of nature into account. *(b) *ibid.,* pp. 303ff. In this interesting paper, Arendt advances the thesis that it is not merely the utopian nature of the ideology but its alleged logicality that leads to the terror. Based on a "scientific" law of movement, these ideologies are "literally the logic of an idea," which is carried through with "ice-cold reasoning" (Hitler) or with the "merci-

lessness of dialectics" or the "irresistible force of logic" (Stalin). We believe the point Arendt makes to be a significant aspect of totalitarian
ideology, but not to have the broad importance she attributes to it. *(c)
Karl Wittfogel, "The Historical Position of Communist China: Doctrine
and Reality," 16:463ff (1954), for further detail.

448. *Revue de internationale droit comparé*, 1963. Jovan Djordjevic, "Les
Characteristiques fondamentales de la nouvelle constitution yougoslave,"
pp. 689–703.

449. *Slavic Review.* *(a) Paul M. Cocks, "The Purge of Marshall Zhukov,"
22:482ff (1963. *(b) Harold J. Berman, "The Struggle of Soviet Jurists
Against a Return to Stalinist Terror," 22:314ff (1963).

450. *Sotsialisticheskaya zakonnost,* no. 4 (1953), special supplement.

451. *Social Research.* George K. Romoser, "The Politics of Uncertainty: The
German Resistance Movement," 31:73ff (1964).

452. *Sovetskaya pedagogika,* no. 1 (1955), holiday work plan for students
in an agricultural area.

453. *Sovetskoe gosudarstvo i pravo.* *(a) 6:16–23 (1954). *(b) *ibid.*

454. *Sovetskaya kultura,* January 18, 1955, p. 2, for a recent attack on hooli-
ganism.

455. *Soziale Welt.* Otto Stammer, Gerhard Schulz, and P. C. Ludz, "Totalis-
musforschung," 12:97–145 (1961).

456. *Survey.* *(a) Melvin Croan, "The Dialectics of Polycentrism," 48:130–
144 (July 1963). *(b) Leonard Schapiro, "The Party and the State,"
38:130–144 (October 1961), referring to a piece by M. Ivashechkin in
Nash sovremennik, 1961.

457. *Trybuna Ludu,* June 7, 1953.

458. United States Congress. See ref. 363.

459. *United States Department of Agriculture,* Agricultural Research Service
and Foreign Agricultural Reports. *(a) *Economic Aspects of Soviet
Agriculture — Report of a Technical Study Group,* Washington, 1959.
*(b) Economic Report No. 13. *Soviet Agriculture Today,* Washington,
1963.

460. *U.S. News and World Report.* Reports of N. and H. Dodges, September
16, 1955. This is also the conclusion of two American educators who
have recently spent some time in the USSR studying the educational
system.

461. *USSR Information Bulletin,* October 20, 1948.

462. *Vechernaya Moskva,* August 12, 1955.

463. *Vedomosti verkhovnogo soveta SSSR,* 9 (827): 259–267 (June 20, 1954).

464. *Vestnik instituta po izucheniyu istorii i kultury SSSR.* *(a) Sencha-
Zalesky, on the Soviet school, 2:69 (1955). *(b) "Po stranitsam
Zhurnala Moskovskoi Patriarkhii," 1 (14):76 (1955). *(c) D. Kon-
stantinov, "Sovetskaia molodezh v borbe za Tserkov," 1 (14): 61–72
(1955). *(d) E. Kyrymal, "Polozhenie musulmanskoi religii v Krymu,"
2 (15): 55–68 (1955).

465. *Vierteljahrshefte für Zeitgeschichte.* *(a) Karl O. Paetel, "Geschichte

und Soziologie der SS," 2:15–17 (1954); however, he neglects the Italian Fascist antecedents of this kind of conception. *(b) *ibid.,* p. 3. *(c) *ibid.,* pp. 1–33.

466. *Voprosy filosofii.* F. N. Ileshchuk, "Religious Survivals and Ways of Overcoming Them" (trans.), 6:79 (1954).

467. *Voprosy trudovovo prava.* N. G. Aleksandrov and V. M. Dogadov, p. 241; quoted in Kulski (ref. 189), p. 414; see also ref. 189c.

468. *Washington Law Review.* Harold J. Berman and James W. Spindler, "Soviet Comrades' Courts," 38:842ff (1963).

469. *World Politics.* A. Eckstein, "Conditions and Prospects for Economic Growth in Communist China," 7:1–37 (October 1954).

470. *Yale Review.* C. J. Friedrich, "The Peasantry — The Evil Genius of Dictatorship," 26.7:724–740 (1937).

471. *Zaria vostoka.* L. Klimovich, "Origin and Reactionary Essence of Islam" (trans.), October 10, 1954.

472. *Zentralinstitut für Erziehung und Unterricht,* Deutsche Schulerziehung (ed. Rudolf Benzed), 1940, containing a report about the development of German schools between 1933 and 1939.

INDEX OF AUTHORS CITED

INDEX

[See also Index of Authors Cited.]

Index

DATE DUE

FEB 13 '69			
FEB 27 '69			
MAR 19 '69			
Apr 1 '69			
MAR 24 '70			
APR 7 '70			
APR 28 '70			
MAR 11 '71			
AP 5 '79			
MY 1 '79			
GAYLORD			PRINTED IN U.S.A.